RETHINKING RACE AND ETHNICITY IN RESEARCH METHODS

RETHINKING RACE AND ETHNICITY IN RESEARCH METHODS

John H. Stanfield, II

Editor

Routledge
Taylor & Francis Group

LONDON AND NEW YORK

First published 2011 by Left Coast Press, Inc.

Published 2016 by Routledge
2 Park Square, Milton Park, Abingdon, Oxon OX14 4RN
711 Third Avenue, New York, NY 10017, USA

Routledge is an imprint of the Taylor & Francis Group, an informa business

Library of Congress Cataloging-in-Publication Data:

Rethinking race and ethnicity in research methods / John H. Stanfield, II, editor.
    p. cm.
Includes index.
ISBN 978-1-61132-000-8 (hbk. : alk. paper) — ISBN 978-1-61132-001-5
1. Ethnic relations—Research. 2. Race relations—Research. 3. Ethnology—Methodology.
4. Sociology—Methodology. II. Stanfield, John H.
    GN496.R46 2011
    305.80072—dc22

2011006967

ISBN 978-1-61132-000-8 hardcover
ISBN 978-1-61132-001-5 paperback

CONTENTS

Part III: Comparative and Cross-National Studies

PREFACE

Rethinking Race and Ethnicity in Research Methods is the long overdue se-
quel to *Race and Ethnicity in Research Methods* edited by John H. Stanfield,
II and Rutledge M. Dennis (1993, Sage). Chapter 1 is my revisit to the introductory piece, "Epistemological Considerations," in the 1993 book.

This edited volume is then divided into three sections. As in the first book,
authors offer intellectual histories and critical assessments of methods they
use in racial and ethnic studies in sociology and in other sociologically oriented fields. Articles in Part I, Qualitative and Quantitative Methods, are written by researchers who offer assessments of novel nontriangulated methods
seldom addressed comprehensively in racial and ethnic sociological research.
The areas covered are: restorative justice (John H. Stanfield, II), discourse
analysis (Teun A. van Dijk), qualitative interviewing (Eileen O'Brien), archival methods (Mary Jo Deegan), emancipation practices (Elizabeth Hordge-
Freeman, Sarah Mayorga, Eduardo Bonilla-Silva), and experimental designs
(Henry A. Walker).

In the chapters in Part II, Mixed Methods, authors present innovative approaches to triangulating qualitative methods such as using historically oriented archival, secondary historical documents, observational techniques, and
interviews (Stephen Small), triangulating qualitative and quantitative historical methods (Yvonne Walker), triangulating quantitative methods (Quincy
Thomas Stewart and Abigail A. Sewell), case studies, focus groups, and long
interviews (Dawn Brotherton), and psychohistorical textual analysis of autobiographies, archival and secondary historical documents analysis, and oral
histories (John H. Stanfield, II).

Part III, Comparative and Cross-National Studies, includes two examples
of innovations in cross-national methodologies: ethnography (L. Janelle
Dance and Johannes Lunneblad) and my piece; Weberian ideal-type methodology in comparative historical sociological research.

ACKNOWLEDGMENTS

As is the case for most writing projects, especially of this collaborative genre, there are many people to thank. First, I thank my wonderful colleagues who agreed to contribute to this volume. They did not have to take the time out of their hectic schedules but honored me and the academy by doing so and did so unselfishly. I am proud to say they represent a rich mixture of baby-boomer and Gen-X scholars who have established their names in the social sciences or are well on their way in doing so. The range of their provocative perspectives assures the long-lasting value of this edited volume as a source of needed discussion and innovation in the underresearched area of race and ethnicity in research methods as matters of intellectual histories, epistemologies, ethics, politics, theories, and technical relevance and creativity. Thank you all so very much.

To really show my chronological age as I come to my sixtieth year on July 9, 2011, I am also grateful that three of the contributors are former students of mine: Dawn Brotherton and Yvonne Walker, Fielding Graduate University Human and Organization Studies doctoral students, and Eileen O'Brien, my extraordinary College of William and Mary undergraduate student who went on to receive her doctoral studies mentorship under Joe Feagin then at the University of Florida. It is always an immeasurable honor when one's former students agree to do intellectual work with you as colleagues and friends.

I thank my publisher Mitch Allen, who, as a Sage Publications editor, recognized the potential significance of the bundle of papers I gave to him in the aftermath of the 1984 American Sociological Association Meeting. The paper drafts of those became *Race and Ethnicity in Research Methods*. *Rethinking Race and Ethnicity in Research Methods* comes to published light due to Mitch's continued encouragement to me over the years to get the next cows born. I wish to also thank Carole Bernard, our copy editor, for her superb work.

The completion of this edited volume project was made possible through the organized research program I direct at Indiana University, Bloomington. This is the Research Program on Transcultural and Intercultural Philanthropic Studies, which is funded by the BEA Foundation, administered through the Silicon Valley Community Foundation, and housed in the Department of African American and African Diaspora Studies. I cannot thank enough the members of my research assistance staff who worked diligently with me on this project: Stacy Ballam, Pilar Britton, Dana Collins, and Suzanne Faulk and my grant administrators: Louise Brown and Melissa Stewart. The funding support of the BEA Foundation allowed me—like my Fulbright Teaching Award to Sierra Leone and Social Science Research Council Fellowship for Advanced Foreign Policy Studies, my participation in two Salzburg Seminars and in two Council for the International Exchange of Scholars Seminars (to Brazil and Thailand), and my Catholic University–Rio de Janeiro Distinguished Fulbright Chair award—to travel, live, teach, and do research abroad, meeting colleagues and making friends along the way who contributed to my expanding globalizing reflections about race and ethnicity in research methods as pressing concerns in the global social sciences. Thanks to all of you for helping me to grow and to think in new ways.

This volume is dedicated to my marvelous mother, my three lovely sisters, and the memory of my dear father who made his transition to the other side of the River Jordan in the midst of the completion of this collaborative writing project.

John H. Stanfield, II
January 2011

1 EPISTEMOLOGICAL RECONSIDERATIONS AND NEW CONSIDERATIONS: OR WHAT HAVE I BEEN LEARNING SINCE 1993

John H. Stanfield, II

The 1993 volume of original essays, *Race and Ethnicity in Research Methods*, has for years enjoyed global influence in graduate education and professional work within and outside sociology, in other academic social sciences, in allied health and social service fields, in marketing, and in numerous other fields. That the introduction, "Epistemological Considerations," has been so well cited over the years worldwide is indicative of how much the published text was in step with the post-Cold War cultural and political critiques of American and other westernizing social sciences.

Race and Ethnicity in Research Methods was conceived a number of years before it was published. The text originated from a 1984 American Sociological Association roundtable on methodological considerations in the sociological study of Blacks.* Now that topic seems to be rather tame if not a bit trite, but in those days, organizing an ASA roundtable on race and ethnicity in research methods focusing on the study of Blacks was quite radical.

The controversy was not only because of the subject matter but also because I and all the original roundtable participants were black. One of the original roundtable colleagues voiced the usual racialized concern that the roundtable would never get off the ground since no Whites were included. The paternalistic presumption that nothing can happen without Whites is still prevalent in some black academic circles in sociology and elsewhere in the academy. Those who make this presumption do not realize that we blacks, especially those of us who are tenured and senior in our fields, are now liberated from the traditional patronizing enslavement of our minds and bodies.

When the roundtable papers were organized as an edited volume, other colleagues were invited to contribute papers, based on their competencies as scholars rather than the color of their skin or their gender. How hypocritical it would have been had I organized a volume that critiqued racial motivations as to how methodologies were fashioned and used while practicing racism in the

11

process. That has happened in white supremacy-driven text frameworks in the past. Such works paid lip service to racial justice but ignored Blacks and other non-Whites as authors or subjects, racially stereotyped them in labeling them (e.g., a black sociologist), or gave them only certain topics to pursue (usually on race relations or on the experiences of a non-white population). I refused to allow my ethnic pride as a black man get in the way of developing a text created by colleagues who admirably critiqued race and ethnicity in various research methodologies without the usual contradictions of preaching liberal inclusiveness while practicing racist exclusivity.

My motivation for organizing the 1984 roundtable stemmed from my concern as a historical sociologist of knowledge about the historical rarity of black critiques of theories and methods in the academic profession of American sociology. That became apparent while I was doing my doctoral dissertation research at Northwestern, which required seemingly countless hours of recovering and analyzing American texts on the sociology of race relations between the late nineteenth century and World War II. Even black sociologists who raised their voices about theoretical and methodological issues—scholars such as William E. B. Du Bois, E. Franklin Frazier, Charles S. Johnson, Oliver C. Cox, Lewis Jones, and much later Joyce Ladner and James Pitts—were either ignored or marginalized in their time. Trivializing their contributions or ignoring them altogether was in keeping with the Jim Crow presumptions then prevalent. These derived from Social Darwinist reasoning that the inferiority of Negroes made their critiques of, and attempts to contribute to, mainstream knowledge about epistemologies, theories, and methods of no intellectual value in the emergence and institutionalization of sociology as a social science.

Not until the 1980s and 1990s did this view begin to change somewhat. Black baby boomer sociologists and other younger sociologists began to critique dominant theoretical and methodological paradigms and offered their own insightful epistemological, theoretical, and methodological perspectives. These scholars included Elijah Anderson in urban sociology, Larry Bobo in social psychology, Aldon Morris in social movements, Patricia Hill Collins and Karen Fields in gender studies, Eduardo Bonilla-Silva in critical race theory, and Tukufu Zuberi in demographics. Still, even as a growing number of black sociologists contribute to expanding and transforming mainstream paradigms in sociology and other social sciences and humanities, we should remember how recent the mainstream acceptance of this work is and how black sociologists were allowed to make only provincial contributions about black people. They were considered irrelevant when it came to making major epistemological, theoretical, and methodological contributions, especially conceptual and technical claims with universal application potentialities. Even today, we are far from being out of the Jim Crow woods. Though there has been a growing acceptance of significant black contributions to mainstream theoretical ideas and methodological techniques, their impressive efforts are still largely focused on racialized issues rather than on the broader foundational issues that define sociology as an academic field.

Toward Global Consciousness, Personally and Professionally

The time lag between the 1984 roundtable and the 1993 publication date and beyond were contexts of personal life events that would very much make *Race and Ethnicity in Research Methods* a transitional text in a number of ways. In 1981, I was offered a seven-year nontenurable contract at Yale,[1] which gave me time to complete *Philanthropy and Jim Crow in American Social Science* as well as receive my first major research grants and fellowships. My publisher did not expect the book to stay in print long since it was such an odd topic, so it was never brought out in paperback. Over the years, it became a key text on the history of race in American sociological thought and in contextual studies in the history of social sciences. It is still in print. It also became a methodological model for sociologists interested in archival research methods.

The book would become the basis of another source of amazement. In 1988, I was promoted, tenured, and offered an endowed chaired professorship in American Studies and Sociology at The College of William and Mary in Virginia. *Philanthropy and Jim Crow in American Social Science* and other publications were derived from my doctoral dissertation that focused on American Studies, matching the seat of my endowed chair. I was a stone-cold Americanist. The same was also true of my personal life. Coming from an upstate New York poor family, I ventured only as far as a few camping trips to Canada as a child and brief tourist visits to the Caribbean and Latin America as a young adult. So, it should not be surprising that *Race and Ethnicity in Research Methods* was very American focused.

My shift into a global consciousness and life-style began when I arrived in Williamsburg, Virginia, in 1988. When I attended the 1988 American Studies Association Conference, I came across the Fulbright booth in the exhibit hall. I asked the Fulbright representative if there was an opening at the University of Liberia since in 1987 I had just published Charles S. Johnson's *Bitter Canaan*, a fascinating historical sociological manuscript on the Americo-Liberian slave trade. "No," the representative said, but they had an opening for a sociologist for the University of Sierra Leone. I was in Sierra Leone and then London for eighteen months.

I spent the first ten months of the 1989–90 academic year teaching at the Fourah Bay College of the University of Sierra Leone as well as taking holiday trips to Senegal, Gambia, Mali, and the Canary Islands. I also took my first trip to Europe when I attended and spoke at my first international conference in Utrecht, The Netherlands while on Fourah Bay College spring break. I also spent two weeks touring Western Europe by train.

I spent eight months in Great Britain on a Social Science Research Council Fellowship in 1990. While a visiting scholar in the Department of History of the University of London School of Oriental and African Studies, I spent a great deal of time traveling to different British cities. I consulted archives and met leading race relations sociologists to recruit for my emerging Race Relations Series for Sage Publications, which developed an international focus.

The global focus launched by my experiences in Europe and in Africa were expanded on over the past twenty years. In addition to visits to my new friends in Europe and Africa, I traveled to South Africa once every twelve to eighteen months to engage in research projects initiated at the Andrew Young Center on International Studies at Morehouse College; attended seminars in Salzburg; did research at the Catholic University in Rio de Janeiro as a Distinguished Fulbright Chair in American Studies; and developed other re-search projects in Brazil focused on comparative race and restorative justice issues.

All of this travel has transformed me from being an American with international interests to being a global citizen who happens to be an American. This global consciousness and life-style has meant that I spend anywhere from six weeks to four or five months each year abroad, usually in Brazil or South Africa, though now I travel and do research in Asian contexts as well.

My growing global consciousness has also greatly impacted my pedago-gies, ranging from what I require students to read and write to using global technologies for students to garner information around the world and to meet people in places outside the United States. It has influenced immensely how I structure my globally focused organized research programs and projects such as my Indiana University research program on Transcultural and Intercultural Philanthropic Studies as well as the consulting work I do for distributive edu-cation doctoral studies universities such as the Fielding Graduate University School of Human and Organization Development. And certainly, my global sense of self explains why several essays in *Rethinking Race and Ethnicity in Research Methods* are cross-national in emphasis.

Now, early in the twenty-first century, Americans are finally living in an era in which we are being encouraged if not forced to move beyond the myth of American exceptionalism and embrace the importance of understanding that the United States is an integral part of the world not above it or in any other way disconnected from it. This is an essential epistemological consid-eration missing in the original *Race and Ethnicity in Research Methods*. Like most American sociologists, as a product of my own society I was entrapped by my own nationalistic ethnocentrism. This was the case even though, like many American sociologists, I was very much interested in cross-national studies and trends in my area of specialty. But I lacked a global sense of consciousness and identity that rendered my international interests theoretical and quite secondary to my nascent Americanism.

This is similar to people of Euro American background who make progressive claims about people of color but who have never closely befriended us, lived with us, or culturally become like us, which leads to occasional slips of racist presumptions in the mind or out of the mouth. And certainly, it is like sociologists of color and of all ancestries who, as middle-class researchers, write all kinds of progressive things about the poor but have never been poor or have forgotten about their impoverished days and subjected to the Jungian shadow effect of their from time to time say things about the poor that are less than generous and humane.

Global consciousness and its influence on research questions, theories, methods, data interpretations, and research applications has numerous effects that are worthy of mention. One effect is understanding the now old cliché that the local is linked to the global and to everything in-between. We simply cannot, at the end of the day, assume that what we are observing or gathering locally just stops there; somehow it keeps on going, some way or another to the global level. Even though it may be beyond the scope of a study to explore the complexities of various levels and degrees of impacting processes and structures beyond the local, the researcher should at least acknowledge being aware of the probable ways in which what is being studied locally has linkages, from the most immediate layers after the local well into some global context. This acknowledgment is just as important as a disclosure as the researcher disclosing the basic awareness of the impact of her or his values on what is being observed or surveyed.

Another way the global consciousness of the researcher cuts is deromanticization. Just as it is important to avoid romanticizing the local community or population I am observing or surveying through impartial collection and analysis of data, the same can be done if I am globally aware. For instance, there is nothing romantic about homelands when exploring the home origins of immigrants. This is what happens in Afro-centric research too often. There is a tendency to embrace a romantic sense of the African past to explain the history and values embedded in African American human development and communities. Once I was able to travel and to live in an African country, and to do so beyond the comforts of a five-star hotel and without my tourist guide, it became apparent that reducing Africans down to one people (such as ancient Egyptians or Yoruba or Zulu) is absurd; assuming that there is one African language is silly (usually Swahili); and narrowing down African values down to one belief system (usually communalism) has no place in empirical reality. The name Africa is a European construct, even when we alternate the term and call it Afrika as is the case of many of my Afro-centric friends and colleagues.

Traveling around the continent and taking in the vast complexities and paradoxes of cultural differences in Africa—exacerbated by tribal, language, religion, national, and ethno-regional distinctions—it is apparent that much of our historiography of the slave trade into the Western Hemisphere, Europe, Asia, and the South Pacific and the consequential formation of slave-based plantations and societies and development of urban and rural settlements of free African-descendent populations and communities after emancipations are grossly overly simplistic. What we are as black people—with intricate multiple ancestries and understudied or unstudied transnational interpersonal, institutional, and movement linkages—is a question we sociologists have yet to adequately grapple with.

As noted in the first volume, we continue to homogenize blackness in the same box. In recent years, however, we have begun to get a bit better because large numbers of African and African diasporic immigrants have come to the United States since the liberalization of U.S. immigration policies in the 1960s. But the important diversification of the black box work will not be completed until we do the empirical work of homelands work reminiscent of the transnational work that W. I. Thomas and Florian Znaniecki did in the seminal *Polish Peasant in Europe and in America.* That multivolume work was important not only for its qualitative methodology but also because it is a model for understanding the importance of keeping the study of flows of immigration experiences embedded in empirical analyses of where they came from as well as where they landed and settled, whether voluntary or involuntary.

Traveling to other countries and observing, or even living elsewhere, is no guarantee that global consciousness and sensitivities will develop about what is really going on in the local setting. This is especially true when we go to a country once or twice briefly but basically remain in our own nationalistic and/or cultural comfort zone and/or when we go briefly or live there for a long period of time, socially and culturally cloistered from local and societal contexts. This is common for academics from other lands who never leave the comforts of the campus or college town and military personnel who never mix with the locals.

This certainly was the case for Robert E. Park, the great iconic University of Chicago sociologist who traveled to Brazil twice toward the end of his life in the 1930s. Park, a world-renowned sociologist by the end of the 1920s, influenced Brazilian social scientists such as Gilberto Freyre and Arturo Ramos before stepping foot on the country. Park became intensely fascinated by Brazil after a 1934 visit to Rio de Janeiro and Salvador, just before he retired from the University of Chicago to historically black college Fisk University via the invitation of his former student Charles S. Johnson (Valladares 2010).

Park was so taken by what he observed about the seemingly fluid "melting pot" nature of white-black relations in Bahia which was more apparent than in the United States that he recruited his last student, Donald Pierson to do his doctoral dissertation on the Negro in Bahia. Park returned briefly in 1937 to Salvador to assist Pierson with his fieldwork. In 1938, Park and Pierson offered a Fisk University seminar on Brazil, probably the first-ever sociology course on Brazilian race relations offered in the United States (Valladares 2010).

Pierson's dissertation was published as *Negroes in Brazil: A Study of Race Contacts at Bahia* by the University of Chicago Press in 1942 (his only major scholarly study), with the introduction written by Park. His published dissertation was well embedded in the Park assimilation-oriented race-cycle model. Pierson continued to embrace the Park model through his long years in Brazil, where he established a Chicago School-style Sociology Department in São Paulo (Valladares 2010). Pierson's importation of the Park model for interpreting white-black Brazilian race relations is an example of a researcher becoming a long-time resident of a country and even part of its intelligentsia while continuing to believe in an imported paradigm that simply does not fit the realities of their adopted country and accommodating to national ideology, in this case, the Brazilian racial paradise myth.[2]

This discussion about Park and his student Pierson entering Brazil with preconceived ideas about white-black relations there and about Pierson actually living there for years shows how easy it is for researchers to develop blinders and continue to misunderstand what they are seeing, feeling, hearing, and touching. This, of course, speaks of the more general problem that social scientists, especially anthropologists, have written about from time to time about projecting imported paradigms of data collection and interpretation grounded in biases, be they ethnocentric, nationality, religious, or class. And if such mistaken ideas are published by a well-connected researcher, the publications can become sources of professional canonization that can influence a discipline for years if not decades. This is certainly the case of Pierson's study, which was the leading sociological text on white-black race relations in Brazil for years. It contributed to an assimilationist perspective that confirmed the long-held racial paradise myth in the country, which has only recently begun to be extensively questioned and dismantled through empirical evidence-based theories and methods.

Still another way the global consciousness of the researcher can cut is understanding how those of us interested in African-descended experiences in the United States must work much more toward not only not romanticizing but also not essentializing black experiences. This was said in the original text but it needs to be emphasized here from a more global perspective. Just like in the American context, in comparative global contexts there is the need to make sure we do not reify blackness. The question of what is blackness, which translates into who has black African ancestry and how far back it is in family tree histories, is a subject of empirical analysis that should always remain on the forefront in any diasporic research project. In Brazil, blackness is a matter of appearance. One can have numerous black African ancestors, but if you look white, you are white, unless you choose to be black. In the United States and in South Africa, blackness is a matter of ancestry. You can look white, but if you have black African-descendent ancestors, you are black. Whether or not your black ancestors matter in your racialized status as a white person depends on the local, state, and regional "drop of black blood" rule. But the rule of thumb is really no matter how far back the black ancestor is, as a white in America, it will always culturally compromise one's sense of being white.

So, even with changing demographics in the United States making racial identity much more flexible and increasingly a matter of choice, when it comes to whiteness, discovering a black relative in the family is still a topic of widespread media controversy and the subject of good scholarly exposés. This helps explain the public fascination about Thomas Jefferson and Sally Hemmings and the eminence of the historian who recently empirically grounded this liaison between an iconic white American and his slave lover and their offspring.

This raises another point about epistemological considerations from an expanded "What have I been learning all these years' perspective"—namely, whiteness studies. Over the past fifteen years, whiteness studies have increased immensely in the United States and to a lesser extent in other multiracialized countries. It can even be said there is now a whiteness cottage industry in the American academia. This certainly reflects the growing demographic realities of the decline of white supremacy in a nation and in a world that is politically shifting to non-Whites, especially in Asia and in Africa.

The whiteness studies field, though, is reified too often. What is sorely needed, as an epistemological consideration, is developing theories and methods of data collection and analysis that reminds us that whiteness, blackness, and other kinds of racializations are relational phenomena. White people create black people; black people create white people; and people in general create each other and structure each other in hierarchies, communities, movements, and societies, and global spheres. As we study what is going on in among the racialized oppressed—whether poor health, underemployment or unemployment, undereducation or no education, or street violence—it is about what is going on with Whites and other racialized populations creating, institutionalizing, and transforming the norms, values, and practices constructing, sustaining, and changing the socially defined racialized dehumanization.

This reminds me of James Pitts's marvelous work (1974) on race consciousness, which was never fully developed by him or by his students. He was my Northwestern race relations sociology professor who had recently completed his doctoral degree under Arnold Feldman shortly before my arrival to pursue doctoral studies in 1973. Pitts began theorizing about race consciousness as a relational and structuring phenomenon in his article "Race Consciousness: Comments on New Directions," but soon thereafter he embarked on a career in academic administration. Pitts argued that race as relational and as a structuring manifestation of consciousness racialized in historically specific societies and communities and systems within them is an interesting way of exploring the normality of race as an outcome of multigenerational socialization. As alluded to above, Pitts's race consciousness concept was not picked up in mainstream sociological literature since it presumed that race was the seemingly natural way in which Americans define themselves and develop their structured environments, not because of genetics but because of multigenerational socialization—and the same is true of other multiracialized societies. This kind of thinking is antithetical to American sociological ontology that presumes that racialized prejudice is individualized and institutionalized, in contradiction to the supposed universal norms of fairness in democratic America. In this sense, sociologists have canonized the study of racial prejudice as conventional or intentional individual bias, while discrimination was the thinking or practice of discriminating based on racialized views of the Other.

There is a host of epistemological problems with this split between racial prejudice and racial discrimination, which actually began with Myrdal's *American Dilemma* (1944) and Merton's (1948) response to it, for decades the American liberal's holy text on race relations (see my chapter on holistic restorative justice in this volume).

When it comes to racialization, we are referring to a societal experience, not merely a specific dominant or subordinate experience somehow disconnected and in other ways reified from each other. Concretely, the problem of race in America and how it is reproduced, institutionalized, and transformed is not merely a white or non-white population problem regarding privilege or oppression. Race is a societal problem. Specifically, race is the very historical way in which the United States has originated and evolved structurally over the decades, indeed centuries with economic, psychological, cultural, and political consequences such as quality-of-life disparities and mental illness outcomes of possessing privileged and subordinated racialized group feelings. This generation-to-generation persistence of race in America and other multiracialized nations with historically specific transformations is due to racialism, the engine of race and racism that is much more fundamental than both.

Specifically, racialism is the routine, the everyday, the taken-for-granted ways in which we are taught to use race in making normal and extraordinary decisions such as where to live and where not to live, who to befriend and who to fear, who to trust and who not to trust, who to hire and promote first, who is smart and who is dumb, who would make a good spouse and who would not, who can dance and who cannot, etc., etc. Racialism cognitively triggers mental images of the Racialized Other that are connected to the one-to-one presumptions about phenotype and behavior or social or cultural characteristics.

Racially embedded everyday language is used to racialize and therefore dehumanize ourselves and the Other, using ordinary words like racialized modifiers to describe self and Others typically or intentionally, such as that black man or that white woman or that asian student or that latino artist.

The caricatures, that is, the stereotypes that racialism produces ever so mundanely and ordinarily in a race-centered society, make us innocently and sometimes quite intentionally assume that certain qualities of our racialized selves or of the Racialized Other are natural. So, you see a black male and assume that he is naturally not too bright, works with his hands rather than his mind, is a low academic achiever, is lazy, is a great dancer, knows about sports, is a ladies' man, and is morally irresponsible when it comes to women and family issues. He may even be a thief, so hold on to your wallet. Or he may be a rapist, so if you are a woman, walk quickly or avoid his eyes when he looks at you too intently in the elevator. And by all means, if it is dark and he is crossing in front of your car at the traffic light, lock your door. Driving while black as a form of racial profiling used by law enforcement agencies is a formalization of racialism.

Until very recently (i.e., the cultural impacts of the women's liberation movement), the racialization of white males portrayed the white male as being typically strong, aggressive, highly intelligent, a morally responsible leader, and the fountainhead of civilization. If you are Asian and male or female, you must not be all that aggressive; you are good when it comes to science and math and weak when it comes to art and literature and competitive sports. And we know that Latinos are slow academically and have major language problems.

Racialism stereotypes geographically in that "we know" that inner city means black or brown and poor and dangerous and suburbia means white and affluent and safe. Mastery of the English language is also racialized, the more you speak what is called good English, the more white you are and the less racial or let's say, ethnic you are. People are surprised to find that well-educated black people can speak well and write well or doubt they can, so they suspect that, for instance, a black student must be from the hood and therefore the excellent paper he submitted to his professor must be due to cheating.

Racialism also naturalizes the commodization of racial status to such an extent that the Racialized Other is viewed as a nonliving object, a piece of furniture if oppressed or an object to manipulate to get resources from if dominant. And racialism legitimates functionality in how dominant and oppressed people interact. This means that interaction is for the most part restricted to impersonal exchanges with no or little interest in getting to know the Other as a human being. At best, people of different racialized backgrounds may share the same classroom space and may even study together but rarely are interested in getting to know each other. Interactions with the bus driver or with the cashier who is a Racialized Other is only for the sake of getting a transaction done. That is why people of different racialized backgrounds can spend years in close proximity as employers and employees, as teachers and students, as pastors and parishioners or even as peers such as classmates, coworkers, members of the same church, and may even be cordial with each other but never take the next steps of becoming knowable, of becoming intimate friends if not even more intimate as lovers, spouses, and forming families. This functionality norm is central to intergenerational racialism since it reproduces the social distance, the presumption that the Racialized Other is of no relevance beyond functional use.

Racialism is created, sustained, and changes through normative cognitive dissonance, generating a split self character. It allows residents of a racialized centered society to construct and live within self-conceptions embedded in notion of good moral character on the one hand, while dehumanizing the humanity of others they racialized presumptively or through conscious thoughts and acts on the other. Indeed, one can even speculate that in racialized-centered societies and communities within them, or racialized communities in nonracialized societies, notions of moral goodness and altruism tend to be extended to senses of one's own racialized people. Therefore, good and altruistic gestures toward Racialized Others tend to be problematic if not controversial. This is apparent in the on-going controversy about racialized-based affirmative action policies meant to extend access to educational and economic markets to the historically excluded in multiracialized societies such as Brazil, India, South Africa, and United States. The dominant have no quarrel with their privileged access to such markets, though many have problems when the same privileges are extended to Racialized Others. The same goes for efforts to extend universal worker and welfare benefits to the poor in multiracialized societies in which low-income people are disproportionately oppressed Racialized Others.

The histories of Jim Crow in the United States, apartheid in South Africa, and the paradoxical racialized history of Brazil have involved formalized and informal segregative interpersonal attitudes and policies. Those were and are maintained through widely embraced presumptions that Blacks should not be treated altruistically regarding emergency medical treatment, social services, and insurance. Further, black communities should not be given resources to develop schools and other social institutions that would make them competitive with if not structurally more dominating than Whites. Too often, the Whites who created, managed, and changed such modes of racial segregation as traditions and intentional thoughts and actions were within their own population contexts morally upright people, great parents, civic leaders, business people, and faith leaders who viewed it not to be a self-definition contradiction to be racially prejudiced if not a racial discriminator.

The societal focus on race-making and transformation should encourage us to introduce new epistemologies, theories, and methodologies, some derived from long-standing paradigms from other social sciences and from humanities such as psychohistory, cross-national autobiographical and bio-graphical analyses, theology, discourse analysis, visual anthropology, experi-mental methods, and psychoanalysis. There is also a need to go beyond the conventional and to design and test new theories and methods such as re-storative justice. In this vein, the authors in *Rethinking Race and Ethnicity in Research Methods* attempt to be innovative in how they expand traditional, theoretical, and methodological perspectives and offer new ones at a time when the demand for theories and methods that adequately capture the complexities, paradoxes, and contradictions of racialization is increasing dramatically.

Four major changes in logic of inquiry discussions in sociology since *Race and Ethnicity in Research Methods* was published have been the grow-ing respect for autobiographical and biographical analysis, methodological triangulation as mixed methods, sexual orientation sensitivity, and transna-tionality. I will briefly discuss each of these, since most are addressed in more detail in this volume.

Autoethnography. For years, sociologists resisted the claim that the dis-cipline is a value-embedded intellectual practice just like all other sciences. Part of that resistance was refusal to understand the value of incorporating the autobiography of the researcher into the research design explanation—disclosing researcher human biases. That resistance began to progressively crumble since the late 1960s and is now very much gone (assisted by the advent of government and university ethics guidelines concerning human sub-jects from the 1970s forward).

Autoethnography is also being seen as being an increasingly appropriate alternative methodology. Autoethnography means that the primary research instrument is the subjectivity of the researcher, whose product derives from the unfolding of a life historical narrative. This methodology is much more acceptable in anthropology than in sociology since autoethnography is one step back from traditional ethnographic logic of inquiry. That is, the former embraces and uses the subjectivity of the researcher to explain something under study; the latter, though a first-hand observer, defines his or her role as that as a detached observer—as a data collector rather than as the data themselves. Some of the most significant studies done in the global race relations field have been those in which the researcher not only makes first-hand observations but also intertwines aspects of her or his life history. This has been the case when the researcher is a novelist, a short story writer, or even a poet or a playwright using autobiography disguised as fiction or just engaging in autobiographical fiction to address sensitive racial issues that would be too explosive to explore using empirical data usually collected and analyzed by sociologists and other social scientists. Richard Wright (America), Jorge Amado (Brazilian), and Philip Abrahams (South African) are examples of novelists who have either used their autobiographies or engaged in autobiographical fiction to construct sociological critiques of racialization.

Triangulation of methods as mixed methods. Triangulation of methods as mixed methods, like the integration of ideas drawn from two or more theoretical frameworks, breaks down long-held walls between quantitative and qualitative techniques and techniques within each broad sphere. Triangulation has been occurring increasingly in sociology and in other social sciences over the past twenty or so years in recognition of the growing complexity of the world and the acknowledgment that there is nothing sacred about any one method. What matters is how adequate a method can test and revise theoretical hunches. Triangulation is very important in racial and ethnic studies, especially between quantitative and qualitative techniques. The former are important for trend analyses and for formulizing patterns and exceptions, particularly when using large data sets; the latter are important for capturing deeply rooted immeasurable subjective experiences such as emotions and spirituality, so crucial for grasping racialized experiences.

Sexual orientation. A major absence in this text is a chapter on sexual orientation in racial and ethnic research because the author assigned to this topic was unable to remain in the lineup. When *Race and Ethnicity in Research Methods* was conceived in the mid-1980s and published in the early 1990s, sexual orientation in sociological research focusing especially on Blacks and other people of color was just beginning to emerge. Consideration of the broad spectrum of sexual orientation in sociology and other social sciences was long a taboo that extended easily into racial and ethnic studies. This is quite unfortunate considering the centrality of sexual orientation in human experiences. When it comes to black experiences in the United States and other Africa diasporic countries as well as African countries, sexual orientation studies remains acutely underdeveloped. This is seen in the absence of sexual orientation concerns in social studies of African-descended communities, families, faith communities, media, sports, and politics.

White gay, lesbian, bisexual, and transgender studies in sociology and other social sciences are much more advanced and even normalized when compared to black gay lesbian, bisexual, and transgender studies. Black gay male studies, for instance, are very much centered on a disease model (i.e., HIV/AIDs), rather than exploring the ways in which black gay males construct their everyday lives historically and contemporarily. Aside from a trickle of biographical accounts, there has been little historically grounded sociological analysis of the participation of black gays, lesbians, bisexuals, and transgendered people in the formation and transformation of institutions such as faith communities, education, media, sports, and business and movements such as civil rights within and outside traditionally black communities.

Transnationality. Comparative literature scholars and historians have been much more into transnational studies than sociologists in this emerging field of research in the American academy and around the world. With respect to sociology as an academic discipline, the focus on transnationality continues to move us away from Social Darwinist and functional conceptions of the closed society and closed institutions, systems, and communities within closed societies. Transnationality encourages the examination of networks, movements, communities' ethnic and other cultural formations, and stratified orders that do not pay attention to sovereign state boundaries. Processes become just as important as structures in transnational studies.

The epistemological challenge of transnationality is to avoid either or myths such as the tendency for some scholars to claim that what matters most are transnational processes and structures rather than paying attention to nation-states. This is the flip side error of assuming that what matters is the sovereign state, paying no attention to what is occurring outside it. It is critical to understand how both transnational structures and processes and sovereign states matter in formulating research questions and in the designs and implementation of research projects. This is especially important in global racial studies research since so much of global trends of voluntary and involuntary population movements of the racialized oppressed stemmed from both the oppressive behaviors of sovereign states and resistance efforts as responses to oppressive sovereign states.

This cannot be said enough when we consider the kind of African and African diasporic research, which began with William E. B. Du Bois's (1896) seminal *The Suppression of the African Slave Trade to the United States* published as the first volume as the Harvard Historical Studies Series. Du Bois's research on the international and U.S. domestic suppression of the African slave trade to the United States became representative of the dominant canon in history and in the historical social sciences and comparative literature studies in the twentieth and early twenty-first centuries. That is, they focus on the pre-twentieth-century international African slave trade, which involved sovereign states and generating transnational flows of dominating and oppressed peoples, creating and changing identities, institutions, systems, communities, and social movements. Thus, in scholarly literature about African Americans in the nineteenth century, the transnational literature is centered for the most part on the slave trade and institutionalized slavery (i.e., plantation experiences), and little attention was paid to the societal and connecting global experiences of free black people and their large variety of domestic and transnational identities, institutions, systems, communities, and movements.

The issue of transnational convergences and divergences from sovereign state ideologies and practices is particularly important in post-1990s America, given the extraordinary growth of the African as well as Asian and Latino immigrant population in the United States. This brings up one last point about transnationality studies in important essential integral balance with sovereign state studies.

One of the most significant academic outcomes of the on-going erosion of the Cold War in global studies research in the United States and abroad is the growing awareness of the need to break down and even integrate balkanized area studies. Area studies in American universities and foreign universities that followed suit, were very much products of the research and surveillance needs of both the American and Soviet governments during the 1950s–1970s. The funding streams and development of specialized careers that followed for at least three generations of scholars doing area studies greatly limited understanding of globalized and globalizing experiences that did not and still do not fit easily into one geographical area, commonly labeled in Cold War terminology. We are still recovering from the nearly three generations of Cold War–area studies specialization. Too often, the recovery is interpreted in terms of where we are sitting or standing. So, in much American sociology and other American interpretations of academic disciplines, there is a tendency to define global issues, some transnational patterns, or trends in American terms.

In globally important fields such as racial and ethnic studies, much critical work still needs to be done to tear down area studies walls and to develop global studies approaches that recover the complexities of transnational processes and structures and their tensions in the ebbs of the emergence, stabilization, and transformations of sovereign states in their continent contexts. In this volume, I provide a glimpse of this breaking down and out of area studies through my methodologically oriented article on bringing India into African diasporic studies as well as my essay on restorative justice as a methodology.

Global technological revolutions. In conclusion, one last trend not considered in *Race and Ethnicity in Research Methods* that is not included in this volume is global technological revolutions. Needless to say, 1993 was in the anteroom of global technological revolutions that would break loose in the 1990s, changing us all forever. The ways in which the Internet, emailing, cell phones, iPods, videoconferencing, YouTube, and other technologies are changing constructions of race and other human differences is a hot area of research. It is possible now for people to develop relationships identities, alliances, and even adversarial relationships inconceivable even fifteen years ago due the liquid nature of the world wrought through post-Cold War global technologies.

One question that is likely to be with us for quite some time how Barack Obama, the first noticeable African-descendent president of the United States, was able to emerge so rapidly and get elected, catching all the usual indicators of presidential electoral politics off guard. Certainly, as noted by many, mastery of cutting-edge technology holds the key to the answer of that question. This opens up many other issues about how we need to study racialization and other human differences that have been so transformed beyond traditional theories in need of radical reconsideration and methodologies in need of radical redesigning and application. This is especially the case in traditional social science literatures such as in sociology, which continues to miss predicting historical events in the transformation of racialization such as the 1950s and 1960s Civil Rights movements and the seemingly sudden emergence and success of a black man who ran for and made it to the White House as a guru of global technology. This is the result of the racialized biases in sociology and other American social sciences being so deeply institutionalized in the canons of the discipline. They have a fixated focus on traditions and systems of prejudice and discrimination while ignoring, overlooking, or simply not believing in the possibilities of human openness and its mobilization for the sake of the dehumanized and therefore for the rehumanized sake of society as a whole and perhaps the entire world.

Notes

* The use of upper- and lower-case letters for describing racialized ethnic peoples in this book is in keeping with standard publisher template style but as will be seen in future publications of mine, my preference is to put black and white in lower-case letters at all times and in places and to democratize this writing practice across all other racialized ethnic groups and communities when named (e.g. latinos, asians, and indigenous peoples). This is my way to minimize symbolically the use of racialized terms as much as possible since "race" is such a deeply culturally ingrained dehumanizing mythology. Upper caps are preferred only when referring to nationality such as Asian American or African American or Latino Americans or Native Americans.

1. To my utter surprise, I became the first American-born black to be promoted to associate professor without tenure in the Department of Sociology as well.

2. E. Franklin Frazier was another student of Park's who went to Salvador in the early 1940s.

References

Du Bois, W. E. B. (1896). *The suppression of the African slave trade to the United States.* Vol. 1 in the Harvard Historical Studies Series. Cambridge, MA: Harvard University Press.

Johnson, C. S. (1987). *Bitter canaan.* New Brunswick, NJ: Transaction Books Press.

Merton, R. K. (1948). Discrimination and the American creed. In R. M. MacIver (Ed.), *Discrimination and national welfare* (pp. 99–126). New York: Harper & Brothers.

Myrdal, G. (1944). *American dilemma.* New York: Harper & Brothers.

Pierson, D. (1942). *Negroes in Brazil: A study of race contacts at Bahia.* Chicago: University of Chicago Press.

Pitts, J. 1974. Race consciousness: Comments on new directions. *American Journal of Sociology 80*, 3, 665–687.

Valladares, L. 2010. Robert Park's visit to Brazil, the "marginal man" and the Bahia as laboratory. *Caderno CRH* (Brazil), vol. 23 no. 58 (April).

PART I: QUALITATIVE AND QUANTITATIVE METHODS

2 HOLISTIC RESTORATIVE JUSTICE METHODOLOGY IN INTERCULTURAL OPENNESS STUDIES

John H. Stanfield, II

SOME FAR AWAY MEMORIES

I was born in Rome, New York. When I was six, my parents moved their young family of three daughters and one son eight miles outside the city limits into the rural Holland Patent Central School District. When it came to school records, my mother seemingly kept everything. One day a few years ago while visiting my parents, I stumbled across my primary school report cards. My sixth-grade teacher Mr. O'Brien wrote two comments to my parents on my report cards, one in the beginning of the year and the second at the end of the year.

The comment at the beginning of the school year was "John needs to work harder; he can do better than this." The end-of-the-year comment was "John was the best bathroom monitor I ever had." Those comments brought back some far-away memories.

Anyone who knows sixth graders, at least when I was one as a baby-boomer, knows that the most crucial ploy was finding ways to manipulate the bathroom pass rules so that two or more of your buddies or girlfriends and you can end up in the bathroom together, away from the eyes and ears of the teacher. Thus, becoming bathroom monitor was even more important than getting elected class president. Being an effective bathroom monitor was akin to being an effective department chair in the adult university world as the liaison between department faculty and the dean. As bathroom monitor, you were a temporarily displaced peer who had the respect of your classmates since you knew when to and when not to tell the teacher and because your peers were inclined more or less to "cut it out" when you told them to. This meant, of course, that you said nothing or little of much significance about your peers' behavior to the teacher lest you become accused of being a squealer. And by telling the teacher that "nothing is wrong, no one is disobeying the rules" (at least not enough to warrant the teacher's attention), the teacher comes to consider you to a most effective leader among peers—"the best bathroom monitor I ever had."

Mr. O'Brien was that balding, overly strict teacher every fifth grader in our small rural primary school, Stittsville Elementary, dreaded having the next year. He was the zealot gatekeeper to that big next step to seventh grade. At the end of the year, he made many arrogant sixth graders cry in the hallway when he told them they were being held back. Over the years, I remember seeing some of those tear-drenched faces as a lower primary student as I passed in the hallway seeing Mr. O'Brien's stern stare while he proclaimed the bad news.

To my amazement and fear, I was nominated to run against one of the popular kids to become the grand bathroom monitor. I was not a very popular kid in my sixth-grade class. I assumed that was because I was rather puny and so was not usually the first choice as a kick ball or soft ball playmate and certainly not when it came to tag football. Perhaps it was because I was a stutterer, which made me shy and rather quiet. Or maybe it was because I was the only black boy in the Holland Patent Central School District, not just in class.

My popular peer and I, competitors for the esteemed position in question, were both told to leave the room for the voting. When we were told to come back in, it was announced I had won and was the bathroom monitor for the year. The ringing sound of hands clapping followed. My life changed in ways that I did not have the emotional maturity to understand then, but did later as my life moved on.

Where and when we spend our formative years has much bearing on who we become as a sociologist focused on a particular research topic. My long-time career and personal interest in how Blacks, Whites, and other racialized people become open human beings in prejudicial environments have much to do with growing up on a farm (from the age of six to sixteen) in that overwhelmingly white upstate New York rural community.

Not until my mid-fifties did I find out from my parents why they decided to move us to the country. I do remember as a six year old being told or overhearing that we had to move from the air force base where my father worked since civilians could no longer live there. But why move us out into the sticks? The answer to that question had to wait for over fifty years.

I found out that my parents decided to buy a house and become the first black couple of their generation in the Rome, New York area to become homeowners. My grandfather, whose name I proudly have, was the most prominent black civic leader in Rome, where I was born. He was seemingly respected enough across the small city to have the largest funeral in the city's history in the early 1960s. Yet, paradoxically, given the insane ironies of race, my paternal grandfather was not respected enough as a black man for the white bankers to extend a mortgage loan to his son and daughter-in-law.

So my parents turned to the lily-white countryside eight miles outside the city limits, without any black family for miles. They found a ten-acre farm being sold by a Polish American farmer. The farmer did the unspeakable by selling his property to Negroes, and many of his neighbors refused to speak to him again. Specifically, he gave my parents an owner mortgage loan since it was impossible for them to get one through a bank.

There was plenty of racial prejudice to go around when my three sisters and I began school in that rural school district, but by the time we moved to California shortly after my tenth year in high school began, we were a well-respected family still remembered in the community to this day. The journey of becoming a well-respected black family certainly was not easy; at times, my parents had to make it clear that we were there to stay even if it meant NAACP intervention, a vibrant and effective civil rights organization back then. Certainly the long meetings my parents had with school authorities and community leaders and their involvement with the PTA and other formal and informal groups of parents caused the local culture to open up a crack or two.

Also, my sisters and I went to school every school day, where we were all competitive academic performers, where we played, and yes, even at times, fought with classmates who dared to insult us due to our complexion. Over time, we transformed each other. We transformed each other to such an extent that it was just a matter of time before no white kid in his or her right mind would bother a Stanfield on the bus or on the play ground or they would be confronted with our white peer allies while we took a back seat and watched. And we Stanfield kids stood by and stood up for our underdog white friends— or at least I did.

And this had a spillover effect on my parents in unimaginable ways. One night, my parents driving back home on one of those old single-lane country roads with no street lights were hit head on by a drunken dairy truck driver, though not injured. The white deputy sheriff who came to the scene was the future brother-in-law of the drunk driver. To cover it up, the deputy cited my father for reckless driving or something like that. Some days later, in mid-evening, the deputy came by our house to arrest my father and take him to the local justice of the peace to make the charge official (I was a seven-year-old boy sitting next to my father watching television with him when the deputy came in and arrested him, which was certainly my initiation into the meaning of being a black man in America).

We had been in the country for about three or four years at the time. The deputy took my father, accompanied by my mother, to the justice of the peace that night and told his fabricated story. The justice of the peace stared at my parents for a few seconds and then asked, "Stanfield... is your daughter

Andrea?" My father said, "Yes." "My wife," the judge began, "is Andrea's fourth-grade teacher. She is such a wonderful smart little girl." Turning to the deputy, the justice of the peace continued, "These are good people, let them go." My parents sued the dairy company eventually and won.

TWO MISSING IDEAS IN AMERICAN SOCIOLOGICAL THOUGHT: THE UNIVERSALITY OF AMERICAN RACIAL PREJUDICE AND INTERCULTURAL OPENNESS

Over the decades, we American- and European-educated sociologists and non-Western sociologists professionalized within Western frames of references have published reams of empirical studies exploring with more or less methodological rigor how racial prejudice produces disparities in quality of life and causes superiority and inferiority complexes in human development. On the other hand, there is little theoretically sophisticated sociological literature with adequate methodological design, implementation, and evaluation about how people who grow up or move to multiracialized societies or institutions, systems, and communities become interculturally open. This is to claim that intercultural openness is a state of becoming rather than a state of being, given the traditions, rituals, and expected attitudes and behaviors of race-centered societies embedded in multigenerational mundane racial prejudice.

To engage in openness studies theoretically and methodologically requires a confession sociologists and the public in multiracialized societies hotly resist genuinely expressing and doing. Namely, everyone who is born and reared in a multiracial society or moves into one, develops racial prejudicial attitudes, opinions, values, inclinations, and practices, whether conscious, semiconscious, unconscious, intentional, unintentional, insidious, or blatant. And no matter how much a person tries to be open-minded, we all have a bit of racial prejudice until we die. This is a hard pill for sociologists to swallow.: Most Americans, and those who internalize American ideological values and norms, consider themselves racial-prejudice free and become quite upset or defensive or both when told otherwise.

The presumption among American and Americanized and Europeanized sociologists that it is possible to be without racial prejudice is apparent in two themes. The first is the white anti-black prejudice and discrimination thesis in American sociological literature that began with the publication of and response to Gunnar Myrdal's *American Dilemma* in 1944. Swedish economist Myrdal, an idealistic admirer of the United States, viewed America as a democracy with the strange contradiction of having a long history of discriminating against blacks. The second is Robert Merton's (1948) response to Myrdal. In conceptualizing his notions of all-weather (white) and fair-weather (white) liberals, Merton formalized the presumption, now a well-institutionalized and erroneous norm in sociology as well as in the dominant U.S. culture, that Whites can be free from racial prejudice.

With no significant empirical evidence, Merton's (1948) think piece laid out four different individual white anti-black prejudice inclinations in conjunction with whether the institutional cultures Whites find themselves in either support or oppose racial discrimination against Blacks. There were the Mertonian all-weather liberal Whites who never discriminated because of their nonprejudical views about Blacks, even when institutional roles and values sanctioned discrimination against Blacks. Fair-weather liberals are Whites who are free from anti-black prejudice but discriminate when institutional roles and values require it. Fair-weather nonliberals are prejudiced against Blacks but will not discriminate if institutional roles and values require nondiscrimination. All-weather nonliberals are Whites who are prejudiced against Blacks and discriminate even when institutional roles and values require nondiscrimination.

This now decades-old folk wisdom in American sociological thought that it is possible for Whites to be without anti-black prejudice—though sometimes feel forced to discriminate against Blacks—has been enshrined for years in textbooks. These ideas were also prevalent in studies done by Merton and other third-generation sociologists and other social scientists coming of age in the 1940s and 1950s (Allport 1979; Simpson & Yinger 1953) about prejudice caused by discrimination. Separating prejudice from discrimination and claiming to be or do neither made it easy for liberal white sociologists to hide their prejudices behind claims of being nonprejudiced while becoming defensive and resentful toward anyone who dared question it.

A common response by Whites to someone trying to explain white prejudice as something most Whites are socialized into is: "Are you trying to call me a racist?" Usually what follows is a lecture on all the things they have done for Blacks and the list of black friends with whom they occasionally eat collard greens and cornbread with chitterlings on the side (a distinguished liberal white sociologist actually said something like this to me the moment we first sat down to meet each other). This denial of being prejudiced allowed post-1960s white sociologists who were liberal before affirmative action forced them to open the doors of their student bodies and departmental faculties to reverse themselves and become anti-affirmative action conservatives. They pointed to their 1950s and 1960s civil rights records (i.e., sending white students south to march with King) or to their abolitionist ancestors when accused of being racist.

Peggy McIntosh's check-list regarding white privilege as well as the recent new area of whiteness studies certainly calls into question this well-established presumption. The prejudice-free white presumption is still prevalent in American sociological research and in the politics of career-making (see Bonilla-Silva [2006] and the article by Elizabeth Hordge-Freeman, Sarah Mayorga, and Eduardo Bonilla-Silva in this volume).

The free-from-racial-prejudice myth has also been extended to non-whites but in a different way. A popular false presumption is that blacks and other non-Whites cannot be racist since we do not have dominant group power with which to discriminate, exploit, and exterminate. As a demographic group, we Blacks cannot be racist in America in the power and authority sense of the word, but we cannot divorce ourselves, either as a population or as individuals, from the racialized historical origins and development of this country and the racialized culture that continues to be passed down from generation to generation in locally- and regionally specific ways.

In mainstream American sociology, the focus in prejudice studies is usually on Whites. We rarely have studies on black prejudice against Whites and other non-Whites. We can appreciate this observation only when we come to realize that prejudgment and preference is more basic than matters of power and authority.[1]

When we consider racial prejudice in this way, we understand that like most Whites in America, most Blacks prefer their own kind when it comes to marriage, adoption, faith community, and other Charles Cooleyian primary group formations. This is why even though black anti-white prejudice is commonplace in traditionally segregated black church circles under the guise of "cultural uniqueness ideologies, values, and ethnic traditions," it becomes a dismal surprise when such anti-black racial prejudice comes to national attention and is rationalized as a "cultural thing or an ethnic tradition" black preachers do to cater to their congregational consumers. This was more than apparent in the Rev. Jeremiah Wright controversy during Barack Obama's campaign for the presidential nomination of the Democratic Party.

"Racialism" (see Chapter 1 in this book) is the term I use to refer to the universal racial prejudice that Americans in general and those in other multiracialized societies are socialized into multigenerationally. In a "race-centered" society that embeds "race consciousness" (Pitts 1974) as well as individual socialization, racialism is the mundane, taken-for-granted written, verbal, and body language, behavior, and decisions premised on false correlations between "real" or imagined phenotypical features and human attributes such as intellectual abilities, moral character, values, identity, leadership abilities, emotional expression, and cultural tastes. Using the term "racism" in the usual power and authority terms and now being introduced to the more basic dehumanizing experience of racialism means that it is necessary to be a racialist if one is a racist, though not all racialists are racists.

Thus, to be black and grow up in America is, under most circumstances, to become normatively racialist. Again, however, from the standpoint of power and authority, for the most part, Blacks and other non-Whites in America cannot be racists. It will be interesting to see how patterns of racial prejudice will shift or remain the same as Whites become the demographic minority in the United States in the twenty-first century.

It is important to discuss black racialism because this hot-button issue has rarely been studied by sociologists. At best, there has been focus on black anti-white religious and political movements such as the Black Muslims and the Black Panthers, with little attention being paid to everyday black racialism. The modest sociological literature on skin color prejudice among Blacks in the United States and other multiracial societies such as Brazil, South Africa, Martinique, and Great Britain is the closest we come to having a noticeable black prejudice literature, but it is focused on intra-racialized populations rather than inter-racialized ones.

Black prejudice against Latinos and vice versa is becoming a matter of significant political interest and concern, given the changing ethnic demographics in the United States. But we have yet to have extensive sociological studies of such patterns as black anti-Latino and Latino anti-black prejudice. The same is true of relations between Blacks and Asians. Also ignored is black-on-black prejudice, which is quite prevalent between Blacks "born and raised here for generations" and recent African-descendant arrivals from African countries and the Caribbean. How much such prejudice is racialism, xenophobia, or nativism needs to be studied empirically.

The universality of racialism requires new theory-driven methodologies to explore how members of such societies become what I call "interculturally opening." To be interculturally opening is to be initially normatively closed and exclusionary and at best cosmetically, symbolically, and marginally intercultural, which is the way most Americans and immigrant residents in America live their lives. Over time, through exposure to and quality-of-life dependency on other racialized populations, tolerance begins to occur. Then, over a lifetime, other experiences allow the interculturally opening person to gradually move beyond just being tolerant to gradually embracing, if not living, the humanity of those deemed to be racialized others. How this intercultural opening happens individually and collectively needs to be studied.

TOWARD A THEORY OF RESTORATIVE JUSTICE AS METHODOLOGY

Restorative justice is a unique qualitative methodology (Stanfield 2006b) that can, I believe, effectively address how interculturally open people become so over time, through small-group dynamics experiences that are observed, recorded, and evaluated. The more historical question is how intercultural openness developed in those who have left autobiographies, oral histories, oral traditions, and personal archival materials and who have had biographies and other secondary histories written about them.

As a lived experience, either normatively or/and through public policy design, implementation, and design, restorative justice is the recovery of our humanity by embracing, respecting, and living the humanity of those we have been socialized to routinely dehumanize. Restorative justice as a national public policy was popularized in the early 1990s by Bishop Desmond Tutu with the Truth and Reconciliation Commission in the earliest years of black majority rule in post-apartheid South Africa. More fundamentally, restorative justice is a community and a societal practice dating back to ancient times as a way indigenous people restored human dignity after something terrible has happened.

Restorative justice, indeed, what I call "multicultural restorative justice," has been written about and debated about all over the world as alternative public policies in regions such as East Europe and East and Central Africa as recent sites of massive genocide (Volf 1996, 2006). In this emerging literature, the process of becoming human is rooted in the assumption that when something terrible happens that destroys human beings en masse, whether be it episodes such as genocide or slavery and their institutionalizations or routine systems such as poverty, ageism, sexism, or anti-religiosity it dehumanizes the entire society. Such horrible human episodes and systems dehumanize perpetrators as well as victims. Indeed, in the restorative justice framework, all involved are both perpetrators and victims. This is why the labor-intensive and deeply painful process of restorative justice involves perpetrators and victims sitting around the same table and taking turns in articulating memories of what happened. They must confess that they all had a part in the horrible deeds in some way. Then they must take responsibility by apologizing and asking for forgiveness (i.e., mutual understanding of each other) so that they can at least coexist and at best embrace each other and live together. Then they must restore what was taken symbolically—such as names or material things such as land—and what represent human dignity. Finally, they must enter the phase of a new way of living sustained through new support systems and new social circles that continue to confirm the humanity of those who they used to see as less than human.

This intense process of becoming human again, which takes much humility and transparency, makes restorative justice a difficult perspective to grasp, let alone embrace and implement in daily life and in public policy formation and implementation in societies based on cultures of retribution and cultures of blame and in cultures which place no value on self reflection and accountability. It is no wonder, then, that aside from some criminal justice concerns (Zehr 2002), there is little mention in the United States or many other societies of restorative justice as a viable public policy alternative let alone as a way of daily life and as a type of valuation and even identity.

Whether restorative justice as an alternative public policy and/or as the way people come to live through generations of changes in a multiracial society such as the outcomes of living in progressively integrating residential communities or participating in increasingly integrating schools of all levels, armed forces, consumer popular culture, written, electronic, and Internet media, medical and legal systems, and electoral and appointive political processes, intentional restorative justice methodology can be used to assist people on the way of becoming interculturally opening. This is an important living process in a country stunned by the election of Barack Obama to the U.S. presidency in 2008. How did it happen? His seemingly sudden emergence caught orthodox media heads and social scientists completely off guard because we are used to focusing on the negative rather than on the positive, on exclusion and discrimination rather than on openness (Stanfield 2008). The racial studies industry has been just too lucrative, as has the way race is used to make careers of politicians who get voted into white or black districts, for it to be dismantled or balanced in studying trends in openness. We are now scrambling to find out what happened and lapsing back into the same routine racialized thinking rather than forging ahead and helping people become much more culturally literate about the dehumanizing character of multiracialism so they can continue to transform their lives in ways which are humane to others who have been racialized and therefore humanize themselves.

The vast literature on what works and what does not work in transforming racially inclusive environments may question a wide range of effective indicators, but one factor matters more than any other. Namely, any kind of transformation, especially that involving race, must have clearly committed senior leaders. So this restorative justice methodology is for any chief leadership in an institution or system or community, or national government wishing to invest deeply in a labor-intensive process of transformation centered on the premise that a horrible monster like the terrible beast of race impacts the entire society. It is a methodology that can be utilized even in a nonreflective blame-oriented society such as the United States in which all must embrace and practice accountability in regard to self and others.

THE SUGGESTED HOLISTIC RESTORATIVE JUSTICE MODEL

Ideally, restorative justice methods are labor-intensive processes of humanity recovery for all concerned, in which dehumanizing perpetrators come to the table, so to speak, with dehumanized victims to create a safe space for sharing interpretations (memories) of what happened, confessions (accountability), apologies (never-do-it-again covenants), forgiveness (understanding), reconciliation (embracing each other), reparations (giving back symbolic, cultural, emotional, and material dignity), and going out together as one (sustaining networks and communities of opening values and identities).

The basic phrase in restorative justice methodology as a goal is "the coming together of perpetrators and victims in synchronic accountability which comes to constitute or reconstitute a community which is healthy and functional since the human dignity of all is embraced, lived, and preserved." Thus, each step is deemed to be complete when those at the table can agree to recip-rocal accountability unification. It looks like this:

1. remembrances between perpetrators and victims bear the fruit of recip-rocal historical interpretation acceptance;

2. confession between perpetrators and victims generates mutual acknow-ledgment of blame—perpetrators for doing the deed or supporting it or being bystanders and victims through being collaborators in their own dehumanization by being passive bystanders; apologies between perpet-rators and victims, from the Judeo-Christian concept of repentance, gener-ates sustaining covenants with promises never to engage in the deed again or support it, perpetrators' covenants never to dehumanize again, and vic-tims' covenants never to allow themselves to be dehumanized again;

3. forgiveness between perpetrators and victims, as what happens is mutual understanding of "the other," which may generate agreements to embrace by living together or co-existing, recognizing, and respecting diversity in values or recognizing the dangers of trying to live together again but re-specting each other to take care the human needs of the community. The option of co-existence as a concept is taken from the divorce literature re-garding parents who divorce since they cannot or should not live together as spouses but wish to do the best for their children and/or their pets and property, so they agree to cooperate with each other though not caring to become emotionally involved with each other again;

4. reconciliation between perpetrators and victims through the reciprocal material, emotional, cultural, and symbolic reparations to restore the human dignity of all and to sustain it; and

5. unification of perpetrators and victims to live intercultural lives, as reflected by changes in their social circles, life decisions and choices, vocations, and so on.

This ideal process of holistic restorative justice rarely if ever occurs or if it does, the time framework can last for years if not decades or centuries. Another problem is that too often restorative justice scholars as well as influ-ential community leaders fragment the ideal holistic process by focusing on one or more aspects of the process or on one population.

Consequently, the restoration process never gets completed and can actu-ally make things worse since piecemeal applications disrupt the healing pro-cess. For instance, to offer reparations to victims without going through the preceding steps can cause resentment or anger among dominant populations and shame and/or rejection of entitlements by representatives of victimized populations. Without the antecedent steps, the terrible things that happened remain buried or minimized. Thus, most people from both perpetrating and victimized populations are utterly ignorant about, for example, the dehumanizing operations of race or have naive understanding of the experience. Before reparations can be effectively justified and allocated, mass education must take place so the general public understands why they are necessary.

All criticisms aside, there is still great value in attempting to develop an effective step-by-step holistic restorative justice process that deracializes an institution, a system, a community, or society. When leaders express genuine inclusion values and have effective leadership styles, holistic restorative justice processes do occur. An example of an implicit restorative justice intercultural opening process is Moskos and Butler's (1997) study of how the U.S. armed forces desegregated, which they argued could be applied to civilian sectors such as universities. What matters is having the leadership skills to design, implement, and evaluate formalized holistic restorative justice processes, as illustrated by the chapter by Dawn Brotherton in this volume.

The Moskos and Butler and the Brotherton models suggest that the best strategic strategy to follow is to organize restorative justice processes as small groups in institutions, communities, and systems led clearly and boldly by the most senior leadership.

Here is how it works. The group, no more than nine, sits in a circle with a moderator-researcher. He or she explains the ground rules. There is the round-robin rule—each person talks with no interruption from others; the time-and-length rule—each person has so many minutes or so many words to use to answer each question; and the break rule—every ninety minutes there is a ten-minute break. The session lasts for no more than seven hours, with a ninety-minute wrap-up time for a round-robin (forty-five minutes) review of how everyone feels and a forty-five-minute free-for-all discussion about what happened. There also has to be a ground rule regarding confidentiality and another regarding meeting schedules.

The moderator-researcher has a cane or some other object meant to encourage intense focus while being held by each participant as the person is answering a question asked by the moderator-researcher. When a person finishes, the cane is passed to the next person. Once the cane gets back to the moderator-researcher, the moderator-researcher pauses in reflection for a minute or two and then asks a deeper question. The cane goes around again and the process continues. This deeper and deeper questioning by the moderator-researcher is metaphorically peeling an onion, which begins with surface, nonthreatening questions and become increasingly threatening, making participants much more vulnerable to exposure. This is actually a process of trust building and deepening transparency so that each person becomes figuratively unclothed before the group as to who they really are and what they really think.

Each component of the process is a series of "onion-peeling questions" that the moderator-researcher asks. Since this is a labor-intensive immersion methodology, it is essential that the process lasts one or two years, perhaps bi-weekly, with observational follow-ups once every other year. An observational follow-up involves the moderator-researcher spending three or four days interviewing each participant and watching him or her in and out of the relevant environment to determine the impact of the process on the person's life.

The pace of the group from beginning to end (indicated by unification agreements) depends on the group's unconscious and conscious emotional work. This might involve asking for counseling services for one-on-one sessions for participants who experience emotional problems as they become unraveled and exposed.

Each component also entails assigned tasks that the group must complete on their own time in conjunction with the component being unfolded. If it involves memory, there may be a group visit to different memorials representing different versions of history about what happened to each population. Or it may be community-based oral histories of people representing different racialized populations in their communities. In the last phase, going out together, the group might spend a month or two in each other's community in a private household. The tasks become integrated into the moderator-researcher series of questions.

Each component of this process is also accompanied by readings—autobiographies, biographies, diaries, and secondary histories documenting or illustrating a particular component—and the requirement that participants must engage in journaling daily or weekly or monthly about their experiences. Key issues from these writings and participant journaling experiences are integrated into the questions the moderator-researcher asks in selected rounds.

Every six months, each participant presents either a tape-recorded or self-written summary about what he or she is learning about themselves, about other group members, and about the relevant environment.

Conclusion

There can be at least three senses of restorative justice processes in multiracialized societies and institutions, communities, and systems within them with logic of inquiry questions and strategies.

First there is normative restorative justice: the everyday experiences resulting in people deracializing through daily encounters with racialized others in integrated living, working, and consuming environments. Oral histories, autobiographies, biographies, journals, archival materials, and ethnographic observations can be used to reconstruct the lives of those who become progressively interculturally open.

This is especially an important line of research now, when the election of Barack Obama as the first noticeable African American president of the

United States indicates the profound and too-often understudied positive impacts of the civil rights movements, including the desegregated work, education, military, and popular cultural environments in the lives of Americans, especially post-baby boomers (Stanfield 2008). But, even going back to the colonial era, some lived opening intercultural lives, irrespective of their racialized ancestry roots. We should find ways to reconstruct their lives and the historically grounded contexts in which they lived (see Chapter 12 in this volume and Stanfield 1983, 1985). What is most exciting is doing such research cross-nationally, for example, comparing and contrasting the life journeys of white female novelists who have lived intercultural opening lives, such as American Smith Lillian and South African Nadine Gordimer, or anthropologists with intercultural openness qualities, such as Margaret Mead of the United States and Gilberto Freyre of Brazil. Using long interviews and ethnographic observation to compare the life flows of people of more modest means and backgrounds in South Africa and in the United States of numerous ancestral backgrounds would make the study of the normative restorative justice basis of intercultural openness life development even more fascinating.

Second is the alternative public policy restorative justice perspective, which is the approach of a national government to resolve any historical horror of race. This is usually done through a standing national court or, in the case of South Africa, through an independent commission. National public policy approaches with a restorative justice ring tend to be plagued with serious implementation problems. Restorative justice as alternative public policies in multiracialized societies is the most common area of focus and debate in the global restorative justice literature. It also tends to have a heavily legal studies bias with little input from the social sciences and humanities. That is changing, though, with, for instance, the growing literature on theological concerns in restorative justice measures. But what the legal studies approach often means is that methodological analysis is too confined to finding ways to critique legal decisions or legal procedures.

Third, and as the focus of this chapter, I am proposing that holistic restorative justice is a labor-intensive transparency process that can be used in multiracialized institutions, communities, systems, and societies as a small-group-immersion experience. Restorative justice as a holistic methodology recognizes that those who are socialized in multiracialized societies can learn to appreciate and embrace the humanity of those they have learned to dehumanize through small-group processes involving several holistic restorative justice steps. All of the steps must be adhered to for a healthy community to be realized.

Over the past five years, I have been testing this theory-driven holistic restorative justice model both in a community setting in southern Indiana, which has a harsh race relations history (Stanfield 2006a), and in Fielding University School of Human and Organization Development workshops for doctoral students, which is beginning to produce scholar practitioners who are using focus group methodologies (see Chapters 9 and 11 in this volume) to study this holistic restorative justice small-group approach. I have also been fine-tuning this approach through classroom-based research on the Indiana University campus in which students conduct research on the racial healing needs of the campus. And a colleague and I are attempting to employ this approach in Indianapolis and Indiana as a whole, which still feels the effects of the 1920s Ku Klux Klan movement that transformed Indiana into a statewide arena of racial prejudice.

Finally, I have been exploring how to use this holistic restorative justice approach in my research travels to Brazil and to South Africa and have plans to do the same in future trips to India (see Chapter 14 in this volume).

Note

1. This point was made clear to me at a meeting I attended in Indianapolis about adopting children. After the meeting, the speaker insisted that birth families had the right to select adoptive parents. A white woman asked if it made any difference about the race of the child in terms of placement—in other words, can white adopted parents be considered for a black child's adoption? The speaker said yes, in theory, but that most birth families, including African Americans, preferred their own kind to adopt their child.

References

Allport, G. (1979). *The nature of prejudice*. Addison-Wesley.

Bonilla-Silva, E. (2006). *Racism without racists*. Rowman & Littlefield.

Merton, R. (1948). Discrimination and the American creed. In R. M. MacIver (Ed.), *Discrimination and national welfare* (pp. 99–126). New York: Harper & Brothers.

Moskos, C., & Butler, J. S. (1997). *All that we can be. Black leadership and racial integration the army way*. New York: Basic Books.

Myrdal, G. (1944). *An American dilemma: The Negro problem and modern democracy*. New York: Harper & Brothers.

Pitts, J. (1974). Race consciousness: Comments on new directions. *American Journal of Sociology, 80*, 3, 665–687.

Simpson, G., & Yinger, J. M. (1953). *Racial and cultural minorities: An analysis of prejudice and discrimination*. New York: Harper & Brothers.

Stanfield, J. H., II. (1983). Leonard Outhwaite's advocacy of scientific research on blacks in the 1920s. *Knowledge and Society, 4*, 87–101.

Stanfield, J. H., II. (1985). *Philanthropy and Jim Crow in American social science*. Westport, CT: Greenwood Press.

Stanfield, J. H., II. (2006a). Psychoanalytic ethnography and the transformation of racially wounded communities. *International Journal of Qualitative Studies in Education, 19*, 3, 387–399.

Stanfield, J. H., II. (2006b). The possible restorative justice functions of qualitative research. *International Journal of Qualitative Studies in Education, 19*, 723–727.

Stanfield, J. H., II. (2008). The Obama phenomenon: The promise of a restorative justice micro-revolutionary paradigm in multiracial America. *PU-Rio Journal of Sociology.*

Volf, M. (1996). *Exclusion and embrace.* Nashville: Abingdon Press.

Volf, M. (2006). *The end of memory: Remembering rightly in a violent world.* Grand Rapids, MI: William B. Eerdmans Publishing House.

Zehr, H. (2002). *The little book on restorative justice.* Intercourse, PA: Good Books.

3 DISCOURSE ANALYSIS OF RACISM

Teun A. van Dijk

INTRODUCTION

The usual study of racism takes place in social sciences such as sociology, political science, anthropology, and social psychology. In the last decades, other disciplines—e.g., studies of language, discourse, and communication—have also contributed to our understanding of racial and ethnic domination.

This chapter focuses on the theories and methods in these latter fields and shows how these are able to study subtleties of everyday racism that are difficult to assess in other disciplines and with other methods. In any case, the complexity of racism requires a multidisciplinary approach, given the manifestation of racism in such diverse phenomena as ideologies, attitudes, text, talk, communication, interaction, institutions, group relations, official policies, international relations, and ethnic diversity in multicultural societies.

Discourse Studies (DS) is one of the cross-disciplines of the humanities and the social sciences that offers a unique perspective in these multidisciplinary approaches. This is especially so because discourse is at once text and a form of social interaction; expresses and forms underlying prejudices and racist ideologies; and plays a fundamental role in the (re)production of domination in intergroup relations, society, politics, and culture. Although much contemporary racist practice is discursive and hence only seems to consist of words, the consequences of these practices on the minds and moods of both the dominant and dominated groups are critical. This does *not* mean that all forms of racism are discursive, but that discourse plays a central role in the reproduction of racist attitudes and ideologies that are the socio-cognitive basis of the social system of racism.

Besides aggregate statistics of various forms of racist inequality in society, discourse analysis (DA) offers the most sophisticated form of qualitative data analysis (e.g., of personal stories of experiences of racism, interviews, government policies, parliamentary debates, racist propaganda, textbooks and classroom interaction, legal discourse as well as the text and talk of mass media, all fundamentally involved in the daily reproduction of racism).

RACISM AND ITS REPRODUCTION

Before reviewing the discourse analytical approach to the study of racism, I will summarize the more general theory of racism I have developed over the last three decades (for details, see van Dijk 1984, 1987, 1991, 1993, 1998, 2005, 2009, 2008a; Wodak & van Dijk 2000; for references to other theories of racism, see the other chapters of this volume, as well as below).

Racism is a social system of ethnic or "racial" domination, where domination is a form of power abuse of one group over another. It consists of two major subsystems: various kinds of discriminatory practices in all domains of social life, on the one hand, and underlying ideologically based ethnic prejudices as forms of socially shared (distributed) cognition, on the other.

Racist discourse plays a crucial intermediary role in this system, since it may be both a discriminatory practice in its own right and, at the same time, the primary source and medium for the acquisition of racist prejudices and ideologies.

Discriminatory practices are illegitimate forms of power abuse exercised by dominant ethnic group members—such as people of European origin in Europe, the Americas, Australia, and New Zealand—against ethnic/racial Others. Such abuse may be in the form of preferential access to or control over scarce material or symbolic resources such as land, jobs, housing, residence, salaries, reputation, or public discourse, among many others (van Dijk 2008a).

Discriminatory practices are cognitively based on and legitimated by shared social attitudes, ideologies, norms, and values construed to be in the interest of the dominant group. These shared ideological representations may, for instance, emphasize superiority or priority of the dominant white group and the inferiority of the ethnic Others in many relevant areas and criteria of social evaluation, such as intelligence, attractiveness, honesty, creativity, dynamism, work ethic, and so on. Racist ideologies, in turn, control specific negative attitudes (prejudices) about the Others, in the fields of immigration, neighborhood integration, the labor market, security, crime, marriage, and so on.

Ideologically based racist attitudes form the evaluative basis of the formation of the specific, personal mental models that control all action, interaction, and discourse of individual group members and hence the social practices that constitute the discriminatory manifestation of racism. And, vice versa, racist discourse may give rise to biased mental models that can be socially shared, generalized, and abstracted as racist attitudes and ideologies.

This closes the vicious circle of the reproduction of racism and, at the same time, allows its (gradual) change if there are many and influential antiracist discourses in the public sphere and if dominated groups engage in various (other) forms of resistance. This theoretical framework may be briefly summarized by the schema shown in Figure 3.1.

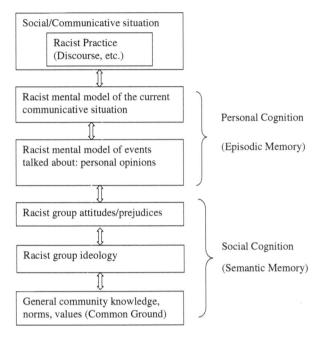

Fig. 3.1 Schematic representation of the (discursive) reproduction of racism

Note in this schema that racist ideologies, attitudes, and models—as well as the concrete discriminatory practices controlled by these underlying representations—are ultimately based on the shared knowledge, norms, and values of a community or society, that is, the sociocultural common ground. This explains why different ideological groups in society (say, racist and anti-racist groups) need a common basis to be able to communicate and interact in the first place. For instance, they may have very different attitudes about immigration, but they all need to know what immigrants are in the first place, what the dominant norms and values are, and so on.

As we shall further see below, racist discourse practices need two kinds of personal mental models. One kind is when language users ongoingly construct a mental model of the communicative situation (for instance, an informal conversation, a news report in the press, a speech in parliament, etc.), that is, a context model (van Dijk 2008b, 2009b). These *pragmatic* context models ensure that what we say or write is adapted to the relevant parameters of the communicative situation, such as the setting, participants (and their identities, roles, relationships), the current social actions performed (e.g., informing the citizens, teaching a class, etc.), the current goals, and intentions as well as the (assumed) knowledge and ideologies of the participants. Indeed, even if speakers have racist mental models, attitudes, or ideologies, they may adapt their talk to the occasion, those they are talking to, and so on—or they may not say anything racist at all. This explains, among other things, why people may use such disclaimers as "I am not a racist, but ..." when they are not sure whether their recipients share their opinions and attitudes. Even racists do not act as racists all the time.

The other mental models used or construed in communication are semantic; that is, they are subjective representations of what people are talking or writing *about*, for instance, an ethnic event they have experienced, observed, or heard/read about. It is this (possibly biased) mental model that is the basis of stories or news reports about such ethnic events. Note, though, that the context model, as discussed above, controls whether or not the (racist, etc.) opinions of this model of an ethnic event will be expressed in the discourse or not: It all depends on the situation (especially who the interlocutors are) and how participants understand or construe it.

The Social Structure of the Discursive Reproduction of Racism

We have seen that discourse plays a central role in the reproduction of racism because of its intermediary role between discriminatory practices and racist social cognition. Text and talk of dominant group members—*as* group members—may be biased and hence itself be a form of discriminatory social practice. At the same time, it is through discourse, interaction, and communication that the contents of ethnically biased mental models, attitudes, and ideologies can be formulated, spread, and acquired by its new members, such as children. We shall see below what kinds of structures and strategies of discourse are particularly relevant in this reproduction and acquisition process.

The Role of the Symbolic Elites

Not all dominant group members are equally responsible for the discursive reproduction of racism because not all of them have equal access to public discourse, the main conduit of the reproduction of racism: the discourse of politics, media, education, science, and bureaucracy. Those who control public discourse, whom we call the symbolic elites, have special power and special responsibilities in spreading—but also combating—the ethnic prejudices that are the basis of the system of racism. All research to date, in many countries, confirms that the symbolic elites, both formerly and today, have played a major part in the problem of racism and a minor part in its solution.

This does not mean that the elites are more racist than the population at large, but only that the attitudes of a small but influential number of them may reach millions through authoritative political, media, educational, or scientific discourse. In today's information and communication societies, the symbolic elites play an especially crucial role, together with the corporate elites who own and manage the mass media, textbook publishing, and related industries. It is important to stress the special role of the symbolic elites in the reproduction of racism because they are the first to deny that they are racist (van Dijk 1992) and generally attribute racism to others, for instance to people with less education or those in working-class neighborhoods.

"Routine" Racism

Most racist discourse today need not be engaged in intentionally or blatantly. It may be a "normal" part or consequence of institutional routines and arrangements that are in the interest of the (white) dominant group in complex systems of power networks and that marginalize or exclude minorities. For instance, research shows that immigrants and minorities have less access to mass media, as news actors written about and as journalists, because most (newsworthy) organizations and news actors the news is about are white. Hence, they will be selected as more reliable sources by white journalists than minority news actors and organizations.

This kind of systematic discrimination is not just caused by racist attitudes of owners and editors of the press, it is indirectly also conditioned by the structure of press routines. Daily routines of newsgathering contact the powerful organizations, which happen to have the press agencies that preformulate news and opinion through tailor-made press conferences, press releases, interviews, and other source discourses, and which are consistently formulated in the best interest of these institutions and organizations (Tuchman 1978). And since the latter are largely controlled by the dominant white elites, it is their ideologically based opinions that dominate in the mass media as long as the journalists do not see an inconsistency with their own ideologies and interests.

Because most journalists in the Americas and Europe are white, and critical minority journalists are even more discriminated against than others, the media routinely tend to accept and adopt dominant ethnic attitudes of these powerful institutions and organizations.

Journalists thus legitimatize racist cognitions for the public at large, which will therefore be more easily persuaded to adopt these attitudes, as long as these mental models and attitudes do not conflict with their own interests.

The Subtle Racism of the Hegemonic Consensus

Because of the resistance of ethnic minority groups and some "antiracist" change agents within the dominant groups themselves, as was the case for the civil rights movement in the United States, the last decades have delegitimized blatantly racist discourse. Such discourse is now associated with the extreme right, neo-Nazis, and various fringe groups, although in some countries racist or xenophobic parties may occasionally be part of coalition governments, as in Denmark, Holland, Austria, and Italy.

At the same time, racist attitudes and ideologies of the extreme right have influenced those of mainstream parties and institutions in a somewhat less blatant and democratically more presentable format. This allows mainstream parties, media, and organizations to continue to accuse the more extreme racist groups and organizations of being the "real racists," thus denying their own attitudes of racism.

Hegemonic contemporary attitudes on immigration and minorities thus converge in what has variously been called "new racism," "symbolic racism," "aversive racism," and others forms of "lite" racism, manifesting itself in more subtle discourses and other practices of exclusion, problematization, and inferiorization of ethnic/racial Others (Barker 1981; Dovidio & Gaertner 1986).

In this chapter, I do not limit my discussion of racism to the extreme right, which is where the symbolic elites say it is. On the contrary, I am specifically interested in the mainstream racism of the powerful elites and institutions that exercise the most control in our everyday lives: local, state, and national governments; political parties; the mass media; schools at all levels; the courts; and all bureaucracies. Also, I am not as interested in the analysis of occasional blatantly racist discourse as in the more subtle mainstream forms of text and talk that are not even seen as racist by the dominant consensus. It is precisely in the analysis of such racist messages and interactions that DA shows its methodological advantages.

Racism and Discourse: General Principles

If discourse plays such a crucial role in the communicative and cognitive reproduction of racism in society, it is equally crucial to pay special attention to the discursive structures and strategies that optimally contribute to this process. Thus, we shall see that specific properties of discourse show the structures of underlying biased models, prejudices, and ideologies and may thus be efficient in the formation of racist mental representations among the population at large.

The Discipline of Discourse Studies

DS developed in most of the humanities and social sciences, often independently and more or less at the same time—between 1964 and 1974—with the first books appearing around 1972. Here is a brief summary of its main approaches, showing the broad diversity of the research in the field—each approach with its own handbooks, introductions, journals, academic specializations, and congresses. (For details, general introductions and handbooks, see, among others, Schiffrin et al. 2001; van Dijk, 2007, 2011.)

- **The Ethnography of Communication.** Anthropology has probably been the first discipline that, since the mid-1960s, explicitly aimed to study the structures of "communicative events" in different societies and cultures, including both text, talk and contexts, in what was first called the "ethnography of speaking" (see, e.g., Saville-Troike 1989). Later, **linguistic anthropology** related this study of culturally variable properties of talk to other developments mentioned below, such as conversation analysis and interactional sociolinguistics.

- **Interactional Sociolinguistics.** Closely linked to work in the ethnography of communication, since the early 1970s interactional sociolinguistics focused on the detailed study of the linguistic properties of talk in institutional settings, with special attention to the way such setting are subtly signaled in what are called "contextualization cues" (Gumperz 1982).

- **Semiotics.** Starting in France in the mid-1960s, semiotics (French: *sémiologie*) set the stage for a structuralist paradigm, which paid particular attention to narrative structures, besides other nonverbal communication such as films. Today, **social semiotics** focuses specifically on nonverbal communication such as the study of images and multimodal messages (e.g., Internet communications) (Van Leeuwen 2005, 2008).

- **Pragmatics.** Another sister cross-discipline developed in parallel with DS since the 1960s and the work on speech acts and the work on conversational maxims by Grice (1989). Though first limited to one-sentence speech acts, later work also focused on sequences of speech acts and in general on the pragmatics of discourse, including, for instance, studies of politeness (Levinson 1983).

- **Text Grammar.** Both structuralist and generative grammars were sentence grammars, and most of them are until today. However, toward the end of the 1960s, there were several attempts (e.g., in Germany, the United Kingdom, and the United States) to develop text or discourse grammars. These grammars accounted for linguistic structures beyond the sentence to account for cohesion, local and global coherence, pronominalization, discourse topics, topic-comment structures of sentences, focus, presupposition, and so on (Givón 1979, 1983; van Dijk 1972, 1977).

- **Conversation Analysis.** One of the most successful and influential directions of discourse studies, with roots in qualitative micro-sociology, phenomenology, and ethnomethodology in sociology, CA has been the study of conversation and verbal interaction since the early 1970s. At first focusing on everyday, informal conversation, CA today also pays attention to many forms of institutional talk (ten Have 2007).

- **The Cognitive Psychology of Text Processing.** Whereas the various approaches mentioned above focused on the situated structures of text and talk, cognitive psychology since the early 1970s specifically examined the mental processes and representations involved in the production and comprehension of discourse and how information of discourse is being stored and recalled in memory. Special attention was given to the role of knowledge in text processing (Graesser et al. 2003; van Dijk & Kintsch 1983).

- **Artificial Intelligence, Computer Linguistics, Corpus Linguistics.** Related to the cognitive psychology of text processing, since the early 1970s, and mostly in the United States, artificial intelligence (AI) focused specifically on the automatic production and comprehension of discourse by computers, specifically examining how world knowledge should be represented (e.g., as mental "scripts") and applied to enable such automatic text processing (Schank & Abelson 1977). **Corpus linguistics** also makes use of computers, but does so by examining the use of words and structures in large data bases (e.g., by a study of "collocations" of specific words) (Connor & Upton 2004).

- **Discursive Psychology.** Starting in the United Kingdom, one of the branches of social psychology called "discursive psychology" rejected classical concepts of the discipline such as attitude as well as laboratory experiments and quantitative accounts of data. Discursive psychology advocated that instead, one should qualitatively study the ways these psychological constructs show up in natural text and talk; hence, its later focus on CA as a method of detailed study of interaction (Edwards & Potter 1992).

- **Genre Studies, Narrative, and Argumentation.** Among the many other approaches in contemporary DS is the development, since the early 1970s, of general discourse genre studies (e.g., of scientific discourse genres) as well as of specific studies of narrative (Phelan & Rabinowitz 2005) and argumentation (Van Eemeren & Grootendorst 2004). The latter are now more or less autonomous fields, with their own handbooks, introductions, journals, and congresses.

- **Critical Discourse Studies.** Whereas all other approaches focus on the analysis of discourse, critical discourse analysis (CDA) or critical discourse studies (CDS), since the early 1980s advocated a more sociopolitically committed, critical approach—focusing on the role of discourse in the reproduction of power abuse, for instance of sexism, racism, and neoliberalism (Fairclough 1995; van Dijk 2008b; Wodak & Meyer 2008).

Each of these approaches developed its own way of studying the structures of text and talk, more formally in linguistics, AI, CA, and partly in genre studies; the other approaches are less formal and explore structures of discourse and contextual conditions and consequences that were hitherto ignored in the study of language use, communication, and text.

The general tendency of most of these approaches, as well as of linguistics as a discipline, has been to progress from smaller and more superficial and "observable" units—such as phonemes, words, and syntactic sentence structures—to more complex underlying structures, such as sequences of sentences, speech acts, or turns at talking; coherence and functional relations between turns or sentences; overall semantic macrostructures (topics); argumentation and narrative structures and other conventional text formats (e.g., of news reports or scholarly articles); and images, multimodal messages, rhetorical, and other persuasive moves and strategies, among many others.

At the same time, the focus has not remained on text or talk itself, but has been extended, first, to the cognitive psychological study of the ways such structures are produced, understood, stored in, and retrieved from memory and how they are related to mental representations such as knowledge of the world. Second, DS had extended to the social, political, and cultural contexts of interaction and communication. It is not surprising, therefore, that nearly all the more socially oriented approaches mentioned above, have (also) paid attention to racist discourse.

In other words, after four decades, DS today is not only multidisciplinary but has moved from a very limited linguistic approach to isolated abstract sentences to the study of naturally occurring, multimodal, socially situated, multilevel and complex structures text and talk, and their cognitive processing and sociopolitical and cultural conditions and consequences.

DA Is NOT A Method but a Discipline

The theory and methodology of the discursive reproduction of racism is, of course, closely tied to the developments, briefly summarized above, of the discipline of DS. The first crucial remark about this discourse approach to the study of racism is that *discourse analysis is not a method, but a (cross- or trans-) discipline of all the humanities and social sciences.* This is crucial, because the concept of "method" in the social sciences suggests that DA is merely a more qualitative alternative to traditional content analysis.

However, just as there is no such thing as a general method of social analysis, there is no general method of DA. This is also one reason we prefer to use the term DS, referring to a discipline, rather than DA, which might suggest that this is just a method of research. Rather, as we have seen, DS is a vast trans-discipline with many different approaches and represented in many disciplines, each with their own theories, methods of observation, data collection, and analysis. Thus, we may find very formal (e.g., logical) analyses of text and talk (e.g., in formal linguistics and AI); experimental methods and protocol analysis in cognitive psychology; fieldwork, ethnography, participant observation, and interviewing in virtually all social and cultural approaches to discourse; historical document research; and systematic and explicit structural description of specific (multimodal) discourse structures or interaction strategies in all approaches. In sum, there is no such thing as *a* method of DA. There are many methods, as many in the joint set of methods available in the humanities and social sciences, all depending on the goals and objects of description and explanation as well as of the kind of discourse or social issue studied.

The Crucial Role of Context

To understand the role of discourse in the reproduction of racism, it is crucial to recognize that text and talk do not come alone, but are socially situated. Although there are countless definitions of discourse—depending on the approaches mentioned above—discourse may be defined briefly as language use and communicative interaction in social situations. We have seen that the properties of situations as found relevant by the participants systematically control discourse production and comprehension. Such contexts are also mental models—namely, subjective definitions of communicative situations we call (pragmatic) context models. Just as the (semantic) mental models of the actions or events a discourse is about (say an ethnic conflict), context models may be influenced by underlying racist attitudes and ideologies. This explains how and why speakers and writers may not only engage in racist practices when writing *about* immigrants or minorities, and generally about ethnic Others, but also when speaking *with* or to *them*, namely by derogating interlocutors, more or less subtly, as being inferior or otherwise unequal to the speaker as a dominant group member.

Since context thus defined controls all contextually variable properties of discourse production and comprehension, this also means that the racist nature of text and talk always depends on the context. This is as it should be, first of all theoretically, as only those social practices that are based on racist attitudes and ideologies will be called racist. Moreover, because these attitudes and ideologies are relevant properties of speakers (and hence of context) and not of text or talk itself, we should always first study the context when we examine discourse as racist practice. This may imply that exactly the same discourse (or discourse fragment) may have a racist function in one communicative situation and not in another—as we know so well from the use of the N-word among black youth, on the one hand, and as used by a racist white speaker, on the other hand, among many other examples.

Intention is one of the parameters of action and hence also of communicative interaction. It is not surprising, therefore, that many white people accused of racist discourse defend themselves by claiming that they did not mean it that way. This suggests that racist discourse is not necessarily intended as such, for instance because dominant speakers have a dominant concept of racism limiting it to extremist forms of racism or because they ignore or do not reflect about the possibly racist consequences of their discourse. In this respect, racism is not an actor category but an observer (analyst or recipient) category, as is also the case for many other forms of crime and deviance. It is therefore methodologically unsound to limit the study of racism to how the speakers define the communicative situation, because they may deny that their discourse is (intended as) racist.

DA of racist discourse needs to examine, among other context properties: (1) the underlying ideologies of the speakers or writers, for instance, as they have emerged in other communicative and interactional situations; (2) the relation with the intended audience (people tend to be less self-controlled among in-group members, family, friends, etc.); (3) the overall goals of the discourse; and (4) the institutional situation and action currently being engaged in (a parliamentary debate on immigration has goals other than articles on immigration on the website of a racist organization).

Such analysis especially needs to study the patterns of access and control in the communicative situation. For instance, reporters may write a news item about crime that has racist implications, but may be less responsible if the story was their idea because their editor had given them the assignment. Or reporters may write about something negative a politician has said about immigrants, thus possibly contributing to the spread of racist prejudice. In that case, the first responsible party may be the politician, although the journalists may be equally responsible when failing to take discursive distance from such opinions. We see that in complex situations of institutional public discourse, the responsibility of racist discourse and its implications and consequences may need to be established by a careful analysis of the context.

As discussed above, racism may be studied by a systematic analysis of discourse. We must therefore account for how discourse structures are related to racism. We saw how practices become racist when based on racist attitudes and ideologies and how the latter are largely acquired, confirmed, and changed by discourse. It is plausible that there are special discourse structures that express or promote mental representations (such as mental models) based on racist ideologies. Trivially, explicitly racist name-calling or derogation is more obviously involved in the expression of racist ideologies than many syntactic structures. However, many indirect and subtle ways underlying racist representations (mental models, attitudes, ideologies) may be expressed or signaled in the structures of text and talk—and these structures may in turn influence the mental representations of the recipients, contributing to the spread and reproduction of racism.

To systematically explore these special discourse structures, we shall assume that at least some of the structures of underlying ideologies also appear in discourse. Thus, ideologies may show the following major categories representing the self-schema of ideological groups (van Dijk 1998).

- **Identity** (Who are we? Who belong to us? Where do we come from?)
- **Activities** (What do we usually do? What is our task?)
- **Goals** (What do we want to obtain?)
- **Norms and Values** (What is good/bad, permitted/prohibited for us?)
- **Group Relations** (Who are our allies and enemies?)
- **Resources** (What is the basis of our power or our lack of power?)

We easily recognize the structure of racist ideologies as they have characterized many white Europeans for centuries and as it is based on the sole symbolic power resource of skin color. The core of racist ideologies, however, is the construed relationship of superiority to the Others, mainly non-white other peoples, mentally represented as a polarization between positive characteristics attributed to the in-group and negative ones attributed to the out-group. This value polarization also determines the structures of more specific negative attitudes (prejudices) and mental models about the Others in general and "ethnic events" in particular, for instance in domains of territory, work, income, housing, status, and civil rights.

These underlying structures of polarized racist representations systematically affect the structures of discourse, primarily according to the following meta-strategy we have called the "ideological square" (Van Dijk 1998):

- Emphasize Our good things
- Emphasize Their bad things
- Deemphasize Our bad things
- Deemphasize Their good things

Applied at all levels of text and talk, we have a systematic discovery procedure for studying the manifestation of racist ideologies in discourse. For instance, immigrants and ethnic minorities are typically represented in dominant discourse in terms of difference, deviance, and threats in all social domains such as drug abuse, crime, violence, or welfare abuse. Such representations will tend to be enhanced by their treatment as main discourse topics (semantic macrostructures), headlines, front-page coverage, photographs, or metaphors, among many other discourse structures. In contrast, our negative characteristics—primarily prejudice, discrimination, and racism—tend to be mitigated, for instance, by denial, legitimatization, euphemisms, or simply exclusion from dominant discourse.

More systematically, we may apply this general principle to all levels and dimensions of discourse, as follows:

(INTER)ACTION

- **Turn taking**: In conversation, *They* may be given less opportunity to speak than *We*.
- **Speech acts**: *They* may typically be confronted with speech acts such as threats, accusations, etc.

SEMANTIC STRUCTURES: MEANING AND REFERENCE

- **Negative topics** (semantic macrostructures): Any overall discourse topic describing *Them* as breaching our norms and values: deviance, threat, insecurity, criminality, inability, etc.
- **Level of description** (generality vs. specificity): *Their* negative properties or actions tend to be described in more specific (lower level) detail than *Ours*.
- **Degree of completeness** (at each level of description): More details will be mentioned, at each level of description, about *Their* negative properties or actions.
- **Granularity** (preciseness vs. vagueness): *Their* negative properties or actions tend to be described with more precise terms than *Ours*.
- **Implications** (propositions implied by propositions explicitly expressed in discourse): Propositions may be used that have (many) negative implications about *Them*.
- **Presuppositions** (propositions that must be true/known for any proposition to be meaningful): Presupposing propositions (negative about *Them*) that are not known to be true.
- **Denomination** (of propositions: participant description): *They* tend to be named or identified as different from *Us* (precisely as *Them*)—strangers, immigrants, Others, opponents, enemies, etc.
- **Predication** (of propositions: meanings of sentences): Any predicate of a proposition attributing negative characteristics to *Them*.
- **Modality** (modal expressions modifying a propositions: necessity, probability, possibility): Negative properties of *Them* may be attributed as inherent, and hence as "Necessarily" applying to *Them*.
- **Agency** (role of the arguments/participants of a proposition): Emphasizing *Their* (and deemphasizing *Our*) agency or active responsibility of negative actions.

- **Topic versus comment organization** (distribution of given/known vs. new information in sentences): As with presuppositions at the propositional level, negative participants may be assumed to be known, etc.

- **Focus**: Any participant, property, or action may receive special focus (e.g., by special stress, volume, size, color, etc.) (see below) to draw attention of the recipients (e.g., to emphasize negative agency of *Them*).

FORMAL/EXPRESSION STRUCTURES

- **Superstructures** (general formats, schemas, or overall organization of discourse)—specific semantic categories (e.g., with negative meanings about *Them*) may be **foregrounded** when placed in irregular (first, earlier) position (e.g., in headlines or leads).

- **Visual structures** that emphasize negative meanings: Foregrounding negative acts or events in images; type, size, color of letters and headlines; prominent position on page or medium (e.g., the front page of a newspaper); photographs representing *Them* as actors of negative actions; derogatory cartoons; preciseness, granularity, close-ups, etc., of negative representations in images or film.

- **Sound structures** that emphasize negative words: Volume, pitch, and so on of phonemes; intonation of sentences (e.g., expressing irony, distance, skepticism, accusations, etc.); music associated with negative emotions (e.g., signifying threat, danger, violence, etc.).

- **Syntactic structures of sentences** (word order, order of clauses, hierarchical relations between clauses, etc.): Active sentences to emphasize *Their* negative agency (vs. passive sentences or nominalizations that deemphasize *Our negative* agency); initial dependent clauses using that may express unknown or false presuppositions about *Them*.

- **Definite expressions**: May express unknown or false presuppositions about *Them*.

- **Pronouns**: May signal in-group and out-group membership, as in *Us* versus *Them*, and in general different degrees of power, solidarity, intimacy, etc. when speaking to *Us* versus *Them*.

- **Demonstratives**: May signal closeness or distance to people being described (e.g., *those people*).

- **Rhetorical moves**: Hyperboles, repetitions, enumerations, rhymes, alliterations to emphasize and hence draw attention to emphasize negative meanings about *Them*, and euphemisms to mitigate the negative meanings about *Us*.

We see that the complexity of discourse, only partly reflected in this list, allows for a large number of ways for dominant racist discourse to express and convey negative representations of ethnic/racial Others, while protecting the reputation and hence the symbolic power white in-group by many forms of denial and mitigation.

One might say that these forms of discursive discrimination are only words and that what is at stake is only the representation and hence the reputation of in- and out-groups. However, such an assessment seriously underestimates the crucial role and power of mental representations as a basis of all social action and interaction. As explained above, all social practices are based on socially shared representations as are the way majority group members and organizations treat minority group members in immigration, admission, hiring, firing, housing, health care—as well as access to public discourse.

In other words, the system of racism is based on, and legitimatized by, underlying prejudices and racist ideologies and these affect all social practices of multi-ethnic societies. Since these underlying ideologies are largely acquired and confirmed by discourse, systematic analysis of discourse structures is one of the most powerful means to understand how racism is reproduced in society (for other studies, mostly in English, of racist discourse, see the following, among others: Blommaert & Verschueren 1998; Henry & Tator 2002; Hill 2008; Jäger 1992, 1998; Jiwani 2006; Kushner & Lunn 1989; Reeves 1983; Reisigl & Wodak 2000, 2001; Smitherman-Donaldson & van Dijk 1988; Van der Valk 2002; Wetherell & Potter 1992; Wodak et al. 1990; Zapata-Barrero & van Dijk 2007).

TOWARD A METHOD OF DISCURSIVE ANALYSIS OF RACISM

The list of ideologically controlled discourse structures also provides suggestions for a focused methodology for the analysis of racist discourse. Indeed, some structures of discourse contribute to the formation of racist mental models among the recipients more systematically and more prominently than others.

First, as suggested, one always needs to start with a systematic account of the context: *Who* is speaking, in what *role*, and to *whom*, in what spatiotemporal *setting*, with what *goals*, etc. Here we are able to gauge the *consequences* of racist discourse. Obviously, a racist joke in the family or among white people in a bar has far less social consequences than a derogatory term about immigrants or minorities used by a member of the government, a newspaper editorial, or a textbook lesson—discourses aimed at hundreds of thousands or even millions of recipients. Similarly, one may discuss problems of immigration with the goal of limiting the immigration rights of immigrants or with the goal of protesting such forms of discrimination. Veiled negative references to immigrants or minorities by a racist party are understood and represented differently than when minority group members self-describe negative group characteristics.

There are virtually no inherently (context-free) racist discourse structures and this is as it should be because the general properties of language can be deployed by all language users for many different goals. That is, the list of discourse structures above is merely a checklist of the ways ideologies and racist ideologies and attitudes may show up in text and talk in specific contexts whose consequences are detrimental for the position, rights, and opportunities of minorities. Once analyzed for such contexts, systematic DA may focus on the structures and strategies of text and talk itself.

Most directly signaling underlying racist ideologies are the semantic structures of meaning, whose propositions may represent the underlying propositions of ideologies such as the alleged bad properties of minorities. This is especially so at the macro level of overall discourse topics, because these control the coherence and interpretation of the whole discourse. We also know that these are the properties of discourse that are most explicitly attended to, most accessibly stored in mental models of recipients, and hence best recalled by them in future discourses and other social practices (van Dijk & Kintsch 1983).

Local meanings of discourse will then fill in the details of the semantic model, with a more precise description of the actors, their properties, and their actions as well as the explanation of these actions (Van Leeuwen 2008). Note that such meanings need not be explicit. As is the case for discourse in general, most meanings are implicit and can still be understood by the recipients because of their socially shared knowledge from which the implicit propositions can be derived by inferences. Much contemporary racist discourse is therefore not very explicit. Still, one should understand what is written between the lines, that is, what can be inferred from what is said or written because we are members of the same epistemic and discourse community.

All the other structures of discourse are geared toward the expression, communication, and interaction based on these meanings, making these more or less efficient or appropriate in the current situation. Thus, we can express the "same" underlying meanings by mitigating them or by emphasizing them in headlines, summaries, front-page coverage, argumentation, size, type and colors of letters, pictures, cartoons, and hyperboles as well as syntactic structures, as indicated. This enhances the probability that the recipients will form or update the details of the mental model as intended by the speaker or writer. This is what language and discourse are all about. The vast resources of language variation, as well as their uses as a function of the context, thus allow speakers to subtly and persuasively convey their racist ideologies.

AN EXAMPLE: STRUCTURES OF PRESS DISCOURSE

To illustrate the theoretical and methodological issues of the discursive reproduction of racism dealt with above, let us examine in some detail an example that may show how this is done for a concrete text. Although there are many discourse types we might select, arguably the most influential, after television, is the press—especially among the elites. Hence, we shall examine some fragments of an opinion article in a popular daily newspaper from the United Kingdom with millions of readers. This does not mean that all these readers passively believe what they read in their newspaper, or that their ethnic attitudes are only formed by the newspaper. However, unless they have other personal experiences, a different (antiracist) ideology, or other reasons to reject the preferred reading of the articles in the press, they will tend to adopt or reinforce many of opinions they read in the press, especially if these are consistent with their own interests (van Dijk 1991).

Here is a typical article on asylum seekers in *The Sun*:

ASYLUM TEARING UK APART

BRITAIN'S asylum system is today revealed as a total SHAMBLES from top to bottom. A shock report by MPs shows bogus refugees are flooding into the country. Yet the Government seems unable to deal with the growing crisis. The report by the all-party Home Affairs Select Committee also reveals that:

THE number of asylum-seekers arriving on our shores has soared from 4,223 in 1982 to 110,700 last year.

THE Home Office has no idea how many who have been refused asylum have stayed and slipped into the population.

GANGS of traffickers have grabbed control of the immigration system.

PROMISES made by ministers to eject thousands of fake refugees are impossible to keep.

OUR benefits system makes Britain a magnet for cheats.

The study by the Labour-dominated committee published days after the racist British National Party gained footholds in several town halls also warned the problem could lead to extreme politics. The MPs fear "social unrest" could erupt across the land unless solutions are found by the Government.

They demanded the immediate removal of cheats, saying they should be locked up prior to deportation if they are likely to go on the run or are seen as a criminal threat.

They called for deals with other countries so bogus refugees can be easily repatriated.

And they warned PM Tony Blair the crisis will deepen until the public sees that cheats are being turfed out.

Liberals who refuse to acknowledge the scale of the problem were accused of sticking their heads in the sand.

The report calls the rising number of asylum-seekers "clearly unsustainable".

The MPs declared: "If allowed to continue unchecked, it could overwhelm capacity to cope, leading inevitably to social unrest. It's evident the efficient removal of asylum-seekers whose claims have failed is a precondition for the credibility of the entire asylum process."

The MPs blasted the Home Office's inability to say how many cheats have slipped the net.

(Nic Cecil, Political Correspondent, *The Sun*, May 8, 2003)

It should be stressed that this article is explicitly about asylum seekers and not directly about African or Asian people. Hence, most likely the editors of *The Sun* would vehemently deny that it is racist. Indeed, they will say and show that in their columns and editorials they have critically reported on racism—especially as directed against black sportsmen.

True, but the record also shows that *The Sun* is a populist newspaper, usually backing the Conservative Party and attacking the Labour Party, especially Labour's immigration policies. For decades, *The Sun* derogated immigrants and asylum seekers, especially those it accuses of "scrounging" (abusing welfare or other social services), as well as black youths, Muslims, and the (white) "anti-racist brigade" it sees as the traitors of the interests of white Britain. As analysts, we need to read and understand this article against the background of many others that have been published in *The Sun* (see the analyses in van Dijk 1991).

Note also that the attack on immigration policies is not only informed by underlying racist ideologies, but also by political ones, namely as one of the easy populist topics on which to attack Labour governments, especially what it used to call the *Loony Left*. Indeed, anti-racism and political correctness are even more vehemently attacked than asylum seekers because of the clashing ideologies concerned and because attacking anti-racism will not usually be seen as a form of racism.

Given this context and background about *The Sun*, it is not surprising that asylum seekers, specifically immigrants, are represented negatively, as predicted by the theory outlined above. Given the current context, the article may be expected to manifest the dominant anti-immigration ideology and attitudes espoused by the editors of *The Sun*. This representation is expressed by the following lexical items that are interpreted as saying negative things on immigrants or immigration:

tearing apart
shambles
bogus refugees
fake refugees
flooding
crisis
soared
slipped
gangs
criminal
threat
traffickers
grabbed control
cheats
overwhelm
unsustainable

Note that some of these negative expressions are classical metaphors used to enhance the supposed threats of immigration: flooding, overwhelming, etc. These metaphors semantically and cognitively imply and convey the fear of drowning in the (floods of) immigrants. It is standard to associate immigrants with fraud (*fake, bogus, cheats, slipped*) and crime (*criminal, traffickers*), threat, and the allegedly negative results of immigration (*tearing apart, crisis, grabbed control, unsustainable*).

This negative representation of immigration as a threat to the country is accompanied by a political attack against Labour. It is represented as not being tough enough on immigration, if not as friends of immigrants, and by ideological inference as Our enemies for two reasons: for being our political enemies and for their policy that favors our enemies (asylum seekers, etc.). Hence, the Labour government (as well as the Liberal Democrats) is attributed its own lexically expressed negative characteristics:

shambles
unable to deal
has no idea
promises are impossible to keep,
(welfare system is) magnet
(politicians) sticking their heads in the sand.
inability
failed

Incompetence is the major evaluative attribute implied by these lexical items, partly emphasized by metaphors as *magnet* and *sticking their heads in the sand*.

According to the general strategy of the ideological square, the article in *The Sun* will not simply say it is against welfare cheats or Labour policies, but it will systematically engage in emphasizing negative attributes of its ideological enemies. It does so, in this text, by the following textual moves:

- **Metaphors** (*top to bottom, flooding, shambles, shock report, growing crisis, numbers soared, grabbed control, benefits system is a magnet, social unrest may erupt, crisis will deepen, rising number blasted*);
- **Hyperboles and Worst-case Formulations** (*crisis, gangs, grabbed control, impossible to keep, scale of the problem, overwhelm, inevitably*);
- **The Number Game**, rhetorically enhancing a threat or a crisis by accumulating many numbers, while at the same time suggesting precision, objectivity, and reliability of the report (*thousands*; ***THE*** *number of asylum-seekers arriving on our shores has soared from 4,223 in 1982 to 110,700 last year; the rising number*).

Recall that this article is not based on data or investigation of *The Sun* itself but is a report on a report by MPs of the Home Affairs Select Committee. The news report rarely quotes directly but reformulates the report in its own rhetorically much more negative terms as it is highly unlikely that the committee report used words such as *bogus, cheats, turfed out*, etc. Besides the reformulation of the report in accordance with its own anti-immigration ideology, *The Sun* selects and highlights as major topics what it sees as the most important findings and opinions of the report such as:

- British asylum system is a disaster (*shambles, magnet, control by traffickers*).
- Bogus refugees are flooding the country.
- The government is incompetent and unable to stop the crisis.
- Social unrest could erupt as a consequence of immigration crisis.
- Cheating refugees should be repatriated.

We see that what the committee intended as a parliamentary critique of (Labour) government policies is now reformulated as a worst-case scenario of a profound crisis, a major threat to the country, and looming social unrest facing a totally incompetent government that requires extreme measures (locking up cheats, repatriation, etc.). This emphasis on the crisis is further sustained by reference to the gains of the racist BNP—with the implicit argument, both of the committee as well as of the newspaper, that if no action is taken, the "real" racists will take the power, which would be another threat to the democratic state.

Note also the use of the cited word *unsustainable*, which associates both the committee report and the news article with climate change as well as environmental disasters, a major metaphorical construct to emphasize the alleged threat of increasing immigration, artfully adapted to general contemporary worries.

Finally, the populist style of this news item itself allows for various forms of emphasis on the alleged immigration crisis, the failing immigration system, and the incompetence of the government, as is shown in such popular expressions as:

> tearing apart
> total shambles
> from top to bottom
> bogus refugees
> the home office has no idea
> refugees have (...) slipped into the population
> gangs of traffickers have grabbed control of the immigration system
> our benefits system makes Britain a magnet for cheats.
> they should be locked up
> (politicians are) sticking their heads in the sand.
> the MPs blasted the home

In sum, this article clearly shows the polarization of the underlying ideology according to which We (white) British are confronted by the threat of Them (immigrants). These immigrants are associated with various negative characteristics that together represent a major threat to the country.

It is this threat, as well as the alleged failure of the Labour government to deal with it, that is discursively enhanced in the text by many typical moves and strategies of exaggeration, suggesting a major national crisis: metaphors, hyperboles, worst-case scenario, lack of control, and the number game, among other structures intended to enhance the representation of the threat and the crisis that form the main topics of this news item as it represents the upshot of a parliamentary report on immigration.

CONCLUSIONS

Discourse is one of the major means for the ideological reproduction of racism defined as a social system of ethnic-racial domination resulting in social inequality. It consists of discriminatory practices sustained by racist social cognitions. Discourse is crucial in this system: It may be a discriminatory practice in its own right but, at the same time, it is through text and talk that racist beliefs are acquired and confirmed. The symbolic elites who control access to public discourse are therefore especially responsible for the discursive reproduction of racism in society.

Given the discursive nature of the reproduction of racism, DS offers many theoretical and methodological instruments for studying how discourse structures are involved in the formation of racist mental models, attitudes, and ideologies. This chapter shows that the polarized nature of underlying racist ideologies may be expressed and emphasized by many types of structures at several levels of text and talk. It is also emphasized that DA is a discipline and *not* a method of analysis. Hence, it is better to speak of DS as a cross-discipline in the humanities and social sciences that may use all the relevant methods of its neighboring disciplines.

An analysis of a *Sun* news item on immigration shows how such structures can be analyzed in a systematic way by examining how the strategy of ideological square, involving enhanced out-group derogation, is implemented at various level of the text, all contributing to the overall emphasis of the definition of immigration as a major national crisis.

REFERENCES

Barker, M. (1981). *The new racism. Conservatives and the ideology of the tribe.* London: Junction Books.

Blommaert, J., & Verschueren, J. (1998). *Debating diversity. Analysing the discourse of tolerance.* New York: Routledge.

Connor, U., & Upton, T. A. (Eds.). (2004). *Applied corpus linguistics. A multidimensional perspective.* Amsterdam: Rodopi.

Dovidio, J. F., & Gaertner, S. L. (Eds.). (1986). *Prejudice, discrimination, and racism.* New York: Academic Press.

Edwards, D., & Potter, J. (1992). *Discursive psychology.* London: Sage.

Fairclough, N. (1995). *Critical discourse analysis. The critical study of language.* London: Longman.

Givón, T. (Ed.). (1979). *Syntax and semantics*, vol. 12: *Discourse and syntax.* New York: Academic Press.

Givón, T. (Ed.). (1983). *Topic continuity in discourse. A quantitative cross-language study.* Amsterdam: John Benjamins Publishing Company.

Graesser, A. C., Gernsbacher, M. A., & Goldman, S. R. (Eds.). (2003). *Handbook of discourse processes.* Mahwah, NJ: L. Erlbaum Associates.

Grice, H. P. (1989). *Studies in the way of words.* Cambridge, MA: Harvard University Press.

Gumperz, J. J. (1982). *Discourse strategies.* Cambridge: Cambridge University Press.

Henry, F., & Tator, C. (2002). *Discourses of domination. Racial bias in the Canadian English-language press.* Toronto: University of Toronto Press.

Hill, J. H. (2008). *The everyday language of white racism.* Chichester, UK: Wiley-Blackwell.

Jäger, S. (1992). *BrandSätze. Rassismus im Alltag.* ("Brandsätze"—Inflammatory sentences/Firebombs. Racism in everyday life). Duisburg, Germany: DISS.

Jäger, S. (1998). *Der Spuk ist nicht vorbei. Völkisch-nationalistische Ideologeme im öffentlichen Diskurs der Gegenwart* (The ghost is not gone. Populist-nationalist ideologemes in contemporary public discourse). Duisburg, Germany: DISS.

Jiwani, Y. (2006). *Discourses of denial. Mediations of race, gender, and violence.* Vancouver: UBC Press.

Kushner, T., & Lunn, K. (Eds.). (1989). *Traditions of intolerance: Historical perspectives on fascism and race discourse in British society.* Manchester, UK: Manchester University Press.

Levinson, S. C. (1983). *Pragmatics.* Cambridge: Cambridge University Press.

Phelan, J., & Rabinowitz, P. J. (Eds.). (2005). *A companion to narrative theory.* Malden, MA: Blackwell Publishers.

Reeves, F. (1983). *British racial discourse. A study of British political discourse about race and race-related matters.* Cambridge: Cambridge University Press.

Reisigl, M., & Wodak, R. (Eds.). (2000). *The semiotics of racism. Approaches in critical discourse analysis.* Vienna: Passagen.

Reisigl, M., & Wodak, R. (Eds.). (2001). *Discourse and discrimination. Rhetorics of racism and antisemitism.* London: Routledge.

Saville-Troike, M. (1989). *The ethnography of communication. An introduction.* Oxford, UK: Basil Blackwell.

Schank, R. C., & Abelson, R. P. (1977). *Scripts, plans, goals, and understanding. An inquiry into human knowledge structures.* Hillsdale, NJ: L. Erlbaum Associates.

Schiffrin, D., Tannen, D., & Hamilton, H. E. (Eds.). (2001). *The handbook of discourse analysis.* Malden, MA: Blackwell Publishers.

Smitherman-Donaldson, G., & van Dijk, T. A. (Eds.). (1988). *Discourse and discrimination.* Detroit: Wayne State University Press.

ten Have, P. (2007). *Doing conversation analysis. A practical guide.* 2nd ed. London: Sage.

Tuchman, G. (1978). *Making news: A study in the construction of reality.* New York: Free Press.

Van der Valk, I. (2002). *Difference, deviance, threat? Mainstream and right-extremist political discourse on ethnic issues in the Netherlands and France (1990–1997).* Amsterdam: Aksant.

van Dijk, T. A. (1972). *Some aspects of text grammars. A study in theoretical linguistics and poetics.* The Hague: Mouton.

van Dijk, T. A. (1977). *Text and context. Explorations in the semantics and pragmatics of discourse.* London: Longman.

van Dijk, T. A. (1984). *Prejudice in discourse. An analysis of ethnic prejudice in cognition and conversation.* Amsterdam: John Benjamins Publishing Company.

van Dijk, T. A. (1987). *Communicating racism. Ethnic prejudice in thought and talk.* Newbury Park, CA: Sage.

van Dijk, T. A. (1991). *Racism and the press.* London: Routledge.

van Dijk, T. A. (1992). Discourse and the denial of racism. *Discourse and Society, 3, 1,* 87–118.

van Dijk, T. A. (1993). *Elite discourse and racism.* Newbury Park, CA: Sage.

van Dijk, T. A. (1998). *Ideology: A multidisciplinary approach.* London: Sage.

van Dijk, T. A. (2005). *Racism and discourse in Spain and Latin America.* Amsterdam: John Benjamins.

van Dijk, T. A. (Ed.). (2007). *Discourse studies.* 5 vols. Sage Benchmarks in Discourse Studies. London: Sage.

van Dijk, T. A. (2008a). *Discourse and context. A socio-cognitive approach.* Cambridge: Cambridge University Press.

van Dijk, T. A. (2008b). *Discourse and power.* Houndmills, UK: Palgrave Macmillan.

van Dijk, T. A. (Ed.). (2009a). *Racism and discourse in Spain and Latin America.* Lanham, MD: Lexington Books.

van Dijk, T. A. (2009b). *Society and discourse. How context influences text and talk.* Cambridge: Cambridge University Press.

van Dijk, T. A. (Ed.). (2011). *Discourse studies.* Second Edition. London: Sage.

van Dijk, T. A., & Kintsch, W. (1983). *Strategies of discourse comprehension.* New York: Academic Press.

Van Eemeren, F. H., & Grootendorst, R. (2004). *A systematic theory of argumentation. The pragma-dialectic approach.* Cambridge: Cambridge University Press.

Van Leeuwen, T. J. (2005). *Introducing social semiotics.* London: Routledge.

Van Leeuwen, T. J. (2008). *Discourse and practice. New tools for critical discourse analysis.* Oxford, UK: Oxford University Press.

Wetherell, M., & Potter, J. (1992). *Mapping the language of racism. Discourse and the legitimation of exploitation.* New York: Columbia University Press.

Wodak, R., & Meyer, M. (Eds.). (2008). *Methods of critical discourse analysis.* 2nd ed. London: Sage.

Wodak, R., Nowak, P., Pelikan, J., Gruber, H., de Cillia, R., & Mitten, R. (1990). *"Wir sind alle unschuldige Täter". Diskurshistorische Studien zum Nachkriegsantisemitismus* ("We are all innocent perpetrators." Historic discourse studies in post-war antisemitism). Frankfurt/Main: Suhrkamp.

Wodak, R., & van Dijk, T. A. (Eds.). (2000). *Racism at the top. Parliamentary discourses on ethnic issues in six European states.* Klagenfurt, Austria: Drava Verlag.

Zapata-Barrero, R., & van Dijk, T. A. (Eds.). (2007). *Discursos sobre la inmigración en España. Los medios de comunicación, los parlamentos y las administraciones.* Barcelona: Cidob.

4 THE TRANSFORMATION OF THE ROLE OF "RACE" IN THE QUALITATIVE INTERVIEW: NOT IF RACE MATTERS, BUT HOW?

Eileen O'Brien

In traditional methodology courses, qualitative interviewing is often presented as a method choice for researchers seeking to give voice to experiences that cannot be adequately tapped through closed-ended survey questions. The gap between what social scientists can explain with statistics and the lived experiences of those individuals behind the statistics is particularly wide in research on race and ethnicity. From its inception, the field of "race relations" in sociology operated from the ideological premise that assimilation to a Eurocentric cultural ideal was the desired end goal for all racial/ethnic groups. Little attention was paid to: (1) the cultural strengths and contributions of other non-Western groups; or (2) the racism woven into the structural fabric of society (Bonilla-Silva 1997; Feagin & Feagin 2008; Stanfield 2008).

Race relations has historically operated in sociology and other disciplines as a way for members of the dominant group to attempt to explain the behaviors and condition of racial/ethnic Others through their own privileged lens rather than through the eyes of those experiencing oppression and subjugation (Zuberi & Bonilla-Silva 2008). Because qualitative interviewing gives the researcher an opportunity to give voice to diverse experiences and to resist assumptions of homogeneity within categories, it is an ideal vehicle through which to challenge some of this previous research, dubbed "white sociology" (Ladner 1998), "white logic," and "white methods" by some (Zuberi & Bonilla-Silva 2008). However, there are different ways to approach qualitative interviewing. I contend that in today's "colorblind" society, we need an approach to in-depth interviewing that does not reduce "race" and "ethnicity" to formulaic categories, but approaches them as ways of relating to each other that vary not just by phenotype, but by the way each of us "activates" race (or not) in our everyday conversations and lives.

IN-DEPTH INTERVIEWING AS AN ALTERNATIVE TO "WHITEWASHED" STATISTICS—GETTING "CLOSER TO" THE ACTION

Many of us gravitated toward qualitative interviewing out of disappointment that quantitative methods and preexisting data did not ask the questions for which we wanted answers. This has been particularly true of the history of race relations research in the academy. Because sociologists, especially race/ethnicity sociologists, often seek to analyze changes over time, and standard survey methodology expects question wording to remain constant over time, being stuck with the same old questions year after year does not enable the kind of flexibility that an interview guide and interviewing allows. Moreover, recent research (e.g., Bonilla-Silva 2006; Carr 1993; Frankenberg 1993) has shown a shift in the ways we as a society conceptualize race and racism, so the ways we ask our respondents questions should be changing as well, yet such methodological changes have been slow in coming. This lag in methodology has led some critics to question the relevance of social science for shedding light on race and ethnicity. As John Stanfield wrote in the introduction to his earlier volume on race and ethnicity in research methods:

> [T]he growth of large scale quantitative research that includes racial and ethnic variables is proving to be a lucrative career path. But even as researchers who embrace such methodological perspectives become well-published in top journals and are otherwise rewarded by their professional colleagues, the disturbing question remains, given the cultural hegemonic biases of their aggregate data manipulations, are they really explaining anything all that relevant outside the walls of their cozy offices and computer labs? (Stanfield 1993b:13–14)

Statistical manipulations are done in "cozy offices and computer labs," far removed from the human experiences that the numbers are purported to represent. Also because those manipulations have been performed by members of the dominant group who often have little meaningful contact with the human beings whose behaviors they are attempting to explain, qualitative interviewing becomes all the more attractive to those of us who are attempting to avoid the pitfalls of earlier race/ethnic scholarship. Indeed, fifteen years after publishing the above words, Stanfield continued to observe:

> The tendency to view race as a homogenous, quantifiable variable rather than as a complex human experience of multiple identities with a vast range of heterogeneous cultural experiences both conscious and unconscious, within, outside, and across racialized categorical boxes, makes much of what gets published in major sociology journals and book-length

sociological studies quite divorced from the real experiences of racialized populations, be they dominant or subordinate. (Stanfield 2008:277–278)

While quantitative methods can help us understand overall patterns in many race/ethnic inequalities—income and wealth disparities, residential segregation, criminal sentencing, birth and death rates, and rates of intermarriage, just to name a few—the way we often fall into interpretations of such data makes race and ethnicity seem like essentialized qualities of human bodies and obscures our understanding of how these categories of identity really operate. I recall this approach being problematized and referred to "race as a dummy variable" during multicultural student protests in the 1990s at my top-ranked graduate program. For example, scholar Tukufu Zuberi offers the following critique:

[W]hen we discuss the "effect of race," we are less mindful of the larger social world in which the path to success or failure is influenced. Usually someone ... argues that "race causes a person to be in a certain condition." This is like arguing that race is a proxy for an individual's makeup, or like smoking causes cancer. Alternatively, I suggest that we place statistical analysis of race within a historical and social context. It is not a question of how a person's race causes disadvantage and discrimination. The real issue is the way the society responds to an individual's racial identification. The question has more to do with society itself, not the innate makeup of individuals. Racial identity is about shared social status, not individual characteristics. Race is not about an individual's skin color. Race is about an individual's relationship to other people within the society. (Zuberi & Bonilla-Silva 2008:7)

Although Zuberi calls for a more critically oriented use of statistics, this same critique has led other scholars to abandon statistical/survey methods altogether and instead look to the qualitative interview as a methodology that will frontline the human experience behind the statistic. For example, Young (2008) points out that some liberally oriented white sociologists in the 1960s began publishing ethnographies of black urban space and culture (e.g., Liebow's *Tally's Corner* and Rainwater's *Behind Ghetto Walls*). These gave voice to the experiences of racial/ethnic Others at a time when statistics describing their experiences (like those reported in the Moynihan Report) often dehumanized them and rendered them and their cultural practices (as opposed to racist social structures) responsible for their own plight. Such qualitative work challenged the dominant social science discourse about race by putting a human face on the outcomes reported by the statistics, revealing that such outcomes were the result of a series of choices forced by multiple social-structural constraints, rather than because of any presumed cultural deficiencies of black Americans.

Most social scientists have tended to do either quantitative or qualitative interviewing, but Bonilla-Silva's (2001, 2006) work, which combined both survey *and* in-depth interview methodology, expertly analyzed this disjuncture between what statistics tell us and what qualitative interviews can tell us about racial attitudes. Bonilla-Silva challenged the "declining significance of race thesis" dominant in the social sciences. He showed that, although Whites have with increasing decades been able to produce the socially desirable responses to racial prejudice questions on surveys, when they can frame their own answers to essentially the same questions in in-depth interviews, the picture of "race relations improvement" is hardly as optimistic.

Results from standard survey questions like "Do you approve of interracial marriage?" and "Do you have any black friends?" have been used by quantitative researchers to proclaim that Whites' prejudices have been steadily declining over the last few decades, but Bonilla-Silva's interview data revealed something altogether different. The same white respondent whose survey answer says she or he approves of interracial marriage will often state in an in-depth interview that she or he personally has never been attracted to someone of a different race and expresses substantial hesitation and questions about anyone in his or her immediate family doing so. Similarly, a large percentage of white survey respondents who stated they had a close black friend, in an in-depth interview format did not list that person in their list of five closest friends, or mention the person when discussing who they regularly hang out with. Bonilla-Silva's research skillfully used the interview method in conjunction with survey data of the same respondents to demonstrate how outmoded the questions being used by researchers of racial attitudes are, so that any conclusions drawn on the basis of such questions about racial attitudes alone are misguided, at best.

Qualitative interviewing allows social scientists to keep their ears open for what is "going on on the ground," as opposed to reproducing the same survey questions year after year hoping for good longitudinal reliability/validity. There has been a significant shift in how people think and talk about race and racism since the 1960s U.S. civil rights legal reforms, and our research will no longer produce valid results if our methodologies do not keep abreast of such changes. As Charles A. Gallagher writes: "We can no longer continue to ask questions crafted for cohorts that had church bombings, poll taxes and lynchings as their cultural and racial reference point, just as we cannot use questions that do not take into account the fact of colorblindness" (2008:167). Bonilla-Silva's use of the interview method (in conjunction with surveys) empirically solidified what many other scholars (e.g., Carr 1993; Frankenberg 1993) had been saying for some time: An ideological shift to "colorblindness" as a society does not indicate the declining significance of racism. On the contrary, it allows racism to continue in more insidious ways that are increasingly difficult to challenge.

The white sociology that proclaimed the declining significance of racism was able to be challenged via the interview method. This made room for powerful new questions about race and ethnicity that previous paradigms had stifled. And as Zuberi and Bonilla-Silva (2008:21) write: "White analysis need not be done by Whites." It is a mistake to assume that if we simply "add diversity and stir"—that is, replace biased white sociology with research done by social scientists of color—a more valid body of scholarship on race and ethnicity will eventually result. Bonilla-Silva's research also reminds us that ideologies are not successful unless members of subordinated groups buy into them at some level. His interview data with black Americans revealed that, while certainly not as colorblind as Whites, some Blacks sometimes reproduce certain colorblind ways of making sense of the world. Thus, white sociology cannot be debunked simply by including non-Whites in the interviewing process (both as researchers and as subjects).

Some have attempted to challenge colorblindness by insisting that whites cannot possibly understand fully (and thus cannot represent adequately) their nonwhite research subjects, just as nonwhite researchers could not hope to interview and fully understand/interpret Whites. While this is a well-intentioned approach for countering the previous "Whites-can-do-all" status quo of race/ethnic research, it is still too formulaic and short-sighted to take into account the current complexities of how race and ethnicity are lived out. Interviewing that included a fuller range of realities of people of color (not just those interpreted by Whites) was an important first step in challenging the hegemony of "white" statistics. However, I believe that we are in a second moment of challenging white sociology now, which may be better suited to "active" interviewing due to the disconnect between raced bodies and raced ideologies in a colorblind society.

MOMENT #1 OF CHALLENGING COLORBLINDNESS: LET'S NO LONGER PRETEND WE'RE ALL WHITE

Part of the problem with so-called white sociological methods obscuring the realities of people of color stemmed from the relative absence of non-Whites in the academy as respected producers of knowledge and research. Reformers began to argue that once non-Whites were able to interview other non-Whites about their experiences, greater insight into those experiences would result.

In the past, members of subordinated groups were reluctant to open up to dominant-group researchers for fear that such information would be used against them (Cannon et al. 1988; Few et al. 2003). African Americans complaining to a white interviewer about their dissatisfaction with the racial status quo during the Jim Crow era in the U.S. South were basically inviting the Ku Klux Klan to come to their house that night. And the infamous Tuskegee experiment that promised some African Americans with syphilis a cure through participation but really allowed their disease to continue untreated is just one of the more well-known examples of researchers treating certain populations as if they were expendable and beneath basic human rights.

Cannon and colleagues (1988) criticized researchers who went about their subject recruitment in a colorblind manner, without taking into account the "special" accommodations participants of color might appreciate, given such history of abuse and suspicion. These researchers write during what I would call Moment #1 of challenging colorblindness by making it a priority to have co-investigators of different races available for interviews in a racially heterogeneous study. They challenge colorblindness by rejecting the assumption that a white team of researchers could expect to have adequate participation of non-Whites in their study without making any race-conscious effort to recruit them and accommodate them. As a part of Moment #1, feminists of color, in particular, argue that they are uniquely placed to give voice to non-white experiences by being able to tap into populations previously unavailable to dominant-group researchers because of the above-cited historical distrust.

White feminists began to follow the lead of feminists of color, calling for an end to colorblindness in the research process by scrutinizing their own cross-racial interview research and acknowledging their lack of cultural competence in interpreting the experiences of women of color. For example, Riessman (1987) reflected on the cultural competence (or lack thereof) of Whites interviewing non-Whites in her study of over 100 women's experiences with separation and divorce.

Using excerpts from two interviews, Marta (Puerto Rican) and Susan (white), Riessman shows how Marta begins repeating herself because her white interviewer is unable to follow her episodic narrative. Marta's repeated references to the wider extended family and how it bore on her marriage were misunderstood by her white interviewer, who had difficulty grasping how any third parties outside of the marriage could have had that much effect on it. Riessman contrasts this transcript with the interview with Susan, whose narrative is temporally ordered and more readily followed by the white interviewer. Riessman concludes by suggesting that the ideal interviewer for Marta would have been another Puerto Rican woman. As her title suggests, "gender is not enough" to create rapport during the interview, thus same-race pairing in an interview is ideal, even when the presumed topic of the research is not race.

White feminist researchers Andersen (1993) and DeVault (1995) agree that same-race pairing is ideal, but make a more nuanced argument in an examination of their own interviews with women of color. Andersen interviewed low-income/education black (and white) women, and DeVault interviewed black (and white) female nutritionists. Both examine how gaps in racial understanding influenced the dynamic of their cross-racial interviews, even where race was not the primary topic of investigation. To bridge that gap, both researchers stress a grounded knowledge of their own racially privileged location (as opposed to colorblindness), while acknowledging that their own racial identifications and experiences shaped the degree to which they were able to understand, interpret, and elicit information from their nonwhite female respondents.

The clear position of interview researchers studying race during this "first moment" of challenging colorblindness (spanning about the late 1980s–the mid-1990s) was: When at all possible, match interviewers on race; if not possible, be aware at how one's interview data might be limited due to a lack of cross-racial understanding, and perhaps also a lack of fuller self-disclosure. In other words, don't pretend that the race of the interviewer doesn't matter.

However, this position was not all that different from that taken by quantitative survey researchers during this time. Numerous articles have been written by quantitative social scientists about the race-of-interviewer-effect (e.g., Cotter et al. 1982; Davis 1997; Finkel et al. 1991; Krysan & Couper 2003; Schuman & Converse 1971). They consistently show that even in a survey interview, whether over the phone or a virtual interview, Blacks are likely to downplay their racial concerns and support for liberal policies on race to a white interviewer, and Whites are likely to exaggerate the extent to which they support racial equality to a nonwhite interviewer. This became of great concern to political scientists, particularly when the previously "exact" science of pre-election polling became increasingly unreliable whenever African American candidates entered the picture (e.g., the "Bradley effect," the "Wilder effect," and more recently, the surprise victory of Hillary Clinton over Barack Obama in a 2007 New Hampshire primary). White respondents tended to exaggerate their support for African American candidates during such polls, presumably out of concern for appearing racist. The conventional wisdom gleaned from such studies was clear: Respondents should be interviewed by interviewers of the same race. This reflected the acknowledgment that our social worlds are so divided that we can no longer pretend, even post-civil rights, that race does not matter.

MOMENT #2 OF CHALLENGING COLORBLINDNESS: LET'S NO LONGER PRETEND THERE'S ONE WHITE EXPERIENCE OR ONE BLACK/NONWHITE EXPERIENCE

By the mid-1990s, a "new language" of qualitative interviewing practice had begun to take root in the social sciences. It rejected the positivist stance that an interview was the practice of a neutral researcher extracting knowledge from a subject. In its place was the acknowledgment among qualitative researchers that the in-depth interview was itself, in fact, a contextualized social product (Gubrium & Holstein 1997; Holstein & Gubrium 1995). This view does not assume that a same-race interviewer automatically elicits the best version of the truth from the interviewee. Instead, *each* interview context, whether same- or cross-race, has something to tell us about the ways in which race as a social construction shapes our communications with each other and how we tell our stories.

As we move toward a more diversified era of academe that begins to acknowledge intersections of race, class, gender, sexuality, nationality, age, and other social statuses, researchers are engaging in reflexivity about their interviewing practices, thus challenging the notion that a same-race interviewing dyad can be automatically assumed to have the most ideal rapport. This multiple-lens reflexivity echoes the age-old insider-outsider question in qualitative research: Should we assume that the racial insider can get the better "scoop" on the data?

In a discussion of race and interviewing, Dunbar (Dunbar et al. 2003) shares his experience as an African American male researcher doing interviews at an "alternative" high school with young men labeled "at risk." He points out how a "common ground" of race was an insufficient basis for close rapport in the interview dyad. Dunbar's respondents' backgrounds were otherwise significantly different—the youth were often from nontraditional families, living either with grandparents or in foster homes, and had been barred from the very university that Dunbar attended. Despite being the same race as his interviewees, Dunbar still faced the outsider problem with his respondents, who viewed him as culturally different from themselves in significant ways (class status, family background, etc.). However, Dunbar also felt there were certain cultural conventions (e.g., subject raising his voice in anger when talking) that he shared with his respondents. He wondered whether interviewers of other racial backgrounds might have walked away offended or not understood. So, while there were some shared cultural conventions with his respondents, there were still a number of barriers despite being same-race.

Similarly, Few et al. (2003) state: "Despite the fact that we were all black women studying black women, we never assumed that we would be granted unmitigated 'insider' status .... Issues of race, color, class, gender, sexuality, nationality, and power were at work from the moment we engaged them" (p. 207). One author shared an account from a same-race/gender interview between two black women that was so jarring it momentarily silenced the interviewer. After discussing episodes of teen motherhood and brief incarcerations in her family, a respondent sharply said: "I may not have as much money as you, but I am a good mother" (p. 209). This exchange underscored to the African American female researcher that, despite her financial status as a struggling graduate student, her educational status clearly drove a perceptible wedge between her and her same-race respondent.

Likewise, Charles Gallagher's research with Whites yielded him some surprises. As a white interviewer studying racial attitudes, he assumed his white respondents would automatically be candid with him due to same-race status. He found, however, that being a "Northerner raised in a working class section of a big city" interviewing whites in "rural Southeast Georgia" presented unanticipated challenges: "My Yankee dialect and professor status with 'big city' university affiliation made me a cultural outsider" (Gallagher 2008:170). There was also an assumption that he might have been Jewish, as evidenced by one interview stopped in midstream as the respondent exclaimed, "Why, ya a Jew-boy, ain't ya?" (Gallagher 2008:170). These perceptions on the part of respondents challenged Gallagher's expectations that same-race status alone would create a situation of candid self-disclosure during an interview.

In his essay on epistemological considerations in race/ethnic research, Stanfield (1993a) discusses both the fallacy of homogeneity and the fallacy of monolithic identity—both paths of false logic that contribute to assumptions that a same-race interviewer is automatically a shoo-in for gaining rapport with interviewees. Indeed, race does matter in the interview dyad, but not in formulaic, simplistic ways that can be quickly attended to by simply pairing people up matched on race. Although the experiences in a particular racial or ethnic group have never been monolithic, in the 1960s and before, *de jure* racial segregation placed relatively more limits, both on the diversity of experiences possible/accessible for people of color and on the amount of contact between members of different racial groups (presenting less diversity of cross-racial experiences and views on race for whites as well).

It was pretty safe to assume that a single black person's life experiences and views were probably closer to another black person's than they would be to another white person's. Likewise, it was pretty likely that the average white person had more in common with another white person than they did with a nonwhite person. Kitwana (2005) refers to this period of time (and way of thinking) as "the old politics of race"—it was safe to assume that Whites were in a position to exploit Blacks, regardless of their class status. Banking on same-race interviewers to be insiders with their respondents in various cultural ways was probably a pretty good assumption during this first moment of challenging colorblindness.

However, in what I am calling the second moment of challenging colorblindness, it is not the case that race no longer matters—but it seems to matter in different, less predictable ways than it did in the past. Kitwana (2005) refers to this moment in time as the "new politics of race." Kitwana's sociohistorical analysis of the hip hop generation uses a contrast between 1950s pop singer Elvis Presley and 2000s rapper Eminem to illustrate this point. Elvis is often regarded by African Americans as a "culture bandit" who "stole" black forms of cultural expression (e.g., music, dance) and parlayed them into a huge profit that was simply inaccessible to black Americans in the entertainment industry at that time.

Kitwana criticizes those who equate the success of white rapper Eminem with the same type of "thievery," because Eminem's success occurred at a new moment in time when Blacks were no longer uniformly poor and power-less and Whites were no longer the only oppressors. While race does still matter in some of the old enduring ways (e.g., white males still control the vast majority of the major record labels), it took a black sponsor, producer/record label owner Dr. Dre, for Eminem to be taken seriously—something simply unheard of in Elvis's time. And Eminem's lyrics focused on his life experiences as an impoverished member of the working class—experiences not unlike some of his black peers and listeners.

While it was still predictable that white suburban parents might have felt safer with a face like Eminem's than that of a black rapper, and thus spent their money accordingly, Kitwana argues that the next generation is not as committed to hard and fast racial rules. The existence of a much greater sized black middle class during the second moment of challenging colorblindness means that not only are Blacks more likely to be in positions of power, but Whites (particularly younger ones) are more likely to have interacted with equal-status Blacks and other minorities and even idolized them (even if only as athletes and entertainers). Kitwana points to both structural and cul-tural changes that have resulted in the decline of predictable assumptions one can make about the set of experiences that lie behind someone's racial phenotype.

Another example of old predictable tenets becoming less reliable during this second moment of challenging colorblindness is in the case of the "contact hypothesis." Beginning with Allport's (1958) studies of racial prejudice, and then upheld by various studies for the subsequent two to three decades (see Forbes [1997] for a review of more than forty studies), the contact hypothesis predicts that the more cross-racial contacts people have, the less likely they are to be prejudiced against members of that other group. During the 1950s and 1960s when Allport began this research, anyone who attempted cross-racial contacts, especially in the U.S. South, faced great risks (even death) for such undertakings. Thus, the sociohistorical conditions made it likely that cross-racial contact would be personally transformative.

By the 1980s, so many caveats were placed on the contact hypothesis (e.g., it has to be not just equal status, but higher status contact; it has to be not just one, but multiple contacts; the contacts have to be supported by norms/authorities; the contacts have to be engaged in similar tasks/goals) that inter-racial contact in and of itself became increasingly not as influential on people's racial opinions and outlooks (Forbes 1997; Jackman & Crane 1986). More to the point, interracial contact became more the norm rather than the exception, even if only superficially. As the survey data reported above show, a large number of Whites saw themselves as being open to friendships with Blacks, even if many of them actually did not have such relationships—clearly racial contact was seen as more and more of a non-issue, at least when non-intimate (platonic).

Yet interview research (Childs 2005; O'Brien & Korgen 2007) uncovered what the survey data left unanswered: The *content* of cross-racial contact had changed beginning with the 1980s. While a minority of cross-racial contacts (usually intimate) were still influential on people's racial prejudice and ideology, increasingly people had cross-racial contacts (even interracial relationships and marriages) where the topic of race was seldom addressed openly. In this new moment, then, cross-racial contact exposes Whites to multiple forms of racial difference, which may or may not challenge their racial worldviews. Thus, colorblindness may be continued/perpetuated by cross-racial contact in today's colorblind society rather than challenged by it. From their interview study of seventy respondents, O'Brien and Korgen conclude:

> [B]ecause Americans have moved more and more to "not noticing" race, crossing racial boundaries is no longer having the transformative impact it once did. We find that exposure to an alternative ideology ("the message") is more influential today than cross-racial contact (with potential "messengers"). People of color may or may not be the bearers of alternative ideologies, and even if they hold one, may not choose to share it with whites with whom they may come into contact. (2007:357)

Thus, I may be surprised to find that I do not share "insider status" with another white person who, like me, is married interracially, because that white person has a colorblind relationship with her spouse, stressing what is alike between them rather than what is different (Childs 2005). The nonwhite member of the relationship may be experiencing enough class privileges (alternatively, both spouses could be equally deprived of class privileges) so that racial privilege or lack thereof has not been a pronounced factor in their shared lives. Indeed, I may not be as likely to have good rapport during an interview with such a white person as I would have in earlier decades. This striking dissimilarity between members of the same racial group is similar to what Gallagher found with fellow Whites, what Few et al. (2003) found with black women, and what Dunbar et al. (2003) found with black men. So, in this second moment of challenging colorblindness, race *does* matter, but in increasingly more complex ways than in the past.

FROM RACE-MATCHING TO ACTIVATING A RACIALIZED SUBJECT

In the first moment of challenging colorblindness, researchers interested in studying race/ethnicity in critical ways challenged the hegemony and paternalism of white sociology by refusing to assume that Whites were all-knowing and objective and that their race would not interfere with good social science practices. They acknowledged how whiteness achieved its power by remaining unnamed and unacknowledged (Desmond & Emirbayer 2010; Frankenberg 1993) and sought to acknowledge how white privilege affected the research process. During this moment, having same-race interviewers were an important first step in getting closer to the truth than when it had been completely "whitewashed." Certain white researchers were willing to be reflexive about how their cultural competence was limited, just as scholars of color were excited about the possibilities of widening that limited body of knowledge by researching their racial peers with greater competence than many of their white predecessors had done.

However, in the second moment of increasing diversity of racialized experience, amid the predominance of colorblindness, race-matching alone is insufficient for the challenges facing today's researchers. Race still matters, but *how* it matters has changed.[1] Thus, perhaps how we approach interviewing also needs to change. I am not advocating abandoning race-matching in interview dyads altogether. Researchers cited above, who faced challenges gaining rapport with same-race respondents and even felt as cultural outsiders with members of their same race, also recognized ways in which a shared racial understanding benefited their interview and their interpretation/analysis of meanings presented within the interview.

For example, black feminist researchers Few et al. (2003) found that when they followed the several recommendations outlined in their essay, women approached them to say they had never before felt so respected and connected to their interviewers. The respondents actually felt they benefited from participating in the research in ways they did not from other research settings. It *did* matter to the research process that they were black women interviewing other black women. But they did not count on their racial phenotype alone as a "free pass" to cultural insider status, and instead practiced several reflexive techniques that could also be practiced in cross-racial interview dyads. For example, they suggest "monitoring symbolic power" through such practices as paying careful attention to language, which they argue is a "status marker" (p. 211) that they have observed drives a wedge between same-race interviewer/interviewees.

Several researchers stress "mutual self-disclosure" as the key to establishing rapport in the interview dyad. I argue that, precisely because we are currently living in the colorblind racism era where it is considered in bad taste (and perhaps morally reprehensible) to complain about experiencing racism, it is not as important for respondents to simply perceive a shared phenotype status with their interviewer as it is for them to know that their interviewer would validate and/or be open to their own experiences with race and racism.

For example, Rodriguez's experience interviewing an African American male college student (with whom she shares neither race nor gender) is informative. This particular respondent began relating experiences of self-doubt he felt after experiencing racial discrimination from a professor. Rodriguez decided to break traditional protocol during the interview by reciprocating: sharing her own experiences in grad school facing marginalization as a Latina. Rodriguez argues that this move "activates a racialized subject" (Dunbar et al. 2003:43), which, in effect, gives the respondent permission to speak more about his racialized experiences, without worry that his experiences would be questioned or second-guessed.

Because the dominant colorblind discourse often questions people of color who dare to complain about racism—labeling them as unpatriotic, lazy, expecting a handout, ungrateful, and so on (Bonilla-Silva 2006; O'Brien 2008a)—whether or not the interviewer and interviewee share the same race may be less important than shared racial understandings. In this case, though the interviewer and interviewee may not share phenotypical race, the interviewer strategically uses self-disclosure to alert the interviewee that they share a certain racialized understanding: Racism still exists, and one can be a hard-working, respectable person of color while still publicly discussing how racism limits him or her.

Activating a racialized subject opens up the door to an interviewee to be critical about the racial order of society in an era of colorblindness where race is assumed insignificant, so those who dare to suggest that the racial order may not be fair—"they are the racist ones" (Bonilla-Silva 2006). In other words, the rhetoric of colorblindness blames those who dare to mention race for creating the race problem. In this climate, people of color are reluctant to discuss racism candidly, particularly in "mixed company," since Whites are more likely to subscribe to this colorblindness than Blacks (Bonilla-Silva 2006; Carr 1993). So, in the first moment of challenging colorblindness, race-matching in interview dyads was assumed to be an automatic racialized-subject-activator. That is, it was expected that a respondent of color would automatically feel more comfortable talking about racism to an interviewer of color (thanks to the race-of-interviewer-effect literature) and no particular active effort on the part of an interviewer was needed to activate a racialized subject. However, in the second moment of colorblindness, in the increased diversity of racialized experience, even same-race interviewers begin to realize that activating a racialized subject is necessary, that they can no longer count on shared phenotype alone to build that automatic rapport with such respondents.

While mutual self-disclosure is one technique interviewers have cited as a way to activate a racialized subject, I argue that in this second moment of challenging colorblindness, where the message is more important than the messenger (O'Brien & Korgen 2007), even interviewers who do not share similar racialized experiences personally can still activate or deactivate a racialized subject. Whether my interviewer is willing to openly engage in candid discussions about race and validate my racialized concerns and interpretations of my life's events may be more important to me as an interview subject than whether my interviewer shares my phenotypical race. Again, it is not that race does not matter—if I can establish that understanding with my interviewer and we *also* happen to share the same phenotype, there may be a special rapport that could not be replicated in cross-racial interview dyads.

In my own research, I have used student interviewers of various racial backgrounds and completed many of the interviews myself. Like Gallagher, I became surprised when white antiracist activists occasionally asked me my own orientation during interviews, because I had expected that interviewees would already assume I was an antiracist myself if I had chosen the topic of white antiracists as my dissertation. But, indeed, even my same-race interviewees wanted to be assured that I was "on their team," so they would feel more comfortable during the interview and not feel like they had to constantly defend their views about race (O'Brien 2001).

In later research, when I interviewed latinos and asian Americans about their racial experiences (O'Brien 2008a), I relied on sharing experiences of previous respondents or friends to activate a racialized subject because I had not faced such discrimination myself. For example, in an interview project with biracial respondents (O'Brien 2009), at one point early in the interview, I asked one light-skinned respondent, Alicia: "Have you ever had people who thought you were just white have people start talking about black people in front of you or anything like that?"

In a more traditional, "naturalist" approach to interviewing, this kind of "leading" the respondent with examples they themselves did not provide might be frowned on. However, while traditional interview protocol might be critical of such "spillage" from one interview to the next, when we conceive of the interview as an active co-creation between interviewer and interviewee, we can become more cognizant of the ways in which the subject is hardly led or misled, but instead makes active choices of his or her own (Holstein & Gubrium 1995). Indeed, Alicia responded to my question with "No, I haven't. … I've never been in that situation. That would be really crazy yeah. I've never been in that situation before." In many cases, across several different studies, I have found my respondents perfectly willing to respond to examples I offer by disagreeing with them, or saying that they have never experienced that. So an interviewer should not worry that she or he is tainting or leading a respondent by offering examples with which the respondent can feel free to agree or disagree.

As a white interviewer interviewing non-Whites about race, I have found that when I give my respondents examples of times when Whites were discriminating or just plain ignorant about matters of race, this can "activate a racialized subject." It alerts my respondents to the fact that, although I may not have experienced racial discrimination personally, I am aware that it exists in many different forms and I would not discount or invalidate their experiences. Although I read a standard script at the beginning of the interview that includes the line "there are no right or wrong answers," that is not enough. In a colorblind society, I need to address race specifically and differentiate myself from the dominant colorblind discourse on race if I expect my respondents to feel comfortable sharing their own racialized experiences with me. Moreover, in this second moment of challenging colorblindness, where same-race interviewers are not necessarily insiders, even nonwhite interviewers could find it helpful to offer up examples in this way.

While the biracial respondent Alicia stated she had not experienced Whites assuming she was white and talking negatively about Blacks right in front of her, I believe that my offering up of such an example very early on in the interview (between questions #1 and #2 on the interview guide) paved the way for Alicia later feeling comfortable enough to share examples of Whites discriminating against her later on (questions #6 and #7 on the interview guide). For example, in response to a question about the best and worst things about being biracial, Alicia responds:

Alicia: But I will say that because people know that I'm half black, especially the church that I went to when we first moved to [southern state], being partially black was a negative for us, I mean, we were definitely discriminated against.

Me: So it was a black church?

Alicia: It was a white church!

Me: A white church, mm-hm.

Alicia: And they were [like]: "Oh, hi how are you doing?" [said in high pitched, fakey voice] that kind of thing, and I knew. I mean I was only what 13, 14, 15 years old ... and I knew. I knew how they felt. You know and it's like I'm not even all the way black, but they still treated us as if we were .... You definitely got the looks, especially from the older people in the congregation. They'd come up to you and shake your hand and then behind your back be like "ugh," whatever. I knew it. I knew it, because I think kids are more in tune with that kind of stuff. They can feel when they're not wanted.

Studies have shown that African Americans often underestimate the amount of discrimination they face, or second-guess discriminatory situations, especially when things are not blatant (Essed 1991; Feagin & Sikes 1994). Since nothing was stated to Alicia's face, the above example might be the kind of situation that people of color would not dwell on or bring up in front of Whites for fear of being accused of exaggeration. But her willingness to offer this example reflects a certain comfort level with the interview space. On the next question, when I ask whether she feels more accepted by the "black side" or "white side," or relatively equally accepted by both, we have the following exchange:

Alicia: In most situations I feel like I'm accepted. Yeah.

Me: But when you do experience something it's more from Whites.

Alicia: Yeah, yeah. Yeah I've never had a black person come to me and say, you're a mutt, or discriminate against me because I'm half white, I've never had that, so.

Notice that Alicia's first answer to the question is to say she feels accepted, but when I summarize to her what I think I've been hearing from her—that the examples of friction she offers all seem to have been at the hands of Whites—she agrees. Perhaps she is not willing to blame it all on Whites unless I do it first. I feel it is incumbent as a white interviewer to create the space where my interviewees feel they can critique Whites in front of me. In this way, I activate a racialized subject even in the absence of a same-race interview.

By the time I ask Alicia the next question—whether anyone has seemed to not want to date her because she was biracial—she speaks pretty candidly about her experiences of discrimination:

Alicia: Yes, yes! I've had that happen to me a couple times. Where, you know … it was purely because I was half black. I mean we could have had the best chemistry, we could have been hittin' it off, and that would be the reason—the *only* reason. Yeah. I remember specifically, when I was in 7th grade, there was this guy, and I remember he used to wear cowboy boots to school every day [laugh together] I mean we talked all the time, you know, and I felt like, you know, this guy really likes me, and of course you get your friends to "Hey, go talk to him and see what he says," you know, in so many words it was, "Yeah, she's cool, *but*." Yeah I've had that happen. Not so much as I got older, but in middle school, early high school, yeah, I definitely got that.

Me: And it was mainly white guys.

Alicia: Yeah … I like black men, and white men, I don't have any preference, but for that period I remember having crushes on like three or four white men—boys, I won't say men, boys in a row, and it was pretty much the same thing every time, I felt like. And I mean some of them wouldn't say that straight out because all their whole family— you could tell. You could tell when, that's how it is. So, yeah.

Again, even though these are situations where the discriminators "wouldn't say … straight out" that their rejection was because of race, Alicia assures me that "you could tell." Members of racial/ethnic groups often rely on shared stocks of knowledge—the "uh-huh" nods of understanding—that Alicia shares with me, even across racial lines. These are examples that, in the first moment of challenging colorblindness, researchers feared would not be shared across racial lines, hence the recommendation of same-race interviewing when possible. I argue that the historical conditions of the second moment of colorblindness make this possible, not because we are different racially but because across that difference, I extend an invitation to a racialized subject, and challenge colorblindness explicitly, not with my phenotype but with my counter-ideology that challenges colorblindness.

This strategy may not work every time. Upon reflection, the interview transcripts I have pulled to make my points also happen to be respondents who knew something about my racially mixed family outside of the interview. Alicia is a coworker of my black spouse and knows my interracial children. Wanda, a black Puerto Rican respondent I interviewed for my research on latinos and asian Americans, not only knows of my family, but has taken a community workshop on racism that I led through my church. So she not only knows the phenotypes in my family, but perhaps more importantly, my own racial ideology. Still, I also create space for Whites' behavior to be critiqued during my interview with her. Interestingly, at first Wanda tells me that the demographic group "that was *most* helpful to me and embraced me the most was white women." Yet once we have a conversation where we arrive at an interpretation for why white women seemed receptive to her (they can say they have a "black friend" but she feels "safer" to them because she is not African American), Wanda seems more willing to share with me other times when white women haven't been so helpful or embracing:

Me: And it sounds like, from the way you're talking, *that* piece might be what warms white women up to you in the work place maybe a bit more because they, like you were saying, some of them say, "Well you're not like those other black women, so why can't ..."

Wanda: Ohhh! They're more comfortable ... yeah, yeah.

Me: So they can say, "I have a black friend," but they don't.

Wanda: They don't have to say that I'm Spanish.

Me: They feel closer for some reason.

Wanda: Well, I don't think, you see, I think they don't feel that I'm gonna judge their behavior in a racial kind of connotations.

Me: Ok, so they fear that other blacks would view them with more suspicion.

Wanda: But let me share one [example] ... a couple of years ago that I was in a [book] club, this group, and they were all white, middle class, and we were talking about different things and I was defending the stance and I was saying that the black people in this country have gotten a bad deal and the poor people who are black, and this and that, and one of them said to me, "Well Wanda, I'm sick and tired of you always bringing out that the black people this, and the poor black people this, I was poor and I was this, and I made it so

> I don't see ...." And then we got into this whole thing. And every-
> body kind of was very quiet. That was one situation where I then
> came to the realization of why it is that black American people do
> not tend to be in the mixed group with white women because they
> don't want to deal with being confronted in that way. It's not com-
> fortable and ... they say, "Why do I need to put myself in that kind
> of situation when I can be with my black people, friends."

This transcript exemplifies the idea of an active interview. Here I am offering up interpretations of racial politics that I see in Wanda's life examples.
Wanda can take them or leave them, as respondents definitely do. But I have
found that when I give interpretations that include criticisms of my own racial group, this activates a racialized subject and indicates to the respondent
that I do not share society's typically colorblind stance, perhaps encouraging
respondents to speak more candidly about race during the interview with me
than they would in everyday conversation with someone else of my same race.

Because I am an antiracist and try to approach my everyday mixed-race
conversations in this way even when I am not doing an interview, I had not
thought much about this intentional practice as a crucial component of my
interview methodology until I noticed one of my white student interviewers unwittingly deactivating a racialized subject doing one of her interviews
with a biracial respondent. One of the questions on the interview guide asks
respondents if their identity has ever been "misperceived" and how they respond to that. Other studies (e.g., O'Brien 2008a; Tuan 1998) have shown that
whites commonly objectify racial-ethnic Others by asking them to explain/de-
fend their family origins in a way they do not do with other whites. Tuan calls
this the "ethnic game," and I refer to it as the "where are you from, no, where
are you really from" dance in my own work. In this study of biracially identified Americans, the question is meant to tap into life experiences of being
put on display and/or not fitting in. We want respondents to describe if they
are treated as Others and how this makes them feel, how they deal with it.
However, rather than empathizing with her respondent (Gordon) about these
problematic "othering" questions, the interviewer seems to instead empathize
with the questioner, by asking Gordon, in effect, what is really so bad about
this questioning:

> Gordon: I think it's funny, ... it doesn't really bother me, but ... then
> of course, you have people come up to you and say "What are
> you?" Which is kind of a weird question, for someone to come
> up to you and say "what are you," I have, I'm open to that
> because I just like to talk, I'm open to like being able to say, I
> like to be able to say that I'm mixed and I like for that conver-
> sation to be open you know, and it's become more and more
> open, so for someone to recognize that maybe I'm not, that I

am something, that I am mixed, is kind of cool for me, even if they get it wrong, and say, you know are you Puerto Rican, you know it's still like they recognize that I am not fully one thing or the other. You know? So that opens up the door for me to be able to talk about it, and it doesn't frustrate me, I'm pretty open about it, but, it happens.

Interviewer: Would you rather someone come up to you and say "Gordon, are you Puerto Rican?" or "Gordon, what is your heritage?"

Gordon: I think I'd rather someone come up to me and ask me what my heritage is rather than I guess assume, but then I also, it's funny because I mean I've learned over the years how to like, respond to questions like that because like, it's kind of a hard question to answer, I mean, it doesn't seem hard but it's hard to put it in words I guess, but there have been times when I'd say "My mom's white," or "I'm mixed," or "I'm mixed with black and white," or you know I'll say I'm mixed and they'll say what are you mixed with and I don't know, it's kind of been a process to kind of like, figure out how to respond so that's not like, I don't know, it's—um ...

Interviewer: It just depends on the circumstance, how you'd respond? Or who's asking, or ... ? ... Would you prefer them saying "What's your heritage?"

Gordon: Yeah like I said I'm open to people asking so I mean, I'm cool with them asking.

In this excerpt, although Gordon describes such incidents where his racial identity is questioned as "kind of cool" and that he's "open" about it and it doesn't frustrate him, at the same time, he problematizes these exchanges by saying "what are you" is "kind of a weird question" and it has been a "hard question" for him to answer that has "been a process" for him to come to terms with how to respond to it. Rather than agreeing with Gordon that these are "weird questions" or validating his perception that if not annoying, at least a bit disconcerting, the interviewer seems to be trying to defend the questioners by asking Gordon, what would you prefer? While this is a seemingly benign or neutral/objective researcher question, in the context of a colorblind society where complaints about being racially objectified are often stigmatized as oversensitive, the interviewer's repeated questions of "what would you prefer?" don't allow any space for Gordon to simply vent about the questioning process in general. Gordon soon realizes he will not get any co-commiserating with this interviewer, so he instead resolves the discussion by emphasizing that he's "open to" and "cool with" people asking, backing away from some of his earlier, perhaps subtle comments that suggest at least slight annoyance. But because the interviewer does not create a space for Gordon to further problematize these encounters (the interviewer provides no "uh-huh" nods of understanding), Gordon closes the book on the issue by essentially suggesting it is no big deal.

The above example underscores the default position of colorblindness in today's society, even when the interview topic itself has to do with race. I now begin each semester teaching race by forewarning the students that without fail, some of them will reach a point in the semester when they will ask me why everything has to be about race, although that is the title of the course. Would they ever stop in the middle of chemistry class to ask the professor why we are still talking about chemistry?

Respondents know they are expected to minimize race in today's society, and that it is the socially acceptable position, so it is not until they are assured they have shared racial/ideological understanding with their conversation partner that they will begin to violate the colorblind norms. And in this second moment of challenging colorblindness, I argue that each person's racial ideology (the "message") is more salient than his or her racial phenotype (the "messenger") in this process. That is, in the first moment of challenging colorblindness, there is an underlying assumption that nonwhite respondents will open up to nonwhite interviewers about the discrimination they face (thus violating colorblind norms), where they would not feel comfortable doing so with a white interviewer. Yet nonwhite same-race interviews can reinforce colorblindness as well.

In another interview for my latino/asian American study, I had a presumably same-race interview dyad with my asian American student interviewer interviewing another asian American (although ethnically they were quite different—the student interviewer is fourth-generation Japanese/Irish American while the interviewee is a first-generation Indian American married to a white man). Interestingly, the respondent ("Kali") decides to ask the student interviewer about her own racial/ethnic background about two-thirds of the way through the interview ("By the way, what's yours, what's your background if you don't mind me asking?").

By this time, Kali has spent most of the interview using language that downplays the extent of racial discrimination she's faced in the United States, even as she recounts fairly serious incidents of discrimination during her interview. In one instance, she is blatantly (and illegally) asked whether she is a Muslim during a job interview; in another instance, at a bar, a drink is thrown in her face by someone who feels that Muslim Americans (which Kali is not) are a negative influence on the country. However, Kali repeatedly uses the transitional phrase of "only that one time" or "other than that one time," not unlike many other respondents in the study, downplaying these serious experiences (see O'Brien [2008b] for a fuller discussion and analysis of why this pattern happens).

In the following excerpt, the student interviewer seems to reinforce the same colorblind position ("It doesn't really bother me") that Gordon takes in the interview above, even though this time the interviewer is not white, but explicitly identifies herself as "a minority" with shared racialized experiences similar to Kali's. Just before this, Kali jokes "Now I am interviewing you," and asks the interviewer questions about her own experiences as a "minority":

Interviewer: That's why I think doing this [study] is so interesting to me because when you lived as a minority, you know.... It's funny, how people how you were saying people think you are Latino and stuff, it's, I have a younger brother and we get that, people think we are Latino or more Mexican and my brother looks very, very Hawaiian, which is basically a sub-race of Japanese. But he looks, looks, exactly Hawaiian, as to what you in your mind would imagine as Hawaiian.

Kali: You do too actually a little bit. Does that bother you?

Interviewer: You know it doesn't bother me but it's one of those things that people always ask and I never really contemplated it and then you are learning about this kind of stuff and you think you know I do get asked that a lot. And how you were saying it doesn't bother you to say I'm Indian, it doesn't bother me but I realize that it does happen a lot, you know.... I never have that resentment or anything. I feel like some people are very bitter about it.

Kali: Really?

Interviewer: Yeah, some women I've interviewed have been angered that people ask them so much, like people should know that they're Indian.

Kali: Yeah I've run into that.

Interviewer: I've found that it's a prevalent thing. I feel, I don't mind informing people but at the same time it's like well you know once again, but it's not, I'm not angry about it.

Kali: Yeah, why should you be angry unless it was said in a derogatory way or something.

Interviewer: Exactly. I like hearing you respond to that because I have the same experience.

The end result of this conversation is similar to Gordon's exchange with the white student interviewer—the respondent observes that people may try to make them feel different and although that may bother some, it is not a big issue for them personally. Indeed, although she shares the same "race" as her respondent, this interviewer effectively co-collaborates with Kali in deracializing the encounters she describes. Of course, the way they get there is different: Gordon's interviewer effectively asks him "What's the big deal?" while Kali's interviewer contrasts herself with other interviewees who *do* think it's a big deal by insisting that she does not. Kali's interviewer at least offers up a different interpretation (a more racialized interpretation), whereas Gordon's interviewer does not much allow for possibilities of alternative interpretations (e.g., outrage at the situation). However, it is evident that same-race interviewers can also reinforce colorblindness and deactivate racialized subjects, even when both interviewer and interviewee are not in the dominant racial group.

Conclusion

In this second moment of challenging colorblindness, the reality of race and interviewing is more complex than a formulaic recommendation of "all interviews should be same-race in order to maximize rapport." The evidence demonstrates that same-race interview dyads can also experience the problems of outsider status, both for white researchers and researchers of color. Furthermore, it is possible for cross-race interview dyads (as well as same-race dyads) to produce situations of candid self-disclosure across racial lines, violating social norms of colorblindness, when interviewers "activate a racialized subject." Such steps taken by the interviewer are not possible in a structured survey interview, which is perhaps why so much literature in the positivist quantitative tradition has bemoaned the race-of-interviewer effect. I am *not* asserting that a race-of-interviewer effect does not exist in qualitative interviewing in a colorblind way that suggests race does not matter. Quite the contrary, race *does* matter when doing in-depth interviewing, but race here does not equal a "body" (e.g., "match a white body with a white body").

Qualitative interviewing must pay attention to race, but not in an essentialized way (Frankenberg 1993). Rather, we must take into account race (as well as other socially constructed categories of difference) and the way it works in our everyday conversations. And we must take steps as interviewers to ensure that we are not reinforcing the default of colorblind racism. Such steps would ideally not be practices like simplistic race-matching, but instead practices that acknowledge the diversity of experiences behind any given racial phenotype "box." Steps like this are consistent with the practice of active interviewing that approaches the interview as a social product that the interviewer and interviewee work together to co-create. In this way, an interview with a particular respondent can end up differently, not just because the race of his or her interviewer is different, but because the racialized content of views and experiences shared during the course of the interview also differed.

Our methods are not just a route to our findings; they *are* the findings. Recently, I discussed with some undergraduates my research on latinos' and asian Americans' minimization of the discrimination they experienced in their everyday lives. I focused on the American Dream ideology, and how certain (nonwhite) citizens of the United States are routinely Othered as immigrants (based on phenotype and despite how long they have been in the country). I theorized that my respondents were reluctant to be too critical of their experiences with racism in the United States in order to distance themselves from other minorities such as African Americans who they have observed being criticized for being a bit too willing to "play the race card." They gave many examples of discrimination, from subtle to blatant, but often used similar language to frame their stories such as "other than that one time" to present the examples as exceptions, seeming to cast themselves as noncomplainers (O'Brien 2008a).

One undergraduate student in my classroom asked, "Did you do these interviews?" and "Do you think they would have been less likely to minimize their experiences if a person of color were interviewing them?" Though I used a mix of interviewers, and the pattern seemed to occur across the different ethnic backgrounds of interviewers (myself included), I could not help but acknowledge that this student was onto something. As scholars, we are trained to take every precaution to make sure racial barriers don't deter us from getting as close to the truth as we can, and the way I answered this question was consistent with that classic/standard training. However, the more I consciously reflected on race and methodology for the purpose of this chapter, the more I had to admit to myself that a better answer to that student's question would have been: "Yes, indeed, the findings might have been different, had I explicitly trained my student interviewers, not just to ask good probing questions, but to consciously activate race during their interviews and to resist the temptation to follow their respondents down the default path of 'it's no big deal'/ 'it doesn't bother me' colorblind rhetoric."

Given the slippery way race functions in society, we would not be good social scientists if we did not admit that the pictures of race/ethnicity we present in our research are contextual snapshots. Here I am reminded of Rockquemore and Brunsma's (2007) study of biracial black-white Americans, where one respondent is reported to have shifted to black vernacular at midpoint during the interview when he ascertained that his interviewer was also biracial. Are we to assume that the second half of the interview was the "real" respondent, and the first half of the interview where the respondent was speaking standard English was not really him? Or could it be that the interviewer was lucky enough to be able to converse with two of the many selves that we all have? Holstein and Gubrium (1995) discuss multivocality in their work on active interviewing, pointing out that a respondent can speak "as a mother" and have a totally different view of a question than when she is "speaking as a professional," "as a wife," and so on.

The strength of active interviewing for research on race and ethnicity is that, as we acknowledge multivocality, we can begin to move away from a static view of race that insists that the insider interviewer gets the truth and everything else is a misleading imitation. Active interviewing allows us to see that, as deeply entrenched as racism has been woven into the fabric of our institutions, it is not inevitable. Just as a tick embedded under the skin, we can try many methods to get it out and make it worse (or at least more irritated) in the process, or let it fester by pretending it's not there. But if we acknowledge it, and do the hard work of bringing it to the surface, we will find it doesn't have to stay that way. And, surprisingly, there is more than one way of getting it out. Those of us who study race and ethnicity through interview method may be quite surprised at what we find as we experiment with new ways to allow these multiple truths to emerge.

Interviewing has been heralded for challenging old paradigms in white sociology by giving voice to racialized experiences for which closed-ended questions did not leave room. By placing the researcher one step closer to his or her respondents than the survey researcher, the interview method has been effective in reformulating previously held racial/ethnic knowledge in the field. Because an interview itself is a profoundly social process, it has the potential both to illuminate our understandings about race/ethnicity but also to obscure that knowledge if the interviewer approaches that interaction in a colorblind manner (as if race doesn't matter) *or* in an essentialist manner (as if race can be boiled down to a simple equation of matching interviewer and interviewee race for maximum reliability). Ideally, active interviewing can help remind us that race is a social construction, not lodged inside genetic bodies, but located in social relations with other human beings and in institutions and societies.

Note

1. I borrow this important question, which forms the title I have chosen for this essay, from Williams and Heikes (1993) who write: "The question is therefore not *if* gender makes a difference but, rather, *how* does gender matter?" (p. 283). Williams and Heikes contend that gender matters in *both* same- and cross-gender interviews, but obviously in different ways. This echoes my issue with the contention that in a same-race interview, racial barriers are removed, race is rendered a non-issue, and the interview is closer to the truth.

References

Allport, G. (1958). *The nature of prejudice*. New York: Doubleday/Anchor.
Andersen, M. L. (1993). Studying across difference: Race, class and gender in qualitative research. In J. H. Stanfield, II & M. D. Rutledge (Eds.), *Race and ethnicity in research methods* (pp. 39–52). Thousand Oaks, CA: Sage.

Bonilla-Silva, E. (1997). Rethinking racism: Toward a structural interpretation. *American Sociological Review, 62*, 465–480.

Bonilla-Silva, E. (2001). *White supremacy and racism in the post-civil rights era.* Boulder, CO: Lynn Reinner.

Bonilla-Silva, E. (2006). *Racism without racists*. Boulder, CO: Rowman & Littlefield.

Cannon, L., Weber, E. H., & Leung, L. A. (1988). Race and class bias in qualitative research on women. *Gender & Society, 2*, 107–117.

Carr, L. (1993). *Colorblind racism*. Thousand Oaks, CA: Sage.

Childs, E. C. (2005). *Navigating interracial borders: Black-white couples and their social worlds*. New Brunswick, NJ: Rutgers University Press.

Cotter, P. R., Cohen, J., & Coulter, P. B. (1982). Race-of-interviewer effects in telephone interviews. *Public Opinion Quarterly, 46*, 278–284.

Davis, D. W. (1997). Measurement error and race of interviewer effects among African Americans. *Public Opinion Quarterly, 61*, 183–207.

Desmond, M., & Emirbayer, M. (2010). *Racial progress, racial domination: The sociology of race in America*. New York: McGraw Hill.

DeVault, M. (1995). Ethnicity and expertise: Racial-ethnic knowledge in sociological research. *Gender and Society, 9*, 612–631.

Dunbar, C., Jr., Rodriguez, D., & Parker, L. (2003). Race, subjectivity and the interview process. In J. A. Holstein & J. F. Gubrium (Eds.), *Inside interviewing: New lenses, new concerns* (pp. 131–150). Thousand Oaks, CA: Sage.

Essed, P. (1991). *Understanding everyday racism*. Thousand Oaks, CA: Sage.

Feagin, J. R., & Feagin, C. B. (2008). *Racial and ethnic relations*. Upper Saddle River, NJ: Prentice Hall.

Feagin, J. R., & Sikes, M. P. (1994). *Living with racism: The black middle class experience*. Boston: Beacon Press.

Few, A. L., Stephens, D. P., & Rouse-Arnett, M. (2003). Sister-to-sister talk: Transcending boundaries and challenges in qualitative research with black women. *Family Relations, 52*, 205–215.

Finkel, S. E., Guterbach, T. M., & Borg, M. J. (1991). Race-of-interviewer effects in a preelection poll: Virginia, 1989. *Public Opinion Quarterly, 55*, 313–330.

Forbes, H. D. (1997). *Ethnic conflict: Commerce, culture, and the contact hypothesis.* New Haven, CT: Yale University Press.

Frankenberg, R. (1993). *White women, race matters: The social construction of race*. Minneapolis: University of Minnesota Press.

Gallagher, C. A. (2008). "The end of racism" as the new doxa: New strategies for researching race. In T. Zuberi & E. Bonilla-Silva (Eds.), *White logic, white methods: Racism and methodology* (pp. 163–178). Boulder, CO: Rowman & Littlefield.

Gubrium, J. F., & Holstein, J. A. (1997). *The new language of qualitative method.* Oxford: Oxford University Press.

Holstein, J. A., & Gubrium, J. F. (1995). *Active interviewing*. Thousand Oaks, CA: Sage.

Jackman, M. R., & Crane, M. (1986). "Some of my best friends are black ...": Interracial friendship and Whites' racial attitudes. *Public Opinion Quarterly, 50,* 459–486.

Kitwana, B. (2005). *Why white kids love hip hop: Wangstas, wiggers and wannabes.* New York: Basic Books.

Krysan, M., & Couper, M. P. (2003). Race in the live and the virtual interview: Racial deference, social desirability, and activation effects in attitude surveys. *Social Psychology Quarterly, 66,* 364–383.

Ladner, J. A. (1998). *The death of white sociology: Essays on race and culture.* Baltimore: Black Classic Press.

O'Brien, E. (2001). *Whites confront racism: Antiracists and their paths to action.* Boulder, CO: Rowman & Littlefield.

O'Brien, E. (2008a). *The racial middle: Latinos and Asian Americans living beyond the racial divide.* New York: New York University Press.

O'Brien, E. (2008b). When racism is not black and white: Latinos, Asian-Americans and discrimination in the racial middle. In C. A. Gallagher (Ed.), *Racism in post-race America: New theories, new directions* (pp. 123–134). Chapel Hill, NC: Social Forces Publishing.

O'Brien, E. (2009). Best of both worlds: "Bi" people living above the fray of race & sexuality. Paper presented at the annual meeting of the American Sociological Association, San Francisco, California, August 11.

O'Brien, E., & Korgen, K. (2007). It's the message, not the messenger: The declining significance of black-white contact. *Sociological Inquiry, 77,* 356–382.

Riessman, C. K. (1987). When gender is not enough: Women interviewing women. *Gender and Society, 1,* 172–207.

Rockquemore, K. A., & Brunsma, D. L. (2007). *Beyond black: Biracial identity in America.* Boulder, CO: Rowman & Littlefield.

Schuman, H., & Converse, J. S. (1971). The effects of black and white interviewers on black responses, 1968. *Public Opinion Quarterly, 35,* 44–68.

Stanfield, J. H., II. (1993a). Epistemological considerations. In J. H. Stanfield, II & M. D. Rutledge (Eds.), *Race and ethnicity in research methods* (pp. 16–36). Thousand Oaks, CA: Sage.

Stanfield, J. H., II. (1993b). Methodological reflections: An introduction. In J. H. Stanfield, II & M. D. Rutledge (Eds.), *Race and ethnicity in research methods* (pp. 3–15). Thousand Oaks, CA: Sage.

Stanfield, J. H., II. (2008). The gospel of feel-good sociology: Race relations as pseudoscience and the decline in the relevance of American academic sociology in the twenty-first century. In T. Zuberi & E. Bonilla-Silva (Eds.), *White logic, white methods: Racism and methodology* (pp. 271–282). Boulder, CO: Rowman & Littlefield.

Tuan, M. (1998). *Forever foreigners or honorary Whites? The Asian ethnic experience today.* Piscataway, NJ: Rutgers University Press.

Williams, C. L., & Heikes, E. J. (1993). The importance of researcher's gender in the in-depth interview: Evidence from two case studies of male nurses. *Gender & Society, 7,* 280–291.

Young, A. A., Jr. (2008). White ethnographers on the experiences of African American men: Then and now. In T. Zuberi & E. Bonilla-Silva (Eds.), *White logic, white methods: Racism and methodology* (pp. 179–200). Boulder, CO: Rowman & Littlefield.

Zuberi, T., & Bonilla-Silva, E. (2008). *White logic, white methods: Racism and methodology*. Boulder, CO: Rowman & Littlefield.

5 EXPOSING WHITENESS BECAUSE WE ARE FREE: EMANCIPATION METHODOLOGICAL PRACTICE IN IDENTIFYING AND CHALLENGING RACIAL PRACTICES IN SOCIOLOGY DEPARTMENTS

Elizabeth Hordge-Freeman, Sarah Mayorga, and Eduardo Bonilla-Silva

The native must realize that colonialism never gives anything away for nothing. ... Moreover, the native ought to realize that it is not colonialism that grants such concessions, but he himself that extorts them.

—Fanon (1963:141)

INTRODUCTION

The racist and patriarchal foundations of social science research have prompted numerous critiques of sociology and its research methods over the last several decades. In Ladner's pioneering 1973 book, *The Death of White Sociology*, Albert Murray indicted the social sciences by saying: "[T]he social science statistical survey is the most elaborate fraud of modern times" (1973:112). This statement refers to the ways white social scientists and, in the last forty years, a few conservative scholars of color have used their research to justify social inequality, trivialize the systems that produce it, and misrepresent oppressed populations (Bonilla-Silva 2001).

More recent efforts, such as that of Zuberi and Bonilla-Silva (2008), have argued that these historical tendencies continue in contemporary sociology. In their book, *White Logic, White Methods,* Zuberi and Bonilla-Silva use the term "white logic" to describe not only the "the context in which white supremacy has defined the techniques and process of reasoning about social facts," but also the "historical posture that grants eternal objectivity to the views of elite Whites and condemns the views of non-Whites to perpetual subjectivity" (2008:17). This "historical posture" is part and parcel of the dominant racial ideology that shapes the theoretical approaches as well as the methodological and epistemological orientations of the social sciences, in general, and of sociology, in particular.

Critical to the reproduction of white logic is the training and profession-alization process sociologists go through that socializes them to "accept, in-ternalize, and act as though the prevailing norms of the role to which [they are] aspiring 'has validity for [them]'" (Clausen 1968:8). The racial practices[1] that accompany the training of scholars into the seemingly neutral yet highly racialized world of the social sciences exert tremendous pressure on scholars of color to adopt a stance of "race neutrality" in exchange for validation and limited success. This affects not only the individual sociologist of color, it also has structural implications for the production of knowledge and resistance against white supremacy.

In this chapter we will not examine how the logic of white supremacy is inscribed in the methodology of the social sciences. That job that has been done very well by many others (Bulmer & Solomos 2004; Ladner 1973; McKee 1993; Smith 1999; Stanfield & Dennis 1993; Twine & Warren 2000). Here we address how the same white logic also dictates sociologists' behavior and perceptions producing a different "opportunity structure" for Whites and non-Whites in academia. Specifically, we are interested in uncovering how *white rule* is expressed, manifested, and more significantly, reproduced in sociology departments at historically white colleges and universities (HWCUs). Bonilla-Silva has argued that most colleges and universities in the United States that parade as "universal" neutral sites of knowledge production and transmission are, in fact, HWCUs. As such, they have a history, demography, curriculum, traditions, climate, and visual and aesthetic ecology that reflect and reproduce whiteness (Bonilla-Silva 2008).

White rule, or the theoretical, methodological, epistemological, and practical domination of Whites in a setting or institution (in our case, soci-ology departments), can happen without Whites at the helm (having a black president like Barack Obama is perhaps the best example). Thus, even in many HBCUs, white logic and white methods are the order of the day. This should not be surprising, as "the establishment of the [HBCU funding] cir-cuit provided safe, dependable institutions which could be trusted to con-duct research on black problems without challenging the dominant racial attitudes of the time" (Stanfield 1982:198). Furthermore, conservative and accommodationist minority scholars (Marable 1983) who work in HWCUs have labored not only within the parameters of white logic, but functioned as gatekeepers and agents of social control disciplining "unruly" scholars of color.[2] Worse yet, many who wish passionately to go beyond white logic are often trapped in the epistemological and methodological prison white supremacy built for them in white-led departments (Schuerich & Young 1997:141).

Accordingly, when we discuss white logic, whiteness, and white rule, we are referring to a system of oppression rather than to skin color. Albeit within this system skin color is an important marker of privilege and marginalization, the correlation between skin color and racial politics is not perfect. As Lipsitz has observed, "White supremacy is an equal opportunity employer; nonwhite people can become active agents of white supremacy as well as passive participants in hierarchies and rewards" (2006:viii). And, "[w]hite people always have the option of becoming antiracist," although we, like Lipsitz, lament that "not enough have done so" because of the material and psychological benefits of whiteness (2006:viii).

We write this chapter using our experiences as a dark-skinned black woman, a white-looking Latina, and a black Latino. We draw on the tradition of autoethnography (Reed-Danahay 1997), which uses personal narratives to gain clarity into cultural or institutional factors. Like most in this tradition, we "resist the façade of objective research that decontextualizes subjects and searches for singular truth" (Spry 2001:710). We highlight personal experiences in conjunction with supporting quantitative and qualitative evidence, to effectively "transform the authorial 'I' to the existential 'we'" (Spry 2001:711). However, our experiences and trajectories should *not* be interpreted as anecdotal and *sui generis*, but as emblematic of the collective experiences of minority scholars around the country.

The three of us, but most notably Bonilla-Silva, are connected to local and national networks and associations of minority scholars and receive masses of information about the status and experiences of sociologists of color, both students and faculty, in HWCUs. Thus, our collective experiences reflect the typical circumstances of most sociologists of color and should be seen as reliable data on the various *racial practices* behind white rule in sociology. As Charles W. Mills has argued (1998:28), "hegemonic groups characteristically have experiences that foster illusory perceptions about society's functioning, whereas subordinate groups characteristically have experiences that (at least potentially) give rise to more adequate conceptualizations."

We proceed as follows. First, we dedicate the bulk of our discussion to the identification, labeling, and explication of racial practices, with a focus on graduate student life and socialization. We focus on graduate life because "graduate experience is an anticipatory socialization into higher education faculty role" (Weidman & Stein 2003:15). So, what happens to minority scholars once they become professors is preordained and an extension of their graduate school experiences. Whenever necessary, we provide examples of how a practice works for faculty and graduate students and point out practices that affect faculty exclusively. Second, we outline strategies to survive as well as to fight against racial domination (Desmond & Emirbayer 2009) in sociology departments. Finally, we conclude with some perhaps utopian views on how to remake the sociological house and the sociological imagination as truly multicultural, democratic, and progressive.

Racial Practices

Weidman and colleagues (2001) categorized the most prominent paradigms for understanding graduate school socialization into three major approaches: linear, nonlinear, or interactive. Irrespective of the sequences detailed by each approach, a successful outcome is always achieved when the graduate student ultimately adopts and replicates the "values and attitudes, the interests, skills, and knowledge, in short the culture, current in the groups of which they are, or seek to become a member" (Merton et al. 1957:287). Given that the values that characterize socialization and solidify "occupational commitment" (Weidman et al. 2001:6) are not neutral, when a graduate student internalizes the required cognitive, ideological, and affective norms, he or she legitimizes white logic and develops scholars unwilling to challenge the status quo.

While many of the barriers that students of color confronted in the 1960s and 1970s continue to play a prominent role in their experience and socialization in graduate school (e.g., exclusion, overt discrimination, minimization of the value of their work, etc.), contemporary socialization and racial practices of the post-civil rights era pose even greater challenges because white rule has become hegemonic and almost invisible (Bonilla-Silva 2001; Omi & Winant 1994). In the next section, we outline a number of the racial practices that help reproduce white rule in sociology.

Assimilation

Diversity has become an empty ideology (Embrick Forthcoming). In fact, the banner of diversity creates a system that "predispose[s] educated people toward a preference for identifying the common or universal themes in human experiences, which means, in practice, discomfort with approaches that reveal basic, perhaps unassimilable differences" (Chesler et al. 2005:80). Thus, HWCUs, which were totally segregated until the late 1960s, admitted a few people of color in the late 1960s–early1970s. This occurred without changing the balance of racial power or, more importantly, the way they did "business." Hence, departments of sociology, pressured by social circumstances, added a few graduate students and faculty of color in the 1970s. By the 1980s and 1990s, patterns had emerged: Although few departments had no faculty or students of color, most had just a few so as not to be seen as racist (Bonilla-Silva & Herring 1999). (This pattern remains, as documented by Bonilla-Silva and Lee [n.d.].) And these scholars of color, used in HWCUs as evidence of "integration," are partially incorporated into the departments they join. In fact, it is more cohabitation than integration, with the expectation of assimilation (Romero 2000).

Assimilating and "cooling out" students and faculty of color is central to white rule since the mere presence of a few non-whites validates the status quo (Romero 2000). As Feagin and colleagues have argued, "The physical and social spaces of predominantly white colleges and universities generally embody the presumption of one-way assimilation for students of color" (1996:50). Students and faculty of color are expected to internalize the hierarchies of knowledge and research and support its value (Romero 2000). This socialization process is both formal and informal, based on "relatively unstructured experiences that are processed in various ways, depending on individual students" (Weidman & Stein 2003:7). One example is the invited speakers at departmental colloquiums. These gatherings establish the criteria that research students and junior faculty need to be valued and get tenure within elite research institutions. At Duke, as well as all the places Bonilla-Silva has studied, worked, or visited for extended periods (Wisconsin, Michigan, Texas A&M, Washington State University, and Stanford), white males, quantitative methods, and research groups are overly represented at the departmental colloquium. These things are then the intellectual standard against which we should presumably measure our success. Smith and colleagues have defined this as "epistemological racism,"

> [which] means that our current range of research epistemologies—positivism to postmodernism—arises from the social history and culture of the dominant race, that these epistemologies logically reflect and reinforce that social history and that racial group (while excluding the epistemologies of other races/cultures), and that this dynamic has negative results for people of color in general and scholars of color in particular. (2002:231)

The assimilation model acknowledges difference without addressing power relations and the dominance of white logic (Simpson 2003:159; Zuberi & Bonilla-Silva 2008). Davidson and Foster-Johnson (2001) critiqued the liberal assimilation view (espoused by Park) that race is "no longer an important dimension of difference once the members of non-dominant racial groups acquire the behaviors and values of the dominant racial group" (p. 560). While the assimilation model is often presented as an attempt to fully incorporate minority groups, the goal is the control and dominance of minority groups (Glenn 2002). The use of individual explanations for structural problems facilitates the subordination of minority groups and validates the privileged group's position. As Barrera (1979) argued, when a group's disadvantage is identified, their subordination is assumed to be internally produced because, according to the dominant group, stratification and inequality are aberrations within the current system. Rather than point to structural issues like the ones we present below, faculty understand graduate student performances, placements, publications, and success as a result of their individual ability to complete coursework, choose a suitable dissertation topic, and publish articles. We know, however, that evaluations of performance and ability, opportunities for publications, and job placement are heavily influenced by race, class, and gender (Madera et al. 2009).

Microaggressions

"Racial microaggressions" refer to "brief, everyday exchanges that send denigrating messages to people of color because they belong to a racial minority group" (Sue et al. 2007:274). Microaggressions can take the form of individual statements as well as an oppressive environmental surrounding. With regard to the latter, the "sheer exclusion" of prominent researchers of color (including W. E. B. Du Bois) in graduate-level sociological theory courses and the limited number of both faculty and students of color in sociology programs reflects environmental microaggression (Sue et al. 2007:274). Indeed, Romero (2000) suggested that despite the lip service and curriculum revisions, "*less than 25%* [of sociology programs] include the study of race in the required theory courses" (p. 285; emphasis added). Moreover, "the centrality of texts written primarily by white people ... immediately establishes all other knowledge as peripheral and as legitimate only to the extent that it does not contradict the knowledge represented in the text" (Simpson 2003:168).

These environmental microaggressions provide the necessary structural setting for interpersonal microaggressions to occur, which, consistent with contemporary theories of color-blind racism, often take the form of more "benign requests, expectations, or pressures" (Chesler et al. 2005:101). For many graduate students of color, racial microaggressions may go unnamed as a daily part of what it means to be a racial minority in the United States, yet they do not go unnoticed. They have significant consequences for graduate student performance and the production of knowledge. For example, white students interested in confessing their racial sins have often approached one of the graduate co-authors of this chapter. White students usually approach her because they are upset that a behavior or comment they have said has been "unfairly" labeled as racist. Not only do the white students burden the minority student with their racist concerns (despite not being friends with her), but after recounting the scenario (in which they have, in fact, said something racist), they dismiss her critique of their comment. It is as though their willingness to address the incident with an "authentic" person of color is enough to grant racial absolution and permits them to completely ignore her critical response. As Smith and colleagues stated, the difficulty of being ignored is in "some ways harder to deal with than malicious interactions" (2002:131).

Other forms of microaggressions take the form of more explicit casual comments. For example, white sociology students' casual use of the term "ghetto" to jokingly describe foods, clothes, and any other object that is dirty or poorly made is common in casual conversations. In another instance, unaware of the black student working in the adjacent office, two white sociology graduate students had a conversation where one woman expressed dislike for her body, lamenting "I have a body like a freakin' African woman." The power of these interactions is that their oppressive results are not predicated on malicious intent. In fact, it is the "benign" nature of these comments that betrays the racist structure and culture of the "white habitus" (Bonilla-Silva 2009).

These slights continue as students of color become faculty of color. Bonilla-Silva, for example, was told by white colleagues after his 1997 article appeared in ASR that racism had no conceptual standing, that they had no clue he was talking about, and that he was racializing issues when race was declining in significance. The worst offender was a somewhat prominent white female colleague, who after congratulating him on having a solo piece in ASR, told him, "I did not know ASR had an affirmative action program." Those slights have continued throughout his career even now that he is a senior scholar with national visibility. He may have achieved and accomplished many things, but he is still a scholar of color, thus most white sociologists see his accomplishments as the product of preferential treatment. As he writes these lines, he heard through the grapevine that a colleague tells his students in a seminar that the work Bonilla-Silva and other race scholars do is not research but "ME-search!"

Differential Response and Expectations

Graduate students of color enter programs where faculty members already have preconceived notions or expectations about student performance, and their responses to student difficulties and/or progress reflect this. These expectations lead to differential treatment, lowered expectations for academic performance, unclear norms, and unsatisfactory advising (Feagin et al. 1996).

The notion that "minorities must work harder and be smarter" because they are "judged at a higher standard" (Bowen & Bok 1998:131) can be partially attributed to the differential expectations of faculty members. The graduate student coauthors provide several examples where important achievements and successes are dismissed entirely or challenged as undeserved. For example, one of them was awarded a competitive fellowship in her first year; when she shared this news with a white faculty member, she was told, "You should reevaluate your reasons for being in graduate school." When she was awarded another fellowship the following year, instead of offering congratulations, this same faculty member expressed regret and frustration because it meant he had to reorganize RA positions.

The faculty presumes, often paternalistically, to know the graduate student of color better than the student knows herself (see Romero [2000] for additional examples). Even when faced with contrary information (high achievement and fellowships), the student of color is presumed to be misdirected or off-track.

Similarly, a male graduate student of color was awarded a prestigious national fellowship available to graduate students of any race/ethnicity. A faculty member in the department assumed, however, that the student's fellowship was a minority fellowship, directly challenged the student about the validity of his racial identity, and asked the student to ponder whether he should have been awarded the presumed minority fellowship. The faculty's racist assumptions and his attempt to police the racial identity of the graduate student reflect dominant notions about minority students' capabilities and paternalistic assumptions about racial categorization. Finally, an excited student of color completed his dissertation proposal defense and informed a white faculty member of his new ABD status, to which the faculty member responded smugly: "Well, you know levels of attrition are the highest at the dissertation stage."

When success is not trivialized, it is dismissed as random. In one cohort of students taking the comprehensive exams, only two students (both students of color) earned high passes. In discussing the exam results with the other white students (none of whom earned high passes), the white students described the grading system as "random," as though the students' expertise and effort were not responsible for their high performance.

At the same time, faculty responses to minority students are problematic, even when seemingly positive because, as Feagin and colleagues noted, "a white gesture that might be seen as complimentary if it were solely based on achievement criteria is taken as offensive because of the racial stereotype implied in the white action" (1996:66). For example, at the end of a statistics class, a faculty member showered the sole black student in the course with overwhelming praise, calling her overall performance in the course "great" and "impressive." The professor's excitement reflected his surprise at her performance and, hence, his initial low expectations for the student's performance, as he made no comments about the A performances of other students in the course.

Bonilla-Silva can attest that this practice continues as one becomes a faculty member. He has pondered many times why he has to work to make sure his awards are mentioned and forwarded to all the faculty in his program, or why he sometimes is not congratulated after receiving a national award (such as the 2007 Coser Award for Theoretical Agenda-Setting) or acknowledged for being cited in the *New York Times*. And we, as graduate students and faculty, see the differential treatment when we observe how white students and faculty react when "good things" happen to them.

Disengagement of Faculty

Weidman and Stein's (2003) study found that "socialization of doctoral students to the scholar role is directly related to student perceptions of departmental faculty encouragement for students' engaging in such activities" (p. 653).

Therefore, differential expectations (noted above) have ongoing consequences for network-building, collaborations, and professionalization. Collaborative projects are a central avenue for graduate students to gain research skills and build relationships with faculty. These projects lead to conference presentations, access to research networks, and publications. Recommendation letters for fellowships and employment opportunities are largely based on these informal professional relationships. We know the opportunities for these collaborations with faculty are not equitably distributed and the subsequent benefits are then disparately distributed. Turner and Thompson's (1993) study of 200 graduate women found that white women report more mentoring experiences and apprenticeship experiences, both student- and faculty-initiated. In fact, upon entrance into the program, many faculty seem to have made decisions about which students are worth investing in, and students of color typically are not part of this group (Romero 2000). A respondent from Turner and Thompson's study recognized that at her institution some students are tapped as "special people ... mostly the white men. They're the ones that start getting everything right from the beginning" (1993:364).

When one of the authors first started graduate school, she met with several white faculty members to discuss her research interests. During and after these meetings, she was surprised at the limited interests white faculty members expressed, especially when she saw the enthusiasm they had for other incoming students and their interests. Now an advanced graduate student, she sees her colleagues reaping the benefits of these initial and subsequent meetings: grant funding, publications, and the psychological benefits of knowing you have been supported by your department since the beginning and believing that this is because you are great. Even students of color who have been praised as top students are not brought in on these more informal, yet resource-rich relationships. Turner and Thompson (1993) offer a revealing excerpt from faculty correspondence, which states blatantly that racial minorities, women, and disabled students are the least desirable graduate students for faculty, particularly when a white male student is available. These initial encounters are fundamental to the entire graduate student experience because, "Given the power differential between professors and students, few students have the psychological and social resources to alter dramatically the social position crafted for them by professors" (Feagin et al. 1996:15). Moreover, these ties work in a cumulative manner, wherein one network leads to inclusion into another project; therefore, patterns of exclusion lead to cumulative disadvantages for students of color.

Minority students must constantly be aware of the "white gaze" and be particularly attuned to how their social ties and racial identity may influence the labeling process. Labeling students and their projects as "high risk" has been discussed by Chesler and colleagues in their book *Challenging Racism in Higher Education.* They report that students of color felt "they were perceived as high risks by professors, teaching assistants and students," who would subsequently lower their expectations of the minority students (2005:114).

This process of disinvestment is something both graduate student authors have experienced. We were enrolled in the same dissertation proposal development course and were called "high risk" and "ambitious" by the faculty course advisor. Although at first glance they may seem like benign comments, these assessments led to minimal feedback from the faculty member and the other students. The central purpose of the required course is to give and receive feedback while constructing the dissertation proposal; essentially, we were excluded from that process. We were seen as "beyond help" because we wanted to collect our own data and study micro-level racial stratification processes. Although ambition can be a positive trait, here it was used to indicate that we were on our own. The dismissal of student interests and lack of advising are themes presented in prior studies of minority experiences in higher education (Feagin et al. 1996:90, 120; Smith et al. 2002:27). Other aspects of the labeling process are discussed later in this chapter.

Disengagement from faculty also has implications for the graduate school process. Students of color are often instructed to include strategic white faculty members on our committees to give our work validation or the white seal of approval. We are encouraged to develop ties with white faculty who will vouch for our potential and accomplishments, while facing simultaneous disengagement from many. Moreover, we often edit our language and claims in our research (dissertation proposals and projects) to make our arguments more palatable for white audiences who may feel discomfort with strong statements about white supremacy and racialized power relations. Davidson and Foster-Johnson (2001) argued that:

> With the scarcity of mentors in graduate school who are knowledgeable about culturally appropriate ways of guiding women and students of color, these students are likely at greater risk of (a) not receiving sufficient training in research and specialized content areas, (b) not completing their degree programs, and (c) not being well positioned to readily succeed in their postdoctoral careers. (p. 550)

Almost every professor of color can attest to how the disengagement and labeling that begins in graduate school continues when one becomes a professor. Few sociologists of color are incorporated into projects, added to grants, made to feel they belong in sociology departments, and treated as equals in both interpersonal and professional interactions. Bonilla-Silva has been a professor for eighteen years and, except for his tenure at Texas A&M (the department was chaired by a Mexican-American sociologist and had ten scholars of color), has never felt included, appreciated, or respected. He has never been asked to work on a grant or a paper with a white colleague. He has never been considered for any administrative post in departments except at Texas A&M, although he had held important national positions in the ASA (as a member of the association's council and chair of the section on racial and ethnic minorities).

Over the years, Bonilla-Silva has been labeled "controversial," "political," "one-sided," "racial," "not methodologically rigorous," and many other things. Although he most often learns about these labels from others, colleagues occasionally have told him so. Once, the director of NSF called Bonilla-Silva to let him know that he was not going to receive a grant. After informing Bonilla-Silva that his proposal was in the bottom tier, the person said: "You need to decide if you want to be a scientist or a sociologist."

Expectation of Uncontrolled Emotion

Not only are our intellectual arguments controlled by the racial structure, but our emotions and bodies are as well. Often students of color are seen as hypersensitive and overly emotional. These characterizations have been well documented (Bonilla-Silva 2010). When we bring up issues related to racial inequality or injustice, we are told it is just a joke and that we need to lighten up. White students and faculty fail to see that "black students' individual and collective experience with whites is the foundation on which they base evaluations of recurring white actions and motives" (Feagin et al. 1996:65). Past experience guides the reactions of students of color, not "shoot-from-the-hip paranoia" like it is often perceived by white observers (Feagin et al. 1996:65). Feagin and colleagues further stated, "Ironically, although blacks are often accused of being overly sensitive, it is white hypersensitivity to blacks, rather than the reverse, that is at the heart of most racial difficulties in white 'home territories'" (Feagin et al. 1996:65).

An extension of this process is the expectation that we are incapable of controlling our emotions. One of us has been complimented twice by a faculty member and a university administrator for reacting to less-than-positive news with restraint and professionalism. Their comments betray the presumption, most likely influenced by gendered expectations as well, that if something does not go the way she wanted, she would be angry and defensive as opposed to open-minded and professional. The idea that a graduate student would lash out against two white male superiors is an absurd premise that makes these compliments more insult than praise.

Sociologists of color know very well about the importance of handling emotions. For example, Bonilla-Silva counsels young sociologists of color on the importance of smiling in job talks, as Whites prefer those of us who, to use their term, do not have an "attitude." This speaks volumes about white normativity and how they expect people of color to behave. White sociologists can express emotions, but we must "keep it together" or we are labeled "angry," "anti-white," and many other things.

Labeling: Racial Stereotyping and Grouping

Two major ways that nonwhite students are labeled and marked by Whites as Other are racial stereotyping and group-based identification. Racial stereotyping can take place along both academic and behavioral dimensions (Chesler et al. 2005:102). By group-based identification, we mean that white students see nonwhite students as parts of a larger whole, as opposed to individuals with independent identities, histories, and issues.

Racial stereotyping includes multiple elements, but we want to highlight a handful of characteristics that influence how students of color are perceived by white students and faculty: gender, class background (real or imagined), substantive interests, and methodological ability. These cues are used to label students and predict the relationship they will have with the department's white habitus (Bonilla-Silva 2009). In other words, these labels help white students and faculty navigate people of color: Are you hypersensitive or rational? Are you colorblind or racially conscious (read: political)? Are you subjective or objective? How white colleagues answer these questions influences how they interact with scholars of color.

The labels can vary within institutional contexts, but from our experiences we generally see three archetypes: the militant minority, the meek minority, and the overachieving minority. The militant minority is the most potentially dangerous for white colleagues and she is often framed as subjective, irrational, hypersensitive, political, dangerous, and self-segregating. The response to students seen as militant is often disengagement or punishment. Punishment and sanctions embarrass students as well as socialize them. The meek minority is typically a term attached to female graduate students, but can also be attached to international students with limited English-language proficiency. These students are generally read as apolitical, safe, and vulnerable. As a result of their vulnerability, students are seen as needing protection. This can lead to extremely paternalistic relationships between graduate students and advisors. The third archetype is the overachieving minority. This student is also seen as apolitical and reasonable as well as a guaranteed success. This view often leads overachieving minorities to receive minimal mentorship and faculty support.

Often, white students and faculty respond to minority students based on the assumptions of these archetypes. Knowing a few details about the person (e.g., where they went to college, what they are interested in studying, and the like) is often enough to place someone in a category. Sometimes assumptions about a person's background are made based on the archetype he or she is placed in. One of the graduate student authors, who has been placed in the overachieving minority group, had a conversation with a white faculty member during which the professor incorrectly assumed she had an upper middle-class background without ever asking her about her life history. The important element here is not whether she was middle class or not, it is that whites can assume they know people of color without ever talking to them. This pattern is seen in sociological research as well, where policies and theories about minorities are created without ever talking to non-whites but rather based on problematic assumptions about culture and behavior.

In addition, when students of color do not fit into the prescribed archetypes or phenotypic expectations of non-whiteness, whites challenge their racial identity. One of the authors, who is a light-skinned Latina, has been told on multiple occasions that she is not *really* a scholar of color because she looks white. The need to authenticate and validate one's racial identity is a function of a limited understanding of whom these identities refer to. Also, telling someone who she is and challenging her history is another way of labeling and asserting dominance over non-Whites. Although it is important to acknowledge the privileges afforded to those with light skin, we must also be aware that light-skinned minorities come from groups whose presence in academia is negligible and whose interests are secondary to those of the dominant group (Vega 2010).

When scholars of color create groups to respond to the intellectual shortcomings of their departments they are also subject to labeling. For example, the authors are all founding members of a race and ethnicity workshop in their department. The students who started this workshop are mostly students of color and have been described by our colleagues as the anti-social and exclusionary "race faction." This label illustrates whiteness at work. We are considered a faction, while other groups are simply friends, colleagues, and classmates. Additionally, students of color are seen as part of a larger contingent, rather than as individuals with particular histories, interests, personalities, and issues (Feagin et al. 1996:14, 93). Recognition and misrecognition are central to cross-racial social interactions in predominantly white universities (Feagin et al. 1996:15). As Smith and colleagues argue, however, "The concept of a critical mass has significance for the retention of African American and other underrepresented students. These students provide support for each other, and the saturation also encourages the continuation of support services provided for these students" (2002:38).

The racist labeling that begins when we are graduate students continues as we become professors. Bonilla-Silva has been labeled a "militant minority" since his days in graduate school at Wisconsin and that label has remained affixed to him. No matter his accomplishments and success, this label has severely limited his academic life chances. For example, after receiving a verbal job offer at a prestigious midwestern university, the offer was rescinded. Later he learned that senior faculty had gone above the chair of the department and sabotaged the hiring. More recently, he learned that a certain latino sociologist from an Ivy League university called colleagues at Duke and urged them "not to waste a line on this fool." This same sociologist had referred to Bonilla-Silva in an ASA meeting as "the Hispanic terror."

Psychological Cost/Isolation

The costs and benefits for minority students who attend HWCUs have been well-documented (Feagin et al. 1996). Although HWCUs tend to have better resources (e.g., funding, training opportunities), the resources and rewards are not equitably distributed. Similarly, Chesler and colleagues have discussed how scholars of color, particularly African Americans, "succeed more" and "enjoy it less." They have explained that "blacks find it more difficult to maintain the view that if only one does everything 'right' all will work out for the best" (2005:190). The differential treatment of minority students (discussed in more detail above) emphasizes the disconnection between what the department says students need to do and how the department responds to student achievements. This creates a situation where departmental norms are unclear, producing what Feagin and colleagues labeled "anomie" (1996:98). The resulting confusion and psychological distress hinders students' emotional health as well as their physical and professional health.

Exclusion from peer and professional networks is another psychological cost that can lead to isolation. Sometimes "students feel that dominant student networks are closed off, that a set of informal boundaries to acceptance is difficult to cross, or even that they are not wanted" (Chesler et al. 2005:104). A recent study at MIT indicated that 40% of black students felt "a sense of racial isolation" (Chesler et al. 2005:104). As a result, "in the face of such feelings of discomfort and alienation many students of color seek out members of their own racial/ethnic group and develop their own associations" (Chesler et al. 2005:104). Attempts to cope with this exclusion, however, are often read as self-segregation. At the same time, complete separation from the dominant group networks is not feasible if we want to complete our degree, get a good job, and receive the training we need to be successful. No wonder some students describe a sense of being trapped (Feagin et al. 1996:71).

This psychological cost is accentuated as one becomes a professional sociologist. As bad as things look when we are in graduate school, our isolation and alienation increases exponentially as faculty. We enter departments with one, two, or sometimes no people of color and still have to operate so as to make Whites feel comfortable. Bonilla-Silva, for example, has become the "lone ranger" in race at Duke. The Sociology Department claims to have a "race area," but it only has *one* professor teaching in the area. Thus, if Bonilla-Silva were to leave, the area would disappear. The overall racialized stress one endures in white spaces produces what Smith and colleagues (2007) aptly label "racial battle fatigue."

Nondepartmental Ties

Hurtado (1994) defined the racial climate of a university as the "perceptions of interaction and trust between minority students and predominantly white faculty or students at the graduate school" (p. 347). She argued that when this trust is lacking or nonexistent, minority students have successfully identified strategies that allow them to "maintain their feelings of self-worth in adverse racial climates" (p. 348). Graduate students of color are constantly negotiating faculty expectations, striving to meet department requirements, while also trying to develop a semblance of friendship networks with other graduate students. Early on, students of color usually recognize that even the most liberal white students have views that are "embedded in a vague rhetoric" that seldom highlights white privilege (Chesler et al. 2005:79).

Interracial friendships can be tenuous, as students of color often are required to compartmentalize relationships with white students in order to stay in good social standing and build networks (see Hurtado [1994] and Turner & Thompson [1993] for examples of superficial interracial relationships). For the black female coauthor of this article, this has meant visiting a country bar with Confederate paraphernalia and white patrons who stared at her with unwelcoming expressions. While happy hours may seem like innocent meeting times, some students of color refrain from these events to avoid alcohol-induced racism.

Given the pressure that these relationships create, it should come as no surprise that minority graduate students and faculty proactively pursue avenues to protect their mental health and build a sense of community. Students of color have to be resourceful in their search for ways to combat the alienation and discomfort that they experience in the university setting. For several students of color, it has meant taking elective coursework in African and African American Studies, Women Studies, and Latin American Studies and developing close ties with minority-based organizations. Participation in minority groups serves as "an attempt at self-determination and cultural maintenance in a sea of whiteness" (Chesler et al. 2005:104; Feagin et al. 1996:72). Moreover, the creation of formal workshops reflects efforts to construct spaces for in-group bonding that validate their experiences and offer spaces for more critical theoretical orientations, methodological approaches, and substantive concerns.

Despite the extra energy and time these activities take, which Romero has called the "double day of graduate work" (2000:302), participation in outside groups has been an important source of fulfillment for racial minorities. For example, civic participation of college-educated men from prestigious colleges is significantly higher for Blacks than for Whites. The level of civic participation is roughly equal for white women and black women, although college-educated black women are more likely to be working in full-time positions

(Chesler et al. 2005:160). Moreover, having an advanced degree is correlated with civic leadership for Blacks (Bowen & Bok 1998:167). Minority students often find that they can "achieve a sense of balance in their lives by being part of a broader ethnic/racial community" (Turner & Thompson 1993:101).

Some Whites, demonstrating white racial myopia reinterpret the presence of these spaces as examples of self-segregation (Elfin & Burke 1993; Tatum 1997). They criticize minorities' behaviors, without recognizing how "demeaning behaviors and various organizational pressures or norms promoting separatism" are largely responsible for this occurrence (Chesler et al. 2005: 86).

Many professors of color, like graduate students of color, seek refuge outside sociology. Bonilla-Silva, for example, has benefited from joint appointments in African American Studies and, more recently, from a deep network of scholars of color across the nation in the social sciences and the humanities. He has created and participated in this community and benefits from the support he receives from minority peers. That said, he has to navigate daily life in sociological spaces where few of his colleagues understand and appreciate his work, style, culture, traditions, and the like.

Racial Innocence/Naturalization of Racial Expertise

The groups of white students who work and socialize together are not likely to acknowledge exclusions but are likely to profess racial innocence and superficial progressive politics when their liberalism is questioned. When one considers the classroom, we can observe that interracial encounters are "sporadic and hesitant, and reproduce prior hierarchies of racial advantage and disadvantage" (Chesler et al. 2005:80). That is, white students are vocal on issues that do not directly relate to race and they look to Blacks or students of color to talk about race (Feagin et al. 1996:86). This occurs because white students understand themselves to be "outside of race" or "unraced" (Simpson 2003:47), while students of colors are singled out as natural racial experts (p. 115). The naturalization of racial expertise is highly problematic because it undermines the extensive training that many minority students have received, supports the false assumption that race only impacts minorities, and ultimately leads to the devaluation of our work as subjective and secondary.

At the same time, there are several white students who conduct research where race is central to their arguments, yet they actively avoid enrollment in race coursework and do not directly engage with scholars of race and ethnicity. In fact, one of the coauthors was approached in a hallway by a white student interested in race and asked to "explain the origins of race and how race is different than class." This question is an important one that cannot be fully explained in a casual hall conversation. She recommended a few books for him to read and the graduate-level course on race, neither of which seemed to be of interest. Because race theory is not viewed as objective or valuable, white students do not invest time in developing their expertise. Instead, they tend to construct questions about race that do not highlight power or white privilege, focus on the "race effect" instead of racial stratification (Zuberi 2001; Zuberi & Bonilla-Silva 2008), or ask a minority student when they have a pressing question.

Some white students do have a sincere interest in race, but these efforts are stymied because they are also "seeking the illusion of peace and harmony, [while] often withdrawing from or even denying uncomfortable racial relations" (Chesler et al. 2005:106). In our department as in many others, the unwillingness of students of color to politely ignore race leads whites to claim that they are made to feel as "walking on eggshells." Whites attribute their discomfort not to their own racism, but to the alleged "hypersensitivity" of racial minorities. The critical perspective that minority students offer on race is consistent with the standards of intellectual rigor, but when applied to race, it is dismissed as combative.

The ability to selectively accept or discount racial criticisms relates closely to the Feagin and colleagues argument regarding "selective white amnesia" about U.S. racial history (1996:17). White students pick and choose which aspects of the comments and criticisms to take seriously and dismiss the most critical ones. If a white student's self-assessment is that he or she is not racist, then "that is the end of the issue for that person and the end of her or his responsibility" (Smith et al. 2002:221). In perhaps one of the most explicit examples of both racial innocence and superficial ties, the black graduate coauthor was leading a group of white graduate students back to a dark parking lot after a day at the state fair. A group of young white men drove by and yelled "Niggers!" Shocked, the black student responds, "I can't believe that just happened." Others looked at her cluelessly, saying that they thought the white men screamed "Indians" and "canned food." Once a white woman in the group confirmed that she too heard "Niggers," another white woman says: "Oh, so they actually did say it. Well, they are idiots. Who do they think I am? I mean look at me." Not only was the experience viewed as subjective and unbelievable until the unbiased white observer confirmed it, but the white student failed to problematize the racist event and rather focused on the fact that the plural racist epithet should have only applied to her black "friend." White students are eager to list students of color among their group of friends, but this does not translate into inclusion in private parties, hang outs, or other events. These friendships are nominal at best and used to merely "affirm their liberalism" (Romero 2000:284).

At the same time, some white students and faculty members are important allies and supporters of students of color. In fact, some of the white faculty who may have originally made racist comments or had racist expectations eventually begin to act in ways that support student success. White allies are important and have been historically valuable in efforts to accomplish more revolutionary objectives. Even when white allies do not completely understand the experience of being a student of color in a HWCU, they often understand that students concerns are valid and need to be heard. The challenge students of color and faculty face push white allies to observe and articulate the problem with the white racial structure and participate in efforts to dismantle it.

The racial innocence of white graduate students is typical of post-civil rights racial discourse (Bonilla-Silva 2001). Bonilla-Silva has dealt with this practice as a professor, too. In his fourth year as a professor at the University of Michigan, after giving a talk on race and methodology in the departmental colloquium, several white colleagues who had never asked him to "do lunch" with them asked him to join them. He quickly learned the reason for the lunches was that his white colleagues wanted to scold him for his talk and accuse him of calling them racist. When he told them he had made a structural rather than an individual claim about race in sociology, they dismissed him and one even said: "Despite this, I guarantee you that this matter will not affect how I vote on your tenure case." Veiled threats have been part of Bonilla-Silva's career since he became a sociologist in 1993.

After Graduation

Once students graduate and begin their careers as faculty members, the white logic of sociology departments continues to reproduce racial practices that marginalize them within their new environment. This process has been well-documented by researchers, including Turner et al. (1999), which indicated the following about faculty of color:

> Most acknowledged continuing racial and ethnic biases in their colleges and universities ... [and] repeatedly mentioned the handicaps of isolation, lack of information about tenure and promotion, unsupportive work environments, gender bias, language barriers, lack of mentoring, and lack of support from superiors. They identified racial and ethnic bias as the most troubling challenge they faced in the academic workplace. (p. 41)

In essence, the racial practices of isolation, microaggression, and disengagement continue, as do the psychological and economic costs.

As professors, faculty of color are often not a part of the informal networks of power where decisions are made. Being excluded from departmental in-groups costs more than potential companionship. Friendships lead to nodes of power, especially since important matters are often discussed and decided outside of faculty meetings. Therefore, not being invited to informal gatherings birthdays, dinners, picnics, games, and the like has serious implications (Bonilla-Silva 2011).

Tenure, perhaps the most important process for any faculty member, is also dictated by departmental white logic. During tenure reviews, minority faculty seldom receive the benefit of the doubt. Fenelon (2003) explains:

> Tenure, when conferred or denied in politicized systems like those described previously, is rather like affirmation systems, with an increasingly higher bar for performance by those who may disagree with the dominant meritocratic ideologies, and an increasingly lower set of standards for those scholars in alignment with the official and informal explanations for the general lack of diversity. (pp. 91–92)

Bonilla-Silva has observed the benefits of whiteness during tenure reviews throughout the years and has seen that these benefits can even include promotion through two ranks, with one book as the foundation for the promotions (Bonilla-Silva 2011). At the same time, the type of scholarship scholars of color produce continues to be heavily scrutinized, and assimilation is still the name of the game. As Bess explained, "The heavy informal controls and sanctions laid on the struggling untenured assistant professor serve to orient him toward the path of valued activities and constrain him from deviating too obviously from accepted standards" (1978:297). Therefore, while some of our work is praised as worthy scholarship, other projects are designated "political" explorations based on identity politics. Our publications are regarded as lesser ones, our books are minimized, and the journals we tend to publish in are treated as second-class.

All of us are the product of a discipline that is racialized. And sociologists ought, but do not, accept this point without reservations. They may argue the extent and character, but few would dispute nowadays the idea that organizations are shaped by class, status, and gender. If sociologists accept that the state and civil society are fractured by these social categories, why do they balk at the idea that sociology itself is racialized? The answer lies in the way dominants react to discussions about their role as dominants (Bonilla-Silva 2011). In the sage words of William Ryan: "[N]o one [wants to think] of himself as a son of a bitch" (1976:20). So whites who rule sociology want to "fake the funk" and thus see sociology with Panglossian eyes as "the best of all possible worlds."

ON THE POLITICS OF RACIAL EMANCIPATION WITHIN SOCIOLOGY

In this chapter we have identified some of the major racial practices and socialization processes that stifle the development of graduate students of color and continue as they become professors. Among others, these barriers include assimilation pressures, racial microaggressions, stereotyping/labeling, and differential expectations. While these practices have immediate psychological consequences, their most far-reaching consequence relates to the continuation of epistemological racism (Mills 1998). Accordingly, we must deconstruct how white rule functions through our professional socialization if we wish to change the racial structure and practice of American sociology. Challenging domination is always risky. Faculty and students of color pay dearly for the public positions they take that challenge whiteness in American sociology. But we also know that there is "salvation through struggle," so speaking up against domination is not only liberating, it is also central to the kind of sociological praxis we wish to exhibit (Bell 1993:98).

The notion that one can just "do work" and let the work "speak for itself" is silly, cowardly, and counterproductive. Minority scholars who successfully assimilate into mainstream values, norms, and epistemology may get rewarded by "the man," but in addition to not sleeping well, they ultimately embarrass themselves and their people. At this curious racial moment in American history, when we have a black man in the still very White House, we believe it is imperative to demonstrate how white rule is accomplished and how that affects the lives, research trajectories, and careers of sociologists of color. By doing this, we hope others can understand this reality and develop the necessary skills to survive and fight back.

Although we are deeply embedded in the white racial structure, our presence need not represent the legitimacy or reproduction of white logic and methods. As Lipsitz argued, we may not choose our color, but we do choose our politics (2006:viii). Accordingly, the challenge we pose to the sociology of race relations is preeminently a political one, for white and nonwhite scholars alike. Here we outline strategies for a broader, political strategy in the struggle against white supremacy and offer suggestions about how students can negotiate the daily verbal and interpersonal assaults that emerge in class and peer relationships throughout graduate school and beyond.

1. Scholars should become familiar with the classic canons, but also identify important sociological works that were strategically erased from sociological memory. By doing so, we effectively challenge the trivialization of the contributions of women and students of color and destabilize the position of white men as the founders of "civilization and culture" (Jordan & Weedon 1995:11). This motivation should drive the articulation of our research questions and lead to new theoretical orientations and innovative methodological approaches.

2. Be willing to sacrifice white (mainstream) validation in exchange for research that is heavily self-directed and unapologetically critical of mainstream research. This work is vital because critical social scientists on race matters can provide data, arguments, counter-narratives, and other

intellectual ammunition against dominant representations of racial groups and racial inequality. And to provide better ammunition for the movements against white supremacy, the sociological and social scientific efforts in this field must be race-conscious and engaged in a systematic analysis of racial stratification and its effects. In addition to "mental" liberation from the tentacles of white sociology (Ladner 1973), we have to remain committed to conducting research without regard to external validation and incorporating this praxis in our daily lives.

3. Speak up in class and in social interactions to counter racist assumptions and comments of peers. Pressures to assimilate and desires to avoid labeling and faculty disinvestment are palpable factors that could easily compel a graduate student to develop a so-called neutral stance on race. Race neutrality is never truly neutral and always supportive of white rule. Indeed, liberal sociology at best fosters charitable views of people of color and reformist policies on behalf of the "problem people" (Du Bois 1903/1996). We must avoid neutrality and take a clear stance. If social sciences are going to assist in the emancipation of people of color, their efforts must clearly be on the side of the racially oppressed, for "If there is a hell for social scientists, it is precisely that they only manage to be objective if they are directly involved in a struggle, and that they have no way of escaping, even through wishful thinking" (Casanova 1981:3).

4. Refuse to give in to assimilation pressures and normativity in race research and strive to identify alternative paradigms, develop new projects, orientations, approaches, practices, and knowledge about racial stratification. There is a history of accommodation by sociologists of color, in which "several major foundations perpetuated a status quo approach to racial inequality by selective sponsorship of the development of black social scientists" (Stanfield 1982:200). Minority scholars who support and validate the existence of this system and its racial practices will be compensated in the short term for their loyalty. In the end, however, because their spaces and positions are "bestowed" on them, they do not escape the consequences of its white logic. Although they may be positioned as exceptions to the rule, under white supremacy they are still vulnerable and subjected to oppressive racial practices (Bonilla-Silva 2011).

5. Decolonize your sociological imagination (Guthrie 2004; Oliver 2004) to unlearn received truths about race, race relations, race research, and even ourselves and our own potential. The new generation of race scholars must do their work without much concern for "*el que dirán*" (what others will say). We must do a "For-Us" social science (Mendoza 2006:155) on racial affairs and let the representatives of whiteness continue finding, again and again, that race is "declining in significance." The race rebellions of the future will awaken them from their dream, just as the race

rebellions of the 1960s forced many of them to admit they actually knew very little about racial matters in America.[3]

6. Instead of the superficial ties that are often encouraged, we suggest continued participation in community and political organizations as a means to address some of the negative psychological consequences of microaggressions and intense isolation. Moreover, we believe civic participation is important because the movement we hope to inspire within sociology and the social sciences must be *directly* related to social movement efforts outside academia. This parallels the efforts of older social analysts through organizations such as the Association of Black Sociologists and the Association of Black Psychologists. We know that "professionals will not empower anyone" (Berkowitz & Wolff 1998:299). But we are also aware that in this age when social science data on race have become crucial (maybe even more important than data from the biological sciences) for the reproduction of racialization and racism (Dumm 1993), critical social scientists[4] must do whatever they can to be active in the various social movements against white supremacy. Even if our engagement with these movements is only as supporters (but we plead with social scientists to become scholar activists), we should not evade our historic responsibility[5]; we cannot continue business as usual and act as mere reporters of racial matters.

Our committed practice *for* people of color and *for* the elimination of white supremacy in the social sciences (the need for outing the institutionally dominant white, male, heterosexual *homus academicus*) is still urgent.[6] We believe this will help lift the veil that has prevented Whites (and some people of color) from truly seeing and understanding how racial stratification affects the life chances of people of color. As Fanon writes, "Come, then, comrades; it would be as well to decide at once to change our ways. We must shake off the heavy darkness in which we were plunged, and leave it behind. The new day which is already at hand must find us firm, prudent, and resolute" (1963:310).

Notes

1. We use the term "racial practices" because the notion of discrimination, married to the limiting prejudice problematic (Bonilla-Silva 1997), does not allow us to capture normative, seemingly non-racial, kinder, and gentler forms of reproducing racial domination. Accordingly, by racial practices, we mean behaviors, styles, cultural affectations, traditions, and organizational procedures that help maintain white rule. Because many of these practices become routine ("That's the way things are"), they are not necessarily carried out with animosity and intent, that is, hostility and explicit expressions of racial cognitions and feelings about the Other need not be at the core of these practices. In fact, they tend *not* to be Jim Crow–like

and are more in line with the hegemonic nature of post–civil rights racial domination (Bonilla-Silva 2001; Omi and Winant 2004): with the "now you see it, now you don't" way that race matters in contemporary America.

2. The 1999 controversy about the editorship of the American Sociological Association (ASA) was illustrative of this point, as several notable minority sociologists signed a document supporting the white side on the controversy. Readers interested in details of this case can see the pertinent documents in *Footnotes*, the newsletter of the ASA, late 1999 and early 2000.

3. One of the few sociologists who openly acknowledged the limitations of how social analysts saw race matters in the 1960s was Everett C. Hughes. His insights and commentary, many of which we believe are still valid, can be read in his 1963 presidential address to the American Sociological Association, which is titled "Race Relations and the Sociological Imagination."

4. The critical tradition has been deeply connected to the work of Frankfurt School scholars such as Theodore Adorno, Herbert Marcuse, and Max Horkheimer among others. But that tradition has been safely expanded and revised to include the work and ideas of many in the black radical tradition. For efforts in expanding the former, see Joe Kincheloe and Peter McLaren (2000). For a magisterial work on the latter, see Cedric J. Robinson (2000).

5. This point reminds Eduardo of discussions with fellow minority graduate students and junior colleagues when he was a junior professor. They insisted they would not do "politics" until they were "safe" (i.e., had tenure). I pointed out to these colleagues that such an approach was a betrayal of those who struggled for our right to be where we were and led to accommodation and, ultimately, cooption by the system that had excluded us for so long. Now, twenty years or so later, these colleagues have become part of mainstream sociology and have still not done anything political (that is, they have not raised concerns about racism in academia).

6. This point was well made referring to queer studies by Joshua Gamson (2000).

REFERENCES

Barrera, M. (1979). *Race and class in the southwest: A theory of racial inequality.* South Bend, IN: University of Notre Dame Press.

Bell, D. A. (1993). *Faces at the bottom of the well: The permanence of racism.* New York: Basic Books.

Berkowitz, B., & Wolff, T. (1998). Rethinking social action and community empowerment: A dialogue. In M. B. Lykes et al. (Eds.), *Unmasking social inequalities: Victims, voice and resistance* (pp. 296–317). Philadelphia: Temple University Press.

Bess, J. (1978). Anticipatory socialization of graduate students. *Research in Higher Education, 8,* 289–317.

Bulmer, M., & Solomos, J. (2004). *Researching race and racism.* New York: Routledge.

Bonilla-Silva, E. (1997). Rethinking racism: Toward a structural interpretation. *American Sociological Review, 62,* 465–480.

Bonilla-Silva, E. (2001). *White supremacy and racism in the post civil rights era.* Boulder, CO: Lynne Rienner.

Bonilla-Silva, E. (2008). Teaching while black/brown. *THE BULLETIN of the North Carolina Sociological Association, 34, 2, 1* (April/May Issue).

Bonilla-Silva, E. (2009). Are the Americas sick with racism or is it a problem at the poles: A reply to Christina A. Sue. *Ethnic and Racial Studies, 32,* 1971–1982.

Bonilla-Silva, E. (2010). *Racism without racists.* 3rd ed. Lanham, MD: Rowman & Littlefield.

Bonilla-Silva, E. (2011). The real "race problem" in sociology: The power of white rule in our discipline. Presented as the Keynote Speech at the Southern Sociological Society Meetings, Jacksonville, Florida, April 9.

Bonilla-Silva, E., & Herring, C. (1999). "We'd love to hire them but": The underrepresentation of sociologists of color and its implications. *Footnotes* (Newsletter of the American Sociological Association), *3,* 6–7.

Bonilla-Silva, E., & Lee, K. (n.d.). The white house of sociology is still white! Unpublished document.

Bowen, W., & Bok, D. (1998). *The shape of the river: Long-term consequences of considering race in college and university admissions.* Princeton, NJ: Princeton University Press.

Casanova, P. (1981). *The fallacy of social science research: A critical examination and new qualitative model.* New York: Pergamon Press.

Chesler, M., Crowfoot, J., & Lewis, A. (2005). *Challenging racism in higher education.* Lanham, MD: Rowman & Littlefield.

Clausen, J. A. (1968). *Socialization and society.* Boston: Little, Brown.

Davidson, M., & Foster-Johnson, L. (2001). Mentoring in the preparation of graduate researchers of color. *Review of Educational Research, 71,* 549–574.

Desmond, M., & Emirbayer, M. (2009). *Racial domination, racial progress: The sociology of race in America.* New York: McGraw-Hill.

Du Bois, W. E. B. (1903/1996). *Souls of black folk.* New York: Penguin Books.

Dumm, T. (1993). The new enclosures: Racism in the normalized community. In R. Gooding-Williams (Ed.), *Reading Rodney King: Reading urban uprising* (pp. 178–195). New York: Routledge.

Elfin, M., & Burke, S. (1993). Rage on campus. *U.S. News & World Report, 114,* 52–54.

Embrick, D. (Forthcoming). Corporate diversity in the post–civil rights era: Colorblindness and the diversity ideology. *Critical Sociology.*

Fanon, F. (1963). *The wretched of the earth,* translation by C. Farrington. New York: Grove Weidenfeld [first published in French in 1961].

Feagin, J., Vera, H., & Imani, N. (1996). *The agony of education: Black students in white colleges and universities.* New York: Routledge.

Fenelon, J. (2003). Race, research, and tenure: Institutional credibility and the incorporation of African, Latino, and American Indian faculty. *Journal of Black Studies, 34,* 87–100.

Gamson, J. (2000). Sexualities, queer theory, and qualitative research. In N. K. Denzin & Y. S. Lincoln (Eds.), *Handbook of qualitative research* (pp. 347–365). Thousand Oaks, CA: Sage.

Glenn, E. N. (2002). *How race and gender shaped American citizenship and labor.* Cambridge, MA: Harvard University Press.

Guthrie, R. V. (2004). *Even the rat was white a historical view of psychology.* Boston: Allyn & Bacon.

Hurtado, S. (1994). Graduate school racial climates and academic self-concept among minority graduate students in the 1970s. *American Journal of Education, 102,* 330–351.

Jordan, G., & Weedon, C. (1995). *Cultural politics: Class, gender, race and the post-modern world.* Oxford, UK: Blackwell Publishers.

Kincheloe, J., & McLaren, P. (2000). Rethinking critical theory and qualitative research. In N. K. Denzin & Y. S. Lincoln (Eds.), *Handbook of qualitative research* (2nd ed., pp. 279–314). Thousand Oaks, CA: Sage.

Ladner, J. (1973). *The death of white sociology.* New York: Random House.

Lipsitz, G. (2006). *The possessive investment in whiteness: How white people profit from identity politics.* Philadelphia: Temple University Press.

Madera, J., Hebl, M., & Martin, R. (2009). Gender and letters of recommendation for academics: Agentic and communal differences. *Journal of Applied Psychology, 94,* 1591–1599.

Marable, M. (1983). *How capitalism underdeveloped black America.* Boston: South End Press.

McKee, J. B. (1993). *Sociology and the race problem: The failure of a perspective.* Urbana: University of Illinois Press.

Mendoza, L. (2006). New frameworks in Philippine postcolonial historiography: Decolonizing a discipline. In J. Young & J. E. Braziel (Eds.), *Race and the foundations of knowledge: Cultural amnesia in the academy* (pp. 155–173). Urbana: University of Illinois Press.

Merton, R., Reader, G., & Kendall, P. (1957). *The student physician.* Cambridge, MA: Harvard University Press.

Mills, C. W. (1998). *Blackness visible: Essay on philosophy and race.* Ithaca, NY: Cornell University Press.

Murray, A. (1973). White norms, Black deviation. In J. Ladner (Ed.), *The death of white sociology* (pp. 96–114). New York: Random House.

Oliver, K. (2004). *The colonization of psychic space: A psychoanalytic theory of oppression.* Minneapolis: Minnesota Press.

Omi, M., & Winant, H. (1994). *Racial formation in the United States from the 1960s to the 1990.* New York: Routledge.

Reed-Danahay, D. (1997). *Auto/Ethnography.* New York: Berg.

Robinson, C. (2000). *Black Marxism: The making of the black radical tradition.* Chapel Hill: University of North Carolina Press.

Romero, M. (2000). Learning to think and teach about race and gender despite graduate school: Obstacles women of color graduate students face in sociology. In The Social

Justice Group at the Center of Advanced Feminist Studies (Eds.), *Is academic feminism dead? Theory in practice* (pp. 283–310). New York: New York University Press.

Ryan, W. (1976). *Blaming the victim* (Rev. and updated). New York: Vintage Books.

Schuerich, H., & Young, M. (1997). Coloring epistemologies: Are our research epistemologies racially biased? *Educational Researcher, 26*, 4–16.

Simpson, J. (2003). *I have been waiting: Race and U.S. higher education.* Toronto: University of Toronto Press.

Smith, L. (1999). *Decolonizing methodologies: Research and indigenous peoples.* New York: St. Martin's Press.

Smith, W., Albach, P., & Lomotey, K. (Eds.). (2002). *The racial crisis in American higher education: Continuing challenges for the twenty-first century.* Albany: State University of New York Press.

Smith, W., Allen, W. R., & Danley, L. L. (2007). "Assume the position ... you fit the description." Psychosocial experiences and racial battle fatigue among African American male college students. *The American Behavioral Scientist, 51*, 551–578.

Spry, T. (2001). Performing autoethnography: An embodied methodological praxis. *Qualitative Inquiry, 7*, 706–732.

Stanfield, J. H., II. (1982). The cracked back door. *The American Sociologist, 17*, 193–204.

Stanfield, J. H., II, & Dennis, R. (Eds.). (1993). *Race and ethnicity in research methods.* Newbury Park, CA: Sage.

Sue, D., Capodilupo, C., Torino, G., Bucceri, J., Holder, A., & Nadal, K. (2007). Racial microaggressions in everyday life: Implications for clinical practice. *American Psychologist, 62*, 271–286.

Tatum, B. D. (1997). *Why are all the Black kids sitting together in the cafeteria? And other conversations about race.* New York: Basic Books.

Turner, C. S. V., & Thompson, J. R. (1993). Socializing women doctoral students: Minority and majority experiences. *Review of Higher Education, 16*, 355.

Turner, C., Viernes, S., Myers, S. L., & Creswell, J. W. (1999). Exploring underrepresentation: The case of faculty of color in the Midwest. *The Journal of Higher Education, 70*, 27–59.

Twine, F. W., & Warren, J. (2000). *Racing research, researching race: Methodological dilemmas in critical race studies.* New York: New York University Press.

Vega, B. (2010). Racial microaggressions and the Latino/a experience in postsecondary education. http://www.race-talk.org/?p=5511 (accessed December 17, 2010).

Weidman, J., & Stein, E. (2003). Socialization of doctoral students to academic norms. *Research in Higher Education, 44*, 641–656.

Weidman, J., Twale, D. J., & Stein, E. (2001). *Socialization of graduate and professional students in higher education: A perilous passage.* San Francisco: Jossey-Bass.

Zuberi, T. (2001). *Thicker than blood: How racial statistics lie*. Minneapolis: University of Minnesota Press.

Zuberi, T., & Bonilla-Silva, E. (2008). *White logic, white methods: Racism and methodology*. Lanham, MD: Rowman & Littlefield.

6 ARCHIVAL METHODS AND THE VEIL OF SOCIOLOGY

Mary Jo Deegan

Archival methods of research are crucial to reconstruct, interpret, and evaluate contributions of early sociologists that are hidden behind the veils of racism and sexism. Many of these founding sociologists profoundly shaped their communities and created important organizations to combat social inequality and injustice. Their lives as intellectuals were frequently controversial, which made them political anathemas to mainstream sociologists, usually white males working in prestigious universities who wanted money, fame, and prestige for the new discipline and its leaders.

In this chapter, I recount how I began a career using historical research to understand the rich, alternative history of the profession. First I discuss how my biographical location led to questioning mainstream accounts of the social construction of the profession. Then I discuss four projects to show how this research method emerged from the people and topics I analyze. The first major study in which I used and developed this method was *Jane Addams and the Men of the Chicago School, 1892–1920* (Deegan 1988a). Although this was not a study in race relations, I developed my archival expertise and methods doing it. I subsequently applied this technique to three projects in race relations: "W. E. B. Du Bois and the Women of Hull-House, 1896–1899" (Deegan 1988b), *A New Woman of Color: The Collected Writings of Fannie Barrier Williams* (2002a), and *Race, Hull-House, and the University of Chicago: A New Conscience against Ancient Evil* (Deegan 2002b).

MY BIOGRAPHY AND THE SOULS OF ABLE-BODIED WHITE FOLK

Here are some biographical bits relevant to the study of American black/white relations (Schutz 1962, 1970). I was raised a conservative, Irish American, Roman Catholic who lived in a physically beautiful and wealthy small town on the shores of Lake Michigan. Although I lived in poverty in a female-headed household, I uncritically believed my family, friends, small town, and country embraced the best people and the most perfect place in the world. In 1966, when I was nineteen years old, I had just completed an associate degree in chemistry and mathematics at our local community college. As part of my physical examination to enter a four-year college, I was told that I needed minor surgery on my right knee. Then my life became a living hell.

Being Able-Bodied, Disabled, and Able-Bodied, 1966–1975

After my surgery, I discovered that my handsome, wealthy, and popular surgeon was an alcoholic and probably under the influence while I was under his knife. The cast he put on my leg was too tight and damaged the nerve to the core. I was in constant, unrelieved pain for the next year, my leg from the knee down to the foot was paralyzed, and I had almost no circulation of blood through that area. My family, except for my loyal-yet-resentful mother and my life-long friends, except for my boyfriend, abandoned me. I was suddenly a nobody in the world of medicine, small towns, and the nation. I was told I would spend most of my life in a bed and wheelchair, unemployed, and in great pain. Everyone around me told me to accept my new life and limb and learn to cope.

Instead of adjusting, I became quite bitter. I no longer thought everything was perfect. I perceived of coping as a mechanism used by people in authority to coerce the disabled to accept things that were wrong and unacceptable. Americans in my small town were cruel to me as an emaciated person with an atrophied and black leg—the poor circulation turned my leg black within seconds whenever it was not elevated. People stared at me and visibly were revolted; children pointed in horror; and parents hurried them away from me. I radiated the constant, tortuous pain I experienced in my rare trips outside my home.

I started to sharply question the process of providing medical services and grew to understand the social construction of "able-bodyism"—although I then lacked a word for the process. Later I learned that I became a phenomenologist during this period because the only thing I understood and trusted was my experience of pain and disability. I was surrounded by powerful people who were socially reconstructing my life, identity, and future, but I systematically rejected what they were saying and doing to me. The historical context of my disability is important to understand, too: There were no curb cuts on public streets, no mandatory access to public buildings, no accessible bathrooms in restaurants or highway rest-stops, and no parking spaces for people with physical disabilities. The disability social movement and legislation supporting it occurred much later. If I wanted to leave our home in a wheelchair, I had to be carried whenever I faced two or more steps, a high curb, a narrow doorway, or any other physical obstruction.

Before my traumatic injury, I vaguely had followed civil rights issues on television but personally had been uninvolved. Slowly, I wondered if white Americans were unjust in many unreflexive ways—just as able-bodied people were to the disabled—and I was one of them. With this insight into the souls of able-bodied white folk, I joined the battle for civil rights. Then I wondered if Americans were unjust by fighting in Viet Nam and decided we were: I joined the peace movement. Then I connected a series of experiences I had had as a woman in college majoring in a male-dominated field, chemistry: I joined the women's movement. All of these groups—civil rights activists, war protesters, and feminists were anathema to my circle of family, friends, and small-town life. I went from having an unquestioning view of my home, friends, family, and community to one that was sharply analytical, tough, and critical.

At this difficult time, an important person entered my life: a funny, sarcastic, imperious physical therapist, Mrs. Marjorie Stamm. No matter what misfortune happened to me—black leg, poverty, abandonment, pain—she would laugh, painfully twist a muscle, and pat me on the back. She had been an officer in the Women's Army Corps in World War II and had seen much worse problems than I had. I was in daily physical therapy for seven months including the original two weeks of hospitalization and later for a month in intensive rehabilitation.[1]

In 1969, I graduated with honors from college—making a long story short—with a major in chemistry and a minor in mathematics. I had matured enough to see that bitterness and anger were dead-ends and recognized that I still had a very privileged life—just not the one I had expected. After being unemployed (and miserable about that) for several months, I was employed as a chemist (and miserable about that). I was totally tired of being miserable. I decided to return to college, get a master's degree in a "fluff" field (i.e., sociology), and have some fun.

To my great surprise and delight, I was experiencing a spontaneous remission of my paralysis after three agonizing years. Even more unexpectedly, sociology gave me the tools to study people and society, especially physical disability, pacifism, social class, feminism, and race relations and the social movements surrounding them. I became a graduate teaching assistant at Western Michigan University and had the good fortune of having Cora Bagley Marrett, now an eminent African American sociologist but then fresh out of graduate school, chair my master's committee. I met and studied with many other wonderful faculty there, especially Morton Wagenfeld, Ellen Robin, and Stanley Robin—who inspired my second identity transformation. I changed from being a physical scientist who looked forward to a life spent in a laboratory to being a social scientist looking forward to a career of scholarship and community activism.

For my master's thesis I designed and administered a questionnaire to some of the staff members at the Michigan Department of Vocational

Rehabilitation. I had intended to study identity change in the physically disabled, a topic I was passionate about, but I was persuaded to study bur-eaucracies and changing definitions of services for the poor and culturally deprived (Deegan 1973). I collected my data in 1971 but was unattached emo-tionally to this topic, especially with its focus on bureaucratic change instead of identity change and questionnaire research instead of experiential and/or participant observation research.

Just as I finished collecting these data, a number of black friends and activists confronted me, calling me an outsider to and intruder on the black movement for power and justice. If I continued to study race relations and got a good job, they argued, I would be stealing it from a black person. I thought these were fair criticisms about my white privileges and a significant barrier to my continuing to work in a field where I did not belong. I had a deep, lived experience with anger, too, and removed myself from the study of race rela-tions. Cora told me she did not believe these were valid reasons for leaving my study, but I ignored her. In retrospect, I see how I was part of a generation of white scholars and activists who voluntarily accepted the rationales of the black power movement (see Olson 2001).

With the encouragement of my committee, I applied to and was accept-ed at the University of Chicago after I had finished my coursework for the master's degree. I was immersed then in bureaucratic sociology and quanti-tative methods, drawing on my undergraduate training in mathematics. I had come to hate my master's thesis, however, and had many unresolved, personal issues revolving around social status and the meaning of academic work. I also developed new professional dilemmas because I was becoming a theorist and questioning the validity of quantitative research methods. I recognized that I did not believe the natural science model applied to human behavior, which was buried in ideology; social inequality organized through capitalism, racism, sexism, and able-bodyism; social constructions; and the everyday life-world (see Deegan & Hill [1991] for a discussion of my career crisis at this point).

I entered the University of Chicago in the fall of 1971 without funding. I borrowed money to continue my now-costly education for that first year. From 1972 to 1975, I received a complete fellowship with tuition and full stipend through the Medical Traineeship, sponsored by the U.S. Department of Health, Education, and Welfare, at the University of Chicago, Center for Health Administration, supervised by Odin Anderson and Ron Andersen. I met and studied with many marvelous theorists during these years when I enrolled in forty-five courses. At this point, I was dedicated to studying iden-tity change in the physically disabled and determined to only study what I thought was important for the rest of my life. Thus, I experienced a fourth identity transformation: I was now a theorist who studied only what I wanted, using the methods that I deemed appropriate.

So, in addition to my physical transformations—able-bodied, until the age of nineteen, then told authoritatively that I was permanently disabled, and then around twenty-four I once again was able-bodied—I was stunned to experience yet another identity transformation, my fourth: theorist.

These tales of identity change fundamentally showed me how people are embodied, subject to change, and located in historical and social situations. It also showed me that the everyday and larger social worlds are products of human action and meaning. I reasoned that since we can create an unjust world, we can create a just one. Similarly, institutions are not given but created, and helping change these institutions is a privilege. Sociology gives us the tools to engage in seeing and creating the world, although it, too, is a product of that world.

Given my physical and identity transformation as a re-able-bodied sociology student, I zipped through the University of Chicago, graduated in four years, and my doctoral dissertation was exactly what I wanted: Identity Change in Modern Society: A Study of the Physically Disabled (1975).

ON BECOMING A FEMINIST PRAGMATIST AS A HISTORIAN OF AMERICAN SOCIOLOGY

After graduation, I intended to become a contemporary theorist who studied physical disability. I also knew my multiple political commitments would continue personally and professionally. I became interested in what I thought would be one tiny, easy task: discovering and writing a short paper about one woman in the history of sociology. Two major events sparked my interest in this topic. While studying the sociology of contemporary women, I was shocked to discover hundreds and hundreds of books written by and about women in the basement stacks at Regenstein Library. I had been taught that I was on the forefront of a new area of study, but that was clearly untrue. At about the same time, I wanted to write a short popular essay for Ms magazine, which had a monthly column on heroic tales of "lost women." I was sure that there had been at least one woman in sociology around 1900. Looking only at the American Journal of Sociology from 1892 to 1930 I found dozens. This gave me a list of names.

I began to learn how to use archives and historical methods to study women who were not in the sociological annals. I did not know who they were or how they were connected to sociology. I had learned a great deal about "Chicago sociology" at the University of Chicago, but it was immediately apparent that women who were part of this history were omitted from this teaching process. Every summer from 1975 to 1981, I traveled to archives across the country, gleaning names and information. I had a very basic technique: If the word "sociology" appeared in their correspondence, publications, or job title, I copied their papers. I did not know who they were before I ferreted around in the archives—totally unacceptable behavior to archivists. I was supposed to know my subjects, topics, and the name of my major person of interest.

I knew little about the history of sociology except what I had learned about white men from Chicago and Europe. I soon discovered that stationery letterhead gave the names of officers of groups, sponsors of research, and basic network information. I copied many letters that were "unimportant" to archivists who read letters for content and did not understand using letters for network analysis or trying to construct a lost history. I also studied "unimportant" people (i.e., women) with minor faculty or social positions when the archives were filled with information about important people. Fortunately, most of the archivists were feminists and sympathetic to finding "lost women," but I was a frustrating client for them.

After five years of diligent and financially costly work, I had a disjointed manuscript of over 800 pages with a little bit on this person and a little bit on that person. My former professor, Morris Janowitz, had taught the history of Chicago sociology in a required course segment in 1975, but I regarded this work as irrelevant and boring: I wanted to be a contemporary theorist. Visiting him in 1980, I told him about my gigantic, amorphous work, and he said: "Why don't you study Jane Addams?" His brilliant and quick insight led to my writing about one woman and the eight men at the University of Chicago whom I had studied earlier and grudgingly under Janowitz's tutelage. This book, *Jane Addams and the Men of the Chicago School, 1892–1920* (Deegan 1988a), contradicted everything written about Chicago sociologists that I had learned.

To have a logical counter-argument to the legitimated literature, which did not consider Addams a sociologist, I established criteria for determining who is a sociologist. I drew on the work of Dirk Kaesler who studied German sociologists whose careers were strongly affected, if not destroyed, by World Wars I and II. Kaesler (1981) defines a sociologist as someone who fulfills at least one of the following five criteria: (1) occupies a chair of sociology and/ or teaches sociology; (2) is a member of the German Sociological Society (changed here to membership in any sociological society); (3) is a coauthor of sociological articles or textbooks; (4) defines him- or herself as a sociologist; and (5) is defined by others as a sociologist. Addams, of course, met all of these criteria. I (1988a:7–15) modified this list for women in sociology by adding: (6) is engaged in women's work in sociology in social settlements or women's separate organizations (such as the Women's Educational and Industrial Union); and (7) is engaged in women's work in sociology by using a socially constructed theory to actively organize for social change with a disenfranchised or oppressed group (especially with women, the poor, African Americans, immigrants, children, or physically disabled). These criteria have been extremely helpful for studying any sociologist who has been forgotten, neglected, or subjected to discrimination in the annals of the discipline.

Janowitz commissioned me to write a monograph on Addams for his eminent *Heritage of Sociology* series for the University of Chicago Press. I was thrilled. I was going to be published in the major history of sociology series in the profession. I began work immediately and sent him copies of the work, which was very rough indeed. I had to create an entirely different story of Chicago sociology and to understand Addams, whom I had originally thought was important politically but not intellectually. I had to unlearn what I had been taught and create a new history of the largest and most important early school in the profession. In this book, I analyzed "critical pragmatism" and "cultural feminism" as two sometimes overlapping and sometimes conflicting aspects of her thought.

Janowitz hated my book. The men of the Chicago School, he argued, shaped Addams who was a not-very-bright but good-hearted sociologist. Unless I wanted to commit "career suicide," I had to change the manuscript and get it right. "Didn't I understand anything I had been taught?" he asked me. Thus ended my dream of having a more recognized and prestigious career in my immediate future.

I worked and worked on my manuscript, sending it to several publishers where it was rejected repeatedly. I ran into the political clout of Janowitz everywhere. Publishers would ask reviewers who were the important people in this field and without exception Janowitz was named and he hated my manuscript. With little hope, I sent the manuscript to Irving Louis Horowitz at Transaction Press. He and his more independent reviewers recommended revising and resubmitting. They advised me to remove many references (about half) to patriarchy, which were redundant and distracting, and try again. To my surprise, the text was improved dramatically. I was delighted when it was selected by *Choice* (American Library Association) as one of the Outstanding Academic Books of 1988–1989. About then, I returned to my earlier interest in American race relations.

Returning to the Study of Race Relations with My Skills in the History of Sociology, 1985

Two things happened in 1985. I had finished the Addams book and I was reading a considerable amount of literature claiming she was, at best, an unreflexive, white, middle-class women biased against black Americans and, at worst, an active racist. How could I have missed this major point? Was my white privilege blinding me to injustice? I began to research her work with W. E. B. Du Bois, using documents in her papers. Again I was in new territory, contradicting the standard accounts of how *The Philadelphia Negro* (1899) was written, including Du Bois's (1903/1961, 1920, 1968) own reflections on the process.

That summer, I also was enrolled in the Women, Health and Healing Institute at the University of California–San Francisco and the University of California–Berkeley. I was surprised to hear young women involved in black women's health care state that they had never worked with a white person—those people with so many resources and so much racism. They pleaded with their audience to get involved: "Wouldn't we help?" I considered their presentation, my previous experience, and my power as a tenured white professor and decided to return to the study of race relations, this time in my specialty, the history of sociology.

I immediately began to use references to Du Bois and to Fannie Barrier Williams that I had discovered during my earlier work with women in sociology. I started systematically reading and researching these two sociologists and other black sociologists and interviewing older black sociologists when I went to sociology meetings to understand more about their lives and eras. The impact of racism was clear, but their trained skills and empowerment were also evident. I called this convoluted and often discriminatory process shaping their black experience in sociology "the veil of sociology," drawing on the work of Du Bois (1903/1961; see Deegan 2002a). Black women's deeper exclusion from the annals of the profession, in comparison to black men and white women, became immediately evident as I constructed new lists. Their differential, black female experience in sociology emerged from "the Gendered Veil of Sociology" (Deegan 2002a, 2002b).

Some new methodological problems appeared. There was a lack of black archives, different call numbers and physical locations for sociology and for black studies ("HM" and "HN" for mainstream sociology and "HV" for early women sociologists classified as social workers versus "E" for African American Studies), and different languages, references, events, interpretations, and people in this literature compared to those in my original training in mainstream sociology and my subsequent learning in the history of women in the profession.

Work on W. E. B. Du Bois and *The Philadelphia Negro* (1899)

I used the Addams and Du Bois microfilms to document the mutual influences between these two organic intellectuals who had changed the world. This alliance was underresearched because of the plethora of studies claiming Addams discriminated against blacks. As noted above, I had studied Addams's work on *Hull-House Maps and Papers* (Residents of Hull-House 1895) for my Addams book. Isabel Eaton (1895) had written a chapter in this edited book, was a Quaker, and was a sociology graduate student at Columbia University. Eaton's (1899) analysis of black women's domestic labor was a significant section of

The Philadelphia Negro and her master's thesis. Du Bois used the questionnaire and insights from *Hull-House Maps and Papers*, and Addams was involved in the early selection of candidates for this new project. I built on my earlier work in this area and extended this knowledge to a new social settlement, Starr Center, in Philadelphia, and dove into the huge literature on Du Bois.

I began teaching Du Bois's *Souls of Black Folk* in 1985 and since then I have taught it twenty or more times. Du Bois is one of my major intellectual anchors to understand the world and the particular insights of prophetic pragmatism (West 1989). I published my first article on Du Bois for John Stanfield's special issue of the *American Sociologist* on race relations and socialization (Deegan 1988b). It took me seventeen years to pull together my analyses and research on black sociology and Chicago, which resulted in my 2002 book on the subject (discussed further below).

WORK ON FANNIE BARRIER WILLIAMS

While I was slogging away on Addams and U.S. race relations, the name Fannie Barrier Williams appeared repeatedly and I began studying her life and work. This involved many problems: She was largely unknown except for her amazing speech at Chicago's Columbian Exposition in 1893. She had no archival deposits, although her husband S. Laing Williams was a "spy" for Booker T. Washington (see his correspondence in Washington 1972–1989). Williams had two published letters to Washington, and I traveled to the Library of Congress hoping to find more. To my dismay, I discovered that one of the two published letters had faded to illegibility and, instead of finding many more, I could not even read the one that was published in the Washington papers.

Williams was portrayed most unattractively in the scant literature on her as a "Bookerite" accommodationist, a woman who "passed" as white, a traitor to black people's interests, and a venal opportunist who pushed her husband's ambitions. Given this daunting view, I asked myself why I liked her writings so much. I answered this question by intensively studying her life and ideas, largely published in obscure black newspapers, journals, and books, and concluding that she was a "feminist pragmatist," my new concept to study Addams. Williams's and Addams's ideas and work were very similar and echoed those of Martin Luther King, Jr.

Once again I needed to develop criteria to study Williams and other African American women in sociology whose work had been ignored in the sociological canon. These indicators of sociological thought and practice include: (1) engagement in work in black women's clubs; and (2) engagement in work in civil rights organization using a socially constructed theory to actively organize for social change with African Americans. As noted earlier, I called the peculiar barriers facing Williams the Gendered Veil of sociology.

Elizabeth Higgenbotham, the eminent African American scholar, gave a positive review of my manuscript to Northern Illinois University Press (NIUP). Despite this strong support, the stigma against Williams runs very deep: The project manager at NIUP repeatedly "corrected" my interpretation and systematically shifted my language to condemn Williams and praise other black women, especially Ida B. Wells-Barnett and Anna Julia Cooper. I received two extremely favorable reviews by Rosemary Bray McNatt (2002) for *UU (Unitarian-Universalist) World* and Janet Duitsman Cornelius (2003/2004) for the *Journal of the Illinois Historical Society*, but no sociological reviews.

WORK ON ADDAMS AND RACE RELATIONS

Meanwhile, I was trying to write a book on Addams and American race relations. I was well versed in the multiple literatures I use: history of women, women in sociology, Black Studies, sociology of race relations, American pragmatism, Chicago sociology, and the history of black women. I combined these literatures, massive archival data, and some interviews into one manuscript: *Race, Hull-House, and the University of Chicago: A New Conscience Against Ancient Evils* (2002b). I tried to brutally confront the signs of Addams's racism: her friendship with Washington, a thoughtless withdrawal from a confrontation between black and white women on a ship sailing to a peace conference, her lack of explicit work with black Americans, and her comparison of their lives with the experiences of immigrants from Europe, which ignored or distorted the unique experiences of black Americans. I balanced these "signs of racism" with her significant friendships with Du Bois, Williams, and Wells-Barnett. Other positive ties with black Americans included her founding work with the NAACP, the National Urban League, and the interracial Frederick Douglass Centre.

My historical skills were stretched in new ways. I began to study Washington and his network for the first time. I had ignored this literature because of my long-standing commitment to Du Bois: I unthinkingly had adopted his antipathy to Washington. I also researched the work of about seventy-five other people who worked in Chicago race relations and moved beyond sociology networks. I examined new social events, literatures, biographies, etc.

When the book was completed, I really disliked it! I had scrupulously attended to all the evidence—in books, scholarship, archives, newspapers, etc. But the writing in the manuscript see-sawed: This is racist evidence, this is nonracist evidence; this is good, this is bad. I was unwilling to send my book to a publisher, what was happening to me?

Again I had to search my own emotions and beliefs. I was angry that several well-respected publications had asserted that the white press in Chicago was so biased that black news was not covered (e.g., Spear 1967). As I gradually found first this newspaper item and then that one on Addams and Chicago race relations, I concluded that I had wasted a lot of time accepting this false argument. I started looking for items around Lincoln's birthday and specific dates, such as the founding of the NAACP or the 1908 Springfield, Illinois, race riot. Then I compared events in black newspapers, especially *The Chicago Defender*, to news in white newspapers, especially *The Chicago Tribune*. So I had to follow new evidence. (This work was done before the digitization of newspapers.)

Finally, I resolved my crisis concerning my disliked book: I established a new thesis. As a pacifist and feminist pragmatist, Addams did not share the fight between Washington and Du Bois. She had a "third way" to view American race relations. It was cooperative and supported both the talented tenth[2] and the illiterate tenant farmer. Using my new thesis, it took me two years to rewrite the manuscript. I liked this new version, which fit the evidence and theory. Sociologists generously accepted my work, and the book received the ASA Section on the History of Sociology, 2003 Distinguished Scholarly Book Award and the ASA Section on Racial and Ethnic Minorities 2003 Honorable Mention, of the Oliver Cromwell Cox Book Award.

AUTOBIOGRAPHICAL TIPS ON TECHNIQUES IN THE ARCHIVES

The Veil and Gendered Veil of sociology distort and hide the contributions of African Americans to the society, community, and world. Historical, archival methods, combined with experiential understanding from phenomenology and political activism, can help us transcend these barriers to understanding the history of black sociologists. In addition, new information and technologies now provide access to long-obscure documents, newspapers, pamphlets, and correspondence. Black newspapers, in particular, documented the lives and ideas of black America over the last century. Chicago, moreover, was the home of several major black newspapers and is a rich resource for studying black Chicago, sociology, and community events. Newspaper items, however, are often brief and list multiple names and places, making filing and cross-referencing complex.

I have developed a series of methodological aids to systematize how I research sociologists explicitly ignored or distorted in the canon. First, my life-partner, Michael R. Hill (1993), has been a rich resource for developing and exploring archival data. He codified his insights in a book I use often. Second, I have developed new ways to organize and file data from newspapers and the Internet, resources particularly important for scholars without archival deposits. Third, I have developed a theory and praxis based on the work of

Addams and her allies in sociology. They were usually based at Hull-House or the University of Chicago but often in other settings underresearched by sociologists, such as the Frederick Douglass Centre or the Negro Fellowship League in Chicago. I discuss these tools next.

Hill's and Stanfield's Influence

Michael Hill (1993, 2001; Hill & Hoecker-Drysdale 2001) is a leading international scholar in the sociology of Harriet Martineau and archival research. His techniques are also mine, and I explicate them briefly here. Hill wrote the first book in sociology on how to conduct archival research: *Archival Strategies and Techniques* (1993). This seminal book can be used by specialists and students. It is short, readable, and theoretically organized by a dramaturgical framework. It draws on his years of doing historical sociology and his theoretical training in dramaturgy, phenomenology, systems theory, and interpretive sociology. He also drew on my experiences (which he meticulously acknowledges) and years of breaking the rules of archival research, which helped me learn what those rules were. I engaged in a kind of unintentional series of breaching experiments (Garfinkle 1967), especially in my work on Jane Addams and predominantly white women in sociology (Deegan 1988a, 1991).

First, Hill discusses how archives are sorted and stored. This is particularly important for black archives because many of these records have been lost or collected haphazardly. Archives, especially well-funded ones, are associated frequently with white enterprises, such as white-controlled universities and private libraries. Until recently, these institutions had few black holdings and did not actively search for more. Even today, many archives do not note the names of black people and organizations making the identification of black archival resources difficult. In 2004, for example, I wanted to find any papers at the Chicago Historical Society that they held on black women. The staff told me they did not have any, so I identified several black women for them. (I am sure some people on their staff did have this information, but none of the staff that I worked with over a four-month period knew it.) This suggests that other papers by black people may be at their institution, but they remain unidentified at this point.

Hill calls the first stage of collecting, tossing, and sorting material by the owner the "primary sedimentation." The "secondary sedimentation" of intentionally collecting, tossing, and sorting material for an archive by the recipient or after the death of the original owner is the next crucial step. Many valuable papers are discarded at this stage because of illness, grief, ignorance, or estate pressures. The final sorting and filing, the "tertiary sedimentation," occurs at the archive. Each stage is fraught with potential errors.

John Stanfield has worked extensively with black historical archival material. His research on *Philanthropy and Jim Crow in American Social Science* (1985) was crucial to my understanding of African American archives, perspective, and participation in the African American Chicago school of race relations (Deegan 2002b). Stanfield (1987) raises many of the same questions that Hill does, but he also focuses specifically on the voluminous papers of E. Franklin Frazier, which have significant gaps despite their size. Stanfield (1985) made the first critical analysis of Robert E. Park's approach to race relations based on archival methodology, and this was a significant aid in my understanding of Park and Addams (Deegan 1988a). Stanfield's (1993) interviews of the "first generation" of race relations research helped me see the mixture of biography and scholarship that is vital to my work on Addams, the "segments" of Chicago race relations schools, as well as my self-reflections here.

Archivists usually conduct an interview before giving access to archival holdings. They need to understand what is sought and determine whether the archives have such material and if the person asking for entrée has the skills and ability to use the materials correctly. Although archivists want capable researchers to use the materials, sometimes they may not be helpful and this is almost impossible for a researcher to determine. Thus, an archivist disguised information that was unflattering to the University of Chicago, and it took me several years to discover this subterfuge.

Archives have one-of-a-kind material that is accessed through request forms submitted by the researcher that are screened before and after the material is used. This is an expensive and time-consuming process. For example, researchers may ask for material and wait thirty–forty-five minutes for its appearance at a selected table. Timing breaks and meals around this schedule can be difficult, especially if the researcher is unfamiliar with the institution or setting. Copying materials may be expensive (e.g., $.60/page) or unavailable for fragile items. Researchers are often visually under surveillance because these one-of-a-kind materials are irreplaceable and sorting and organizing them is technical and costly. A researcher may consult several papers at one institution and then visit a number of institutions that also have multiple files of interest. The researcher quickly amasses a large amount of material that needs to be stored and sorted. One item, moreover, may be relevant to several different people and topics.

Learning to File Archival Material

Filing the copies of material obtained from archives is expensive and daunting. One letter, for example, may mention three or four people, as many topics, and a narrative about these things. Personal and public events intertwine, and multiple projects can use the same letter. Filing is a huge and complicated problem, one that I have not resolved. Sometimes I file items in paper folders identified by the name of the person or organization, or interests organized by race, gender, or interracial categories. Sometimes I use notebooks to do so, and these are very bulky and heavy. The advantage of the latter system is that I can quickly re-sort material and visually see patterns that are hard to discern otherwise.

When each piece of paper is put in a plastic sleeve with a three-hole punch, these notebooks provide easy access to different items. This is an expensive and laborious project but it pays off when working with thousands of items with potentially several projects on each page. I have dozens of such notebooks for my present projects and they are extremely awkward to handle. Each notebook, however, allows me to check and organize my material quickly for a given topic or person.

An example of a total reorganization of all my archival material is my rewriting of *Race, Hull-House, and the University of Chicago*. It took two years to rewrite the book because every item had to be connected in a different pattern. Originally, I had used the Du Bois-versus-Washington categorization, where Du Bois held the "correct" position on race relations. This dichotomization was part of a conflict model. This was such an accepted approach in the sociology of knowledge that I did not even imagine a different way to interpret my material. Addams, however, advocated the elimination of dichotomies and the consistent use of cooperation. This third way to view black and white social relations not only organized her work, but recognized that she was part of, and sometimes led, a large social movement also supporting these values and patterns of interaction. Thus, Addams and her allies created a pattern of race relations that characterized a city and its race relations organizations that contradicted my filing system. The contemporary scholarship on Chicago race relations, moreover, shared Du Bois's opposition to Washington and a cooperative model and ignored the considerable evidence of the friendship between Du Bois and Addams.

Using the Internet

The Internet expands our access to original documents. Some large-scale projects on black Americans have made previously obscure papers and publications accessible. I have increasingly used newspaper items as a resource to augment the many gaps in existing records. Each newspaper column requires a separate plastic sleeve. To gauge how complicated this process is, I can combine "Addams" and a topic, such as "Urban League," and get fifty to a hundred items. Since many scholars assumed that these were not useful categories, this is all new material, often loaded with different names and subtopics, and linked to other categories for different projects. I can quickly change the order and topics using a new notebook if I want to write a different article or chapter. I try not to make copies of these items because that is more paper, but occasionally a new topic crosses several existing notebooks, and I make a new notebook to accommodate it.

Material originally available only on microfilms is appearing on the Internet, too. An archival resource on a topic that might have taken months, if not years, to research on microfilm can be done in hours or days. Often these digitized materials contain bulky items such as organization's reports or pamphlets, and storing them in a plastic sleeve is difficult. So I use different colored paper files for these items, but it is easy to fill an entire file drawer quickly with this material. This, too, creates a storage problem involving expense, space, and cross-categorization.

Although this filing of archival material is cumbersome, it provides quick and complex access to the material. Each item must be accurately identified, or the system is useless. Although digitized items could be left in a digital format with a complex naming system, I cannot keep complicated information in this format and use it well. I need to see the names, the organizations, and the topics displayed before my eyes. I need to be able to change their order and categories to see new patterns and relationships. Sometimes I even need to see the mass of information to perceive changes through time and controversies. I am working on a project now, for example, that appeared to some scholars to have no newspaper coverage, but I have collected over sixty items from different newspapers on this topic. I can identify what happened, when, and to whom. When this type of information is combined with original archival papers, digitized books or journals, and scholarship, I can generate new insights about important people considered "lost" or "forgotten." Given the problems of distorting scholarship and lack of established archives, complex information can reappear with depth and complexity.

In addition to these methodological steps, I use theory to interpret archival material.

CONNECTING THEORY AND METHODOLOGY: FEMINIST PRAGMATISM

My archival material is intellectually organized by "feminist pragmatism." This theory and practice draws heavily on the work of Addams, Du Bois, and dozens of women in sociology who lived at or were associated with Hull-House; who taught or studied at the University of Chicago where they developed or applied the Chicago pragmatism of John Dewey and George Herbert Mead; and/or who worked with or applied the black feminist pragmatism of Williams and Wells-Barnett, which was anchored at the Frederick

Douglass Centre, the Negro Fellowship League, or black women's clubs. I also draw on the work of the Chicago school of race relations, including Oliver Cromwell Cox, Wilmoth Carter, the Haynes family (Birdye, Elizabeth Ross, and George E.), E. Franklin Frazier, Charles S. Johnson, Richard Wright, Jr., and contemporary theorists in dramaturgy, women's studies, Black Studies, and pragmatism (Deegan 2002b, 2008). Feminist pragmatism underlies the approach of "the Hull-House school of race relations." Sometimes this is distinct from the Chicago school of race relations: Sometimes it complements the latter school, and sometimes it conflicts with it.

Conclusion

My biography and interest in the methodology of historical race relations research are intertwined. I am historically and biographically located in a particular era, just as my predecessors were. My experience of disability, feminism, pacifism, and the civil rights movement in the late 1960s and early 1970s emerged from a particular context that was tied dramatically to sociology. In fact, I doubt if I would have become a sociologist had I not experienced medical malpractice and a severe physical injury. My experience of multiple identity transformations broke my connections to everyday reality and showed me hidden sides of American life and institutions. Although these were often confusing experiences, they expanded my sociological understanding and poignantly revealed the flexibility of social definitions and perceptions. I deeply enjoy this historical, intellectual, political, and spiritual work and admire the people I study. They enrich my understanding of society and my profession.

In addition to the feminist pragmatists noted in this chapter, I am now studying the work of more than twenty-five black women, primarily located in Chicago. Many white female sociologists worked closely with these black women between 1889 and 1935 in "the Hull-House school of race relations," during the years of Addams's greatest work and the emergence of sociology as a profession. Thus, there is no end to my historical examination of black sociology, the interaction of sex, class, and race in the city of Chicago, and the possibility of recovering significant work that has been long forgotten.

Notes

1. I dedicated my first book, coedited with Nancy A. Brooks, to Mrs. Stamm: *Women and Disability: The Double Handicap* (Deegan & Brooks 1985). Although Mrs. Stamm knew I was getting it published and dedicating it to her, I did not know she was dying of an aggressive cancer. I mailed a copy of the book to her, and

her brother showed it to her on her deathbed. She smiled while he held it up and slipped into unconsciousness. She died the next day. I mention this dramatic moment because she was so important to me and it shows the power of sociology to move our biographies into a social, structural process. It reveals that Du Bois (1903/1961:15) was quite correct when he noted that "being a problem is a strange experience." He added it was "peculiar even for one who has never been anything else." In my case, I was "something else," became a problem, and then looked as if I were not one.

2. This is a Du Boisian term for the African American elite of the early to mid-twentieth century.

REFERENCES

Cornelius, J. D. (2003/2004). Review of *The New Woman of Color. Journal of the Illinois State Historical Society, 96*, 401–403.

Deegan, M. J. (1973). Organizational traits affecting change in the Michigan Division of Vocational Rehabilitation. M.A. thesis, Western Michigan University.

Deegan, M. J. (1975). Identity change in modern society: A study of the physically disabled. Ph.D. dissertation, University of Chicago.

Deegan, M. J. (1988a). *Jane Addams and the men of the Chicago School, 1892–1920.* New Brunswick, NJ: Transaction Books.

Deegan, M. J. (1988b). W. E. B. Du Bois and the women of Hull House, 1896–1899. *American Sociologist, 19*, 301–311.

Deegan, M. J. (Ed.). (1991). *Women in sociology.* Westport, CT: Greenwood.

Deegan, M. J. (Ed.). (2002a). *A new woman of color: The collected writings of Fannie Barrier Williams.* DeKalb: Northeastern Illinois University.

Deegan, M. J. (2002b). *Race, Hull-House, and the University of Chicago: A new conscience against an ancient evil.* Westport, CT: Greenwood Press.

Deegan, M. J. (2008). *Self, war, and society: George Herbert Mead's macrosociology.* New Brunswick, NJ: Transaction Books.

Deegan, M. J., & Brooks, N. A. (Eds.). (1985). *Women and disability: The double handicap.* New Brunswick, NJ: Transaction.

Deegan, M. J., & Hill, M. R. (1991). Doctoral dissertations as liminal journeys of the self. *Teaching Sociology, 19*, 322–332.

Du Bois, W. E. B. 1899. *The Philadelphia Negro: A social study.* With a special report on domestic service by I. Eaton. Publication of the University of Pennsylvania, Series in Political Economy and Public Law, No. 14. Philadelphia: Ginn and Co.

Du Bois, W. E. B. (1903/1961). *Souls of black folk.* Greenwich, CT: Fawcett Premier Book.

Du Bois, W. E. B. (1920). *Darkwater: Voices from within the veil.* New York: Harcourt Brace.

Du Bois, W. E. B. (1968). *The Autobiography of W.E.B. Du Bois.* New York: International Publishers.

Eaton, I. (1895). Receipts and expenditures of cloakmakers in Chicago. In Residents of Hull-House (Eds.), *Hull-House maps and papers* (pp. 79–88). New York: Crowell.

Eaton, I. (1899). Special report on Negro domestic service in the Seventh Ward. In W. E. B. Du Bois (Ed.), *The Philadelphia Negro: A social study* (pp. 427–509). New York: Schocken.

Garfinkle, H. (1967). *Studies in ethnomethodology.* Englewood Cliffs, NJ: Prentice-Hall.

Hill, M. R. (1993). *Archival strategies and techniques.* Qualitative Research Methods Series, Vol. 31. Newbury Park, CA: Sage.

Hill, M. R. (2001). Of time, space, and the history of sociology: Methodological rules in archives and archival research. In J. Mucha, D. Kaesler, & W. Winclawski (Eds.), *Mirrors and windows: Essays in the history of sociology* (pp. 326–336). Torun, Poland: Nicholas Copernicus University Press.

Hill, M. R., & Hoecker-Drysdale, S. (Eds.). (2001). *Harriet Martineau: Theoretical and methodological perspectives.* New York: Routledge.

Kaesler, K. (1981). Methodological problems of a sociological history of early German sociology. Paper presented to the Department of Education, University of Chicago, November 5.

McNatt, R. B. (2002). Review of *The New Woman of Color. UU (Unitarian-Universalist) World, 6,* 72.

Olson, L. (2001). *Freedom's daughters.* New York: Simon and Schuster.

Residents of Hull-House. (1895). *Hull-House maps and papers.* New York: Crowell.

Schutz, A. (1962). *Collected papers.* Vol. 1: *The problem of social reality.* The Hague: Martinus Nijhoff.

Schutz, A. (1970). *Reflections on the problems of relevance.* New Haven, CT: Yale University Press.

Spear, A. H. (1967). *Black Chicago: The making of a Negro ghetto.* Chicago: University of Chicago Press.

Stanfield, J. H., II. (1985). *Philanthropy and Jim Crow in American social science.* Westport, CT: Greenwood Press.

Stanfield, J. H., II. (1987). Archival methods in race relations research. *American Behavioral Scientist, 30,* 366–380.

Stanfield, J. H., II. (1993). *A history of race relations research.* Newbury Park, CA: Sage.

Washington, B. T. (1972–1989). *The Booker T. Washington papers,* 14 vols. Urbana: University of Illinois Press.

West, C. (1989). *The American evasion of philosophy.* Madison: University of Wisconsin Press.

7 RESEARCHING RACE AND ETHNICITY: (RE)THINKING EXPERIMENTS

Henry A. Walker

> Theory is the method of the sciences.
>
> —David Willer (1987:ix)

INTRODUCTION

This chapter is concerned with the experiment as a technique for investigating phenomena in the field of race and ethnic studies. My view is that a discussion of experiments, or of any other research method, is incomplete unless it is embedded in a discussion of the role that research plays in the scientific process.[1] Science is concerned with developing and testing explanations for relationships between phenomena (i.e., theories). Mature sciences like chemistry and physics are marked by two characteristics: (1) they have well-developed bodies of theory; and (2) they make extensive use of experiments. In contrast, theory is underdeveloped in the study of race and ethnicity, and social science experiments on race matters are statistically rare.

Disciplinary differences in theory development and in the incidence of experimental research are quantitative not qualitative but they reflect a deeper problem for the social sciences. Theory is *the* method of science; it distinguishes the sciences from other academic disciplines. The degree to which theory is central to the research process differs in the physical and social sciences. Physical and social scientists test hypotheses but, unlike their physical science counterparts, social scientists typically derive their hypotheses from ad hoc speculation and prior observations rather than theory. It is not coincidental that experimental studies of race are rare and that theory development in the study of race and ethnicity lags behind theory development in fields that make greater use of experimentation.

By and large, the mature sciences and the social sciences take different approaches to science. An *empiricist* approach to science dominates work in sociology and race and ethnic studies. The approach taken in the mature

141

sciences is more often *theory driven*. In this chapter, I argue that widespread adoption of the theory-driven approach is necessary to transform race and ethnic studies from a field that amasses unexplained empirical observations to a science that offers more, and better, understandings of human behavior. Experiments are an important element of the approach. I also assert that combining a theory-driven approach with the norms of scientific conduct can reduce (if not eliminate) many of the problems that critics ascribe to research methods. The time is ripe for social scientists to reconsider an investigative tool to which most have received only a cursory introduction. But we must understand the nature of experiments and their role in the scientific process before we can seriously *rethink* their use. I came to this position easily, but the path may be more difficult for some.

I have designed and run many sociological experiments during a career that spans almost four decades. Before embarking on a career in sociology, I spent countless hours running biology and chemistry experiments in high school and college laboratories. My earliest exposure to social science research methods came in courses that fulfilled requirements for an undergraduate degree in sociology. Each methods course included material on experiments and there was much talk of theory in those courses. But there was little actual theory. Sociology introduced me to the empiricist approach to science.[2]

I got my social science introduction to theoretical methods as a graduate student at the University of Missouri at Kansas City. The late Ernest Manheim[3] required students to read Hempel and Oppenheim (1948), Nagel (1961), Kaplan (1964), and others. At Stanford, I got more exposure in course work with Joseph Berger, Bernard P. Cohen, and Morris Zelditch, Jr. Collectively, those instructors reintroduced me to the theory-driven approach to science and its connection to experimentation. Given my earlier experiences as a student in the physical sciences, I had no difficulty adopting an approach that conceived of science as a continuous process of: (1) theory development; (2) theory testing; and (3) theory refinement.

To make the case for a theory-driven approach, the remainder of this chapter is organized as follows: In the next section, I discuss problems associated with the conduct of inquiry in race studies, including the statistical rarity of experiments as an understudied phenomenon. I discuss empiricist and theory-driven approaches to science in the third section. There, I argue that adopting a theory-driven strategy is crucial to advancing science. The fourth section is devoted to a discussion of data collection and reasons that scientists collect data. The discussion locates research and research methods in the larger scientific enterprise and corrects common misunderstandings about science, experiments, and experimental research. In the fifth section, I give examples of experiments to show how they have been used (and misused) to study race and ethnic issues. The last section includes an appeal for more theory-driven research and more extensive use of experiments in studies of race and ethnicity.

SOCIOLOGICAL STUDIES OF RACE AND ETHNICITY: DILEMMAS AND PROBLEMS

The field of race and ethnic relations encompasses a broad range of phenomena. At the microsocial level, investigators are concerned with patterns of conscious and unconscious bias (Greenwald et al. 1998), the relationship between individuals' prejudices and discrimination (LaPiere 1934), and how discrimination affects the well-being of its targets (Allport 1954). Macrosocial researchers study societal patterns of ethnic and race relations such as lynchings in the nineteenth-century United States (Wells-Barnett [1892–1895/2002]), global patterns of slavery (Patterson 1982), and race and class stratification in modern America (Wilson 2009). Between the micro and macro extremes, students of race and ethnic relations study every imaginable human behavior, including crime and punishment (Mann 1993), academic achievement (Ogbu 2003), patterns of family formation and family structure (Moynihan 1965), and preferences for the race composition of neighborhoods (Clark 2002; Williams 1975).

Social scientists engaged in the systematic study of race and ethnicity have a wide array of research techniques at their disposal. That is as it should be in a field that encompasses such a broad range of phenomena. The new field began to blossom at the turn of the twentieth century, as did criticisms of researchers and the methods they used to study race. Minority scholars were among the earliest contributors to the critical literature.[4] Du Bois proclaimed more than a century ago: "[Sociologists] simply collect the facts. Others may use them as they will" (cited in Green & Driver 1976:313).

Du Bois understood that collecting facts is not a simple matter and that interpreting and applying facts to problems of the human condition are difficult at best. As a septuagenarian reflecting on his youthful search for scientific truth, Du Bois pointed out that "[At the time] the difficulties of applying scientific law and discovering cause and effect in the social world were still great" (Du Bois 1940:50–51). His concerns were not limited to questions of theory development (i.e., discovering cause and effect) or the application of theory. Nor did he claim that those problems—as important as they are—were the most important barriers to developing knowledge about race matters. He said:

> Most unfortunate of all, however, is the fact that so much of the work done on the Negro question is notoriously uncritical; uncritical from lack of discrimination in the selection and weighing of evidence; uncritical in choosing the proper point of view from which to study these problems, and,

finally, uncritical from the distinct *bias* in the minds of so many writers. (Du Bois 1898:12–13; emphasis added)

Du Bois's concerns presaged unfavorable evaluations offered by contemporary scholars who have studied the history of research on race and ethnicity—fact collection—and found it wanting. Mainstream sociology is taken to task on epistemological grounds (Ladner 1973:xx), with some labeling its logical positivist foundation a flawed or limited approach (Stanfield & Dennis 1993:16ff.). Critics also raise ontological concerns about the meaning of race as a biological construct (Graves 2004; Montagu 1942) and question the use of specific research techniques. (See papers on survey research, community studies, participant observation, demographic analyses of population data, etc., in Ladner [1973], Stanfield & Dennis [1993], and Zuberi & Bonilla-Silva [2008].)

Modern-day criticisms center on additional issues that include but are not limited to: (1) underrepresentation of minority scholars and minority subjects in sociological research; (2) cultural, political, and ideological biases that affect researchers' observations, their interpretations of research, and the explanations they offer for race and ethnic phenomena; (3) unethical behavior, including maltreatment of minority subjects and their communities; (4) researchers' positive evaluations of the status quo (i.e., majority dominance) vis-à-vis alternative ways of organizing social life; and (5) the difficulty of translating sociological knowledge into policies that secure *positive* results. With increasing frequency, contemporary critics express skepticism concerning the capacity of sociology to uncover social facts and to develop valid explanations for them. Many reputable scholars also question the ability of sociological research to inform policies that can advance the human condition (Cole 1994).

Experimental studies of race have generally escaped the criticisms directed toward other research techniques. Goar (2008) calls attention to the oversight and points out that many early experiments on race and ethnicity are contaminated by bias. Moreover, she asserts that white privilege has sustained the pattern in subsequent experimental research. Importantly, Goar uncovers reasons for the scarcity of critical commentary on experimental methods. She points to evidence from Hunt et al. (2000) that race and ethnicity are understudied topics in social psychology. Social psychologists use experiments more often than any other sociologists and *Social Psychology Quarterly* (SPQ) is the leading journal of research in sociological social psychology. Hunt and colleagues analyzed 954 articles published in SPQ from 1970 to 1999 and reported that only 8.3% "seriously considered" race and ethnicity. Unfortunately, Hunt and colleagues did not report data on research techniques.

To correct this omission, I reviewed all articles published in four leading journals (*American Journal of Sociology* [AJS], *American Sociological Review* [ASR], *Social Forces* [SF], and *Social Psychology Quarterly* [SPQ]) and two specialty journals (*Ethnic & Racial Studies* [ERS] and *Social Problems* [SP]) that are more likely to include studies of race. I counted 482 articles, including eighty-eight in ERS, published in calendar years 2007 and 2008.[5] Using less stringent inclusion criteria than Hunt and colleagues, I found that 180 articles (37.3% of the total) focused on race or used race (ethnicity) as an explanatory variable. Omitting articles from ERS, 107 of the remaining 394 articles (27.2%) focus on race. Fifteen articles (3.1% of 482) reported using the experimental method, but only two race studies (.4% of all studies and 1.1% of 180 race studies) reported using experiments. SF and ERS each published a single race experiment. Despite publishing only thirty-nine articles over the two-year period, SPQ published two-thirds of the experiments (ten of fifteen) but none on race.

Hunt and colleagues data and my findings support the claim that social psychologists understudy race and ethnicity. Our combined results are also important for understanding why critics of other research methods have rarely trained their sights on experiments: Sociology experiments are statistically rare. Taken together, the studies raise two important questions. Why are experimental studies of race so scarce? Why should sociologists look more often to experiments to study issues in the field of race and ethnicity? In the next section, I begin answering these questions with a discussion of science and theory development.

SCIENCE AND APPROACHES TO THEORY DEVELOPMENT

Basic science has as its objectives, identifying, classifying, and explaining recurrent relationships between phenomena. Science achieves these objectives by answering an ordered series of questions as follows (Walker 2002): (1) What is the phenomenon y? (2) What phenomena (xs) are correlated with y? (3) What accounts for the relationship between y and x? Scholars answer the first type of question by introducing definitions and classification schemes. The second type of question motivates a search for relations between phenomena. Finding patterned relations can trigger the development of *empiricist* or historical explanations. Alternatively, finding patterned relations motivates researchers to ask questions of the third type. Scientists answer the third type of question by devising *theoretical* explanations. Empiricist explanations and explanations by theory reflect two different approaches to science. I describe each approach below.

Empiricist and Theory-Driven Approaches to Science

On their faces, empiricist and theory-driven approaches to science appear very similar. Each approach treats the discovery of laws or theory as the ultimate objective of science. In each approach, experiments are also important tools in the scientist's toolkit. The approaches advocate fundamentally different strategies for creating bodies of laws.

The Empiricist Approach and Empiricist Explanations

The empiricist approach presumes that laws are found by observing the world of phenomena. Mill's five canons (1843/1967) are the logical foundations for empiricist research. The methods of (1) agreement; (2) difference; (3) agreement and difference; (4) concomitant variation; and (5) residues are often described in social science research texts. Mill's idea of an experiment is epitomized by his description of the method of difference, which, for him, is *the* experimental method:

> If an instance in which the phenomenon under investigation occurs, and an instance in which it does not occur, have every circumstance in common save one, that one occurring only in the former; the circumstance in which alone the two instances differ is the effect, or cause, or an indispensable part of the cause, of the phenomenon. (Mill 1843 /1967:452)

As the method of difference is described in most texts, it is the standard to which every other method aspires and which social researchers claim to emulate (Lieberson 1985). The "phenomenon under investigation" is an effect or dependent variable. The "circumstance in which alone the two instances differ" is the cause or independent variable. The cause occurs in the experimental group and does not appear in the control group.

Mill argued that scientific knowledge is found by applying his methods to the world of phenomena and uncovering regular patterns of cause and effect. He presumed that statements describing invariant cause-effect patterns are laws.[6] They are not. Nor can they be treated as laws. Laws are general statements that describe invariant relationships between classes of phenomena (e.g., social status and competence evaluations) and do not refer to particular events, times, or places. Here are two examples of laws:

1. "The alteration of motion is ever proportional to the motive force impressed; and is made in the direction of the right line in which that force is impressed" (Newton 1686/1966:83).

2. An actor's resistance to accepting a given exchange is equal to the ratio of (1) its interest in gaining its best payoff to; (2) its interest in avoiding its worst payoff (see Willer & Anderson [1981:122] or Willer [1999:43]).

The first statement is Newton's second law of motion and, after Newton's clarifications and extensions, it has been passed down to contemporary students as Equation 1. The idea that the quantity, force, is equal to mass times acceleration has been memorized by generations of high-school physics students.

$$f = ma \tag{1}$$

The second statement is unfamiliar to all but a few social scientists in the subfields of social psychology and exchange network studies. It is the law of resistance drawn from the Elementary Theory (Willer & Anderson 1981). The resistance law specifies the degree to which an actor, i, resists a proposed exchange with another, j. It is expressed as Equation 2:

$$R_i = \frac{P_i \max - P_i}{P_i - P_i \, con} \tag{2}$$

where R_i is an actor's resistance to a payoff, P_i, P_i max is i's highest possible payoff, and P_i con is i's payoff at confrontation when i fails to reach agreement with its negotiation partner, j. Elementary Theory (ET) and the related Network Exchange Theory (NET) are sociological theories of social structure and behavior. The resistance law is important because a principle of ET asserts that two actors exchange at the point of equiresistance (Equation 3). I shall use ideas from ET and NET below.

$$R_i = \frac{P_i \max - P_i}{P_i - P_i \, con} = \frac{P_j \max - P_j}{P_j - P_j \, con} = R_j \tag{3}$$

Neither of the two laws above is equivalent to an aggregation of observations (e.g., Observation$_1$, Observation$_2$, ..., Observation$_n$) because neither refers to specific events, places or times or aggregations of such events. That they are not demonstrates the failure of Mill's method.

Mill's method fails to find laws. It fails because there is no logic that permits an observer or generations of observers to infer general statements from an empirical observation or a collection of observations. Observations are described in concrete terms whereas laws and law-like sentences (Hempel 1966; Nagel 1961) employ theoretical constructs (Willer & Webster 1971).

Mill's method also fails because it is impossible to use one or a million observations to claim evidence of an absolute regularity. Observation 1,000,001 may be inconsistent with the previous million. As a result, Mill's project was modified to focus on *probable regularities* (i.e., patterns that are unlikely to occur by chance). Fisher (1935, 1956) is widely recognized for establishing the statistical foundations for inferring probable regularities from a set of concrete observations. The Mill-Fisher method is today the hallmark of academic social science and empiricist research, including empiricist experiments. Despite its failure to find laws, the Mill-Fisher approach is an excellent one for finding empirical regularities and developing empiricist explanations.

There are two types of empiricist explanation—qualitative and quantitative (Walker 2002). Qualitative empiricist explanations are understandings of a concrete event. Quantitative empiricist explanations offer understandings of collections of concrete events. Empiricist explanations are data driven; their content depends entirely on a set of putative facts.

Consider the Matewan Massacre. On May 19, 1920, a violent shootout took place in the small coal-mining town of Matewan, West Virginia (Bailey 2008). Ten people were killed and the battle triggered events that led to a coal war that took the lives of approximately fifty people over the next two years. A qualitative empiricist explanation of the massacre describes the causal connections between the gun battle (a fact) and events preceding it. Relevant events include the migration of ethnic Hungarians and blacks to the area, the reactions of old or native stock to the new residents, local political structures and actions taken by the Republican and Democrat parties, mine owners' interests and actions, and so on. These spatially and temporally constrained events and structures can only be employed to explain the Matewan Massacre.

By way of contrast, Lichter and colleagues (1997) used quantitative analysis of county-level data to explain the likelihood that families are headed by women. Their article is a textbook example of quantitative empiricist explanation. It shows that thirteen factors—including percent black—are significantly associated with the likelihood that families are headed by females. The thirteen concrete factors are said to explain variation in the dependent measure, family or household type—an aggregation of concrete events. Lichter and colleagues research, like many quantitative empiricist explanations, appears all the more impressive because it gives precise estimates of its explanatory effectiveness (measured as R^2). Their analysis explains 83.4% of variation in the dependent measure. However, like all empiricist explanations, there is less than meets the eye. Such explanations typically fail to offer insight into *why* any two phenomena are related.

The Theory-Driven Approach

As stated earlier, the theory-driven approach is concerned with developing and testing explanations by theory. The empiricist approach finds patterned relations between phenomena and presumes that the patterns are laws. In contrast, the theory-driven approach is concerned with developing theories that explain *why* two general phenomena are related. A theory is a set of interrelated, universal statements (laws or law-like statements), to which a set of rules or procedures can be applied to create new statements (Willer & Walker 2007:20). Universal statements contain constructs (i.e., general terms that do not refer to specific places or times). Consider the *abstract empirical generalization*:

For members of task groups, social status is correlated with perceptions of competence.[7]

Social status and perceptions of task-group competence are general terms. Why social status and perceptions of competence are correlated is a question that motivates theory development (Walker 2002). Theories are deductive systems that can be represented as follows:

$$E: \quad _AR_{2D}$$
$$P1: \quad _AR_{1B}$$
$$P2: \quad _BR_{1C}$$
$$P3: \quad _CR_{2D}$$

where E is an abstract generalization requiring explanation; each P is a proposition or argument; the subscripted terms A, B, C, and D are theoretical constructs that represent phenomena (e.g., social status, competence evaluations); and R is a relation (e.g., positive association, ownership). The statements 1–3 are universal in the algebraic sense (i.e., their terms can represent any phenomena or relations). P1 is interpreted as "A stands in a particular relation, R_1, to B," and similarly for P2 and P3. The representation includes R_1 and R_2 because theories often include statements about different types of relations.[8]

The theory of Status Characteristics and Expectation States (SCT) offers an explanation for the generalization above (Berger et al. 1977). The theory consists of interconnected propositions or arguments that explain the connection between social status and perceptions of competence (e.g., "A" and "D" in the schema above).[9] As a general theory, SCT can explain a host of phenomena including the correlation between race/ethnic status and perceptions of competence, sexual orientation and perceptions of competence, and so on.

Theories are data generating rather than data dependent because they must be tested against empirical reality. To do so, a researcher first uses the theory to build a model. Next, she or he identifies measures of: (1) a theory's concepts; (2) conditions that realize the theory's scope of application; and (3) its initial conditions to create a research design that generates data. A research design is a replica of its theoretical model (Freese & Sell 1980). Data that fail to fit hypotheses drawn from theory put the theory in danger of falsification (Popper 1934/1958). Theories that fail to find empirical support from carefully designed studies must be revised or discarded. Data that fit hypotheses deduced from a theory support the theory's conditional truth.[10] Theories that find empirical support can be refined and improved to explain a broader range of phenomena or to explain phenomena more precisely. Figure 7.1 describes theory-driven research and the first phases of a strategy for developing cumulative theoretical knowledge.

Important differences in the empiricist and theory-driven approaches to science are reflected by research carried out under those approaches. I discuss research and experiments as a research method in the next section.

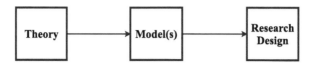

Fig. 7.1 Relations between theory, model, and research design

RESEARCH: OBJECTIVES AND TECHNIQUES

Two types of research follow from the empiricist and theory-driven approaches to science. Empiricist research uncovers phenomena and triggers the development of empiricist explanations. Theory-driven research tests theories. Explanations by theory can exist independently of data, but *theory testing* requires data and that requirement motivates research design and data collection (see Figure 7.1). There is an important implication of the research process: Any evaluation of research techniques must include evaluations of the approach taken as well as the soundness of designs.

Empiricist research falls into two broad categories. The first is exploratory research that involves a search for patterned behavior. It is not guided by hypotheses in any meaningful sense of that term. The second type of empiricist research is the de facto standard for sociological research. It tests hypotheses drawn from hunches and extrapolations from previously published research. As stated above, experiments are the ideal method for research conducted in the Mill-Fisher approach.

Theory-driven research is very different than empiricist research. Its objective is to test hypotheses drawn from research designs that, in turn, are drawn from theoretic models. Theory-driven research is the key to scientific advance, and experiments are the best method for testing theory. I turn now to experiments and experimental research.

What Is an Experiment?[11]

An experiment is "an inquiry for which the investigator controls the phenomena of interest and sets the conditions under which they are observed and measured" (Willer & Walker 2007:2). Experiments are rarely used in sociology. There are several reasons why this is so. First, sociologists-in-training rarely learn the purposes of experiments or how to design and conduct them. (See Webster & Sell [2007] for an excellent introduction to experiments in the social sciences.) Second, poor training promotes and sustains popular misconceptions about experiments. Many sociologists believe that laboratory experiments are only useful for studying microsocial phenomena. Third, many sociologists believe or have been taught that the *artificiality* of experiments makes generalizing experimental findings difficult if not impossible.

Fortunately, all of these barriers to increasing the numbers of experiments that study race and ethnicity are surmountable.

Training

Courses in research methods and statistics typically offer sociologists-in-training limited exposure to experimental methods. Students learn that

> The most conventional type of experiment, in the natural as well as the social sciences, involves three major pairs of components: (1) independent and dependent variables, (2) pretesting and posttesting, and (3) experiment and control groups. (Babbie 1998:233)
>
> *True experiments* must have at least three things: Two comparison groups (in the simplest case, an experimental and a control group), variation in the independent variable before assessment of change in the dependent variable, [and] random assignment to the two (or more) comparison groups. (Schutt 2006:201; emphasis in the original)

These descriptions and those in other textbooks focus on *empiricist* experiments, the standard model for sociology experiments. The Mill-Fisher empiricist experiment can be summarized by four maxims that mirror the definitions of empiricist experiments given above. (See Willer and Walker [2007] for a more detailed discussion and illustration of each maxim.)

1. Create at least two study conditions that are initially as identical as possible.
2. Introduce a single difference (a presumed cause) between the two conditions and observe the result.
3. Restrict all inferences about the result to the effect(s) of that single difference.
4. Infer relative regularities only if it is unlikely that they are due to chance.

The empiricist experiment as refined by Fisher is a very effective tool for uncovering and verifying probable regularities if research conforms to the maxims above.

Beginning students are rarely exposed to theory-driven experiments—a form known from antiquity and institutionalized in the physical sciences since Galileo (Willer & Walker 2007:12 ff.). Theory-driven experiments test theory. *Theory designs methods of test* that generate evidence for or against a theory's knowledge claims. Theories that garner substantial empirical support can be applied for prediction or explanation. The design of theory-driven experiments is given by the following maxims:

1. Derive one or more models from the theory to be tested.

2. Use the theory to generate predictions by linking initial conditions to end conditions.

3. Build experiment replicas, set initial conditions, and observe the end conditions.

4. Compare results to predictions and decide whether the theory is supported.

5. Make inferences from theory with greatest confidence to instances most theoretically similar to experiments supporting the theory. Predictions are not formally limited by that similarity. (Again, see Willer and Walker [2007] for detailed discussion of these maxims.)

Experiments are the best methods for testing hypotheses and theory because they give researchers the greatest control over test conditions. Experimental control serves different purposes in empiricist and theory-driven experiments. Empiricist experiments control test conditions in order to create experimental and control conditions that are as similar as possible. The Mill-Fisher method requires their essential similarity to infer that putative causes are probable causes of effects.

Theory-driven experiments control test conditions to create conditions that satisfy conditions described by theory. Put another way, test conditions are controlled by (i.e., established by) theory so that results can be credibly evaluated as supporting or disconfirming the theory. Because theory designs the experiments, theory-driven experiments will have designs that reproduce—in concrete form—the general relationships found in the theories they test. It follows that the designs of theory-driven experiments will vary as widely as the theories that are tested.

Social Science Experiments with Applications to Race and Ethnic Studies

Varieties of Experimental Designs

Scholars can use research to uncover patterned relations or to test theory. Empiricist research can be used to study any phenomenon that piques the spirit of human inquiry. Theory-driven research can be used to study any phenomena that are explained by theory. Researcher control is the criterion that distinguishes experiments from other research techniques. Laboratory experiments offer researchers the greatest control of study conditions but there are other experimental designs. In what follows, I give examples of natural, field, survey, and laboratory experiments. Some examples are hybrids of pure types but the sample demonstrates the wide range of issues that can be investigated experimentally.

Natural Experiments

There are instances in which the world of phenomena offers researchers conditions that imitate experimental control. Natural experiments can produce interesting discoveries and, in some cases, offer unusual tests of theory. The draft lottery implemented in 1969 spawned several natural experiments. The Selective Service System randomly assigned a number to each day of the calendar year to establish the draft order for eligible men. Draft-eligible males born on June 8 "won" the first lottery held in December 1969. The date was assigned the number 366, whereas those born on September 14 got number 1. Men with low lottery numbers were drafted first, so the lottery neatly partitioned more than 5 million men into two groups, those certain to be drafted and those almost certain to remain undrafted. Alternatively, draft numbers can be treated as continuous measures of exposure to the draft.

A decade after the Vietnam War ended, Hearst et al. (1986) reported that men with low draft numbers were more likely than those with higher numbers to commit suicide and to die in traffic accidents. The findings were interesting, provocative and were used to justify providing increased medical and social support services for Vietnam-era veterans. A quarter century later, Conley and Heerwig (2009) reported findings from a draft lottery experiment that included race as an independent variable. Their study of more than 372,000 deceased members of the 1950–1952 birth cohorts failed to find a draft lottery effect. Their finding is robust and consistent across race and ethnic subgroups (white, non-Hispanic black, Hispanic, and non-Hispanic others). Conley and Heerwig conclude that special assistance for health effects of draft status may not be needed over the long term. Hearst and colleagues cannot explain why there appear to be short-term draft-lottery effects on health, nor can they or Conley and Heerwig explain why the effects disappeared two decades later. Answering those questions requires theoretical analysis.

Field Experiments

Field experiments are conducted in natural settings and exercise greater control over research situations than naturalistic observations (e.g., ethnography or participant observation). Audit studies that use testing teams or telephone audits (Massey & Lundy 2001) to detect housing discrimination are field experiments. LaPiere's (1934) study of attitudes and actions is a classic field experiment. LaPiere traveled around the country with a Chinese couple visiting 251 hotels, restaurants, and campgrounds. The group was refused service at one establishment. Six months after the last visit, LaPiere mailed the proprietors and asked if they would serve Chinese, Negroes, or other ethnic patrons. Of 128 responses, only one proprietor responded with an unqualified "yes" to the query about serving Chinese patrons. The findings show extremely poor fit between attitudes (prejudice) and actions (discrimination). LaPiere could not h his findings but speculated that subtle and uncontrolled differences in eanor (e.g., the couple spoke impeccable English and smiled a lot), not nnicity, may have determined proprietors' positive reception of the traveling party. Ayres and Siegelman (1995) offer similar post hoc speculation concerning findings of their field experiment in which white males got better offers for new car purchases than black males or black and white females.

Survey Experiments

Survey experiments control the content of survey items and the order in which they are presented. Respondents often differ on many characteristics and are typically drawn from a variety of social and personal situations. Most survey experiments are empiricist studies that apply the Mill-Fisher paradigm in an efficient and effective way. However, some survey experiments are used to test theory.

Krysan's (1998) research on white racial attitudes is an example of a survey experiment. Krysan began with an apparent paradox. Surveys show that white support for principles of race and ethnic equality has risen over time. Yet, the same body of research finds declining white support of policies that are proposed to ameliorate race and ethnic inequalities. Krysan speculated that normative pressure (independent variable) influences public expressions of racial attitudes (dependent variable) and designed a survey experiment to evaluate the idea. The survey included traditional items used to measure race prejudice like support of a black presidential candidate, support of intermarriage of Whites with members of various race or ethnic groups, tolerance of black neighbors, attributions of black disadvantage to social or personal (i.e., innate) conditions, etc. Krysan asked white respondents to answer questions under three experimental treatments as follows:

1. Public: Respondents answered questions in face-to-face interviews (high pressure).
2. Semi-private: Respondents answered some questions in face-to-face interviews but were interrupted periodically to complete some paper-and-pencil items (moderate pressure).
3. Private: Respondents answered survey questions mailed to their homes (low pressure).

Krysan reported partial support for her first hypothesis that white respondents would express less liberal attitudes as the privacy of their responses increased. The positive finding did not hold for some attitude items. Her second hypothesis that privacy effects would be greater for items about principles of racial equality than items about racial policies was disconfirmed. She also found mixed support for a third hypothesis that privacy effects were more pronounced for the highly educated. College graduates who responded privately expressed more negative attitudes than other combinations of education and mode of administration but, again, only for some items.

Krysan's research addressed issues of theoretical and practical importance but she was unable to find strong support for the three regularities she expected to find. As a next step, the findings of empiricist experiments like this one suggest mounting additional studies to answer conclusively whether there is a regular relationship between privacy and expressions of race tolerance.

Laboratory Experiments
Laboratory experiments are conducted under highly controlled conditions. Researchers exercise maximal control of important variables for empiricist and theory-driven experiments. Here, I describe an empiricist laboratory experiment and a series of theory-driven experiments that demonstrate the range of phenomena that can be investigated with theory.

The Obama Effect

A series of recent papers focuses on what some label the "Obama effect." The idea is that the success of Barack Obama's presidential campaign has had or can have positive effects on the aspirations and behaviors of black Americans. Several experiments draw on the concept of *stereotype threat*, a reaction that individuals experience when evaluations of their performances have the potential to verify negative stereotypes of their ingroup (Steele & Aronson 1995). Stereotype threat is assumed to degrade the performances of those who experience it.

Aronson et al. (2009) used a laboratory experiment to study the Obama effect. In July 2008, they administered portions of the Medical College Admission Test (MCAT) to aspiring medical students enrolled in summer programs at three universities. The experiments were conducted before the political conventions had officially designated Barack Obama and John McCain as presidential candidates. All participants received an instruction that described the test as an important measure of ability that predicted success in gaining admission to either medical or graduate school. That instruction was designed to activate stereotype threat.

Students were randomly assigned to one of four treatments: (1) Obama treatment; (2) McCain treatment; (3) American politician treatment; and (4) control. Subjects in each of the four groups were given a test booklet that contained a cover sheet, test instructions, and the MCAT items. Test booklets for treatments 1–3 included a short survey of political issues designed to get subjects to think about and offer positive comments about Obama, McCain, or "an American politician." Participants in the Obama and McCain conditions saw three small color photographs of the candidate at the top of the sheet

>miling on a *Time* magazine cover). A series of politically ambiguous .ations taken from speeches, news conferences, etc., was printed under the .1otos. The quotations were attributed to Obama, McCain, or to "an American politician." The quotes were identical with one exception. The phrase "my friends," uniquely identified with McCain during the campaign, was added when the quotes were attributed to McCain.

Aronson et al. (2009) tested the hypothesis that black students who are primed to think positively about Obama before taking a difficult test will have higher scores than Blacks who are not primed. Their hypothesis was not supported. Blacks in the Obama treatment did not have higher test scores than Blacks in the other treatments. Further analysis showed that test performances were not affected by the degree of positive sentiment expressed toward Obama, engagement with the presidential campaign, mentioning Obama's race, mentioning Obama's intelligence, or the subjects' SAT scores. In fact, students who showed greater engagement with the election (measured by how closely the respondent followed events on television during the previous three months) had lower test scores.

Aronson and colleagues findings are interesting but answer no important questions. There is no evidence of an Obama effect and their findings are inconsistent with those of Marx et al. (2009), who asked 472 adult Americans to answer items from the Graduate Record Exam. Marx and colleagues predicted that Obama's candidacy could reduce black-white differences generated by stereotype threat. They report smaller black-white differences in test scores immediately after "stereotype-defying" actions during the Obama campaign. Differences in the studies' findings are intriguing, but strict comparisons are not possible because the experiments differ in many ways. Marx and colleagues study combined elements of a natural experiment with typical laboratory procedures. It was a web-based study in which respondents answered items under two conditions (relatively active or relatively inactive periods of the Obama campaign). Aronson and colleagues research was conducted in labs at three universities with students contemplating medical careers. Is there an Obama effect? These studies leave the basic question unanswered.

But Is It a Real World? Theory, Micro Experiments, and Macro Application

Two related criticisms are often directed toward social science experiments. First, some critics argue that research labs are contrived social situations and that findings from experiments cannot be generalized beyond the lab. Second, given constraints on space, laboratory groups are small. As a result, even if they could be applied outside the laboratory, findings from such studies would not be useful for understanding meso- and macro-level phenomena. Each criticism is important but neither is an impediment to using experiments as an integral part of the scientific process, nor are they barriers to scientific progress. In fact, the features of experiments that appear most problematic make experiments the most suitable method for theory-driven science.

Laboratory experiments that test theory are contrived situations but they are also real situations. Researchers can exercise the greatest level of control in the lab. They use theory to build situations that are stripped of the baggage found in natural settings—baggage that proves detrimental to tests of theoretical understandings of social life. The claim that their artificiality makes it impossible to generalize laboratory findings misunderstands the role of data in the scientific process. As stated earlier, there is no logic that permits an investigator to generalize one or a million research findings to find laws as Mill presumed. Nor can findings (e.g., sample data) be generalized to a population. That reality is devastating for scholars who take an empiricist approach to science, but generalization, as espoused by empiricists, is irrelevant to theory-driven research.

Theory-driven research does not try to find laws. It tests laws and the theories in which they are embedded. Moreover, theory-driven research is not concerned with applying patterns observed in the lab to situations beyond the research setting. For theory-driven research, generalization is a process through which *theory* is applied more generally, first within a specified scope and, as scope restrictions are relaxed, over an ever-expanding scope.

Physical constraints limit the size and range of social systems created in research labs. Most laboratory situations do not qualify as microcosms of any known universe. In that sense, uninformed critics have every reason to be concerned about using experiments to study meso- and macro-level phenomena. Armies cannot be brought into research labs (Zelditch 1969). Some critics misunderstand that elemental truth to mean that researchers cannot use experiments to study organizational life or life in other large-scale social institutions. Nothing could be further from the truth. Researchers can use laboratory experiments to gain vital information about processes that play out among military units or between nation states (Zelditch 1969). I use experiments that test predictions of Elementary Theory (ET) to illustrate.

As mentioned previously, ET (Willer & Anderson 1981) is a theory of network structures and social behavior that describes and explains processes of exchange, coercion, and conflict. The experiments I describe below use the coercive structure reproduced as Figure 7.2. The Ds possess resources that are of value to them and to C. C is an actor who controls negative sanctions that can be used against actors at D_1–D_4. As is true of the "real world," C's decision to use sanctions is costly.

Experimenters use student volunteers to fill the positions in Figure 7.2. Subjects are given chips at the start of each experiment trial. Position C is given 4 red chips that it can send to any or all Ds. Each D is given 10 white

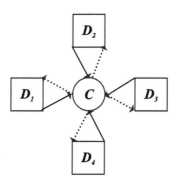

Fig. 7.2 A coercive network structure

chips, any number of which can be kept or sent to C. Red and white chips are worth 1 point each to C. White chips are worth 1 point to Ds, but the point values of any white chips a D holds are lost if D gets a red chip from C. That is, C can use red chips as negative sanctions against any or all Ds. C can refuse to accept white chips but Ds are obligated to accept red-chip sanctions. Subjects are told that researchers will record the points earned after each trial, convert points to money at the experiment's end, and pay them by points earned.

The experimental situation establishes coercive relationships. Position C has an incentive to gain white chips from the Ds, but every rational D prefers to keep its chips and 10 points by doing nothing. C's sanctioning capacity gives it leverage against D so that D now has an incentive to send some chips to C to avoid receiving a red-chip sanction. However, even under the threat of sanctions, no rational D will send 10 resources to C. It would be left with nothing of value and C would have gained 10 units of value without incurring the cost of sending a sanction (-1 point). Negotiation is the solution for C and D in this situation.

Much simplified, ET's resistance law (Equation 2) predicts the amount of resistance to any given exchange. Principle 2 of ET asserts that two actors (e.g., C and D_1) will agree to deals at the point of equal resistance which is predicted by Equation 3. The first experiment in the series created a situation like that in Figure 7.2 with 3 Ds rather than 4. Position C gains its maximum payoff (or gain) if D gives 9 white chips and C does not send D a red chip, whereas D's maximum payoff is 0 when it does not get a red chip (p_c max $= 9$ and p_d max $= 0$). D's payoff is 0 because it neither gains nor loses value. At confrontation (failure to reach agreement), C sends a red chip to D. Confrontation costs C one point, the value of its red chip, but D loses the value of all 10 white chips (10 points). For quantities in Equation 3, p_c con $= -1$ and p_d con $= -10$. Solving Equation 3 for p_c and p_d, the payoffs at equal resistance, ET predicts that D will agree to send C an average of 4.5 white chips and lose their value (i.e., $p_c = 4.5$ and $p_d = -4.5$).

Next, consider a second experiment identical to the first except that C is required to punish at least one D by sending it a red chip. Under that scenario, every D has an interest in avoiding punishment and the Ds compete to avoid punishment by offering better and better deals to C. ET predicts that Ds will strike deals such that p_c approaches p_c max = 9.

These experiments, run more than twenty years ago, found that Ds sent an average of 3.67 white chips (theoretic prediction = 4.5) to C in the first experiment (see Willer 1987). The second experiment for which punishment was certain for one D found an average of 7.3 chips sent to C with a maximum of 9 sent (theoretic prediction = 9). Finally, a variant of the second experiment increased the number of Ds from three to five and required C to send at least 2 red chips per trial. For that study, C received an average of 8.5 chips and the modal rate was 9 chips.

Critics of experimental research question the importance of experiments like those just described. Data collected from college students playing chip-trading games may support theoretic predictions but the experiments are not real-world situations. The findings cannot be generalized to situations outside the lab so they must certainly be irrelevant to issues that concern students of race and ethnicity. The critics are wrong.

Coercive structures like that in Figure 7.2 model ET's theoretical structure and the experiments test the model and in turn ET. Support for ET (or any theory) gives theorists confidence that the theory can be applied to any phenomena that satisfy the theory's scope and initial conditions. Real-world coercive relations like those modeled here include muggers (C) and victims (D), nation states (C) and their citizens (D), and masters (C) and slaves (D). The last example brings us back to the topic at hand.

Race-based slavery as practiced in the Western Hemisphere could be particularly cruel, but the harshness of treatment is difficult to quantify (Degler 1971). There is general agreement on two points, however: First, there was substantial variation across slave owners in the harshness of treatment; second, cruelty to slaves varied across slaveholding societies. On the second issue, evidence suggests that slavery in the United States was harsher in the Deep South than in slave states closer to the Mason-Dixon line. Being sold down the river was not an idle threat. Similarly, slavery in Brazil and the Caribbean is widely believed to have been harsher than in the United States. Ironically, slavery appears to have been more profitable in the harshest environments (e.g., Jamaica and Brazil).

Marx (1867/1967) and Weber (1896/1963) speculated that slavery was more profitable in Brazil than in the United States because slave holders had a supply of cheap slaves. Importation of slaves to the United States was banned after 1808, although slavery was not effectively abolished until the Civil War ended in 1865. The U.S. slave population grew by natural increase after the 1808 ban. Brazil did not ban the importation of slaves until 1850 and did not end slavery until 1888.

Application of ET to the study of slavery in Brazil and the United States is more than an exercise. ET predicts that harsh sanctioning of slaves (Ds) will increase their marginal productivity as they compete to avoid punishment. On the other hand, confrontation is costly to slaves and slave holders (Cs). Slaves must bear the psychic costs associated with living under threat of bodily harm and the physical costs of severe injury or death. Slave holders lose the value of dead or incapacitated slaves and must incur the costs of replacement. The costs of confrontation for slaves (p_d con) are assumed to be relatively stable across slaving societies, but a plentiful supply of slaves lowers the cost of replacing them and reduces the cost of confrontation (p_c con) for slave holders. Consequently, p_c con is lower in countries that had plentiful supplies of slaves (e.g., Brazil between 1808 and 1888) than in countries like the United States where the supply was less plentiful. Application of ET (Equations 2 and 3) leads to the twin predictions that slaves are treated more harshly and their labor exploited to produce greater profits in countries where supplies of slaves are bountiful. ET's predictions are consistent with historical observations and are based on well-supported theory rather than informed speculations like those of Marx and Weber.

Concluding Remarks and an Appeal

Theory is underdeveloped and researchers rarely conduct experiments in race and ethnic studies. This chapter advocates a shift from empiricist to theory-driven research as a corrective for both problems. Theory development is the ultimate goal of basic science, and theory-driven research is more productive of theory. Theory designs methods of test and experiments are the best method for testing, given researchers' ability to exercise control of the research setting. Additionally, researchers properly trained in experimental techniques can more easily apply tested theories to situations outside the lab. Any discipline that amasses a larger storehouse of theory than another also has an advantage in using theory—rather than ill-informed speculations—to design policies. Better theoretical understandings increase the odds that policies have positive results (i.e., produce intended outcomes). There are other salutary effects of using a theory-driven approach that develops more theory and makes more extensive use of experiments.

Critiques of race and ethnic studies find myriad problems. Many studies reflect various forms of race and cultural bias. Bias taints the research process by leading researchers to misperceive phenomena, misinterpret observations, and offer explanations for phenomena that either do not exist or have been described inaccurately by biased observers. Some bias follows from the under-representation and underutilization of researchers and research subjects who are members of race and ethnic minority groups. All too often, researchers have made observations of dominant race and ethnic groups and *assumed* that the same patterns ought to be reflected among members of subordinate groups. The failure of some groups to exhibit expected patterns has often been treated as an aberration to be accounted for by empiricist explanations. Finally, cultural and race prejudices contribute to malfeasance and maltreatment of minority participants in research and the communities from which they are drawn.

There are many valid criticisms of specific race and ethnic studies, and I applaud those who point them out. However, I raise several general concerns about critical commentary. First, critics all too often fail to identify correctly the sources of the discipline's troubles. Second, few of the criticisms are constructive. Third, our discipline and its practitioners have not addressed clearly and specifically the difficulties Du Bois associated with finding and applying scientific laws. I address these objections in turn.

Many of the most vocal critics of research in our field attribute problems to the logic and origins of modern science and research methods. However, since Du Bois (1898), it has been clear that the actual culprits are social scientists who misunderstand or misuse research techniques and scientific method. Neither the logic of modern science nor the research methods scientists use can be held accountable for underrepresentation of minority scholars, bias in research, or malfeasance of researchers and research institutions. However, the approach a scientist takes can exacerbate or ameliorate problems identified by critics.

My second objection is to critics who describe problems but don't offer plausible solutions. If solutions are offered, they are often based on untested hypotheses or are so vague that they are useless as guides to corrective action. Consider criticisms of the Moynihan (1965) report. Moynihan reported a negative statistical association between the number of adult heads of families and family poverty. Critics claimed that what Moynihan saw as weaknesses were really strengths when viewed from a minority rather than majority perspective (Billingsley 1968; Hill 1972). However, the critics failed to describe procedures that would produce a set of contrary findings (e.g., a zero or positive correlation).

My final and most strenuous objection concerns the failure of sociologists—not just scholars of race—to fully specify and address adequately Du Bois's (1940) concerns about "difficulties of applying scientific law and discovering cause and effect in the social world." In contrast, I argue that lagging theory development is due in part to a reliance on an empiricist approach to science. There is an additional disadvantage of the empiricist approach. The current period is one in which *public sociology* is appealing to a growing proportion of sociologists (Burawoy 2005). Public sociology incorporates a number of ideas, but one of them reflects Du Bois's interest in applying sociological knowledge to public issues. I agree with Weber (1918/1958) that speaking out—and taking action—on public issues is our "damned duty." At the same time, I argue that mixing social activism and science creates bad results.

Taking active positions on social issues requires activating and acting on values. Activists value some social arrangements more than others (e.g., integrated vs. segregated schools). Activists are more likely to value observing the correlates of outcomes (empiricism) rather than explaining relations between outcomes and their correlates (theory). Injecting values into scientific work ensures that sociological research is affected by bias. A half-century has passed since Rossi (1960) asserted that without overarching theory, investigators typically find exactly what they are looking for rather than what exists. Making public whose side we are on (Becker 1966) does nothing to mitigate the negative effects of activist bias.

There is a way out of the conundrum, but it requires embracing science—the enemy many critics have named. Sociologists of race and ethnicity can lead the way by reforming not science but scientists. To do so, scientists must embrace theory—the method of science. Not method as investigative technique but method as the logic that justifies accepting or rejecting theory. We can make headway in the fight to resolve problems raised by critics if we recognize that doing science is a public process. As scientists we comprise a public community, and external funding exposes our actions to a much larger public. Only public scrutiny can prevent abuses like some of those from the past. The Tuskegee Experiment (Jones 1981) was immoral and unethical, and ethical safeguards introduced after it was brought to light make future Tuskegees less likely. But we must be vigilant. Today, many people are repulsed by the idea of harvesting embryonic stem cells from aborted fetuses just as an earlier generation was repulsed by revelations of the Tuskegee study. Women from some groups are disproportionately more likely to have abortions—a potential source of stem cell material—than are members of the majority. Scholars of race can play an important role in regulating the actions of scientists.

On the main criticisms of race and ethnic research, theory and data collection are objects of scrutiny by the scientific and lay communities. Theory can be tested by anyone with the requisite knowledge, skills, and resources to do so. Interested and independent analysts can check data that purport to support theory. It is still possible to claim that American Blacks do less well academically than Whites because they are genetically inclined to poorer performances. And some researchers continue to make such claims. But theories that purport to explain how genetic characteristics produce poorer performances must be tested. And tests can be conducted by qualified members of the groups that have been described as genetically inferior.

The distinction between empiricist and theory-driven experiments raises a caution. Experimenter control is the hallmark of both types of research but the nature and purpose of control is different. Empiricist experiments seek answers to "which *x*s are related to *y*" questions. Aronson et al. (2009) asked whether seeing positive images and making positive statements about Barack Obama (*x*) overcame the negative effects of stereotype threat (*y*). They used experimental control to isolate key independent and dependent variables. Using standard Mill-Fisher logic, they examined the question and found no support for their hypothesis.

Theory-driven studies rely on theory to design experimental controls. Theory-driven experiments are designs that establish conditions that satisfy a theory's scope and initial conditions and use reliable and valid measures of a theory's concepts. For theory-driven experiments, experimental control means *controlled by theory*. Willer (1987) created coercive structures in his laboratory because ET required them. The theory predicts payoffs for *C* and *D* in lab studies and for master-slave relations in slave-holding societies. The theory is supported by observations from the lab and from two slave-holding societies.

Empiricist and theory-driven research can be complementary. Scholars can repeat Aronson et al.'s (2009) or Willer's (1987) experiments. Perhaps, members of Aronson and colleagues research team supported candidates other than Obama and introduced bias into the study. The public character of the research process permits others to replicate Aronson and colleagues empiricist experiment to find evidence of an Obama effect obscured by bias. After uncovering an effect, researchers would be left to contemplate the next step. Does existing theory explain the Obama effect? If so, patterns found by empiricist research can fuel theory-driven research to replicate and extend the findings. If no theory explains the now-documented phenomenon, science dictates that theorists take up the challenge to build new theory and test it as part of a theory-driven program. But all of this is part of a public process—a process that abhors and corrects bias, misrepresentation, and bad ideas.

The theory-driven approach values theoretical understandings. Theories that find support in the lab can be applied to a variety of micro-, meso-, and macro-level phenomena that satisfy the theory's conditions. Given the proven value of theory-driven lab experiments, scholars of race ought to be more inclined to use them in their research projects. Moreover, findings from such research can be used to inform public policy as "others will." One can only hope that Du Bois would approve.

NOTES

1. Following Rudner (1966:5), I distinguish techniques for collecting and analyzing data (method$_1$) from the logic of justification—a discipline's rationale for accepting or rejecting theories (method$_2$ or methodology). Here and elsewhere, I use the terms "methods" and "techniques" interchangeably. I trust that I am able to communicate clearly whether the terms are intended to refer to method$_1$ or method$_2$.

2. The term "empiricist" is often used as a pejorative. I use the word in its descriptive sense (i.e., that knowledge [theory] can be derived from observations).

3. Ernest Manheim was a remarkable man and brilliant teacher. Fearful that the Nazis would not approve it, Manheim withdrew his habilitation thesis (an academic qualification in Germany that comes after the Ph.D.) in 1933 shortly after the faculty at Leipzig had approved it. He moved to London and worked as an assistant to his cousin, Karl Mannheim, while earning a doctorate in anthropology. Arriving at Kansas City University (later UMKC) in 1938, his research on race relations quickly reshaped the thinking of civic leaders in Kansas City. Later, Manheim volunteered to testify for Brown when *Brown v. Topeka* was heard in federal district court.

4. The volume of criticisms has expanded almost as rapidly as the field. See papers compiled by Ladner (1973), Stanfield and Dennis (1993), and Zuberi and Bonilla-Silva (2008) for a thorough introduction to general criticisms of research on race and ethnicity.

5. SF and AJS split volumes across calendar years. I reviewed articles published in the appropriate volumes for 2006–2008. AJS, SF, and SPQ also published special issues that focused on race during the period of observation. Consequently, the numbers of papers devoted to race may be inflated in those journals. Finally, as expected, all articles in ERS focus on race.

6. An empiricist approach "emphasizes the importance of observation and of creating knowledge by amassing observations and generalizing from these observations" (Cohen 1989:16; and see Popper 1962:21ff.). Mill's logic is empiricist.

7. Examples of empirical generalizations are: (1) Mexican American students earn lower grades than non-Hispanic white Americans; or (2) students give higher evaluations to attractive than to unattractive teachers (Freng & Webber 2009; Hamermesh & Parker 2005). The claim that perceptions of task competence vary with social status is an abstract empirical generalization. The statement describes a relationship between two general concepts (or constructs), social status and perceived task competence, where Mexican American, non-Hispanic white, and attractiveness are examples of status groups, and grades and student evaluations of teaching are perceptions of competence.

8. I simplify the description of theory for illustrative purposes. Willer and Walker (2007:17–30) give an introduction to the structure of theories and Cohen (1989) offers an extended introduction suitable for advanced undergraduates, graduate students, and others who seek a nontechnical introduction to theory construction.

9. SCT consists of five propositions and a number of scope restrictions. I do not present the theory here, but see Berger et al. (1977) for a complete discussion of the theory, including arguments and scope restrictions. See Walker (1999) for an application of SCT to modern affirmative action and interracial relations.

10. Theories are never judged true in an absolute sense. Tests of theories are not tests of reality but tests of sentences that claim to describe reality. Even well-corroborated theories are in danger of falsification if they encounter contrary evidence in future tests. For this reason, it is important that theorists specify the scope limitations of

their formulations (Walker & Cohen 1985) and embed tests of theory in a larger program of theory-driven research (Cohen 1997).

11. Remarks in this section draw extensively on my previous work (Walker 2002) and work with David Willer (Walker & Willer 2007; Willer & Walker 2007).

REFERENCES

Allport, G. (1954). *The nature of prejudice*. New York: Addison-Wesley.

Aronson, J., Jannone, S., McGlone, M., & Johnson-Campbell, T. (2009). The Obama effect: An experimental test. *Journal of Experimental Social Psychology, 45*, 957–960.

Ayres, I., & Siegelman, P. (1995). Race and gender discrimination in bargaining for a new car. *American Economic Review, 85*, 304–321.

Babbie, E. (1998). *The practice of social research*. Belmont, CA: Wadsworth.

Bailey, R. J. (2008). *Matewan before the massacre*. Morgantown: West Virginia University Press.

Becker, H. S. (1966). Whose side are we on? *Social Problems, 14*, 239–247.

Berger, J., Fisek, M. H., Norman, R. Z., & Zelditch, M., Jr. (1977). *Status characteristics and social interaction*. New York: Elsevier.

Billingsley, A. (1968). *Black families in white America*. Englewood Cliffs, NJ: Prentice-Hall.

Burawoy, M. (2005). For public sociology. *American Sociological Review, 70*, 4–28.

Clark, W. A. V. (2002). Ethnic preferences and ethnic perceptions in multi-ethnic settings. *Urban Geography, 23*, 237–256.

Cohen, B. P. (1989). *Developing sociological knowledge*, 2nd ed. Chicago: Nelson-Hall.

Cohen, B. P. (1997). Beyond experimental inference: A decent burial for J. S. Mill and R. A. Fisher. In J. Szmatka, J. Skvoretz, and J. Berger (Eds.), *Status, network and structure: Theory development in group processes* (pp. 71–86). Stanford, CA: Stanford University Press.

Cole, S. (Ed.) et al. (1994). Special issue: What's wrong with sociology. *Sociological Forum, 9*, 129–320. New York: Plenum Press.

Conley, D., & Heerwig, J. A. (2009). The long-term effects of military conscription on mortality: Estimates from the Vietnam-era draft lottery. Cambridge, MA: National Bureau of Economic Research, Working Paper 15105.

Degler, C. N. (1971). *Neither black nor white*. New York: Macmillan.

Du Bois, W. E. B. (1898). The study of the Negro problems. *Annals of the American Academy of Political and Social Science, 11*, 1–23.

Du Bois, W. E. B. (1940). *Dusk of dawn*. New York: Harcourt Brace.

Fisher, R. A. (1935). *The design of experiments*. London: Oliver and Boyd.

Fisher, R. A. (1956). *Statistical methods and scientific inference*. Edinburgh: Oliver and Boyd.

Freese, L., & Sell, J. (1980). Constructing axiomatic theories in sociology. In L. Freese (Ed.), *Theoretical methods in sociology: Seven essays* (pp. 263–368). Pittsburgh: University of Pittsburgh Press.

Freng, S., & Webber, D. (2009). Turning up the heat on online teaching evaluations: Does "hotness" matter? *Teaching of Psychology, 36,* 189–193.

Goar, C. (2008). Experiments in black and white: Power and privilege in experimental methodology. In T. Zuberi & E. Bonilla-Silva (Eds.), *White logic, white methods* (pp. 153–162). Lanham, MD: Rowman & Littlefield.

Graves, J. L., Jr. (2004). *The race myth.* New York: Dutton.

Green, D. S., & Driver, E. D. (1976). W. E. B. Du Bois: A case in the sociology of sociological negation. *Phylon, 37,* 308–333.

Greenwald, A. G., McGhee, D. E., & Schwartz, J. L. K. (1998). Measuring individual differences in implicit cognition: The implicit association test. *Journal of Personality and Social Psychology, 74,* 1464–1480.

Hamermesh, D. S., & Parker, A. (2005). Beauty in the classroom: Instructors' pulchritude and putative pedagogical productivity. *Economics of Education Review, 24,* 369–376.

Hearst, N., Newman, T. B., & Hulley, S. B. (1986). Delayed effects of the military draft on mortality: A randomized natural experiment. *New England Journal of Medicine, 314,* 620–624.

Hempel, C. G. (1966). *Philosophy of social science.* Englewood Cliffs, NJ: Prentice-Hall.

Hempel, C. G., & Oppenheim, P. (1948). Studies in the logic of explanation. *Philosophy of Science, 15,* 135–175.

Hill, R. B. (1972). *The strengths of black families.* New York: Emerson Hall.

Hunt, M. O., Jackson, P. B., Powell, B., & Steelman, L. C. (2000). Color-blind: The treatment of race and ethnicity in social psychology. *Social Psychology Quarterly, 63,* 352–364.

Jones, J. H. (1981). *Bad blood: The Tuskegee syphilis experiment.* New York: Free Press.

Kaplan, A. (1964). *The conduct of inquiry.* San Francisco: Chandler Publishing.

Krysan, M. (1998). Privacy and the expression of white racial attitudes. *Public Opinion Quarterly, 62,* 506–544.

Ladner, J. A. (1973). *The death of white sociology.* New York: Random House.

LaPiere, R. T. (1934). Attitudes vs. actions. *Social Forces, 13,* 230–237.

Lichter, D. T., McLaughlin, D. K., & Ribar, D. C. (1997). Welfare and the rise in female-headed families. *American Journal of Sociology, 103,* 112–143.

Lieberson, S. (1985). *Making it count.* Berkeley: University of California Press.

Mann, C. R. (1993). *Unequal justice: A question of color.* Bloomington: Indiana University Press.

Marx, D. M., Ko, S. J., & Friedman, R. A. (2009). The "Obama Effect": How a salient role model reduces race-based performance differences. *Journal of Experimental Social Psychology, 45,* 953–956.

Marx, K. (1867/1967). *Capital*. New York: International Publishers.

Massey, D. S., & Lundy, G. (2001). Use of black English and racial discrimination in urban housing markets: New methods and findings. *Urban Affairs Review, 36,* 452–469.

Mill, J. S. (1843/1967). *A system of logic*. London: Longmans, Green and Co.

Montagu, A. (1942). *Man's most dangerous myth: The fallacy of race*. New York: Columbia University Press.

Moynihan, D. P. (1965). *The Negro family: The case for national action*. Washington, DC: Government Printing Office.

Nagel, E. (1961). *The structure of science*. New York: Harcourt, Brace & World.

Newton, I. (1686/1966). *Principia mathematica*. Trans. A Motte. Berkeley: University of California Press.

Ogbu, J. U. (2003). *Black American students in an affluent suburb*. Mahwah, NJ: Lawrence Erlbaum.

Patterson, O. (1982). *Slavery and social death: A comparative study*. Cambridge, MA: Harvard University Press.

Popper, K. R. (1934/1958). *The logic of scientific discovery*. New York: Basic Books.

Popper, K. R. (1962). *Conjectures and refutations*. New York: Basic Books.

Rossi, P. H. (1960). Power and community structure. *Midwest Journal of Political Science, 4,* 390–401.

Rudner, R. S. (1966). *Philosophy of social science*. Englewood Cliffs, NJ: Prentice-Hall.

Schutt, R. K. (2006). *Investigating the social world: The process and practice of research*. 5th ed. Thousand Oaks, CA: Sage.

Stanfield, J. H., II, & Dennis, R. M. (1993). *Race and ethnicity in research methods*. Newbury Park, CA: Sage.

Steele, C. M., & Aronson, J. (1995). Stereotype threat and the intellectual test performance of African-Americans. *Journal of Personality and Social Psychology, 69,* 797–811.

Walker, H. A. (1999). Two faces of diversity: Recreating the stranger next door? In P. Moen, D. Dempster-McClain, & H. A. Walker (Eds.), *A nation divided: Diversity, inequality and community in American society* (pp. 52–69). Ithaca, NY: Cornell University Press.

Walker, H. A. (2002). Three faces of explanation: A strategy for building cumulative knowledge. In J. Szmatka, M. Lovaglia, & K. Wysienska (Eds.), *The growth of social knowledge* (pp. 15–31). Westport, CT: Praeger.

Walker, H. A., & Cohen, B. P. (1985). Scope statements: Imperatives for evaluating theory. *American Sociological Review, 50,* 288–301.

Walker, H. A., & Willer, D. (2007). Experiments and the science of sociology. In M. Webster, Jr. & J. Sell (Eds.), *Laboratory experiments in the social sciences* (pp. 25–55). Burlington, MA: Academic Press.

Weber, M. (1896/1963). The social causes of the decay of ancient civilizations. In R. Kahl (Ed.), *Studies in explanation* (R. Frank, Trans.) (pp. 339–356). Englewood Cliffs, NJ: Prentice-Hall.

Weber, M. (1918/1958). Science as a vocation. In H. H. Gerth & C. Wright Mills (Trans. and Eds.), *From Max Weber* (pp. 129–156). New York: Oxford University Press.

Webster, M., Jr., & Sell, J. (2007). *Laboratory experiments in the social sciences.* Burlington, MA: Academic Press.

Wells-Barnett, I. B. (1892–1895/2002). *On lynching.* (Edited and with an introduction by P. H. Collins.) Amherst, NY: Humanity Books.

Willer, D. (1987). *Theory and the experimental investigation of social structures.* New York: Gordon and Breach.

Willer, D. (1999). *Network exchange theory.* Westport, CT: Praeger.

Willer, D., & Anderson, B. (1981). *Networks, exchange and coercion: The elementary theory and its applications.* New York: Elsevier.

Willer, D., & Walker, H. A. (2007). *Building experiments: Testing social theory.* Stanford, CA: Stanford University Press.

Willer, D., & Webster, M. (1971). Theoretical concepts and observables. *American Sociological Review, 35,* 748–757.

Williams, R. M., Jr. (1975). Race and ethnic relations. *Annual Review of Sociology, 1,* 125–164.

Wilson, W. J. (2009). *More than just race: Being black and poor in the inner city.* New York: Norton.

Zelditch, M., Jr. (1969). Can you really study an army in the laboratory? In A. Etizioni (Ed.), *A sociological reader on complex organizations,* 2nd ed. (pp. 528–539). New York: Holt, Rinehart and Winston.

Zuberi, T., & Bonilla-Silva, E. (2008). *White logic, white methods: Racism and methodology.* Lanham, MD: Rowman & Littlefield.

PART II: MIXED METHODS

8   MULTIPLE METHODS IN RESEARCH ON TWENTY-FIRST-CENTURY PLANTATION MUSEUMS AND SLAVE CABINS IN THE U.S. SOUTH

Stephen Small

INTRODUCTION

Thousands of plantation museum sites containing buildings and structures constructed during the antebellum period or earlier still exist across the U.S. South at the start of the twenty-first century, and many of these sites house original slave cabins (Eichstedt & Small 2002; Mooney 2004; Small 2009). Scholars from various disciplines have analyzed these sites, including slave cabins, and most of the research on the cabins has focused on their history and archeology (Singleton 1991; Vlach 1993; Wilkie 2000).

In recent decades, a growing body of research on contemporary plantation museum sites—by public historians, sociologists, anthropologists, and museum specialists—has emerged, and the primary focus of this work has been on the role, operations, and functioning of these sites in the present rather than the past (Eichstedt & Small 2002; Horton & Horton 2006; Mooney 2004). These studies explore how heritage tourist sites discuss or avoid discussion of slavery, racialized segregation and injustice, and their legacies. They focus on the discursive strategies used and the ways in which images and representations work alongside textual language using euphemisms, evasions, and erasures. These analysts raise issues about public history, collective memory, the operation of gender ideologies, and the many aspects of power inequalities underlying the institutions and their operations. Representational strategies of race and slavery at heritage sites have also been linked to similar strategies operating in the realm of politics and the media (Hall 1997; Omi & Winant 1986; Small 2002). And they resonate with broader studies of collective memory (see, e.g., Trouillot 1995).

Studies of plantation museum sites use a variety of methodologies and methods and draw on a wide range of empirical data, including historical archives, archaeology and architecture, site observations and ethnography, discourses, texts, and visual images as well as interviews. Data have also been collected from websites. Analysts of African American Studies and African Diapora Studies have been centrally involved in this work (Horton & Horton 2006). They have deployed multidisciplinary perspectives, added substantial empirical insights, and expanded the sources of data consulted, including African American testimony, folklore and literature, music, art, and performance, and archeology and architecture (Franklin & McKee 2004; Singleton 1991). They have also carried out comparisons across the Diaspora (Horton & Horton 2006).

This chapter discusses research that I'm currently conducting on the organization, operations, and functioning of plantation museum sites in the U.S. South; it describes the multiple qualitative methods I have used to collect data from a wide range of sites, with a particular focus on slave cabins. My primary focus is on the contemporary sites and their representations of the past, rather than on their historical details. In other words, I'm interested in *the past in the present*, in the strategies and tactics used by site professionals today—including the layout of sites, the use of texts and images, and the stories told by tour guides—to convey messages about the nature, significance, and legacy of slavery and southern history.

My previous research persuaded me that most contemporary heritage sites in the South operate to aggrandize elite white southern society and to avoid discussion of slavery and black people (Eichstedt & Small 2002; Small 2009). Other researchers arrive at similar conclusions (Alderman & Modlin 2008; Davis 2008; Harrison 2008; Jackson 2004). Most sites focused on the mansions in which elite Whites lived and marginalized the lives and accommodations of the enslaved. There were determined efforts to avoid or minimize discussion of exploitation and violence, especially sexual violence. And particular efforts were made to avoid any discussion of the connections between slavery and contemporary racial formations.

In this chapter, I highlight how multiple methods can be deployed to collect primary data on the lives, experiences, and aspirations of black people under slavery and to access insights into representational strategies at contemporary sites about black lives under slavery. I argue that a sustained focus on slave cabins (rather than just the main houses where elite Whites lived) can bring significant insights into the processes of power and access to resources underlying the public history and collective memory of slavery at these sites. I believe that a detailed analysis of slave cabins can serve as a key step in highlighting such issues and in moving toward a public history that brings black lives and experiences to the forefront of the discussion.

From the outset, I sought to discover documents and data that directly addressed slave cabins, heard black voices (narratives and testimony, for example, in folklore and music), and engaged with black visions (in art and sculpture). I believe that the best way to address these issues is by using multiple methods to collect diverse sources of data. I address issues concerning the literature review, online research, historical archives, site observations, texts and images, and unstructured interviews. I argue that despite all the progress made in studying slavery and its consequences, a study of representations of slavery and slave cabins at contemporary heritage sites reminds us that we still need to dig deeper and press harder to identify and locate data by and about Blacks, especially data on their lives that humanize and individualize them. This is also true for research on representations and discourses about black lives that prevail at contemporary museum sites. I further suggest that in the future, attempts to document black lives and assess links between the past and the present will become more difficult, in an age in which racisms have been rearticulated and the United States has elected its first black president. We should take nothing for granted as we continue to document black lives.

REFLECTIONS ON PERSONAL AND PROFESSIONAL HISTORY

My path to multiple research methods began before my studies as an undergraduate student in England. I was influenced by my experiences as a child and teenager. I grew up in Liverpool, where I had little interest in local museums because the main images of Blacks there were of savage and barbarian Africans and eroticized or abject black women, typically in grass skirts with breasts revealed. There was nothing critical about Liverpool's role as the biggest slave port in the British Empire or the precious items plundered from Africa during colonialism, many still locked away in the cellars of the museums. There were no exhibits to celebrate human origins in the Rift Valley or the Kingdoms of Dahomey and Ghana, and nothing about Ethiopia. To museum managers at the time, the idea of "slave resistance" was probably an oxymoron, so nothing about that either. I probably learned more about Africa from watching Tarzan on television and the 1960s movie, *Zulu*, for what it was worth. And there was nothing much to offset such images in the books we read at school. However, there were exhibits on the achievement and glory of the British Empire, the march of civilization, and the kind and magnanimous abolition of the slave trade by the British government.

But I had deep interest in other aspects of black life in my local community and across the Diaspora. I was fascinated by the migration of West Indians to England (my father among them), with the power and pride of African Americans in the civil rights movement and Black Power (including Martin Luther King, Jr., the Mexico Olympics, and Angela Davis), with the arrival in Britain of reggae music and Rastafarians, with slave resistance and rebellion in Jamaica, Nanny of the Maroons, Paul Bogle, Marcus Garvey, and Walter Rodney. There were always more men than women, but it was a welcome start. I studied race and ethnic relations as part of my undergraduate work and wrote my senior thesis on Rastafari.

At graduate school in England, I began work in historical archives for my MSC thesis on class and race stratification under nineteenth-century slavery in the British and Spanish Caribbean. As a Research Fellow at the Policy Studies Institute (1980–1984), I worked on statistical studies of racial discrimination, analysis of documents, and ethnography (Small 1983a, 1983b). I continued working in the archives for my doctoral work at UC-Berkeley where I studied black people and Blacks of mixed African and European origins under nineteenth-century slavery in the British Caribbean and the United States (Small 1989). For that research, I spent substantial time in archives (Spanish Town Archives and the National Library in Jamaica, the Georgia Department of Archives and History, the Rare Books and Manuscript Collection in the Hargrett Library at the University of Georgia, and the Georgia Historical Society in Savannah) (Small 2004). At Berkeley, I also continued ethnographic work as a graduate student researcher at the Institute for the Study of Social Change, an institute that specialized in field research methods.

During all this time, I was enraged by the racist images of black people in the media across the globe and had worked on a number of projects in the United States and Britain to examine and challenge such images. I also began teaching qualitative methods. In 1992, I became involved as a curator in a gallery in Liverpool on trans-Atlantic slavery (in 2007, this gallery became the International Slavery Museum). The images, representations, and language used in the exhibits were a major source of contention between museum professionals and the black community in the development of that exhibit; the most vigorous opposition came from black women about hostile images of black women in museum exhibits (Small 1994, 1997).

I became more interested in museums as racialized institutions, and, while carrying out archival research in Georgia in 1994, I began to study plantation museums as tourist venues. At that time, Georgia was preparing for the Olympic Games and began a massive advertising campaign promoting southern heritage to persuade visitors and tourists to remain in the state and spend money. I was surprised by the striking images of plantation mansions and gardens in the promotional literature and glossy magazines. I was startled to learn that so many former slave plantations still existed in the state, along with a host of ancillary buildings. I was stunned to discover that so many of these buildings were slave cabins—shacks, huts, and hovels. As I took part in tours—from the Antebellum Plantation in Stone Mountain, to Alexander Stephens State Park in Crawfordville, and from Bulloch Hall in Roswell to the Hofwyl-Broadfield Plantation in Brunswick—I was outraged by the ways in which slavery and its injustices were so effortlessly circumvented.

Leaflets, glossy literature, tour guides, and tours highlighted the grandeur and architecture of the mansions, the beauty of the gardens, the honor, and civility of elite White lifestyles, while mourning the loss of a so-called golden age in which "cotton was king." White people (especially elites) were everywhere, black people nowhere. Overall, black contributions, lives, and aspirations, along with black suffering, struggles, resistance, and resilience were marginalized, anaesthetized, erased, or annihilated. Fortunately, I found sustained and spirited challenges to these images in some of the exhibits organized and managed by black people at the Harriet Tubman Museum in Macon, and the Negro Heritage Trail in Savannah.

By this time—1994—I had left the Sociology Department and joined African American Studies, where I felt greater affinity with the priorities for research, including the multidisciplinary approaches and the comparative international research central to African Diaspora Studies. This move also reflected my continued desire to identify, embrace, and articulate black voices and black visions in my research. A common element in my professional experience was a concern for the links between past structures, institutions, and ideologies of racialization (slavery, colonialism, racism, "race mixture"), and contemporary expressions of racialization in patterns of inequality, differential access to power, and racist images. These experiences led to my undertaking research on plantation museum sites and gave me the opportunity to connect many of the concerns that were important to me.

Between 1994 and 2001, a colleague (Jennifer L. Eichstedt) and I researched contemporary exhibits on southern history at more than 120 plantation museum sites across three states (Virginia, Georgia, and Louisiana). The main research findings were published in 2002 (Eichstedt & Small 2002). In that study, we carried out site observations, took part in guided tours, and analyzed site promotional literature and visual images to explore representations of slavery, including gender, by private and public ownership, by plantation crop (cotton, sugar, and tobacco), and by geographical region. We found that the majority of sites ignored, marginalized, or trivialized discussion of slavery by deploying a series of discursive strategies. All strategies of evasion were systematically gendered. Most attention was focused on the lives, culture, and achievements of elite Whites. We also analyzed the representations of fifteen sites managed and/or operated by African Americans, sites that provided contested histories. These sites were far more likely to discuss slavery, to bring black people's lives and experiences to the foreground of the exhibits, and to highlight post-slavery experiences of African Americans, especially the civil rights movement. They were also far more likely to make connections between slavery and contemporary racial formations in the United States.

Since 2004, I have been exploring the distribution and representation of twenty-first-century antebellum slave cabins in the contemporary southern heritage industry. I have also focused on the social history of these cabins. The majority of my time has been spent in Louisiana. I am currently preparing a book manuscript on three public sites with twenty-first-century antebellum slave cabins in Natchitoches, Louisiana. My primary goal is to describe the social role and significance of slave cabins in the organization of heritage tourism and public history and assess how various forms of history are deployed to support the narratives prevalent at these sites.

An examination of these cabins raises questions of public history (how certain aspects of southern history and society are institutionally incorporated into tourism and others are not) and questions of collective memory (how certain aspects of southern history are willfully remembered and others willfully forgotten). Relatedly, they raise questions of power, inequality, and the vexing contours of class and gender in a racialized hierarchy. Clearly, there is a long tradition of research on these issues (Blight 2001; Brundage 2005; West 1999), and I seek to add insights to this literature from the study of slave cabins at heritage sites today.

Using Multiple Methods on Plantation Museums and Slave Cabins

Setting up the Study

I began with a literature review and online research, including social history, museum studies, archaeology, and historical architecture. I wanted to find out what existed and where and to identify information on the institutional infrastructure of heritage tourism in the South. Unlike in my previous work on plantation museum sites (Eichstedt & Small 2002), I had not yet decided exactly what I was going to write about or which states I would focus on, so I decided to identify and visit a wide range of sites. Between 2004 and 2006, with two research assistants, I collected information from hundreds of sites across the South. This generated an immense amount of descriptive information, helping me identify which sites had cabins and their distribution. Where there was ambiguity in this information, telephone calls to sites filled in the gaps. Beginning in 2007, and over nine months, I visited more than 150 cabins at more than sixty sites in eight states (Florida, Georgia, North Carolina, South Carolina, Louisiana, Mississippi, Virginia, and Maryland).

Vastly more information about plantation sites and cabins had become available online compared to when I began research in 1996–2001, including descriptive information, photographs, and plantation maps. This was now substantial primary data (such as lists of enslaved persons, reproductions of letters, historical photographs, detailed contemporaneous descriptions, and architectural dimensions of cabins). There was also information on the location, management, staff, and opening hours at the sites, which allowed me early contact and better preparation for visits. In addition, entire copies of dissertations could easily be downloaded from the Internet. I identified top scholars currently working in the field and contacted many of them directly. One of the most fascinating discoveries was the burgeoning literature on archeology, the unique and innovative insights provided, the novel perspective "from the back of the big house," and the impressive original evidence revealed about black voices and visions, including gender and the experiences of women (Singleton 1991; Vlach 1993). Though some research like this had existed for a while, the field was blossoming, as I discuss below.

There is detailed primary information online and access to information on microfilm as well as in specific archives. Descriptions of data archives were readily available, along with summaries of data collections, for example, at University of North Carolina, Chapel Hill. There were also some primary collections available online, for example, audio interviews with internationally acclaimed "primitive artist" Clementine Hunter at Louisiana State University, Lafayette. Other primary documents included access to the original pages from the 1850 and 1860 census via www.ancestry.com. Web research also produces substantial amounts of statistical and quantitative data, secondary data, for example, patterns of employment and educational and housing inequality by race and gender. These broader data are important for people like me who are interested in the demographic and institutional contexts in which sites are located, resource and power inequalities, and how such factors shaped patterns of professional behavior at sites.

There were some challenges. Web searches, in my opinion, should be considered a point of departure, rather than a conclusion. There are massive amounts of information, so you need to exercise caution and not get swallowed up in the black hole of information. When looking for specific topics, most web pages produce little useful information and are repetitious. Persistence produces more useful information, including academic publications, names of scholars, primary data (including state websites), and primary collections on microfilm. Many plantation museums now have their own websites, which helped me identify sites in multiple states, especially those I had not previously visited. For example, I suspected that there were stone and brick cabins still in existence and was able to identify some online, in Texas and Maryland. Practical information, like opening times, can be obtained—most of the sites I visited were closed on Mondays—so call ahead. In other words, gather as much detailed info as you can before you leave home. Note, too, that websites have become so important and ubiquitous that they are now themselves sources of primary data for analysis of sites (see Alderman & Modlin 2008).

Overall, there was still far more information on the houses and lifestyles of elite Whites than on the lifestyles and accommodation of enslaved Blacks. There is still a need to dig deeper and press harder to identify black sources and sources about Blacks (see Camp 2004; Glymph 2008). Not all slave cabins were mentioned on websites or in promotional literature, and I found a number of slave cabins only after I actually visited. In general, National Park

Service (NPS) sites had more information and were better organized than other sites, especially private ones.[1] My experience in Jamaica and Brazil convinces me that research of this kind is far more difficult in the Caribbean and South America, given institutional structures and limited resources, and that's even before we consider the cost involved for research visits.

Historical Archives and Libraries

Because I'm interested in the history as well as the current organization of the sites, I used archives and libraries considerably. I was especially interested in documents for the last forty years or so that document the establishment and development of heritage tourism at many sites, including when and how they opened and the debates that took place about them. I visited state archives (e.g., Georgia Department of Archives, Alabama State Archives, Louisiana State Library and Archives); historical societies such as the St. Augustine Historical Society (Florida); and state and county historical societies (Natchitoches [Louisiana], Savannah [Georgia], and St. Augustine). Many plantation sites also have their own historical archives with rich, detailed information sometimes going back 150 years (e.g., Kingsley Plantation, Florida, and West Baton Rouge Museum, Louisiana).

These archives include a vast amount of data and a wide range of items—including official and unofficial records, manuscript collections, newspapers, diaries and memoirs, minutes of meetings, correspondence, financial transactions, probate records, work schedules, and purchases and sales. They also have a great number of photographs. I obtained substantial information about the recent organization, management, and activities at the sites. These data included personnel, social organization, tour formats, tour texts, and photographs. I accessed statistical information and official data from city, county, state, and federal levels. Many archives had significant data on black voices and visions. I also explored public libraries, some of which also have extensive primary documents. For example, I found "vertical files" in many libraries, including along the River Road and in East Baton Rouge in Louisiana, in Charleston, South Carolina, and in Macon, Georgia. Vertical files have newspaper clippings, some going back to the start of the twentieth century, site literature going back decades, and a range of other local primary documents.

It will come as no surprise to historians that the information in these archives is frequently incomplete. For example, all indications from online research were that most of the data for the plantations of the Prud'homme family of Natchitoches (a very large master-enslaver family, whose ownership of plantations lasted over 200 years) were in the University of North Carolina collection. But when I visited Natchitoches itself, I discovered multiple boxes of documents in the NPS regional headquarters there, including extensive store records, purchases, and payments to laborers and residents of the plantations in the early and mid-twentieth century. These laborers were almost all black or of African origins. These data remain essentially untapped and could provide vast opportunities for research on the lives and labors of black men and women in twentieth-century Natchitoches.

Observations at Sites

I made site observations at the sixty locales I visited in eight states (building on the site visits I had made for my previous book). I eventually choose three main sites in Natchitoches for more intensive observations and analysis. These are Oakland Plantation, Magnolia Plantation, and Melrose Plantation (Small 2009). I carried out more research on these sites than on the others, and many of the comments that follow are greatly influenced by this. My research involved multiple visits to the same site and interviews and discussions with management, staff, and other personnel, as well as discussions with people in the community. Where possible, I examined site files and documents. I took part in multiple tours, guided and unguided, with as many of the different tour guides at each site as was possible. I took hundreds of photographs (later used as an aide-memoire to help with my descriptions of the sites) and even took several mini-videos. Overall, this gave me a wide range of insights from a large number of people associated with each site. My goal was to gain exposure to the common elements of tours and to variations across tours. I wanted to know what issues were frequently or always discussed and what questions may have arisen contingently. I also wanted to identify the messages, direct and indirect, communicated in the tours. And I wanted to know what issues were marginalized, anaesthetized, or obliterated.

One important goal of site observations was to examine the layout of the site overall. Did it have slave cabins, even if they were not mentioned online or in the promotional literature? Where are the various buildings, especially those inhabited by elite Whites and enslaved Blacks, and what does the layout convey about their importance to contemporary representations of slavery and slave cabins? Are the cabins marginal or central to the main site? Are they close to it, or far from it? Are they well sign-posted? What kind of information—texts and images—are provided about the slave cabins and their residents? How does this information compare with the information about elite Whites?

If sites mentioned Blacks at all, most just listed the number of enslaved persons, and occasionally the name of a skilled person or "faithful slave" (e.g., Alexander Stephens's Plantation in Georgia). There were exceptions, which were all the more notable for being so. Boone Hall, South Carolina, provides significant details on the lives and culture of enslaved people; the Booker

T. Washington National Monument in Virginia is one of a tiny number of plantation sites dedicated almost exclusively to a black man; and Frogmore Plantation in Louisiana has slave cabins displayed as the main component of the tour and does not include a visit to the main house. This was a striking contrast with other sites.

I did not use audio or video record tour guide presentations. I felt this would be too intrusive and would disrupt the natural flow of the tours. But I made extensive written notes and took photographs. This did not usually attract attention or disrupt anyone—because often teachers and/or school children on tours were also taking notes. Everyone was taking photos all the time. On less than a handful of occasions, I was asked what I was doing (by a visitor because guides always knew ahead of time that I was a researcher) and I indicated I was a researcher. It was mainly unproblematic. After tours finished, I often dictated summaries into my digital audio-recorder.

Texts and Visual Images

There are numerous kinds of texts and images at the sites; on websites, in promotional literature such as leaflets and booklets, placards, and panels; and in the many buildings and pathways at the sites themselves. Most sites provide maps and guides, with text, drawings, and images, and there are posters, paintings, and portraits. Panels outside and inside buildings have detailed descriptive information about plantation residents. My main goal was to identify the nature and range of texts and images of slavery at sites, especially in the cabins. What pictures, portraits, drawings, photos, and other images of people, places existed and where were they located? Which texts and/or images were highlighted in guided tours? I was also interested in variations across sites.

The basic question was whether the sites displayed images of black men and women, in a range of contexts, and whether they were varied or limited in scope. In conjunction with textual information, this helped me assess how important a value was placed on telling the stories of black people's lives. I also wanted to figure out what messages these images conveyed about slavery and about Blacks, though this was more difficult. How do we know what the message is? And how do we know what message visitors take away? But compare, for example, Hofwyl-Broadfield, Georgia, which has virtually no images, or mention of Blacks and where the slave cabin doubles as the restrooms; with Boone Hall, South Carolina, which provides considerable texts and images about Blacks. It's clear that very different messages are given to at these sites.

I had significant experience in analyzing discourses and images of race in my previous research, for example, working with the Transatlantic Slavery Gallery in Liverpool, England, and in the U.S. South at the end of the 1990s

(Small 1994, 1997). I have been influenced in this work by research in Europe (Hall 1997; van Dijk 1991, 1993, 2002). I continued to study images in websites and promotional literature throughout the early 2000s. This meant examining concrete images of Blacks, especially gendered images, at a range of sites. Increasingly interesting to me were the ways in which racialized messages are conveyed, without explicit mention of race. One technique for doing this involves code words, for example, using the word "servant" or "worker" to mean an enslaved person (see also Omi & Winant 1986). Another is universalism, where, for example, site docents might say "Everyone was welcome to stay at the house," but what they actually meant was only white people were welcome.

During site visits, I recorded every image I observed—paintings, portraits, drawings, signs, and what was on walls inside and outside buildings—and took multiple photographs (thank goodness for digital cameras—and don't forget the batteries). I paid particular attention to the slave cabins: what images, photos, and drawings were inside and outside of them. Again, my main goal was to identify and assess the number and range of images. I was also fascinated by whether images and texts personalized and humanized black people by providing, for example, names, biographies, beliefs, hopes, aspirations, and dreams. As with my previous research, I found this kind of information was invariably provided for elite Whites in the main houses, even down to details about favorite colors—and infrequently for Blacks.

(Unstructured) Interviews

I planned a series of unstructured interviews with management and staff at the sites—including site managers, docents and tour guides, volunteers, and boards of advisors or management committees. I also planned interviews (or conversations) with experts in the field—academics, independent scholars, and other writers working for agencies such as the NPS. I expected them to provide key information on big issues, including debates around options for the goals and organization of the sites; to fill in the gaps, especially when documents were silent; to provide information that only they knew about (e.g., origins of docent scripts); and to direct me to other sources of information. This involved identifying relevant people to interview, and submitting by proposal to the Committee for the Protection of Human Subjects. My view is that an hour with an expert can save you several weeks of independent (and uninformed) research—especially at the start of your research. So I emailed, telephoned, and wrote to many people, and sought out others at conferences, seminars, and workshops. It was a highly productive tactic.

In preparing for the interviews, I contacted as many senior people as possible ahead of time and before I visited sites. Contacting them ahead of time was designed to alert them to my visit, to give me an idea of what kinds of information they had at hand, and get them thinking about information that they might be able to share. I usually did not contact staff below management (e.g., docents) until I got to the sites, because contacting them was less practical (e.g., I did not have access to their names, and many are volunteers). I also wanted an impression of whether the management of the site would welcome the research and be responsive or not. Much of this was clearly based on initial impressions that I had, and I did not come to any firm conclusions upon initial contact. That is, when they seemed uncooperative or even hostile, I did not rule them out—not only because it could have been a bad moment, but because each site has multiple staff and people to whom I could talk.

When I got to sites, I informed site personnel of my research goals and issues. I usually did not give a great deal of information about the exact goals of my project—partly because I felt it was not wanted and partly so as not to increase the risk of researcher effect—for example, by discussing controversial issues (see discussion below). After I had made initial contacts, my plan was to carry out detailed interviews. This required respondents to fill out human subjects reports. Overall, most people did this. One or two refused. This is common. The forms can be intimidating, and some potential respondents interpret the forms to mean they are signing all their rights away. At this point, one does the best one can. I believe that interviews should come after you have collected detailed information and details from many other sources. This will help you identify key issues and questions and frame the questions in a way most likely to elicit complete responses.

I did not plan or do any interviews with audiences. This would have required far more resources than I had and entailed a more complicated methodology. Interviews with visitors would most certainly have produced useful information—on their experiences, on what the sites and images meant to them, why they visited, and what they got from the visit. Other scholars have done interviews of this kind and have raised important issues and provided key insights (Horton & Horton 2006). However, interviews were not an indispensable component of my research—my goal was not to explore how visitors responded to the sites, but to explore the social construction of the sites, the relative importance attached to slave cabins by the people who put the sites together, and the nature and range of information at the sites dedicated to slavery and slave cabins, especially as compared with elite white plantation residents.

I did not do many formal interviews until the research was well under way. I met many scholars, librarians, and archivists and had fascinating discussions with them. But significant delay in formal interviewing occurred mainly because of some health issues that I had during the research process. And at the time of writing this, I'm still conducting interviews. Overall, they have proceeded well, and I have experienced no major problems.

Dig Deeper, Press Harder

Researching slave cabins (especially where there is far greater valorization of elite mansions) reminded me once again that when studying African American history and culture, the researcher often has to dig deeper and press harder to get the necessary data. Vastly more attention in the available historical documents is devoted to the lives of elite Whites, including their mansions and material goods. There are far more photographs of elite Whites than of Blacks. While reading diaries and memoirs by Whites, I occasionally stumbled on mention of slave cabins or saw black people standing in the background of photographs. With one or two exceptions, it is clear that the people who organize and promote the sites expect that the vast majority of visitors are coming to visit the homes of the elite Whites. And many of these staff, with some notable exceptions, seem to think this is appropriate. As mentioned above, some plantation museums websites simply did not mention the cabins at all. I had to dig deeper and press harder to uncover information on slave cabins and I actually went to many sites even if advance information failed to mention cabins.

Another obstacle concerns the reliability and credibility of documents and secondary publications. First, the vast majority of documents about slavery that currently exist were produced by white people for white people (with significant class and gender bias). This has been the basis of much debate, and much has been written about locating and interpreting sources of data and insight left by black people, especially the "slave narratives" (see, e.g., Camp 2004; Glymph 2008).

Also, significant contemporary writing about the history of some of the sites is being produced by the descendants of master-enslavers and mistress-enslavers and their families (Haynie 2002; Hunter 2005). If there is substantial alternative writings this is not a major problem, but where there are few other studies, especially in regions and districts (like Natchitoches) that have not commanded significant scholarly attention, it can be especially problematic. Prima facie, this raises issues of emphasis, framing, and possibly of distortion and bias. Overall, my impression is that many of these writers set out to document and celebrate their families as important and valuable contributors to southern society and culture. There was a marked tendency to speak favorably of the families and to avoid unpleasant or critical issues, especially issues of brutality and violence. There was little condemnation of the system of slavery per se. Bearing this in mind, I believe that we need to scrutinize such accounts very closely.

Research on slave cabins highlights issues that are bound to become more significant in the near future for research on race and ethnic relations. This is because of broad changes in U.S. society as well as changes at plantation museum sites. The broad patterns of the former are directly shaping the institutional dynamics of the latter. So, given the transformations in public expressions of racism, the changing strategies of racialized discrimination, and the hyperbole in the political and public realm about the arrival of a so-called post-racial America following the election of Barack Obama as president, explicit racist enmity is no longer expressed in the forthright ways that it was in the past. It is less visible now, but no less virulent (Brown et al. 2003). And given the tendency to circumlocution, prevarication, and obfuscation—at plantation museum sites, in media, and in political discourse—what is not said will often be as compelling in its implications as what is said. At many plantation museum sites, waxing lyrical about elite white lifestyles frequently highlights the deep silences about black humanity. A single unframed drawing of a black person stands out strikingly when it is surrounded by lush and vivid family portraits in gold-colored frames of elite Whites. We will need to identify and deploy appropriate methods and tactics for documenting such practices, in texts and images, from our colleagues in cultural studies.

For my project, it was crucial to make sustained efforts to identify, document, and incorporate black voices and visions. By black voices, I mean documents that provide black testimony like slave narratives, biographies and memoirs, court transcripts, folktales, and songs (Patterson 2005; Starling 1988). By black visions, I mean creative expressions in material culture, such as art and sculpture. And I mean archaeology. All of these offer invaluable evidence of black people's expressed identities, issues, concerns, and aspirations (Collins 2002). There was much evidence and information on slave cabins revealed in archaeological studies of individual sites as well as profound insights in scholarly writing. Archaeology scholars greatly helped interpret this evidence (Franklin & McKee 2004; Singleton 1991; Wilkie 2000).

For example, at the several sites where I conducted the majority of my research—Oakland Plantation, Magnolia Plantation, and Melrose Plantation, in Natchitoches—I found more than ten archeological studies that had been carried out at the sites, including several dedicated exclusively to the "slave and tenant quarters" (see, e.g., Brown 2006; Miller & Wood 2000). These studies had information on the changing construction, design, structure of the cabins, including consideration of African influences, and offered insights into human agency, cultural practice, and resistance by the cabin residents.

It was not just that such studies supplemented documentary sources, they provided fundamental challenges to evidence from other sources. For example, while tour guides and interpreters at most sites today overwhelmingly represent master-enslavers and their families as good, decent, and honorable people and the enslaved population as largely happy, well fed, and faithful, archeological studies provide convincing evidence of dissatisfaction, hunger, resistance, and sabotage. Archeological studies exist for increasing numbers of sites across the South.

Similar evidence and insights are revealed in art. For example, at Melrose Plantation in Louisiana, one must search for detailed insights into the lives of black people. The art and life of Clementine Hunter, primitive artist of national and international acclaim, can provide a necessary corrective (Lyons 1998; Wilson 1990). But only if one reads between the lines, because Hunter's art on display at the plantation is narrowly interpreted. Born in Natchitoches in the 1890s and raised there her entire life, she worked for the first fifty odd years picking cotton in the fields, cleaning, and cooking in the main house. Her remarkable talent led to the production of several thousand paintings and to national and international acclaim.

At the site, Clementine Hunter is discussed in detail and referred to as an "exceptional black," in stark contrast to the lack of attention given to the majority of Blacks at the plantation. This attention is highly individualized and none of it locates her in the context of a black woman working in Jim Crow America. But a different set of messages is conveyed in her art, where we see family, culture, work, leisure, and pleasure as well as strong and independent black women in the foreground. There are also critical portrayals of the white power hierarchy on the plantation; white people, if they appear in her art at all, are in the background. In her biography and interviews, we find evidence of her subordinate status on the plantation and hear her voice as a black woman who grew up deep in the belly of rural Jim Crow. Other analysts have offered more compelling accounts of the value of art and sculpture, especially in documenting black women's lives, and I urge you to consult them (Collins 1991; Patterson 2005). Historical architecture also provides key insights (Vlach 1993).

Researcher Effect

I did not carry out a typical ethnography—with long-term immersion in a community—but I was present at some of the sites on multiple occasions, over several years, took part in many guided tours with groups of visitors, often with the same tour guide, and was also frequently present at sites for long periods in unstructured ways. Staff saw me on multiple occasions and knew that I was doing research; after all, this was required by the Committee for the Protection of Human Subjects, and I was more than happy to inform them ahead of time of my research plans. In this respect, my research has some resemblance to ethnography.

Researcher effect has been the subject of much discussion in the literature, including chapters in this book (Bulmer & Solomos 2004; Stanfield & Dennis 1993). The main question is how to minimize the impact of the researcher on the people being studied so as to get the most extensive, accurate, and reliable data. This is especially significant in a context in which a researcher of color is working with white respondents and the topic is contro-versial. Potentially greater problems can arise when the researcher is a woman (especially a woman of color) conducting research on men (especially white men). Some of these issues applied to this research. The researcher needs the cooperation of site workers and management, so the priority is to maintain cordial relations to facilitate cooperation. This means avoiding issues that might lead to feelings of unease or discomfort.

This is not so simple. What do you do if staff say something with which you fundamentally disagree (e.g., that slaves were happy, or that slave-masters were good people)? What if they use language that you find offensive (like "mammy")? What if they state facts confidently that you know to be entirely incorrect? And what if the staff ask you for advice? And they do ask for advice all the time—they ask if their site is doing a good job, how it could improve; and they ask for comparisons with other sites that are doing it better. On every occasion, it is possible that you might cause discomfort or unease. There are no easy answers to these questions. But there are many insights to be gained from reading studies that have been done, problems encountered, and prob-lems overcome (as described, e.g., in several other chapters in this book). The best I can say is that you must try to avoid offence or controversy.

I strongly suspect that there was researcher effect in my research, though I can't be sure how extensive it was. I come to this conclusion from my an-alysis of the literature, from my own extensive ethnographic work and inter-views, and from concrete experiences during the research process. To begin with, it is well established that greater insights are achieved when the race and gender of the researcher and the subjects are the same, especially where the topic concerns race or gender inequality or discrimination. At the sites I researched, the vast majority of staff and volunteers are white; a majority of them are southern; and large numbers of them are from the older generation—over sixty years old (I was a younger black man conducting research on over-whelmingly white subjects). All the docents knew I was doing research while on their tours, and I suspect that it likely affected their presentations. My core-searcher on the previous study found that she was addressed in different ways than I was because she was white, northern, and female (Eichstedt & Small 2002). During my research, some staff expressed surprise and amazement that I wanted to look at the cabins not the mansions. It simply did not make sense to them, and several urged me to visit the mansions rather than the cabins. If they pushed me on the issue and I made it clear that I valued the slave cabins more than the mansions, some became indignant.

Almost none of the white staff or docents volunteered detailed stories of the textured lives of the enslaved or of black people. Some offered brief details of the lives of one or two favored enslaved persons (so-called faithful slaves) or perfunctory stories of the lives of enslaved. Almost none described slavery as involving widespread exploitation, violence, or brutality. I did not judge it appropriate to ask direct questions about such issues because I felt this would adversely impact my observations. On its own, the failure to raise such issues may not be considered significant. But my research experience suggests otherwise. For example, it was in stark contrast to the views and options expressed by staff at the black sites, where exploitation and violence were frequently commented on, represented in texts and images, and words such as "brutality," and "rape" were commonly used. Such words were almost never used at the plantation museum sites I visited for this current project. In our 2002 book, Jennifer Eichstedt and I argued that these sites begin from very different premises and assumptions, and it's clear from my ongoing research that this continues to be the case (Eichsted & Small 2002:233).

It is difficult to know the full extent or impact of researcher effect. The vast majority of my respondents were overwhelmingly polite and responsive to the questions that I asked. No one openly refused to respond to my questions or to give me documents that I requested. Many people volunteered additional information. As a black British man with an English accent, I was often welcomed in ways that may not have been extended to an African American (e.g., site staff frequently expressed admiration for the English, for English culture, and English architecture). I am satisfied that the use of multiple methods helped offset some of the likely researcher effects. Information from site staff, while important, was just one source of data, and tour presentations were just one part of my work.

CONCLUSION

For the research described here, I have sought to identify, document, and evaluate representations of slavery and twenty-first-century antebellum slave cabins at contemporary plantation museum sites in the U.S. South. Hundreds of sites exist in a tourist network infrastructure that is highly developed, extensive in scope, and intricately interconnected. The sites convey detailed information, ideas, and interpretations of the nature and extent of slavery and its legacy in the United States and tell fascinating stories about individuals, families, and communities. They convey powerful messages about American values, institutions, and historic events. And they shape, frame, and influence how contemporary visitors to the sites understand U.S. slavery and its legacy. These sites attract millions of national and international visitors each year.

The majority of these sites deploy a series of tactics to symbolically denigrate, marginalize, or trivialize slavery and its legacies. Their representation and treatment of twenty-first-century antebellum slave cabins reveals these tactics in striking ways because these cabins, when compared with mansions, are neglected, distorted, or simply left out of accounts (Eichstedt & Small 2002; Small 2009). Research by other scholars reveals that despite some significant if uneven improvements, significant problems remain (Mooney 2004; Pustz 2010).

The role of contemporary plantations sites in the heritage tourism industry is increasingly capturing the attention of analysts who are engaged in a number of research projects and who are using a wide range of methods. Researching the African American experience in the past at these sites remains difficult, but the obstacles are not insurmountable.

As I prepared to do this research, it was clear to me that I would need to use multiple methods to do it. In this chapter, I have tried to persuade you that multiple research methods for collecting evidence can offer unique advantages that offset the disadvantages of any one method. The problem that confronted me at every stage was how to confront *the past in the present*? How to confront the past in terms of how many cabins existed and what were the experiences of their inhabitants? How to confront the present in terms of the organization, exhibits, and displays about such cabins at plantation sites today? And how to apprehend the ways in which the past was represented at the sites today?

A focus on twenty-first-century antebellum slave cabins reveals some of the innovative methods that can be used and some of the rich data that can be found for those seeking to document the black experience. It brings our attention to important sources, data, and methods for describing black lives and culture; it provides opportunities to identify, challenge, and overthrow old theories; and it demonstrates how established methodological dominance can be challenged. It can open up new vistas. And once again, we are reminded that there are still significant amounts of evidence that remain largely untapped. I have found that some of the most promising opportunities arise from the work being done by archeologists and other analysts of material culture. I believe that researchers must still dig deeper and press harder to attain rich insights. In so doing, they are far more likely to access the multiple sources of data on black voices and visions.

Acknowledgments

I'd like to thank several people who provided valuable feedback on this chapter, including Mark Christian, Trica Keaton, Althea Legal-Miller, Angela Lintz, Alexis Martin, and Kwame Nimako.

Note

1. See, for example, the Kingsley Plantation in Jacksonville, Florida, the Oakland Plantation in Natchitoches, Louisiana, or the Booker T. Washington National Monument in Franklin County, Virginia.

REFERENCES

Alderman, D. H., & Modlin, E. A. J. (2008). (In)visibility of the enslaved within online plantation tourism marketing: A textual analysis of North Carolina websites. *Journal of Travel & Tourism Marketing, 2*, 265–281.

Blight, D. (2001). *Race and reunion: The Civil War in American memory.* Cambridge, MA: The Belknap Press of Harvard University Press.

Brown, K. L. (2006). *A preliminary report on the 2006 excavations in the Quarters Community of the Magnolia Plantations, Cane River Creole National Historical Park, Natchitoches Parish, Louisiana.* Houston, TX: University of Houston Press.

Brown, M. K., Carnoy, M., Currie, E., Duster, T., Oppenheimer, D. B., Shultz, M. M., & Wellman, D. (2003). *Whitewashing race: The myth of a color-blind society.* Berkeley: University of California Press.

Brundage, W. F. (2005). *The southern past: A clash of race and memory.* Cambridge, MA: The Belknap Press of Harvard University Press.

Bulmer, M., & Solomos, J. (Eds.). (2004). *Researching race and racism.* London: Routledge.

Camp, S. M. H. (2004). *Closer to freedom: Enslaved women & everyday resistance in the plantation South.* Chapel Hill: University of North Carolina Press.

Collins, L. G. (2002). *The art of history: African American women artists engage the past.* Rutgers, NJ: Rutgers University Press.

Collins, P. H. (1991). *Black feminist thought: Knowledge, consciousness, and the politics of empowerment.* London: Routledge.

Davis, P. (2008). Ripping the veil: Collective memory and black southern identity. Ph.D. dissertation, University of California, San Diego.

Eichstedt, J. L., & Small, S. (2002). *Representations of slavery: Race, ideology and southern plantations museums.* Washington, DC: Smithsonian Institution Press.

Franklin, M., & McKee, L. (2004). African Diaspora archaeologies: Present insights and expanding discourses. *Historical Archaeology, 38*, 1–9.

Glymph, T. (2008). *Out of the house of bondage: The transformation of the plantation household.* Cambridge: Cambridge University Press.

Hall, S. (1997). *Representation: Cultural representations and signifying practices.* London: Sage.

Harrison, A. Y. (2008). Reconstructing Somerset Place: Slavery, memory and historical consciousness. Ph.D. dissertation, Duke University.

Haynie, S. P. (2002). *Legends of Oakland Plantation.* Shreveport, LA: LaPressCo Printing.

Horton, J., & Horton, L. (Eds.). (2006). *Slavery and public memory: The tough stuff of American memory.* New York: New Press.

Hunter, H. A. (2005). *Magnolia Plantation: A family farm.* Natchitoches, LA: Northwestern State University Press.

Jackson, A. (2004). African communities in southeast coastal plantation spaces in America. Ph.D. dissertation, University of Florida.

Lyons, M. E. (1998). *Talking with Tebé: Clementine Hunter, memory artist*. Boston: Houghton Mifflin.

Miller, C. E., & Wood, S. E. (2000). *Oakland Plantation: A comprehensive subsurface investigation*. Tallahassee, FL: Southeast Archeological Center, National Park Service.

Mooney, B. B. (2004). Looking for history's huts. *Winthur Portfolio, 29*, 43–70.

Omi, M., & Winant, H. (1986). *Racial formation in the United States, from the 1960s–1980s*. London: Routledge.

Patterson, T. (2005). *Zora Neale Hurston and a history of southern life*. Philadelphia: Temple University Press.

Pustz, J. (2010). *Voices from the back stairs: Interpreting servants' lives at historical house museums*. Dekalb: Northern Illinois University Press.

Singleton, T. A. (1991). The archaeology of slave life. In E. D. C. Campbell & K. S. Rice (Eds.), *Before freedom came: African-American life in the antebellum South* (pp. 155–191). Charlottesville: University Press of Virginia.

Small, S. (1983a). *Police and people in London. II A group of young black people* (No. 619). London: Policy Studies Institute Report.

Small, S. (1983b). Black youth in England: Ethnic identity in a white society. *Policy Studies, 4*, 35–49.

Small, S. (1989). Racial differentiation in the slave era: A comparative analysis of people of "mixed-race" in Jamaica and Georgia. Ph.D. dissertation, Berkeley: University of California..

Small, S. (1994). Concepts and terminology in representations of the Atlantic slave trade. *Museum Ethnographers Journal, 6*, 7–21.

Small, S. (1997). Contextualizing the black presence in British museums: Representations, resources and response. In E. H. Greenhill (Ed.), *Museums and multiculturalism in Britain* (pp. 50–66). Leicester, UK: Leicester University Press.

Small, S. (2002). Racisms and racialized hostility at the start of the new millennium. In D. T. Goldberg & J. Solomos (Eds.), *The Blackwell companion to race relations* (pp. 259–281). Malden, MA: Blackwell.

Small, S. (2004). Researching "mixed-race" experience under slavery. Concepts, methods and data. In M. Bulmer & J. Solomos (Eds.), *Researching race and racism* (pp. 78–91). London: Routledge.

Small, S. (2009). Twenty-first century antebellum slave cabins in Louisiana: Race, public history, and national identity. Presented at the annual conference of the Organization of American Historians, Seattle, March 26–29.

Stanfield, J. H., II, & Dennis, R. M. (Eds.). (1993). *Race and ethnicity in research methods*. Newbury Park, CA: Sage.

Starling, M. W. (1988). *The slave narrative: Its place in American history*. Washington, DC: Howard University Press.

Trouillot, M. (1995). *Silencing the past: Power and the production of history*. Boston: Beacon Press.

van Dijk, T. A. (1991). *Racism and the press*. London: Routledge.

van Dijk, T. A. (1993). *Elite discourses and racism*. Newbury Park, CA: Sage.

van Dijk, T. A. (2002). Discourse and racism. In D. T. Goldberg & J. Solomos (Eds.), *The Blackwell companion to race relations* (pp. 145–159). Malden, MA: Blackwell Publishing.

Vlach, J. M. (1993). *Back of the big house: The architecture of plantation slavery*. Chapel Hill: University of North Carolina Press.

West, P. (1999). *Domesticating history: The political origins of American's house museums*. Washington, DC: Smithsonian Institution Press.

Wilkie, L. A. (2000). *Creating freedom: Material culture and African American identity at Oakley Plantation, Louisiana 1840–1950*. Baton Rouge: Louisiana State University Press.

Wilson, J. L. (1990). *Clementine Hunter: American folk artist*. Gretna, LA: Pelican Publishing Company.

9   SMALL-SCALE QUANTITATIVE AND QUALITATIVE HISTORICAL STUDIES ON AFRICAN AMERICAN COMMUNITIES

Yvonne Walker

We are losing the opportunity to capture first-hand stories of African American history from the 1880s to early 1900s as those who heard these accounts grow older and pass on. Do you ever regret missing the opportunity to capture a first-hand account from a family or community member? Do you want to learn more about a particular thread of history, but realize the only connection is now deceased? In some instances, it is too late to capture stories that can help us make sense of our lives and those around us, but we still have many opportunities.

Among other things, social historians keep family accounts that capture crucial parts of the past and allow us to build stepping stones toward a better future. Research methods that weave first-hand stories with historical documentation enable legacies to be passed down from generation to generation. We must not let the traditions of storytelling die in communities. The ability to improve today's communities may be enhanced by capturing and applying the lessons learned by our ancestors. Indeed, being faithful keepers of their lives will not only help preserve what made us a great nation, it will also help guide the next generation.

To better understand and solve some of today's dilemmas, it is imperative to navigate correctly, given the narrowing time constraints to capture these historical studies of African American communities. This quest requires strategically implementing various research methods that will be highlighted in this chapter.

In the first section, I delve into my own research as it relates to methods used to study small rural communities. In the second portion, I focus on three methodologies for studying rural communities and provide examples from various historical researchers who utilized each research method. The description of each of the methodologies will conclude with reflections on their strengths and weaknesses. I hope that this chapter will further encourage you to be a keeper of historical accounts and help recognize the contributions of those once ignored. Although I use the research subject of the African American community in the South, these methods span the human experience in gathering the historical stories that keep the lives of all our ancestors alive.

To depict some strategies of how to conduct research for community and family historical accounts, I will use my research topic to describe the methodologies applied to research stories that depict the legacy of some African American males born between 1850 and 1900. These men developed communities by establishing churches, schools, financial institutions, farms, and rudimentary insurance practices for burial, along with other types of trades that sustained not only their own families but supported others in the community.

Support systems were developed by heroes through the Jim Crow era, one of the most vulnerable periods for southern Blacks. This era was designed to cripple the forward mobility of Africans Americans, thus preventing equal status within the political, social, economic, and educational spheres in the United States. These men were the initial generation of free African Americans impacted by the abolishment of slavery and faced a host of unimaginable challenges along with little, if any, access to social services or government resources. In the midst of these struggles, they developed their own resources and they left legacies. How did these visionaries move past such great opposition? Was it personality, leadership traits, innate skills, mentorship, a rich father, being mixed racially, or some other factor(s) that enabled them to accomplish so much in their lifetime? What can we learn from their lives that will make our own journey more productive and easier?

The answers to these questions are certainly important, especially given the current plight of many young African American males. Their destiny is obscured by numerous obstacles. While today's roadblocks are different from those of the past, the generations can still be linked by determining if there are skill sets and behavior traits that transcend time and will allow young men to achieve their visions and leave a culture that motivates and directs their families and communities.

In analyzing and determining some former successful leaders' traits, I used two qualitative methods: comparative history and hermeneutics layered with quantitative empirical analysis, using a 360-degree questionnaire to gather survey data. My goal is to provide both qualitative and quantitative analyses to explore what style of leadership they predominantly used to accomplish their goals.

Background: African American Transformational/ Transactional Leadership during Antebellum

The period following emancipation was one of tremendous struggle for African Americans; despite those struggles, leaders in African American communities thrived. The concept of transformational leadership was not formulated as a concept until Burns (1978) and Bass (1985) provided evidence that leaders can transform followers to engage in a collective vision based on values. After this vision is established, followers embody the values and move forward. My study focused on former generations to determine whether their leadership skills demonstrated the paradigms of transformation/transactional leadership and whether these skills can be transferred to others.

A transactional leader takes the initiative in making contact with others to exchange something valued. According to MacGregor Burns, "leaders approach followers with an eye toward exchanging." In contrast, transformational leadership is based on more than the compliance of followers; it involves shifts in the beliefs, needs, and values of followers. The result of transforming leadership is a relationship of mutual stimulation and elevation that converts followers into leaders and may convert leaders into moral agents (Burns 1978:4).

Bass (1996) notes: Transformational leaders inspire greater accomplishment in their followers than they would have achieved without the skills set of this type of leadership. Transformational leaders are charismatic; they inspire and motivate and stimulate the intellect by providing individual attention to the needs of followers. Transactional leadership is described as being dependent on using rewards or discipline to motivate followers (Bass 1996). Bass further asserts that there is a connection between the transformational and transactional leadership.

Providing a setting for these leaders to emerge will require a careful review of key systems and their constraints on African Americans within political, educational, economic, social, and religious spheres, especially within the Jim Crow South. The next section of this chapter provides an overview of culture of inquiry to briefly describe these systems. The following sections will review research methodologies applicable to this research topic.

Culture of Inquiry

Historical inquiry is used to identify patterns relating to social, political, religious, and economic factors during the period in question for African Americans or any other group within the context of the specified research topic. It is important for the researcher to respect other researchers' discoveries within the historical reference area and to acknowledge their contributions.

An exemplar of such inquiry was Gunnar Myrdal (1972), who provided a macro-analysis of the plight of an entire race of people. He focused on historical frameworks to identify prevailing schools of thought, social movements, and political constraints and freedoms that governed African Americans. He addressed how schools of thought emerged, provided the context to account for the emergence of thought process, and offered insight on behaviors. Myrdal's objective to provide a comprehensive study of African Americans is a good example of historical inquiry. Myrdal researched race, economics, migration, education, and politics and analyzed social inequalities by comparing laws, class differences, white leadership, segregation, and many other factors (1972). His work uncovered conditions that had led to inequities influenced by Jim Crow laws and it delineated the injustices done, using the dominant culture to determine where injustices occurred.

On the micro-level, Harris (1958) compares Marx's theories on business enterprise with historical perspectives on capitalism. Additionally, he "came to regard Marx, Veblen, Sombart, Commons, and Pesch as representatives of patterns of thought which depart not only from the analytical methods of traditional economic theory but also from the principles of classical liberalism concerning the meaning of freedom and the political conditions under which it can best be realized" (1958:14). Harris's analysis of these theoretical economists' ideologies of reform during the nineteenth century provides a comparative historical analysis that fits the context of what constitutes the culture of inquiry, highlighted by Bentz and Shapiro (1998) as comparative historical inquiry and theoretical inquiry.

Comparative Historical Methodology

I used comparative historical methodology to determine the leadership organizational development efforts of the men who were the first emancipated leaders in the South. I strove to discover uniqueness in their actions in organizational and community development. This methodology allows for a theoretical prediction in the development of future leaders.

One of the weaknesses associated with using this approach topic is the limited amount of literature available that focuses on productive outcomes of black males. Instead of focusing on the contributions from African American men born between 1850 and 1900, much of the literature using the comparative historical approach focuses on the disparate and inequitable treatment of this group. My intention here is to highlight the positive attributes and outcomes created by African American male leaders of the era. Stories of successful African American males lift up not only the African American community but the whole nation, as was the case with the Civil Rights Acts of the 1960s.

Appreciative Inquiry

To counter this methodology's weak factor, appreciative inquiry is an effective tool to use as part of the data-gathering technique to identify some of the positive character traits in small community studies. According to Hammond (1996:20), appreciative inquiry assumes:

1. In every society, organization, or group, something works.
2. What we focus on becomes our reality.
3. Reality is created in the moment, and there are multiple realities.
4. The act of asking questions of an organization or group influences the group in some way.
5. People have more confidence and comfort to journey into the future (the unknown) when they carry forward parts of the past (the known).
6. If we carry parts of the past forward, it should be what was best.
7. It is important to value differences.
8. The language we use creates our reality.

AI focuses on what we do well. In contrast, the research methodologies used by many historians regarding the African American experience has often focused on the negative, which then becomes a perpetual lens for how a community or person is viewed. If Hammond is correct and "what we focus on becomes our reality," then some historical research helps perpetuate negative cycles within the African American community.

Since the comparative historical methodology concludes by providing a theoretical prediction for the future, AI is a complementary technique because it leads to "provocative propositions that are derived from stories that actually took place in the person's life" (Hammond 1996:39). The provocative statement can be used for sparking transformation. When we take what we know and use it to talk about what could be, we bridge the past to a future, which fulfills one of the aspects of comparative historical methodology by providing a theoretical prediction for the future of what worked that is still relevant for today. "Because we derive the future from reality, we know it can happen" (Hammond 1996:46). By reframing the answers to questions into the present tense, the current generation can help others know what to do and how to grow toward a stated ideal (Hammond 1996). In sum, using AI as a framework furthers the positive outcomes manifested under harsh conditions.

Archival Research

Archival research complements comparative historical inquiry and theoretical inquiry. Historical archives can be the object of the study, and historical investigation techniques and strategies for studying archives can be a method of inquiry. Using this method, sociologists can obtain vital historical data that were only previously claimed by historians. It is important to have the skills as outlined in *Archival Strategies and Techniques* by Michael Hill (1993) to properly represent the contents of archives without bias. Treasures are hidden within documents, and thoughtful excavation coupled with careful analysis can inform research in numerous disciplines, including politics.

For instance, the dissertation work developed by Craig Simpson (1973) on politics during 1850–1861 focused on Henry A. Wise, a brigadier general in the Confederate Army, a Virginia congressman, a farmer, and a family man. To get his information, Simpson analyzed Wise's personal papers, family records, and his Civil War minutes and other books donated to the National Archives (Simpson 1973:3). Simpson was given access and permission to quote these documents from a relative of Wise.

Oral History In-Depth Interviews

Oral history in-depth interviews record a personal testimony being taped, hand-written by the interviewer, or somehow transcribed for research. Historical scholars are increasingly using oral history to obtain information through open-ended qualitative interviews. In *Doing Oral History*, Donald Ritchie (2003:20) states that: "An oral history interview generally consists of a well-prepared interviewer questioning an interviewee and recording their exchange in audio or video format. Oral traditions are stories that societies have passed along in spoken form from generation to generation. The in-depth or long interview is a highly efficient type of interview method that is streamlined yet can be broken down into incremental interviews conducted over a period of a few days for at least three hours" (McCracken 1988).

Valerie Yow (2005:2), in *Recording Oral History*, describes the concept of "shared authority" as a shift that has occurred in oral history practices wherein both the narrator and interviewer hold power instead of the researcher being the dominant scholar and where the narrator is respected as an equal participant in sharing knowledge.

The use of memory in recording history goes as far back as the fifth century BC. After World War II, oral history interviews were transcribed on tape, and by 1965 eighty-nine oral history projects were being carried out in the United States (Yow 2005). A key differentiation between oral historians and social scientists is that "historians tend to isolate interviewees from their environment and to put them in a quiet place where they will not be interrupted during the interview, whereas in other disciplines subjects are examined in their natural setting" (Ritchie 2003:107).

Oral history projects vary and include community studies, family studies, historic events (war, tragedies), and others. Public history can be conducted by scholars or by local citizens and is defined by its audience (Yow 2005). Yow specifies that:

> Local history, once slightly denigrated by academicians, is now valued because it inevitably deals with transformation. Studies of communities, focused as they are on a particular group in a particular place, offer the great advantage of allowing us to see in detail how economic and social pressures common to a whole region affect people on a local level. (p. 189)

An example of a community study that combines oral history and ethnography with analytical methodology is the *Philadelphia Negro* by W. E. B. Du Bois. The University of Pennsylvania hired Du Bois as a researcher in 1896 to provide a sociological study on the black people of Philadelphia (Du Bois 1973):

> [Dr. Du Bois] devoted his time to systematic field-work among the Negroes, especially in the Seventh Ward, attending their meetings, their churches, their business, social and political gatherings, visiting their schools and institutions, and, most important of all, conducting a house-to-house visitation in their families, through which he came in personal contact with over ten thousand Negro inhabitants of the city. (p. 7)

House-to-house interviews, general observations, and statistical methodology were applied to analyze crime, organizations, political activity, etc. (Du Bois 1973). Du Bois utilized a combination of quantitative and qualitative methods, using an ethnography approach for general observation, with surveys combined with in-depth interviews as qualitative methods.

Yow (2005:190) suggests the strategy for oral history should be "more of a shared experience than the traditional approach to historical research, where the source is primarily written documents." Indeed, I am interested in using both of these methodologies, but for a different category of oral history: family oral history.

Beginning a Family History

A literature review is a key step in finding information; it is done using books, newspapers, censuses, published records, photographs, and other resources. In the case of ethnic community study, Yow (2005) asserts that building trust within the community is a necessary foundation. The researcher's initial conversations with people in the community will help craft the questions in the interview guide (Yow 2005). As the interviews continue, researchers gain insights regarding other questions to ask. Although the interviews focus on individual insight, the researcher conducting this study for a community considers the individual reflections in the broader context of the community (Yow 2005). One of the steps in conducting this type of research is looking for patterns and reading other research to compare findings (Yow 2005).

I was delighted that my research purpose was aligned with Yow's (2005) philosophy of purpose by presenting my family's past in a way that the community or recipient of the information gains a present notion or tangible sense of meaning. Once the collection is gathered, look for patterns such as repeated stories and the presence of inferred meanings that may reflect shared values and attitudes within the community. Yow (2005:209) reminds the researcher to be diligent in determining whose point of view is represented and others that should be included. It is important to analyze perception differences in similar stories to gauge whether a variety of social classes are adequately represented and if those classes vary in their perceptions of history. The researcher must stay neutral, be prepared to guide the conversation, and remain flexible enough to allow topics that are unexpected to evolve.

One unique challenge of analyzing transcriptions of long oral history interviews is having a clear purpose and a thoughtful interview guide. Accuracy in reporting the interview is extremely important since one of the differences between quantitative and qualitative analysis is the ability to duplicate information. In an interview, the same question asked to a number of individuals will most often have different answers. As in most quantitative studies, the reliability of accuracy falls on the researcher rather than a questionnaire. The challenge is gathering data that truly match the research question. The data should augment the literature review as well as provide interpretations of interview content that are coherent and aligned with the research question.

Challenges with Family Research

Family research poses great rewards and its own challenges. Families may be hesitant to reveal unfavorable information about the subject(s). Further, conflicts in stories from participants can develop into a challenging situation when a neutral interviewer may be construed as choosing sides. Family ties and friendships may create unusual and difficult circumstances for researchers. I had not imagined such considerations until my own research and study of family historical writings revealed well-kept secrets that explained the embarrassing outcomes of slavery and missing pieces of the family puzzle. The truth may be perceived as permanently tainting the image of the family legacy. I designed an approach for this aspect of my research and considered the implications for family members whose stories would no longer be a secret. Circumstances in my family allowed me to weigh the impact of this kind of research on other families. Researchers wield great power; if the power is not handled delicately and thoughtfully, it may have devastating permanent results.

Other challenges include variations of memory for the same event. According to Yow (2005), the key to overcoming this dilemma is to not show partiality in recording the versions. At times, individuals may request that sensitive information be removed. As a researcher, one should find an alternative to deleting material—perhaps a compromise that certain information would be removed from some manuscripts but not the original, or that information can be disclosed upon a family member's death.

I would have overlooked the value of family folklore if it had not been for Yow's (2005) overview. Folklore can be a challenge since these stories are deeply embedded into the family's fabric. At times, there are kernels of truth that can be corroborated, and it is the researcher's duty to verify fact from fiction. Also, the folklore can have an interpretation for expressed family values. These factors make listening to folklore important, but the researcher must determine what the folklore is intended to convey and why—the fact buried within the story. Whatever the reason, the folklore may reveal an aspect of the family dynamic worthy of a historical account.

Benefits of Family Oral History

One key benefit of family oral history is the automatic level of trust typically present between interviewer and family narrator. Similarly, narrators are often more forgiving of a beginner's interviewing mistakes. Familiarity facilitates smooth initial interviews, and family members might disclose more to another family member than to a stranger, allowing for richer contexts for interpretation of facts. A family member researcher is more apt to gain personal insight from the historic contexts of the family exchanges. If managed well, oral family history can deepen family ties.

Suggested Techniques for Capturing Family Histories

One approach to stimulate memory is to have the family member bring artifacts, photographs, quilts, artifacts, Bibles, personal collections, family recipes, and the like related to the interview topic. This brings the family history to life, with the researcher learning through the artifacts (Yow 2005). Yow also expounds on ways to expand the use of photographs by asking questions about the subjects' positions or the clothing they were wearing: Was it their Sunday best? What did they want to project in using the photo location—Was it for posterity or image? What's not in the picture?

Using open-ended questions and gentle nudges toward difficult subject matter by asking "Why is that?" or something like that helps continue the dialog. One should be willing to deviate from the prepared questionnaire and adapt to the direction the narrator's story unfolds. Through careful questioning, researchers can use the interests of the narrator to determine further areas for research.

Ritchie (2003:232) suggests that interviewers "familiarize themselves with some of the history of the larger events, perhaps thoroughly reading basic history textbooks; such preparation generates questions to ask and frames the interviewee's story against a larger backdrop."

Yow (2005) recommends that the scope be appropriately broadened. For example, the researcher can ask interviewers for names of people in the neighborhood who knew the family. This provides a lens that is outside the family circle. I appreciated the fact that the quantitative aspects of this study can include a 360-degree survey wherein neighbors could participate in both in-depth interviews for qualitative data and perspective through the use of quantitative measures.

Storytelling

Connecting historical events through storytelling requires skill in extracting, interpreting, and compiling events to depict a time period or perhaps family dynamics. The interviewer often must get details about their subject from brief glimpses within the narrator's depiction. One must investigate for accuracy and balance one's role as a social scientist with the role of family member. Striving to be nonbiased during the interview takes a tremendous amount of self-control, introspection, and suspension of perceptions. Without this introspection, even the line of questioning can be skewed toward one's biases.

I applied my research questions to a blend of families, including my own. In "cross-pollination," my goal was to weed out bias and drill down to some of the common denominators that define these historical figures. It is important that the researcher attempt to serve a broader public interest; in fact, one concern that historians have raised is that family histories can be superficial in their accounts. In compelling ways, that gap has been bridged by such works as *The Negro Family in the United States* (Frazier 1966), which deals with the evolution of the Negro family in America, and *Black Family in Slavery and Freedom 1750–1925* (Gutman 1976), which strives to unearth the origins of black family beliefs and behaviors in the South. Both authors used archival research methods and historical documents, including narratives, Freedmen's Bureau records, court documents, journals, national census records, and so on to gather information. The weaving together of these historical accounts provided the synthesis for theoretical articulation.

Strengths and Weaknesses of Oral History

Gathering oral history through comparative historical methodology builds trust between the researcher and the community of invitees and their families and friends. In my case, since I was from the community, I was seen as one of them—an insider. I had an even broader appeal by not having lived in the community for a period of time, so I did not have a close alliance with any one clique or political faction in the community. As a neutral party, I enjoyed ethnohistorian advantages.

Allen and Montell (1981) noted that careful use of original historical information could be extremely valuable. There are a number of community stories shaped by men who were the first generation of free African American leadership that have not been recorded. These added accounts will help fill the gaps in the historic documentation. Oral history has at least one advantage over written history in that written records speak to the point of *what happened*, while oral sources almost invariably provide insights into *how people felt about what happened* (Allen & Montell 1981; emphasis added). Although some might dismiss oral history as unreliable and potentially biased, the same could be said about written history.

> Written history is supposedly unbiased but we know that stating just facts without a biased interpretative bent is not always the case given the perspective of the historian. On the other hand, orally communicated history comes from the personal experiences of individuals, tends to be more subjective and evaluative thus individual and community attitudes are clearly expressed in oral accounts of historical events. (Allen & Montell 1981:21)

Certainly, oral history has potential drawbacks, for example, "time warps." Time warps occur when interviewees recall stories that present information in a nonlinear or nonchronological form. The difference between traditional historical accounts and oral history is that historical accounts can be told out of order in the latter. So, the facts may be accurate but the chronology may not be. To counter this weakness in gathering oral history, I conducted several oral interviews to cross-reference stories and to obtain a clear sequence of events. Further, I requested and was granted approval to ask follow-up questions after the interviews were concluded.

Another potential weakness of oral history is "telescoping historical time." This means that as people talk about occurrences that are separated by time, they fail to mention some of the factors that intervened between each episode. Accordingly, events that were really separated by time and circumstances can seem to have occurred back to back. This can cause a distorted picture of overall history and of an individual's life. This type of retelling of events can create a false cause-and-effect relationship between two events by leaving large voids of time unaddressed within the historical context (Allen & Montell 1981).

To avoid the effects of telescoping, I used archival resources to confirm events through newspaper articles, minutes from associations, dated photos, etc., to confirm the order and timeframes of events. I also considered the personality of the research participants, because individuals typically tell events in the way they wish those events had occurred. These wished-for events, once separated from reality, could be part of future interventions or/and recommendations.

Another weakness of oral history is the possibility of "displaced original actors in an event." This occurs when individuals recalling significant events place more emphasis on what happened than on who was involved. As a result, actors in an event may be changed. A less significant actor may be switched with a more prominent historical figure and vice versa. To avoid this phenomenon, I studied written documentation to help confirm events and verify accuracy.

I also kept close watch on "patterning events" in the oral accounts, wherein interviewees emphasize similar characteristics that seem to create particular patterns such as hardships or pioneering events, economic downfalls, etc. As a researcher, I strove to discern if recalled stories were selectively shared. As Allen and Montell (1981) note, it is important for researchers to notice variations in settings of the same story retold by various interviewees. This can indicate the patterns of selective memory. For example, family stories may illustrate the family's role in community politics, financial stability, and social events. While those stories are valuable, I ensured their accuracy and confirmed them with census material and archival data (like letters, articles, business minutes, written interviews, newspaper articles, census records, birth and death certificate, other historical accounts in local libraries, etc.). I verified historical accuracy by using other documentation or by creating a focus group setting where stimulation between participants recounting different aspects of the same story can help bolster the accuracy of the overall historical event. Events or recollections that cannot be verified were eliminated or held back until accuracy could be confirmed.

Hermeneutics

Similar to the comparative historical methodology, hermeneutics has been used to emphasize the oppression and shortcomings of the African American condition. The disproportionate number of accounts of oppression leads to a void in our understanding of the heroic attributes and stories of our ancestors.

For historians, perhaps it is easier to target disparities. Sociologists, however, should endeavor to foster a balanced perspective on the stories they resurrect through hermeneutics. If a weakness of this methodological approach is the emphasis that researchers place on negative historical aspects of a community, then one of its strengths is when we emphasize a community's successes and achievements. Positive written historical research findings could empower remaining community members to continue to fight disenfranchisement. Compiling the positive historical events that occurred during this period for African Americans could enhance one of the potential outcomes of this study, which is to provide written records of prosperity and upward mobility; recipients of this research can be inspired to emulate past success.

The combination of methods increases the accuracy assessment of my subject through the historical comparative lens. I chose to study what made these people powerful rather than powerless. As indicated in *Race and Ethnicity in Research Methods* (Stanfield & Rutledge 1993), archival research works for both methodological approaches.

One key to archival research is to know where to search and to select what is sound theoretical information. "The tricky aspect of reviewing and mastering such literature is that the researcher must remember that historical and biographical interpretations are value-laden human activities" (Stanfield & Rutledge 1993:276). That is why I chose a multifaceted approach to data collection. A multidimensional method not only included interdependent material, normative arguments, and macro and micro arguments but also helped reconcile theory and historical comparative data.

I began with written resources such as newspaper articles, local records, physical artifacts, and archival documents about their local area. Next, I relied on written and orally communicated historical data. Finally, I compared the local community study oral history findings with historical context of classical research work completed by Myrdal (1972), Harris (1958), Du Bois (1966), Frazier (1966), Gutman (1976), and others.

Quantitative Methodology

Quantitative history work has been documented as early as ancient Greek times; it was my third research method. Massive amounts of data can be now compiled, processed, and analyzed with computers. According to Jarausch and Hardy (1991), there are three uses of quantitative history:

1. numbering evidence using tables;
2. evaluating causative connections through testing hypotheses in a more stringent way; and
3. analyzing statistically or textually using the computer.

An example of the first and second use of quantitative history is found in the 1971 dissertation by Charles Seagrave titled "The Southern Negro

Agricultural Worker: 1850–1870." Seagraves evaluates and compares a number of wage earnings by year for field hands and sharecroppers in Louisiana to determine the effects of emancipation on the agricultural workers. The statistical analysis in comparing charts "show a significant improvement in the income positions of Negro workers resulting from the emancipation" (Seagrave 1971:66). However, "the increase is smaller than one would have predicted on the hypothesis that the income position of the workers after the war should have increased to the real value of the marginal product of slave labor prior to the War" (Seagrave 1971:66). In other words, logically after slavery, wages for the former slaves who were now employed for a wage should have gone up. However, in comparison to the rations (clothing, food, housing, etc.) that were provided during slavery, the statistical comparison of historic documents proves otherwise. At the time of his study, there was a limited amount of research on this topic, and his work is a prime example of quantitative history.

When there are a number of variables to consider, Jarausch and Hardy (1991) lay out some basic issues:

1. Can two or more variables be used to predict the values of another variable?

   For example, Seagrave's work (1971), the examination of one variable was the "estimates of the total of the rental costs per slave" and the "maintenance costs per slave" compared with the estimates of the "incomes earned by Negro field hands immediately following the War." This should help predict the variable in question, which is whether the freedmen's income improved.

2. Does an independent variable improve the accuracy of the predictions of a dependent variable beyond the level reached by one or more of the other independent variables?

   According to Jarausch and Hardy (1991):

   > The second question occurs in one form or another in many substantive investigations. It arises most often when a researcher believes that a factor not yet considered by the existing literature plays a role in predicting an important outcome. Because this new variable may be correlated to some degree with other variables already deemed important, the scholar must test its ability to improve the prediction of the dependent variable over and above the accuracy level of the prior variables rather than simply show a bivariate relationship between the new variable and the dependent variable. (p. 141)

3. Is an independent and dependent variable causally related after the effects of one or more of the other variables are statistically controlled?

For instance, to discover the leadership traits of African American men born between 1850 and 1900, I might want to find out whether the relationship between transactional or transformational and charismatic styles of leadership is the same for leaders today.

Empirical Analysis

The third methodology I use is a 360-degree instrument for empirical analyzing leadership traits for African American males who built their communities. Typically, 360-degree instruments are utilized with individuals who are still alive. However, authors James Kouzes and Barry Posner's Leadership Practices Inventory (LPI) to identify leadership behaviors can be utilized, regardless of whether a subject is still living, because the 360-degree tool is used by those who knew the individuals first-hand (2007). Although living subjects can answer the questions about themselves in the LPI, the historic deceased subjects would have only the reflections of their peers and followers rather than answering for themselves. The LPI tool for studying the characteristics of leadership was not available during the 1800s, and the data captured regarding the men who lived during this era can be compared against national averages of contemporary leaders. The 360-degree assessment could validate leadership qualities from a historical perspective. The LPI has been used worldwide and has proven to be a predictor of leader performance. The LPI used as a tool for historic figures can help gauge similarities between leaders today and those of previous generations, with particular emphasis on elements of transformational and transactional leadership.

To analyze the quantitative data, a mean of the ratings from community members and family of the subjects in question would be made regarding their assessment of the leadership styles of the men born 1850–1900. After the quantitative analysis, additional interview questions clarifying the quantitative analysis could be posed.

Strengths and Weakness of 360-Degree Empirical Method

One weakness in using the 360-degree instrument is that although the descriptions used for leadership today may work culturally for corporate America and certain socioeconomic groups, it may be challenging to determine their utility and applicability for leadership traits of African American males during the late 1800s. The terminology may not translate to the vernacular of the time and the leadership styles may not fit within the context of corporate leadership scenarios. However, I believe that the parallels of character traits should be timeless. We will be able to determine whether there are historical parallels once the research is completed.

Another potential problem regards the format itself. As the questions are typically now administered electronically, if the individuals answering the 360-degree questions are elderly, it is necessary to make sure that the responders know how to use a computerized format.

One of the strengths in using this 360-degree tool combined with archival analysis is that it will inform and confirm whether these leaders can now be recognized using a level playing field of unbiased assessment tools. If tools are biased, identification of leadership traits by historical analysis will be contradicted by using the 360-degree instrument. If the methods and tools for research confirm one another, then this study will provide information that will add to the areas that were disproportionately studied by the transformational and transactional leadership theorists whose work often failed to reflect the African American community's experience.

The main point is to garner further insights in leadership theories as they apply to African American culture and historical timeframes prior to work done by Burns (1978), Bass (1998), and others. Using inductive and empirical methods, we can determine whether contemporary leadership theories hold true for this timeframe.

CONCLUSION

The three methodologies used as a triangular approach for research help eliminate the weaknesses of each. It is incumbent on the researcher to be vigilant of the biases within each approach and to carefully strategize to eliminate them.

Qualitative comparative historical, hermeneutics, and quantitative empirical analysis are the methods of research best suited not only for the research question of how leaders were formed and succeeded in a time where few resources, including education, were available but for many other social and cultural research questions. Archival history provides the context for when these men were born and the obstacles they faced. In-depth interviews provide a space for the first-hand stories of these individuals to be told by others who were personally acquainted with their strengths and frailties. This format allows for reflection in privacy on the character traits of these historical figures. Then, using a 360-degree assessment, statistical analysis can ascertain one of two types of leadership styles that made these men successful (transformational/transactional). Triangulation of these methods allows a cross-referencing and intersection of patterns in the study. Using both qualitative and quantitative methods of data collection provides a clearer picture of the research subjects.

Through these methods, we hear these men tell how they became successful at creating bridges for the next generation. And as the next generation continues to develop new approaches for achieving their potential, we continue to create the systems to maintain vibrant communities that we all take part in living in the legacy of unsung heroes—as this poem suggests:

The Bridge Builder
An old man, going down a lone highway
Came at the evening, cold and gray,
To a chasm vast and wide and steep,
With waters rolling cold and deep.
The old man crossed in the twilight dim;
the sullen stream had no fears for him.
But he turned when safe on the other side,
and built a bridge to span the tide.

"Old man," said a fellow pilgrim near,
"You are wasting your strength with building here.
Your journey will end with the ending day;
You never again will pass this way.
You've crossed the chasm, deep and wide,
Why build you this bridge at eventide?"
The builder lifted his old gray head.

"Good friend, in the path I have come," he said,
"There followed after me today;
A youth whose feet must pass this way.
The chasm that was as naught to me.
To that fair-haired youth may a pitfall be;
He, too, must cross in the twilight dim –
Good friend, I am building this bridge for him."

—Will Allen Dromgool

REFERENCES

Allen, B. A. M., & Montell, W. L. (1981). *From memory to history: Using oral sources in local historical research.* Nashville: American Association for State and Local History.

Bass, B. (1996). *A new paradigm of leadership an inquiry into transformational leadership.* Alexandria, VA: U.S. Army Research Institute for Behavioral and Social Sciences.

Bass, B. (1998). *Transformational leadership.* Mahwah, NJ: Lawrence Erlbaum Associates.

Bass, B. M. (1985). *Leadership and performance beyond expectations.* New York: The Free Press.

Bentz, V. S. & Shapiro, J. J. (1998). *Mindful inquiry in social research.* Thousand Oaks, CA: Sage.

Burns, J. M. (1978). *Leadership.* New York: Harper & Row.

Du Bois, W. E. B. (1966). *The souls of black folk.* New York: Modern Library Edition.

Du Bois, W. E. B. (1973). *The Philadelphia Negro.* Philadelphia: University of Pennsylvania Press.

Frazier, E. F. (1966). *The Negro family in the United States.* Chicago: University of Chicago Press.

Gutman, H. G. (1976). *Black family in slavery and freedom 1750–1925.* New York: Pantheon Books.

Hammond, S. (1996). *The thin book of appreciative inquiry.* Plano, TX: Thin Book Publishing Co.

Harris, A. L. (1958). *Economics and social reform.* New York: Harper & Brothers.

Hill, M. (1993). *Archival strategies and techniques.* Thousand Oaks, CA: Sage.

Jarausch, K. H., & Hardy, K. A. (1991). *Quantitative methods for historians.* Chapel Hill: University of North Carolina Press.

Kouzes, J., & Posner, B. (2007). *The leadership challenge.* San Francisco: John Wiley & Sons, Inc.

McCracken, G. (1988). *The long interview.* Beverly Hills, CA: Sage.

Myrdal, G. (1972). *An American dilemma.* New York: Harper & Row.

Ritchie, D. A. (2003). *Doing oral history.* New York: Oxford University Press.

Seagrave, C. (1971). The southern Negro agricultural worker: 1850–1870. Ph.D. dissertation, Stanford University.

Simpson, C. M. (1973). Henry A. Wise in antebellum politics 1850–1861. Ph.D. dissertation, Department of History, Stanford University.

Stanfield, J. H., II, & Rutledge, D. (1993). *Race and ethnicity in research methods.* Newbury Park, CA: Sage.

Yow, V. R. (2005). *Recording oral history: A guide for the humanities and social sciences.* Lanham, MD: Altamira.

10   QUANTIFYING RACE: ON METHODS FOR ANALYZING SOCIAL INEQUALITY

Quincy Thomas Stewart and Abigail A. Sewell

BACKGROUND

Racial inequality is a social experience. Our interest in methodology centers on how to quantitatively model this concept. We each entered the academy with a love for mathematics and an aim to model patterns in the physical world. Though we both lost interest in the physical sciences early in undergraduate school, we similarly turned our attention to studying the social world, particularly social inequality. Our paths crossed when Abigail began graduate studies at Indiana University. At that time, we began an ongoing discussion about how to quantitatively model racial inequality. Our discussion centered on the question: "How can we model the complex, multi-level patterns that constitute the social experience of race and reveal the policy mechanisms needed to undermine racial inequality?"

Over the years, we have had countless spirited interactions in which we often agree, and sometimes disagree, on how to answer this question. We often agreed/disagreed on the extent that a study had great models with little policy relevance, clear policy relevance, and horrible models, and, rarely, both great models and clear insights on policy mechanisms. Each of our interactions, and disagreements, pushed us to a new peak in understanding how to quantitatively model the experience of race. This chapter represents our best mutual solution to date and it is a guide to our ongoing work. Our plan is to use—and build on—this solution to develop a body of research that may be used to guide policy aimed at eradicating racial inequality in the United States and beyond.

INTRODUCTION

Scientific research on racial inequality is academically appealing because it has great promise. For some, it is the promise of eradicating racial disparities in educational achievement that drives their research. For others, it is the promise of identifying the policy mechanisms for realizing racial equality more broadly. W. E. B. Du Bois (1899/1996) discussed the promise of his own research—and perhaps his personal hopes—in *The Philadelphia Negro*. He noted: "The final design of [this] work is to lay before the public such a body of information as may be *a safe guide* for all efforts toward the solution of the many Negro problems" (p. 1; emphasis added). Here, Du Bois invokes the promise of scientific research for advancing humankind and improving the deplorable relative conditions facing black Americans in particular. In the century since Du Bois's publication, the promise of race research has continued to fuel the intellectual fires of countless social scientists.

Quantitative race research plays a critical role in realizing this promise as it is a means to conduct formal—and often generalizable—analyses of racial inequality. This research highlights the: (1) magnitude of racial disparities in an outcome; (2) variables that covary with the disparity; and (3) mechanisms responsible for the creation and/or maintenance of outcome disparities. The difficulty, though, is that racial inequality is a product of a host of variables simultaneously operating in various levels (e.g., structural, intrapsychic), social spaces (e.g., educational institutions), and in the gamut of individual/institutional encounters in a social system (Bonilla-Silva 1996; Reskin 2003; Stewart 2008a, 2008b; Zuberi 2001). This complexity creates endogeneity (i.e., dependence among variables), which undermines traditional quantitative methods' ability to correctly identify the mechanisms that shape the experience—or interactive process—of racial inequality (Stewart 2008a). Our aim here is to review the arsenal of quantitative strategies available for analyzing racial inequality, discuss the benefits and drawbacks of each, and propose a plan for overcoming the deficiencies in each approach.

We begin with a brief review of race research and present a formal model of racial inequality. Then we review six quantitative methods and discuss how each addresses the complexity implicit in racial inequality. We conclude with a prescription for quantitative race research that centers on using multiple techniques.

RACE: THE ENVIRONMENT

A host of factors shape the nature and magnitude of racial inequality. Some argue that socioeconomic (SES) disparities (e.g., education) are the primary mechanism behind racial differences in outcomes (e.g., health); others argue that discrimination plays the most important role (Cancio et al. 1996; Farkas & Vicknair 1996; Neal & Johnson 1996; Wilson 1978). We group these factors into three broad categories that capture the general tenor of the explanation. They are: (1) behavioral; (2) resource based; and (3) structural. We do not endorse any one perspective as a best explanation. Rather, we use the categories as a frame to shed light on the implications—and oversights—of various approaches to studying racial inequality. This allows us to detail the appropriateness of a method for identifying the source of inequality when all of the theories may be operating.

Three Broad Theories

The first broad theory, entailing behavior, locates the source of group outcome disparities within individuals, specifically, in a set of traits that influence behavior. Outcome differences are viewed as a product of this set of behaviors occurring more (or less) in one race group than another. The behavior may be a preference for one group, statistical discrimination against a group, a disinvestment in education, etc. (Du Bois 1899/1996; McWhorter 2000; Ogbu 1974, 1978, 1983, 1987, 1990; Ogbu & Davis 2003). The driving feature of behavioral theory is that members of one racial group enact behaviors that are associated with an increase (or decrease) in an outcome for the underprivileged group. An important aspect of behavioral theories is the general assumption that the behavioral mechanism is largely modifiable. This leads to policy suggestions for inequality that center on modifying the behavior(s) of a specific group (Andreasen 1995; Durlak & Wells 1997, 1998; Eccles et al. 2002).

The second theory, resource based, locates the source of racial outcome inequalities in the distributions of a related, important resource. (See Cancio et al. [1996]; Darity [1982, 1998]; Farkas & Vicknair [1996]; Neal & Johnson [1996]; O'Neill [1990]; and Wilson [1978] for examples of this perspective in regard to wages.) The "important resource" varies based on outcomes from factors such as human and social capital (e.g., education, network connections) to access to important services (e.g., health insurance). The resources allow the actor entrée and/or access to higher outcomes than other similar actors without the resource. Thus, racial outcome disparities are viewed largely as a product of one group having more resources—or more of a set of resources—than another group. Policy suggestions for resource-based models center on changing the underlying distribution of the valued resource (e.g., increasing educational outcomes of a group) (Harvey 1973; Korpi & Palme 1998; Tyler 1997).

The third and last broad theory, related to structure, locates the source of inequality within the spectrum of social relations in society. Structural theory asserts that while the distribution of resources and behaviors of agents are important—and in constant flux—the relationships between the agents conform to a larger *system* of racial inequality (Bonilla-Silva 1996; Oliver and Shapiro 1995; Omi and Winant 1994). Racial differences in an outcome, then, are viewed as products of an array of institutional arrangements (e.g., property tax and educational quality) and rules guiding behavior (e.g., social networks). These arrangements and rules produce a patterned set of relationships and resource distributions that constitute the system (i.e., structure) of racial inequality in the population. Structural theorists argue that the uneven effect of the institutional arrangements and rules across racial groups is the driving force behind racial inequality. Importantly, this theory subsumes that the ideology embedded in the institutional arrangements and rules that guide behavior are the true purveyors of injustice (Bonilla-Silva 2003). Hence, the policy suggestions center on changing the ideologies that create and maintain inequality via the racial structure.

The Formal Model

The theories discussed above present quantitative social scientists with three unique mechanisms to model. An overlooked and, oftentimes, omitted important point in each of the theories is they are interconnected. For example, behavioral theorists often point out that behaviors are a result of systematic discrimination (Fryer & Torelli 2005; Ogbu & Davis 2003). Likewise, structural theorists often identify the summation of behaviors and resource distributions in a population as constituting the system of racial inequality (Bonilla-Silva 1996, 2003; Bonilla-Silva & Baiocchi 2001; Oliver and Shapiro 1995). Moreover, resource-based theorists often highlight the importance of behavior and institutional arrangements in creating the uneven distribution of resources (Bonilla-Silva 1996; Roscigno and Ainsworth-Darnell 1999; Wilson 1978). A depiction of this interconnected model of the three broad theories appears in Figure 10.1. All three of the theories, then, potentially contribute to an actor's outcome in time k+1 and to outcome disparities among actors more broadly.

Indeed, the model of the three theories of inequality presents a considerable amount of complexity. Stewart (2008a, 2008b) suggests this is further complicated by race and racial inequality being an interactive process (Emirbayer 1997; Reskin 2003; Schwalbe et al. 2000; Tilly 1998; West & Fenstermaker 1995). Race, from this perspective, only has meaning in social interactions (i.e., mechanisms) where the concept is used to distinguish the experience of actors from diverse racial groups and facilitate racial inequality. Stewart writes:

> These mechanisms embody social processes that operate at various levels (e.g., organizational, interpersonal) and locations in society to allocate rewards based on actors' characteristics—including race. Each mechanism … represents a social interaction space where an actor's characteristics are translated into some reward or opportunity, and where racial inequalities are created and maintained. (2008a:287)

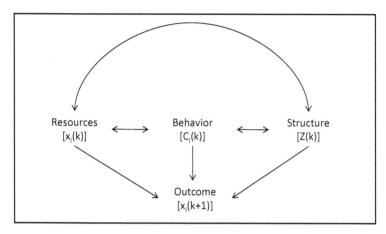

Fig. 10.1 General model of three broad theories of racial inequality operating in time period k

Stewart (2008a, 2008b) formally characterizes this process as the accumulation of countless encounters of the form shown in Figure 10.2. During this generic interaction k, an actor enters with a set of characteristics $x_{i,k-1}$ and a racial identity r_k. She is then exposed to a treatment T_{ik} in the encounter, which may be based on her race (i.e., racial discrimination). After the treatment, the actor perceives the treatment P_{ik} and compares it with past encounters—and the treatment of similar others—to determine the quality of the treatment (i.e., fair/unfair). She then responds to this treatment. This response, C_{ik}, may take on several forms and depends on the perception of treatment by the actor. The

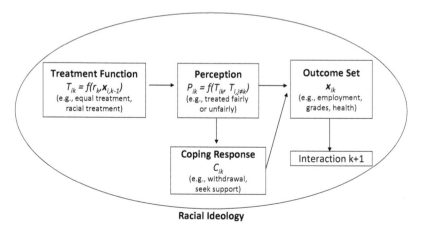

Fig. 10.2 General interactive model of racial inequality: Interaction k

interaction concludes with the actor receiving an outcome—or an update to her set of characteristics—which she carries into the next encounter.

Although Stewart's (2008a, 2008b) model depicts the potential process through which race becomes racial inequality, several mechanisms are not discussed. Specifically, where do the aforementioned behavior, resources, and structure fit into this theoretical model? Albeit overlooked, the general nature of these variables highlights where they fit. First, behavior corresponds with the coping responses of actors C_{ik}. This space identifies the influence of an individual's agency on her own outcomes and to the larger structure (i.e., the system of relations). Second, resources span the treatment, perception, and coping response mechanisms. An actor's resources will govern her treatment, her perceptions of that treatment, and the actions she takes as a consequence of the treatment/perception. Structure, the final—and most complex—variable, enters the model via the treatment mechanism. This space captures the systematic disparate treatment of actors on the basis of their race, which compounds across encounters to become differences in characteristics. It is this systematic disparate treatment of actors that constitutes the racial structure. Hence, Bonilla-Silva (2003) defines the "racial structure as the *totality of social relations and practices that reinforce white privilege*" (9; emphasis in the original).

Summary

The discussion above suggests that resources, behaviors, and structure operate to create inequality in countless social encounters across the course of social actors' lives. We have formalized this model in Equation 1.

$$x_{ik} = f[T_{i,k-1}, P_{i,k-1}, C_{i,k-1}] \tag{1}$$

where

$$T_{i,k-1} = h[r_i, x_{i,k-1}(x_{i,k-2}), (Z_{k-1})]$$

$$P_{i,k-1} = g[x_{i,k-1}, T_{i,d < k-2}(Z_{k-2}), T_{j \neq i, k-2}(Z_{k-2})]$$

$$C_{i,k-1} = z[x_{i,k-1}, P_{i,k-1}, T_{i,k-1}(Z_k)]$$

The terms in Equation 1 are synonymous to those used above—and the terms f, h, g, and z preceding the parentheses refer to functions. Here, the outcomes in the current encounter $[x_{ik}]$ (i.e., resources) are a function of the treatment $[T_{i,k-1}]$, perceptions $[P_{i,k-1}]$ and coping responses $[C_{i,k-1}]$ of all earlier encounters—but only directly tied to the parameters seen in the previous encounter. As indicated earlier, the treatment in the preceding encounter is a function of race $[r_i]$, resources $[x_{i,k-1}]$ and structure $[Z_{k-1}]$ in that encounter. Perception of treatment $[P_{i,k-1}]$ is a function of one's resources as well as one's own treatment in previous encounters $[T_{i,d<,k-2}]$, where d is interaction number] and the treatment of others $[T_{j \neq i, k-2}]$—both of which are tied to the structure of previous encounters $[Z_{k-2}]$. Finally, the current outcomes are also tied to the coping responses $[C_{i,k-1}]$ used by the actor in the previous encounter. These responses are a direct result of the resources $[x_{i,k-1}]$, perception $[P_{i,k-1}]$, and treatment $[T_{i,k-1}]$ experienced in the same interaction.

This model of racial inequality is quite complex. Each of the respective variables becomes nested in others such that an early difference in behavior influences the resources of ensuing encounters (Stewart 2008a). Alternatively, an initial difference in structure may nest itself in behavioral differences. This process complicates our ability to single out any one variable as the primary culprit behind racial inequality. So, how do we model this complexity? We now turn to our review—and critique—of six quantitative methods.

RACE RESEARCH: THE STRATEGIES

There are several ways one may model the general system of racial inequality outlined above. We review six methods ranging from static models of cross-sectional data to dynamic methods that use artificially simulated data. They are: (1) traditional survey; (2) comparative analysis; (3) natural experiment; (4) multilevel analysis; (5) formal experiment; and (6) computational. Each method has a host of submethods (e.g., traditional survey includes both ordinary least squares and logistic regression models). Although some readers may be interested in the specifics of these submethods for a particular research question, we only review the larger method to shed light on the benefits and drawbacks for studying the system of racial inequality.

Traditional Survey

The traditional survey method—or variable analysis—uses individual-level data derived from social and/or demographic surveys (e.g., General Social Survey, U.S. Census data) to assess the nature and magnitude of racial inequities in an outcome (Blumer 1969/1998; Stewart 2008a, 2008b). Traditional surveys collect data on race group membership (i.e., racial identification) as well as a host of other variables such as income and education. These data sets are generally large (i.e., $N > 1000$) and collected using random sampling techniques. Researchers use these data to generate unbiased estimates of the nature and magnitude racial differences in a specific outcome at the time of the survey.

The traditional survey modeling process is done in two (or more) steps. First, the racial difference in an outcome variable is estimated in a bivariate model. Specifically,

$$y_i = f[r_i] \tag{2}$$

where y_i is the outcome for person i, and r_i is the race of person i. This model highlights the nature and magnitude of observed—or "real"—racial differences in the outcome of interest. Researchers then control for theoretically relevant variables that may be correlated with this real difference. For example, an analysis of income disparities typically controls for education, experience, and occupation (Cancio et al. 1996; Darity 1982, 1998; Kilbourne et al. 1994; O'Neill 1990). Similarly, an analysis of disparities in negative health outcomes often includes variables for smoking behavior, body mass index, and physical activity (Adler & Rehkopf 2008; Bell et al. 2004; Dressler et al. 2005; Lantz et al. 1998; Schoenborn et al. 2004; Williams & Jackson 2005). Hence, one controls for variables that are theoretically tied to the outcome variable in a fundamental way. This second step is seen in the multivariate model

$$y_i = f[r_i, x^*_i], \quad \text{where } x_i = y_i \cup x^*_i \tag{3}$$

where y_i is the outcome of interest for person i, r_i is the race of person i, and x^*_i refers to the vector of theoretically relevant variables for person i that are used in the analysis. This multivariate model provides an estimate of the average racial difference between persons with similar characteristics [i.e., $x^*_i \approx x^*_j$]. If the addition of variables to the model reduces (i.e., explains) the race effect to insignificance, scholars interpret the variables as being responsible for the observed racial disparity in the outcome (Darity 1982; Reskin 2003; Stewart 2008a; Zuberi 2001). When the race effect is not explained away, scholars interpret the result as evidence of either continued racial discrimination in the social arena or an omitted variable.

Although the traditional survey method is elegant, cost effective, and easy to apply, the method is severely limited by the nature of the data. Specifically, the method draws on cross-sectional data, where each unit of analysis has only one data point within a time continuum. This creates an epistemological gap as the theoretical models of interest are dynamic (i.e., causal), but the empirics used to examine theory strictly rely on correlation. This gap is best seen in the difference between the dynamic, theoretical model depicted in Equation 1 and the static, empirical model shown in Equation 3. This gap necessitates a "leap of faith" by scholars in which one presumes that the static, cross-sectional model accurately depicts the complex, dynamic relationship between the same variables in the real world (Zuberi 2001).

Comparative Analysis

Comparative analysis explicitly focuses on group similarities and differences to shed light on the social mechanisms that influence racial inequality (Martin 2009; Ogbu 1983, 1987, 1990; Waters 1999). Specifically, this method looks at two or more groups with the same racial classification that vary on a specific characteristic (e.g., immigration status). For example, Dodoo (1997) compares the earnings of African Americans with those of black West Indian and African immigrants, while Stewart and Dixon (2010) compare the wage outcomes of four native-born racial groups with their foreign-born counterparts. Comparative analysis attempts to shed additional light on the mechanisms behind racial inequality by analyzing two phenotypically (i.e., racially) similar groups and modeling how a criterion variable (e.g., immigration status) is correlated with differences in outcomes across the two groups.

Comparative analysis is done in two (or more) steps. First, one estimates the raw outcome disparity between two phenotypically similar groups. Equation 4 shows this basic model where nativity of the respondent, n_i, is the characteristic that differentiates the two groups.

$$y_i = f[n_i] \tag{4}$$

This model provides an estimate of the average difference between persons of the same race group, but different nativity groups (i.e., native-born/foreign-born disparity). Perhaps the most popular statistic among comparative analyses comes from this basic model, which shows that foreign-born Blacks earn significantly more than native-born Blacks (Dodoo 1997; Sowell 1978, 1983; Stewart & Dixon 2010)—a relationship researchers have found also applies to Whites (Stewart & Dixon 2010).

The second step is to incorporate theoretically relevant variables and is functionally written

$$y_i = f[n_i, x^*_i], \quad \text{where } x_i = y_i \cup x^*_i \tag{5}$$

where the variables are synonymous to those used above. Scholars interpret any significant residual nativity—or other—effect in this model as a sign that the factor differentiating the groups (e.g., birthplace) produces or mediates the group outcome disparities and, in kind, racial inequality more broadly.

The benefit of comparative analysis is that by analyzing two phenotypically similar groups that are different in regard to a broad characteristic (e.g., African ancestry with different migration history), one can shed light on the broad social mechanisms that are tied to the criterion variable (e.g., migrant selection). Comparative analysis, though, suffers from the same issues as the traditional survey method: The empirical estimates are simply correlations. Researchers have to make a leap of faith as to how differences in treatment, coping responses, resources, and the like covary with the criterion variable *and* as to whether and how observed relationships capture the deeper dynamic process of racial inequality (Stewart 2008b). An example of this leap is research where scholars presume that the higher SES outcomes of West Indian Blacks is attributable to more motivation and culture and that the poor outcomes of native-born Blacks is attributable to laziness and ineptitude (McWhorter 2000; Sowell 1978, 1983). This problem speaks to the critical issue of research design and theoretical development for comparative analyses (Bashi & McDaniel 1997). The phenotypically similar social groups should not be able to be distinguished by other mechanisms or sources of bias beyond the criterion variable (e.g., language or nativity). When this condition is not satisfied, the results of comparative analysis are biased and the conclusions are off the mark.

Natural Experiments

The natural experiment method draws on naturally occurring data to shed light on the social mechanisms that drive racial inequality. These data must capture a change in one or more of the mechanisms theorized to impact racial inequality. Typically, social scientists draw on spatiotemporal variation (i.e., change) in a social policy or an environment as a means to examine these mechanisms (Marini & Singer 1988; Stewart 2009). This variation in a social mechanism (e.g., policy) creates a large-scale, "quasi" case-control design that one can use to study the effect of a social or environmental manipulation on a given outcome.

The data for natural experiments consist of individual-level survey data as well as aggregate survey and/or administrative data where the units of analysis may be cities, counties, or states. The data must provide information on the spatiotemporal variation in a mechanism (e.g., social policy) and on individual/group outcomes prior to and after the time of implementation in the respective spatiotemporal spaces. One compares group outcomes before and after a period of change to make an inference about the importance of the mechanism (i.e., the quasi-manipulation) for racial inequality. If changes in group outcome disparities occur after the quasi-manipulation—compared to the control areas—then one may infer that the mechanism (e.g., environmental change) is a determinant of racial inequality.

The natural experiment begins with a simple model of group disparities in outcomes across time k and space l.

$$y_{ikl} = f[r_i, k_i, l_i] \qquad (6)$$

Equation 6 indicates that the outcome y_{ikl} of person i at time k and place l is a function of the race r_i of individual i and the respective time k_i and place l_i of the respondent. This simple model gives an idea of how group disparities vary across time and space. After estimating the simple model, we build on it by adding controls for the quasi manipulation variable T_{kl}—this is the change of social policy that mirrors the treatment function discussed in Figure 10.2. We write this as

$$y_{ikl} = f[T_{kl}, r_i, k_i, l_i] \tag{7}$$

where T_{kl} is a dummy—or continuous—variable that measures the spatiotemporal variation in social policy or environment. One should insert an interaction variable in this model to assess the extent to which the manipulation is related to the racial disparities in the outcome variable (e.g., modeling the r_i coefficient at level-1 as a function of T_{kl} at level-2). This model provides an estimate of how group disparities in an outcome covary with changes in a social policy or environment. As a last step, one estimates a full model that includes other individual x^*_{ik} and spatiotemporal X_{kl} variables that are theoretically tied to the outcome.

$$y_{ikl} = f[T_{kl}, r_i, k_i, l_i, x^*_{ik}, X_{kl}] \quad \text{where } x_{ik} = y_{ik} \cup x^*_{ik} \tag{8}$$

Equation 8 allows one to assess the extent to which racial outcome disparities are tied to the quasi manipulation T_{kl} among similar persons who live in comparable social environments.

Natural experiments draw on repeated cross-sections of both observational and survey data to capture more of the complexity spelled out in Equation 1. This allows one to assess the direction of causality between a social policy/environment and racial disparities in a specific outcome. When the method is applied correctly, the natural variation neatly approximates a real social space with an experimental manipulation—as opposed to the contrived (i.e., quasi-) space that is discussed in the traditional survey and comparative analytic methods (see Bansak & Raphael [2001], Chay [1998], and Chay and Greenstone [2003] for examples of natural experiments). This allows one to more effectively test a hypothesis instead of statistically *speculating* on how manipulating one variable (e.g., education) may affect racial disparities in another outcome variable (e.g., income).

Although natural experiments are extremely useful, they are not without criticism. The primary criticism is that the quasi-manipulation may not truly capture the theoretical mechanism in question. In a perfect world, a quasi-manipulation emerges directly from a scholar's theory of racial inequality in a specific outcome. This would allow one to measure the influence of this manipulation on racial inequality. More commonly, the quasi-manipulation is muddied by the real world where natural variation is one dimension of a larger social policy or, in most cases, does not exist at all. This limits the applicability of the method to areas where one can find natural social/environmental variations that are theoretically meaningful to racial inequality.

A second criticism is that using repeated cross-sectional surveys overlooks how the quasi-manipulation affects specific respondents. These pooled samples of theoretically identical people potentially overlook: (1) person-specific variation in the relationship between the quasi-manipulation and other respondent characteristics (i.e., endogeneity); (2) person-specific variation in the coping response of respondents to the quasi-manipulation that may alter the first oversight; and (3) temporal variation in other environmental factors that may be tied to racial disparities in the outcome variable. Thus, the natural experiment method does not fully capture Stewart's (2008a, 2008b) "interactive process" of racial inequality. While natural experiments provide novel insights on how a policy/environment is tied to racial inequality, they still overlook the gamut of interactions that comprise the system of inequality.

Multilevel Analysis

Multilevel analysis is quite similar to the natural experimental method. The method draws on repeated data for a key unit of analysis to infer the mechanisms of racial inequality. The key unit can vary considerably based on one's research question and data availability. For example, the key unit in longitudinal studies where the focus is on the forces driving changes in personal characteristics $[x_{ik}]$ is the individual (Block & Robins 1993; Karter et al. 2002; Lantz et al. 2001; Muthén & Muthén 2000). The researcher in this example would use longitudinal data for a group of respondents over a finite period of time (e.g., a panel study of income dynamics). In contrast, the key unit for hierarchical studies is a macro-unit that represents a theoretically important social or spatial dimension (e.g., neighborhoods). The investigator in this example would use survey data that contains information on individuals within the macro-units (e.g., race) and on the characteristics of the respective macro-unit (Grodsky & Pager 2001; Horton & Sykes 2008; McCall 2001; Stewart & Dixon 2010; Sykes 2003). These two examples represent ideal types of multilevel models. The estimation is synonymous across the different types. For brevity, we will only discuss the longitudinal model as it has a stronger causal claim.

For longitudinal models, one begins with a simple model that highlights time variation in race group outcomes and is written

$$y_{ik} = f[k] \quad \text{where } k = h[r_i] \tag{9}$$

where the time-specific individual outcome y_{ik} is a function of time k, and each time point k (Level-1) is a function of the race r_i of the respondent (Level-2)— such that multiple observations are nested in individuals. This model highlights how race is related to the emergence/change in the time varying outcome of interest.

We build on this by incorporating time-varying Level-1 characteristics x^*_{ik}, which are nested in respondents and modeled as a function of race, as well as the time-invariant Level-2 characteristics X_i [Equation 10].

$$y_{ik} = f[k, x^*_{ik}] \quad \text{where } k = h[r_i, X_i] \text{ and } x^*_{ik} = g[r_i, X_i] \tag{10}$$

The estimation of this function reveals the extent that the observed pattern (e.g., emergence, change) of racial outcome disparities persist among persons with similar time-varying and time-invariant characteristics.

The strength of multilevel models is the fluid estimation of racial inequality. For example, one can model how racial disparities in college persistence emerge among a cohort of incoming college students using a longitudinal method and the factors that temporally precede this event. Alternatively, one can assess racial disparities in educational achievement across schools and assess the extent to which they are related to school composition. The flexibility of the methods allows one to infer either temporal (i.e., longitudinal) or ecological (i.e., hierarchical) causality.

Multilevel modeling has two limitations. First, the method overlooks the treatment, perceptions, and adaptive coping responses that contribute to the social experience—and reality—of racial inequality. Though longitudinal models can capture the emergence or change in racial inequality among a sample of panel respondents, it does not reveal how a respondent's treatment, perceptions, and responses may have altered the racial inequality. In other words, multilevel methods simplify the interactive process that influences a respondent's outcome trajectory in a longitudinal model and overlook the endogeneity introduced by this process—this is seen in comparing Equation 1 to Equation 10 (Stewart 2008a).

The second limitation centers on the conceptual measurement of variables and related interpretation. Although accurate conceptual measurement is important in all research, it poses new issues in multilevel work. Vague measures, such as residential segregation or poverty rates, are often used to measure a theoretically important concept in the second level of a model. The issue becomes acute when the vague measure offers no practical policy insights. For example, a significant correlation between residential segregation and health disparities may be interpreted as either: (1) living around black people is bad for one's health; or (2) residential segregation represents the larger structural phenomenon of race which has an impact on health outcomes (Collins & Williams 1999; Williams & Collins 2001). Unfortunately, the multilevel method often does not allow one to discern which practical explanation rings true.

Formal Experiments

Formal experiments are the product of contrived social situations that are designed to infer the mechanisms behind racial inequality. They may take the form of: (1) lab-studies with respondents interacting with authority figures or "confederates" (Richeson & Trawalter 2008; Steele 2003); (2) audit studies where confederates participate in a discrete social interaction with unknowing respondents (Bendick et al. 1999; Bendick et al. 1994; Bendick et al. 1991; Fix et al. 1993; Heckman & Siegelman 1993; Pager 2003; Saltman 1979; Yinger 1993); and (3) vignette studies where respondents rate/gauge a series of faux materials such as resumes or medical records (Loring & Powell 1988; Perneger et al. 1995). Each formal experiment is designed to approximate a social space in the everyday world. The intent of the method is to examine how stimuli (i.e., manipulations) in a controlled environment elicit various responses (Walker 2011; Walker & Willer 2007; Willer & Walker 2007). The focus of the race researcher is how race influences the response of actors to a stimuli *and* how this may influence the dynamics of race in the real world.

The formal experimental model is written

$$y_i = f[T_i, C_i] \quad \text{where } T_i = h[r_i, x_i] \text{ and } C_i = g[x_i, T_i, P_i] \qquad (11)$$

where y_i is the experimental outcome for respondent i. This outcome is a function of the stimuli T_i and the response to the stimuli C_i. The stimuli is a function of race r_i and other respondent characteristics x_i, while the coping response is a function of respondent characteristics, the stimuli, and the perception P_i of the stimuli by respondent i.

Certainly, formal experiments offer great insights into how social actors experience a finite interaction (Walker 2011). Researchers can vary the form of the interaction, the treatment, and the resources available to respondents. One can assess how a specific manipulation is tied to a specific coping response and outcome. The issue with formal experiments is generalizability. They typically use convenience samples—mostly college students—to examine a social interaction. These samples limit generalizations to the social spaces from which the sample is drawn. Audit studies and vignettes provide more representative alternatives to lab studies as they are conducted outside of the laboratory environment. These type of experiments draw on real-life social interactions (e.g., review of resume) to evaluate how people respond to a stimuli "in the wild." However, they are also limited because they focus on a finite interaction in what is usually a convenient social location for the researcher.

Computational Approaches

The computational (i.e., agent-based) approach to studying racial inequality is considered the latest quantitative method being used in the area. Schelling (1971), however, used it in a pioneering study of residential segregation over thirty years ago. Schelling randomly populated a checkerboard with black and white checkers. He then selected checkers at random and moved them using a simple rule: If your neighborhood (i.e., the blocks surrounding the checker) has at least 50% of checkers of your color then stay; otherwise, move to the nearest open square that satisfies this preference. Schelling showed that perfect residentially segregated communities can result (i.e., emerge) from agents independently using a simple preference rule for living in a neighborhood where one-third of the population is of the same racial group. The micro-level preferences for mixed neighborhoods created a macro-condition of segregated communities.

The computational approach is designed to reveal how several of independent agents may interact to create a larger social phenomenon (Epstein & Axtell 1996; Hanneman et al. 1995; Leik & Meeker 1995; Moss & Edmonds 2002). Macy and Willer (2002:144) precisely describe the aim of the approach noting: "[We] may be able to understand [the] dynamics [of human groups] much better by trying to model them, not at the global level but instead as emergent properties of local interaction among adaptive agents who influence one another in response to the influence they receive." The computational approach, then, is a means to examine how the finite behaviors of artificial agents in repeated social interactions coincide *and* compound to create a larger social phenomenon such as racial inequality (Cederman 2005; Epstein & Axtell 1996; Hanneman 1995; Stewart 2010).

Indeed, each analysis that uses computational approach model is distinct. The two things that connect the models are: (1) Agents interact with other agents on the basis of a set of rules; and (2) They use bounded rationality in their decision making (i.e., they do not have complete information). Each agent is running a simple, logical model in each interaction. Equation 12 details the generic model used by agents in the computational approach.

$$y_{i,k+1} = f[T_{ik}, P_{ik}, C_{ik}] \text{ where } T_{ik} = h[r_i, x_{ik}], P_{ik} = g[x_{ik}, T_{ik},$$
$$T_{i,d\neq k}, T_{j\neq i,k-1}] \text{ and } C_{ik} = z[x_{ik}, T_{ik}, P_{ik}] \quad (12)$$

An agent's outcome in an encounter $y_{i,k+1}$ is a function of the treatment T_{ik}, perceptions P_{ik}, and coping responses C_{ik} of the current encounter. The treatment, perceptions, and coping responses covary with each other (i.e., they are endogenous), and are also a function of agent characteristics (e.g., race, previous outcomes). Using Schelling's segregation model as a frame, one can walk through the functional model where an agent is treated by being placed in a neighborhood. The agent perceives the composition of this neighborhood—in this case, the comparison is to a preference set—and makes an adaptive coping response (i.e., moves) if the racial composition of the neighborhood is not to his or her liking. Altogether, the model allows one to formally imagine the natural consequence of countless micro-behaviors.

Although the computational approach best captures the complexity implicit in racial inequality, it has a huge limitation. Namely, it is based on artificial data. One can examine how various theories may dynamically intersect at the level of individual to produce the larger system of racial inequality, but the analysis is all based on data that is contrived. Epstein (2008) responds to this criticism:

> Anyone who ventures a projection, or imagines how a social dynamic—an epidemic, war, or migration—would unfold is running some model. But typically, it is an implicit [theoretical] model in which the assumptions are hidden, their internal consistency is untested, their logical consequences are unknown, and their relation to data is unknown. ... The choice, then, is not whether to build models; it's whether to build explicit [agent-based] ones. In explicit models, assumptions are laid out in detail, so we can study exactly what they entail. (pp. 1.3–1.5)

The utility of the computational approach is that one can examine the merits of theory and assess the natural consequence of micro-level behaviors observed in a laboratory setting or in qualitative research. These concrete benefits, however, do not change the fact that the computational approach is still a dynamic *artificial* model of the system of racial inequality.

Counting Race: The Master Plan

The quantitative analysis of race and racial inequality presents researchers with an array of dilemmas. "How do we measure race? Can survey data capture the dynamic, interactive process? Are we able to replicate experiments in the real world? Does my residual race effect measure discrimination? How can I model structure?" No technique will sufficiently address all of these and many other dilemmas (i.e., questions). Every method has at least one major limitation that prevents an analyst from strictly confirming/refuting a theory on the emergence, experience and maintenance of race and racial inequality (see Table 10.1). The question remains: How should we conduct policy relevant quantitative race research given the limitations of each method?

There are two solutions to the dilemma. The first solution is to continue the status quo. One can conduct research and mention the limitations in the Methods and Discussion sections of an article. For many, this will be the preferred solution. There are no real costs to this solution other than the addition of text that lists the caveats of the analysis. One may also add qualifying language to the interpretations of the results to better frame the contribution of the study to the literature. The pitfall is this solution does not advance our understanding of the system of race and racial inequality. A researcher must still speculate about the policy relevance of a significant residual correlation between two variables. Or, one must infer what a finite interaction in a laboratory experiment would look like in the real world when it's taking place in millions of interactions in various social realms everyday. The inability to

Table 10.1 Summary of Quantitative Methods for Race Research

Method	Benefits	Limitations
Traditional survey	Easy to apply, elegant design, cost effective	Static data (i.e., not dynamic), causality inferred
Comparative analysis	Easy to apply, elegant design, identification of broad mechanism, cost effective	Static data (i.e., not dynamic), causality inferred, requires good criterion variable
Natural experiment	Elegant design, identification of policy mechanism (i.e., quasi-manipulation), causal model	Overlooks micro-level response to manipulation, requires good instrument (i.e., quasi-manipulation), inflexible manipulation
Multilevel analysis	Flexibility in model specification, incorporates time (i.e., longitudinal) or space (e.g., geography, social), models growth/emergence	Overlooks micro-level processes (e.g., treatment, response), requires good conceptual measurement at each level, causality inferred (geographic models)
Formal experiment	Models micro-level interaction, causal model, flexible manipulations	Small sample size, limited generalizability, mechanisms and manipulations are often contrived (i.e., not real), high costs
Computational	Dynamic data, simultaneously models micro-level interaction and system, causal model, flexible manipulations, large sample size	Contrived data, limited generalizability, difficult to apply

shed light on more than one aspect of the dynamics of race and racial inequality makes this solution undesirable.

A second solution is to conduct research that uses more than one quantitative method. This solution draws on the allegory of the blind men and the elephant. Each of the blind men in the allegory touches one part of the elephant to infer what the elephant looks/feels like. The consequence of this event is that each blind man has a different description of the elephant. This leads to a conflict as to which description is correct.

As in the allegory, a scientist (or group of scientists) who conducts quantitative race research using one method illuminates one aspect of the system of racial inequality. Another, using a different method, sheds light on another dimension of racial inequality. This is further complicated by research being conducted using one social domain, sample, and/or general specification. The conclusion of these separate scientific investigations using different methods is often disagreement—specifically, a heightened conflict about the social experience of racial inequality and the policy solutions.

We can, however, solve this dilemma by taking a lesson from the blind men and the elephant allegory. The blind men were limited to inferences based on touching one aspect of the elephant. As scientists, we are free to study the experience of racial inequality using an array of quantitative methods; we are only limited by our training and imagination! We can advance our understanding of race and racial inequality by using complimentary quantitative methods (i.e., one method overcomes the limitations of the other)—as well as qualitative methods that better capture the immeasurable human experience (e.g., emotion, spirituality). These types of analyses will provide insights into how the concept of race becomes racial inequality across the course of social interaction and better reveal the social experience of race.

Perhaps the best example of this second solution is seen in group processes research. Social scientists in this tradition use an array of methods to reveal the mechanisms behind a particular outcome (e.g., the emergence of status value for a characteristic) (Berger et al. 1972; Cohen 1982; Ridgeway 1991). These scholars use formal experiments, computer simulations, and traditional surveys as well as qualitative methods to ascertain the fundamental mechanisms of a particular social process (Cohen & Lotan 1995; Ridgeway 1997; Ridgeway & Balkwell 1997; Ridgeway et al. 1998; Ridgeway & Johnson 1990; Robinson & Smith-Lovin 2001; Smith-Lovin & Brody 1989; Umberson & Hughes 1987). No one researcher performs all the methods. Rather, they collaborate with methodologically divergent colleagues to assess the different aspects of the system of interest. In race research, this strategy would provide a more nuanced understanding of the social and policy mechanisms that create and maintain racial inequality.

Indeed, triangulation in quantitative race research would be most effective at capturing the multiple mechanisms that create and maintain racial inequality—at once a social identity, an institutional force, and a network structure. One example of the triangulation approach in race research is a disparate outcomes study that employs traditional survey research, multilevel models, and computational methods. Sewell (Forthcoming) is using this approach to analyze racial discrimination as a fundamental cause—or multi-pathway mechanism—of health disparities. In the analysis, she connects a longitudinal survey of youth who are nested in neighborhoods with: (1) data from a community survey of adults living in the neighborhoods; and (2) systematic observations of the institutional and environmental features of the neighborhoods.

Sewell uses traditional survey methods and multilevel analysis to model the emergence of health disparities, and, subsequently, the individual- and community-level characteristics that are related to this emergence. The limitation of this initial analysis is that it ignores the micro-level processes (i.e., agency of actors) that influence the relationship between the variables of interest. To overcome this limitation, she uses the computational approach to estimate how human agency (i.e., selection effects) and health behaviors may bias the results. Thus, Sewell uses triangulation to reveal the nuanced mechanisms that shape the experience of race and racial inequality.

Concluding Thoughts

In his early article entitled "The Study of the Negro Problems," Du Bois (1898:2) defined a social problem as "the failure of an organized social group to realize it's groups ideals, through the inability to adapt a certain desired line of action to given conditions of life." Du Bois viewed the exclusion of Blacks from fully participating in the national life of the United States as a pressing social problem. In the course of his career, Du Bois aimed to use social scientific research to reveal the sources of the race problem so they could be used as guides for policy aimed at eradicating racial inequality.

The continued significant racial disparities in earnings, educational achievement, health outcomes, and countless other measures of social and physical well-being represent a modern social problem (Conley 1999; Grodsky & Pager 2001; Hayward & Heron 1999; McCall 2001; Oliver & Shapiro 1995; Stewart 2009; Stewart & Dixon 2010; Williams & Collins 2001). Though minority groups are no longer excluded from the gamut of social realms through legal means, significant disparities in well-being are signs that the complex system of racial inequality still exists. Our task as social scientists is to shed new light on the mechanisms used to maintain this system. For quantitative social scientists, this means using formal, mathematical techniques to measure the extent to which a social policy, network, or other pattern of social interaction influences the experience of racial inequality in a particular social dimension.

Quantitative race researchers must produce empirically sound estimates of the nature and magnitude of racial inequality and assess the varying degrees to which specific mechanisms act to create and maintain racial outcome disparities. The dilemma is that our methods, when used singularly, undermine our ability to clearly identify the range of mechanisms behind race and racial inequality. We can overcome the limitations in one method by supplementing our analyses with complimentary methods. Data limitations may prevent scholars who study less-developed regions or novel outcomes from using an array of methods. One may have to build the infrastructure to perform complimentary quantitative analyses of racial inequality in a particular environment. The benefit of the complimentary analyses, though, is the ability to circumvent the limitations of single method and shed new light on the social machinery (i.e., mechanisms) that constitutes the system of race and racial inequality. By revealing these mechanisms, quantitative social scientists set the stage for realizing the larger universal ideals of fairness, equality, and justice for all. And then we may begin to see the promise of race research in the United States and beyond.

ACKNOWLEDGMENTS

We thank John Stanfield and Tukufu Zuberi for their comments and conversations regarding earlier drafts of this chapter. This research was partially supported by a National Science Foundation Graduate Research Fellowship and a Ford Foundation Predoctoral Fellowship for Abigail A. Sewell. An earlier version of this chapter was presented at the workshop on Handling Measurement Error in Quantitative Studies of Race and Ethnicity at the 2010 Annual Meeting of the American Sociological Association in Atlanta, Georgia. Direct correspondence to: Quincy Thomas Stewart, Department of Sociology, 1810 Chicago Avenue, Northwestern University, Evanston, IL 60208-1330.

REFERENCES

Adler, N. E., & Rehkopf, D. H. (2008). U.S. disparities in health: Descriptions, causes, and mechanisms. *Annual Review of Public Health, 29*, 235–252.

Andreasen, A. R. (1995). *Marketing social change: Changing behavior to promote health, social development, and the environment.* San Francisco: Jossey-Bass.

Bashi, V., & McDaniel, A. (1997). A theory of immigration and racial stratification. *Journal of Black Studies, 27*, 668–682.

Bansak, C., & Raphael, S. (2001). Immigration reform and the earnings of Latino workers: Do employer sanctions cause discrimination. *Industrial and Labor Relations Review, 54*, 275–295.

Bell, A. C., Adair, L. S., & Popkin, B. M. (2004). Understanding the role of mediating risk factors and proxy effects in the association between socio-economic status and untreated hypertension. *Social Science & Medicine, 59*, 275–283.

Bendick, M., Jr., Brown, L., & Wall, K. (1999). No foot in the door: An experimental study of employment discrimination. *Journal of Aging and Social Policy, 10*, 5–23.

Bendick, M., Jr., Jackson, C., & Reinoso, V. (1994). Measuring employment discrimination through controlled experiments. *Review of Black Political Economy, 23,* 25–48.

Bendick, M., Jr., Jackson, C., Reinoso, V., & Hodges, L. (1991). Discrimination against Latino job applicants: A controlled experiment. *Human Resource Management, 30,* 469–484.

Berger, J., Cohen, B. P., & Zelditch, M., Jr. (1972). Status characteristics and social interaction. *American Sociological Review, 37,* 241–255.

Block, J., & Robins, R. W. (1993). A longitudinal study of consistency and change in self-esteem from early adolescence to early adulthood. *Child Development, 64,* 909–923.

Blumer, H. (1969/1998). *Symbolic interactionism: Perspective and method.* Berkeley: University of California Press.

Bonilla-Silva, E. (1996). Rethinking racism: Toward a structural interpretation. *American Sociological Review, 62,* 465–480.

Bonilla-Silva, E. (2003). *Racism without racists: Color-blind racism and the persistence of racial inequality in the United States.* Lanham, MD: Rowman & Littlefield.

Bonilla-Silva, E., & Baiocchi, G. (2001). Anything but racism: How sociologists limit the significance of racism. *Race and Society, 4,* 117–131.

Cancio, A. S. T., Evans, D., & Maume, D. J., Jr. (1996). Reconsidering the declining significance of race: Racial differences in early career wages. *American Sociological Review, 61,* 541–556.

Cederman, L.-E. (2005). Computational models of social forms: Advancing generative process theory. *American Journal of Sociology, 110,* 864–893.

Chay, K. Y. (1998). The impact of federal civil rights policy of black economic progress: Evidence from the Equal Employment Opportunity Act of 1972. *Industrial and Labor Relations Review, 51,* 608–632.

Chay, K. Y., & Greenstone, M. (2003). The impact of air pollution on infant mortality: Evidence from geographic variation in pollution shocks induced by a recession. *The Quarterly Journal of Economics, 118,* 1121–1167.

Cohen, E. G. (1982). Expectation states and interracial interaction in school settings. *Annual Review of Sociology, 8,* 209–235.

Cohen, E. G., & Lotan, R. A. (1995). Producing equal-status interaction in the heterogeneous classroom. *American Educational Research Journal, 32,* 99–120.

Collins, C. A., & Williams, D. R. (1999). Segregation and mortality: The deadly effects of racism? *Sociological Forum, 14,* 495–523.

Collins, J. W., Wu, S. Y. & David, R. J. (2002). Differing intergenerational birth weights among the descendants of U.S.-born and foreign-born whites and African-Americans in Illinois. *American Journal of Epidemiology, 155,* 210–216.

Conley, D. (1999). *Being black, living in the red: Race, wealth, and social policy in America.* Berkeley: University of California Press.

Darity, W. A., Jr. (1982). The human capital approach to black-white earnings inequality: Some unsettled questions. *The Journal of Human Resources, 17,* 72–93.

Darity, W. A., Jr. (1998). Intergroup disparity: Economic theory and social science evidence. *Southern Economic Journal, 64,* 805–826.

Dodoo, F. N. (1997). Assimilation differences among Africans in America. *Social Forces, 76*, 527–546.

Dressler, W. W., Oths, K. S., & Gravlee, C. C. (2005). Race and ethnicity in public health research: Models to explain health disparities. *Annual Review of Anthropology, 34*, 231–252.

Du Bois, W. E. B. (1898). The study of the Negro problems. *The Annals of the American Academy of Political and Social Science, 11*, 1–23.

Du Bois, W. E. B. (1899/1996). *The Philadelphia Negro: A social study.* Philadelphia: University of Pennsylvania Press.

Durlak, J. A., & Wells, A. M. (1997). Primary prevention mental health programs for children and adolescents: A meta-analytic review. *American Journal of Community Psychology, 25*, 115–152.

Durlak, J. A., & Wells, A. M. (1998). Evaluation of indicated preventive intervention (secondary prevention) mental health programs for children and adolescents. *American Journal of Community Psychology, 26*, 775–802.

Eccles, J. S., Gootman, J. A., & National Research Council (U.S.), Committee on Community-Level Programs for Youth, National Research Council (U.S.), Board on Children Youth and Families, and Institute of Medicine (U.S.). (2002). *Community programs to promote youth development.* Washington, DC: National Academy Press.

Emirbayer, M. (1997). Manifesto for a relational sociology. *American Sociological Review, 103*, 281–317.

Epstein, J. M. (2008). Why model? *Journal of Artificial Societies and Social Simulation, 11*. http://jasss.soc.surrey.ac.uk/11/4/12.html (accessed March 23, 2011).

Epstein, J. M., & Axtell, R. (1996). *Growing artificial societies: Social science from the bottom up.* Washington, DC: The Brookings Institution.

Farkas, G., & Vicknair, K. (1996). Appropriate tests of racial wage discrimination require controls for cognitive skill: Comment on Cancio, Evans, and Maume. *American Sociological Review, 61*, 557–560.

Fix, M., Galster, G. C., & Struyk, R. J. (1993). An overview of auditing for discrimination. In S. Fix & R. Struyk (Eds.), *Clear and convincing evidence: Measurement of discrimination in America* (pp. 1–68). Washington, DC: Urban Institute Press.

Fryer, R. G., Jr., & Torelli, P. (2005). An empirical analysis of "acting white." Working paper, Harvard University.

Grodsky, E., & Pager, D. (2001). The structure of disadvantage: Individual and occupational determinants of the black-white wage gap. *American Sociological Review, 66*, 542–567.

Hanneman, R. A. (1995). Simulation modeling and theoretical analysis in sociology. *Sociological Perspectives, 38*, 457–462.

Hanneman, R. A., Collins, R., & Mordt, G. (1995). Discovering theory dynamics by computer simulation: Experiments on state legitimacy and imperialist capitalism. *Sociological Methodology, 25*, 1–46.

Harvey, D. (1973). *Social justice and the city.* Baltimore: Johns Hopkins University Press.

Hayward, M. D., & Heron, M. (1999). Racial inequality in active life among adult Americans. *Demography, 36*, 77–92.

Heckman, J. J., & Siegelman, P. (1993). The Urban Institute audit studies: Their methods and findings. In S. Fix & R. Struyk (Eds.), *Clear and convincing evidence: Measurement of discrimination in America* (pp. 187–258). Washington, DC: Urban Institute Press.

Horton, H. D., & Sykes, L. L. (2008). Critical demography and the measurement of racism: A reproduction of wealth, status, and power. In T. Zuberi & E. Bonilla-Silva (Eds.), *White logic, white methods: Race, epistemology and the social sciences* (pp. 239–250). Lanham, MD: Rowman & Littlefield.

Karter, A. J., Ferrara, A., Liu, J. Y., Moffet, H. H., Ackerson, L. M., & Selby, J. V. (2002). Ethnic disparities in diabetic complications in an insured population. *JAMA, 287*, 2519–2527.

Kilbourne, B., England, P., & Beron, K. (1994). Effects of individual, occupational, and industrial characteristics on earnings: Intersections of race and gender. *Social Forces, 72*, 1149–1176.

Korpi, W., & Palme, J. (1998). The paradox of redistribution and strategies of equality: Welfare state institutions, inequality, and poverty in the Western countries. *American Sociological Review, 63*, 661–687.

Lantz, P. M., House, J. S., Lepkowski, J. M., Williams, D. R., Mero, R. P., & Chen, J. (1998). Socioeconomic factors, health behaviors, and mortality: Results from a nationally representative prospective study of US adults. *JAMA, 279*, 1703–1708.

Lantz, P. M., Lynch, J. W., House, J. S., Lepkowski, J. M., Mero, R. P., Musick, M. A., & Williams, D. R. (2001). Socioeconomic disparities in health change in a longitudinal study of US adults: The role of health-risk behaviors. *Social Science & Medicine, 53*, 29–40.

Leik, R. K., & Meeker, B. F. (1995). Computer simulation for exploring theories: Models of interpersonal cooperation and competition. *Sociological Perspectives, 38*, 463–482.

Loring, M., & Powell, B. (1988). Gender, race, and DSM-III: A study of the objectivity of psychiatric diagnostic behavior. *Journal of Health and Social Behavior, 29*, 1–22.

Macy, M. W., & Willer, R. (2002). From factors to actors: Computational sociology and agent-based modeling. *Annual Review of Sociology, 28*, 143–166.

Marini, M. M., & Singer, B. (1988). Causality in the social sciences. *Sociological Methodology, 18*, 347–409.

Martin, L. L. (2009). Black asset ownership: Does ethnicity matter? *Social Science Research, 38*, 312–323.

McCall, L. (2001). Sources of racial wage inequality in metropolitan labor markets: Racial, ethnic, and gender differences. *American Sociological Review, 66*, 520–541.

McWhorter, J. (2000). *Losing the race: Self-sabotage in black America.* New York: The Free Press.

Moss, S., & Edmonds, B. (2002). Sociology and simulation: Statistical and qualitative cross-validation. *American Journal of Sociology, 110*, 1095–1131.

Muthén, B., & Muthén, L. K. (2000). Integrating person-centered and variable-centered analyses: Growth mixture modeling with latent trajectory classes. *Alcoholism: Clinical and Experimental Research, 24,* 882–891.

Neal, D. A., & Johnson, W. R. (1996). The role of premarket factors in black-white wage differences. *The Journal of Political Economy, 104,* 869–895.

Ogbu, J. U. (1974). *The next generation: An ethnography of education in an urban neighborhood.* New York: Academic Press.

Ogbu, J. U. (1978). *Minority education and caste.* New York: Academic Press.

Ogbu, J. U. (1983). Minority status and schooling in plural societies. *Comparative Education Review, 27,* 168–190.

Ogbu, J. U. (1987). Variability in minority school performance: A problem in search of an explanation. *Anthropology & Education Quarterly, 18,* 312–334.

Ogbu, J. U. (1990). Minority education in comparative perspective. *The Journal of Negro Education, 59,* 45–57.

Ogbu, J. U., & Davis, A. (2003). *Black American students in an affluent suburb: A study of academic disengagement.* Mahwah, NJ: Lawrence Erlbaum Associates.

Oliver, M., & Shapiro, T. (1995). *Black wealth, white wealth: A new perspective on racial inequality.* New York: Routledge.

Omi, M., & Winant, H. (1994). *Racial formation in the United States: From the 1960s to the 1990s.* New York: Routledge.

O'Neill, J. (1990). The role of human capital in earnings differences between black and white men. *The Journal of Economic Perspectives, 4,* 25–45.

Pager, D. (2003). The mark of a criminal record. *American Journal of Sociology, 108,* 937–975.

Perneger, T. V., Whelton, P. K., Klag, M. J., & Rossiter, K. A. (1995). Diagnosis of hypertensive end-stage renal disease: Effect of patient's race. *American Journal of Epidemiology, 141,* 10–15.

Reskin, B. (2003). 2002 presidential address: Including mechanisms in our models of ascriptive inequality. *American Sociological Review, 68,* 1–21.

Richeson, J. A., & Trawalter, S. (2008). The threat of appearing prejudiced and race-based attentional biases. *Psychological Science, 19,* 98–102.

Ridgeway, C. L. (1991). The social construction of status value: Gender and other nominal characteristics. *Social Forces, 70,* 367–386.

Ridgeway, C. L. (1997). Interaction and the conservation of gender inequality: Considering employment. *American Sociological Review, 62,* 218–235.

Ridgeway, C. L., & Balkwell, J. W. (1997). Group processes and the diffusion of status beliefs. *Social Psychology Quarterly, 60,* 14–31.

Ridgeway, C. L., Boyle, E. H., Kuipers, K. J., & Robinson, D. T. (1998). How do status beliefs develop? The role of resources and interactional experience. *American Sociological Review, 63,* 331–350.

Ridgeway, C. L., & Johnson, C. (1990). What is the relationship between socioemotional behavior and status in task groups? *The American Journal of Sociology, 95,* 1189–1212.

Robinson, D. T., & Smith-Lovin, L. (2001). Getting a laugh: Gender, status, and humor in task discussions. *Social Forces, 80,* 123–158.

Roscigno, V. J., & Ainsworth-Darnell, J. W. (1999). Race, cultural capital, and educational resources: Persistent inequalities and achievement returns. *Sociology of Education, 72,* 158–178.

Saltman, J. (1979). Housing discrimination: Policy research, methods and results. *Annals of the American Academy of Political and Social Science, 441,* 186–196.

Schelling, T. C. (1971). Dynamic models of segregation. *Journal of Mathematical Sociology, 1,* 143–186.

Schoenborn, C. A., Adams, P. G., Barnes, P. M., Vickerie, J. L., & Schiller, J. S. (2004). Health behaviors of adults: United States, 1999–2001. *Vital and Health Statistics, 10,* 1–79.

Schwalbe, M., Godwin, S., Holden, D., Schrock, D., Thompson. S., & Wolkomir, M. (2000). Generic processes in the reproduction of inequality: An interactionist analysis. *Social Forces, 79,* 419–452.

Sewell, A. A. (Forthcoming). Racial discrimination as a fundamental cause of health: A disparate outcomes analysis of multilevel longitudinal data from the Project on Human Development in Chicago Neighborhoods. Ph.D. dissertation (in preparation), Indiana University.

Smith-Lovin, L., & Brody, C. (1989). Interruptions in group discussions: The effects of gender and group composition. *American Sociological Review, 54,* 424–435.

Sowell, T. (1978). Three black histories. In T. Sowell (Ed.), *Essays and data on American ethnic groups* (pp. 7–64). Washington, DC: The Urban Institute.

Sowell, T. (1983). *The economics and politics of race.* New York: William Morrow.

Steele, C. (2003). Stereotype threat and African-American student achievement. In T. Perry, C. Steele, & A. Hilliard, III (Eds.), *Young, gifted and black: Promoting high achievement among African-American students* (pp. 109–130). Boston: Beacon Press.

Stewart, Q. T. (2008a). Chasing the race effect: An analysis of traditional quantitative research on race in sociology. In C. Gallagher (Ed.), *Racism in post-race America: New theories, new directions* (pp. 285–304). Chapel Hill, NC: Social Forces.

Stewart, Q. T. (2008b). Swimming upstream: Theory and quantitative methodology in race research. In T. Zuberi & E. Bonilla-Silva (Eds.), *White logic, white methods: Race, epistemology and the social sciences* (pp. 111–126). Lanham, MD: Rowman & Littlefield.

Stewart, Q. T. (2009). The shape of inequality: Racial disparities in age-specific mortality. *Biodemography and Social Biology, 54,* 152–182.

Stewart, Q. T. (2010). Big bad racists, subtle prejudice and minority victims: An agent-based analysis of the dynamics of racial inequality. Presented at the 2010 Annual Meeting of the Population Association of America, Dallas, Texas.

Stewart, Q. T., & Dixon, J. C. (2010). Is it race, immigrant status or both? An analysis of wage disparities among men in the United States. *International Migration Review, 44,* 173–201.

Sykes, L. L. (2003). Income rich and asset poor: A multilevel analysis of racial and ethnic differences in housing values among baby boomers. *Population Research and Policy Review, 22,* 1–20.

Tilly, C. (1998). *Durable inequality*. Berkeley: University of California Press.

Tyler, T. R. (1997). *Social justice in a diverse society*. Boulder, CO: Westview.

Umberson, D., & Hughes, M. (1987). The impact of physical attractiveness on achievement and psychological well-being. *Social Psychology Quarterly, 50,* 227–236.

Walker, H. A. (2011). Researching race: (Re)thinking experiments. In J. H. Stanfield, II (Ed.), *Rethinking race and ethnicity in research methods.* Walnut Creek, CA: Left Coast Press.

Walker, H. A., & Willer, D. (2007). Experiments and the science of sociology. In M. Webster, Jr. & J. Sell (Eds.), *Laboratory experiments in the social sciences* (pp. 25–56). Burlington, MA: Academic Press.

Waters, M. C. (1999). *Black identities: West Indian immigrant dreams and American realities*. New York: Russell Sage Foundation.

West, C., & Fenstermaker, S. (1995). Doing difference. *Gender and Society, 9,* 8–37.

Willer, D., & Walker, H. A. (2007). *Building experiments: Testing social theory*. Palo Alto, CA: Stanford University Press.

Williams, D. R., & Collins, C. A. (2001). Racial residential segregation: A fundamental cause of racial disparities in health. *Public Health Reports, 116,* 404–416.

Williams, D. R., & Jackson, P. B. (2005). Social sources of racial disparities in health. *Health Affairs, 24,* 325–334.

Wilson, W. J. (1978). *The declining significance of race: Blacks and changing American institutions*. Chicago: University of Chicago Press.

Yinger, J. (1993). Access denied, access constrained: Results and implications of the 1989 housing discrimination study. In S. Fix & R. Struyk (Eds.), *Clear and convincing evidence: Measurement of discrimination in America* (pp. 69–112). Washington, DC: Urban Institute Press.

Zuberi, T. (2001). *Thicker than blood: How racial statistics lie*. Minneapolis: University of Minnesota Press.

11 REHUMANIZING RACE-RELATED RESEARCH IN QUALITATIVE STUDY OF FAITH-BASED ORGANIZATIONS: CASE STUDIES, FOCUS GROUPS, AND LONG INTERVIEWS

Dawn B. Brotherton

A PERSONAL JOURNEY

Tylese was the only person in my fifth-grade class with dark skin, but I didn't consciously think about that until the day she left our school. Of real significance to me was the way she wore her hair. I only wore two hair bobbles at a time—"pigtails"—one on either side of my head, but she styled a dozen in every direction, and her hair stayed beautifully twirled. One day in the middle of the year, our teacher told us that Tylese wouldn't be coming back. She was not in class and our teacher was crying. We had disappointed her in the way we treated Tylese. I don't know what prompted the situation and I don't remember talking with anyone else about it after that moment. It was confusing, but then the day went on and it was never mentioned again. At some point after college, during a training event for my job, a facilitator asked our group to draw a map of significant moments related to race starting as far back as we could remember. The story of Tylese was the first thing that came to my mind.

Race moved from the shadows to the front of my thinking while in Africa for several months during college. In April 1993, I was in East London, South Africa, days after the assassination of Chris Hani, leader of the South African Communist Party and the ANC. While rioters filled the streets of the city, I watched the events unfold on television with strict instructions from my host family to stay inside. Nelson Mandela spoke to the country in an effort to keep tensions from erupting into further violence. The deep complexities of race in South Africa came into view. I started reading, asking questions, and, on my return home, paying attention to race relations in the United States.

For ten years after graduation, I worked in a faith-based organization where conversations and efforts to increase racial diversity were taking place. This led to a lot of frustration and little change. The experience set me on a journey to understand racial inclusion in faith-based organizations. In 1995, I took a class called Africana Ministry in the Twenty-first Century, in which we immersed ourselves in African American history and took a ten-day bus tour to some of the places involved in the civil rights movement. We traveled through Selma and Birmingham, Atlanta, Nashville, Little Rock, and Cincinnati, visiting museums, listening to lectures, meeting with civil rights activists, and watching videos about the freedom struggle and Dr. Martin Luther King, Jr. During that trip, I wrestled with my identity as a Christian in relation to racism undergirded by white Christian theology and the minuscule presence of the white church in the struggle against it (Chappell 2004; Ellis 1996).

My interest in racial inclusion in religious organizations took on new dimensions with the growth of my family. Statements from my preschooler like, "Mommy, I only see peachy skin," created a fresh urgency to address the issues of creating a deracialized world. Race and its subversive powers must be understood and pushed against because it influences everyone to perpetuate the oppressions of race, regardless of deeply held beliefs about human equality and because the effects of internalized racism are not recognized until they have happened (Katz 2003; Omi & Winant 1994; Stanfield Under review).

In the early stages of my journey, fighting racism was like a David and Goliath story. Race as Goliath was an enormous enemy jeering at those tiny few who dared come against it. I now see race and the resulting problems of racialization, racialism, and racism as analogous to a disease of addiction. There is no silver bullet that takes down that giant. The paradigm of addiction presents a long-term, complex, and ingrained process that must be examined and addressed over time, with multiple interventions at individual and systemic levels. The challenge comes in learning to recognize destructive, debilitating responses and the triggers that send one down those dysfunctional paths. New ways of thinking must be created, learned, and practiced with support networks and guides to help along the way. There are communities of people practicing deracialized ways of living and intentional goals of inclusions that derail the process of racialization. We must see and understand how racial harmony is allowed to thrive. My hope is such research will help us understand how to facilitate racial healing in faith-based organizations, among racial groups, between individuals, and within the souls of people so that humanity is restored to us all as we view and interact with ourselves and each other.

Unique Challenges of Race-Related Research

Race-related research presents a number of unique challenges that must be addressed so the integrity of the research process as well as the validity and reliability of the data can remain strong. More harm than good comes from the research process when researchers engage race without paying close attention to the specific meaning of words, the deeply embedded weight of the issue for people in racialized societies, and the difficulty of engaging people in meaningful dialog about it. Race as a category is a dehumanizing process because for hundreds of years it has pressed us to live out the lie that some people are "better than" or "less than" others, based only on phenotypical characteristics. No one escapes unharmed from living this way. Viewing people through this narrow lens and judging behavior and character on those features alone harms the emotional, psychological, and spiritual core of individuals and society as much as overt acts of racism, which harm the physical body.

This dehumanizing process works equally against the oppressor as well as the oppressed, creating an erosion of relational capacity that jeopardizes the social networks necessary for healthy society where people can prosper (Du Bois 1903; Myrdal 1944). An added problem with this type of wound is that when left unresolved it remains, and the story is ultimately passed to future generations who continue to carry it resulting in a further-fractured society where differences seem insurmountable (Stanfield Under review; Staub & Pearlman 2001; Volf 1996). Researchers engage on a large scale to identify and reveal the nature of race in all its insidious forms, because it will not disappear by ignoring it and time will not heal all wounds.

The dehumanization of people involved in research studies starts in the design process and is multiplied in the research process through the temptation to reify race categories. Common descriptors such as black, white, asian, minority, person of color, and so on are overly simplistic and carry little meaning unless the topic of study is actually racial stereotypes. They wrongly erase important distinctions and differences related to things like ethnicity, age, or gender and present a false idea of homogeneous groups (Stanfield 1993). The problem is complicated because addressing the oppression and dehumanization caused by race, racialism, and racism requires using the very terms that need to be erased in order to create a deracialized society (Maylam 2005). As researchers, scholar-practitioners, and students of social and behavioral sciences, we have not yet used enough imagination to create new and different vocabulary to describe the reality of whole and complex human beings. As a result, such race-related concepts have become further embedded and fixed within the social sciences and spread to social thought in general, despite their inaccuracies and lies.

The language surrounding race issues poses another challenge for researchers. Words commonly used in conversation about racial issues such as race, ethnicity, culture, and nationality are often used interchangeably and mistakenly to mean the same things. The confusion of these words and the perpetuation of race as a construct in social thought make it difficult to have clear dialog or study about race issues. Race is a false idea constructed through social and cultural processes created to advance economic, political, and legal

agendas, and the resulting race categories use peoples' phenotypical characteristics to define and predict a person or population's behavior, social characteristics, cultural characteristics, moral fiber, propensity to do good or bad,
and physical, mental, or social abilities (Barndt 2007; Horton 2003; Omi &
Winant 1994).

Race is commonly interchanged with ethnicity or culture to mean a person
with a different color skin, from a different country, speaking a different language, or to refer to a person in the minority population of a group because of
obvious differences with the majority group. This is an important distinction,
because people with different phenotypical characteristics can share a common
ethnicity, culture, or nationality. Ethnicity refers to common societal characteristics and culture shared by a group of people particularly marked by tribal
and/or national heritage, language, and traditions (Cornell & Hartmann 1998).

In racialized societies such as the United States, South Africa, or Brazil,
ethnicity is only assigned to people considered "not white" when, in reality,
relocation of families and peoples across continents, countries, and national
borders has resulted in most people in the world being multiethnic; however,
we are not socialized to understand ethnicity in this way (Stanfield 1995).
Culture is often connected to a particular ethnicity, but it does not have to be.
Different cultures commonly exist within the same ethnicity or nationality.
Nationality is defined by a government holding authority over a geographic
region of land. People of different ethnicities may share the same nationality
through birth or nationalized citizenship. Using these terms synonymously
causes confusion and makes communicating about race more difficult.

A slow shift of focus away from race to tangential topics has weakened
the ability of researchers to confront race issues. It is important to notice the
movement from race to multicultural, multiethnic, multiracial, appreciation,
inclusion, and so on because over time it has shifted education, policy-making,
and potentially healing dialogs about race issues to areas of diversity with
much less historical conflict and repercussions than exist around race such as
gender, sexual orientation, personality type, work preferences, and leadership
styles. The perpetual use of race as a category on mandatory government and
educational forms like census data sheets or applications for monetary aid further confuses the issue. On official documents, people are required to define
themselves according to a predefined category that may not really exist or
does not capture their identity as they know it to be, and then in actual life (or
multiple places of life) claim different racial identities.

A Multimethod Approach

Qualitative data collection is most suitable for race-related research because
it is able to tap a deeper level of consciousness with subtleties and nuances.

It allows a researcher to understand how people see, feel, think about, and understand their experience. The subjective nature of interpreting life as part of a group and making meaning of one's experience requires a methodology that captures depth and complexity. Narrative analysis of interview transcripts and organizational documents help find the deeper meaning of participants' stories (Spickard 2007). Narratives gathered through qualitative methods such as individual and group interviews allow space for stories to emerge while participants speak in their own words without being boxed in by specific answers. They also let the stories be retained in the words of the participants during data analysis.

Case Studies

The case study as a method of inquiry has a long tradition in psychology and anthropology. Early psychologists like Freud used individual people to study interesting phenomena and develop theory. Individuals were observed over long periods of time with detailed notes and interviews. Following the lead of the Chicago School, many early sociologists and social workers in the United States during the 1920s and 1930s used case studies alongside ethnography, surveys, and comparative historical methods to study small towns, urban growth, and immigrant populations (Denzin & Lincoln 2000). In the 1930s and 1940s, statistical surveys became widely used, and the debate about the reliability and validity of qualitative research raged on. Case studies fell out of common use because they were not considered sufficiently valid, and quantitative methods became popular. Case study research has again become common in social science research as postmodern dialog, feminist research, critical theory, and deconstruction of positivism have raised questions about the reliance and faith in quantitative research and argued for the validity and reliability of qualitative research.

A case study must have clearly defined boundaries around a distinct or unique situation and rely on multiple sources of evidence that can include different qualitative and quantitative methods (Hamel et al. 1993; Stake 2003). A case study may include immersion or participation in and direct observation of a group, community, or culture; it may focus on the uniqueness of a group, description, or interpretation and try to see what is hidden to people within the group. In these ways, it uses some elements of ethnography. Ethnography, however, can often encompass more than what would be bounded by a singular case.

Case studies allow a researcher to present a real-life phenomenon or situation in its context (Yin 1994). Case studies can capture the complexity of situations, which is often the case with human systems. They provide a more holistic study of social processes from many different sources over a significant period of time, allow the investigator to see continuity and changes in patterns of the case, and encourage creativity and innovation in making generalizations from the data (Feagin et al. 1991; Yin 1994). This occurs when case studies are used as a prominent mode of research on multiethnic religious organizations (Christerson et al. 2005; Christerson & Emerson 2003; Emerson & Kim 2003; Heffner 2005; Marti 2005; Sanders 2006).

Through focusing on one or just a few cases at a time, researchers have been able to investigate both micro-events as well as the larger social structures of the organizations with rich depth and detail and identify and theorize about how, what, and why they were able to become integrated and remain so. Across these different studies, a mixture of qualitative and quantitative methods have been used including, ethnography, participant observation, surveys, phone interviews, and in-depth face-to-face interviews. Cases are also used to help establish the limits of generalization (Stake 2000) by finding exceptional cases to what is already known. When matched with well-formed questions, case studies can shed more light on a subject than extensive, randomly selected survey research (Williams 1991).

Focus Groups

Interviewing many people together was an innovative and successful experiment developed by Robert Merton (Denzin & Lincoln 2000). It was used in marketing research to study consumer opinions, advertising, and customer service delivery; in politics for voter reaction and opinions; and in sociological research to better understand criminology, aging, medical sociology, social movements, the sociology of work, and in subdisciplines such as program development and evaluation, fertility, family planning, and HIV/AIDS research around the world (Morgan 1997). Feminist researchers are strong proponents of using focus groups as a primary research tool with many minority group populations who are likely to feel threatened by one-on-one interviews and for whom normal life circumstances function around communities rather than as individualistic cultures (Madriz 2000).

A value of focus group methodology is the opportunity to gather a collective story from a number of people talking together that would not arise if these people were interviewed separately. Members of the focus group often feel more secure speaking out on issues if other people in the group hold similar views or if they feel they do not have to defend their views to an interviewer by themselves. Comments by one individual may cause a chain reaction of responses from other participants by triggering their thoughts on certain issues. Because many people are being asked a question at one time, an individual does not feel pressured to come up with a response to every question. Participants question each other, explain themselves to each other, and agree or disagree with each other. This type of interaction allows the researcher to use the group process as a window into the behaviors and motivations of the group that might inform further questions and developing conceptual models or hypotheses of the research.

At the same time, this process requires a greater level of preparation, understanding, and emotional intelligence on the part of the interviewer since that person must be a competent and skilled group facilitator. The importance of having a skilled facilitator is magnified when the interview questions relate to race because of the emotionality, deep-seated pain, confusion, and sensitive nature of this topic.

Morgan points out the need for the facilitator to pay close attention to all aspects of group dynamics. Though the group may only exist for as little as a few hours and for a specific purpose, group formation and dynamics will occur and should be managed well for the group to be successful at discussing the topics relevant to the research question. Any group of people coming together for the first time will experience some level of anxiety and questions regarding their ability to fit into the group, the motivations of others in the group, their safety and freedom in the group, the trustworthiness of the other group members (including the facilitator), and the value of the experience for their investment. For individuals to speak openly and for a collective story to emerge, an environment of trust and safety must be created with the group and be held in place by the facilitator over a sufficiently long period of time for conversation to develop past introductions and awkwardness around sensitive issues toward depth and honest interaction among group members. Attention must also be paid to sustaining the conversation and bringing appropriate closure to the group at its end. Three hours is probably the minimum time needed to work through this process.

Morgan (1997) says a good facilitator should have sufficient understanding of group dynamics to lead the group toward the purpose(s) of the research question. To do this, the focus group facilitator must be able to tactfully and skillfully ensure equal participation by all members so the group is not biased by a couple of outspoken people, facilitate an atmosphere that is not threatening, communicate an appropriate level of comfort and safety in the group, and provide enough distance to appear unbiased. The facilitator must also be able to manage time effectively and keep the conversation on task lest the time runs out and the needed information has not been gathered. If not careful, a facilitator can quickly change the normal course of conversation among group participants in an effort to guide the conversation.

Special attention must also be paid to focus groups' informed consent and confidentiality statements. Unlike individual interviews, there is no guarantee of confidentiality or anonymity because too many people are involved in the information-gathering process. Everyone in the room will hear the statements being made and know who said them. Even if every participant agrees to confidentiality, the researcher has no control over the actions of other participants and therefore cannot ensure the confidentiality of what happens during the focus group. The best a researcher can do is make this situation clear to all involved so that each participant is conscious of his or her ability and responsibility for his or her words and actions. The researcher should also urge participants to respect other group members by keeping confidential the communication within the focus group. The researcher or facilitator of the group should clearly spell out guidelines for respectful communication to which everyone in the group must agree before participating and make clear to all participants the freedom to not answer questions, participate in conversations, or leave the group at any time. These types of boundaries, plus a facilitator skilled at managing small groups, will help ensure a positive experience for everyone involved.

Long Interviews

Anthropologists and sociologists have long been using interviews to obtain information from research participants for clinical diagnosis, counseling, and psychological testing. Qualitative data were the main kinds of social research until the last half of the twentieth century when Paul Lazarsfeld's survey research began to dominate the social sciences with quantitative data gathering (Denzin & Lincoln 2000). In recent decades, interviews have become formalized with methods, theories, critiques, and a growing body of literature because of the increased availability of technology such as recording devices and computers, increased acceptability of qualitative research in social sciences, and postmodern conversation about hermeneutical interpretation, dialectics, phenomenological description, and textual analysis (Lincoln & Guba 2000). Postmodern critiques of interview methods have focused on the specific roles of the interviewer, reflexive stance, highlighting the voices of participants as coresearchers, the interviewer-respondent relationship, and specific factors involved in interviews such as race, social status, and age (Bentz & Shapiro 1998).

The long interview is a specific type of interview method developed "to give the investigator a highly efficient, productive, 'stream-lined' instrument of inquiry" (McCracken 1988:7). It is so named for taking a minimum of approximately three hours or more and can be broken into several segments or days if longer time is required. It is advantageous because it allows a researcher to avoid the prolonged process of ethnographic research, which may inhibit access due to participants' privacy concerns, budget constraints, and time. It takes place between the investigator and one other person and focuses beyond the informant's understandings to cultural categories and meanings shared by many interviewees. For this reason, it is a good fit with focus groups to follow up on topics revealed in the group conversation or to generate topics to be explored later in group interviews.

The long interview allows the researcher to delve deeply into the thoughts and feelings of individual respondents about what he or she began talking about in a group. Choosing one or two participants from the focus group who either agreed about particular issues or disagreed about them allows the researcher to triangulate data, confirm or disconfirm pieces of hypotheses, or follow new research questions. The long interview has been criticized as being too stressful for participants; however, the length of such interviews is generally more taxing for the researcher than for the participant. Interviewees report being energized by the experience and enjoy sharing their thoughts and stories (McCracken 1988).

The long interview is a helpful tool for examining cultural and analytic categories embedded in an organization that are important pieces to understand in analyzing the system being studied. Long interviews provide a space to gather stories, individual experiences, and specific examples of what pieces of the culture mean to different people, serving to sharpen research questions and emerging analytic categories. Data from separate interviews can be compared and compiled to create a fuller picture of the complexities of the organization. Creating questions that draw out this type of information and building report through the interview process is a learned skill that must be developed. Some researchers find carrying the interview past one hour to delve into deeper and more personal information to be one of the greatest challenges of data gathering. An adequate pilot study should help develop such skills. It might also be advisable to review early interview recordings and transcripts with more experienced researchers to receive coaching on interviewing and questioning skills.

Reliability and Validity

Case studies, focus groups, and long interviews face similar challenges in regard to reliability and validity. In quantitative data, the reliability of a study is how well a study can be replicated by the same or a different researcher. Research involving discussions with people poses an interesting dilemma, because even if the same questions are used in every case, the conversation can never be replicated, and generally (unless the interviewer is incredibly inflexible, which does not lend itself toward gathering detailed or nuanced information) questions within the same research project are not asked in exactly the same way to each person, nor are they interpreted the same way by each respondent.

Qualitative research is sometime critiqued because it cannot be duplicated; however, in both qualitative and quantitative research studies are rarely duplicated. It is simply assumed in quantitative research that they are reliable because they can be duplicated. Whether that is really true is not clear (Hamel et al. 1993). In qualitative research (case study research, in particular, because each case is unique), there cannot be exact replication. Reliability, therefore, is about the confidence the reader can place in the reports of the researcher. Has the participant been represented accurately? How did participant checks take place? Why was this part of the interview exemplary as opposed to another? The transparency of the researcher's thought process and theoretical paradigms are critical.

Validity is concerned with how well the research findings match with the research questions and whether the explanations of the researcher are credible. Do the questions gather information that match the purpose of the study? Do the arguments presented make logical and coherent sense and find a place in relation to other literature on the topic? Are the conclusions reached by the researcher justified by the information presented in the study?

Answers to these questions are not found by plugging information into a formula that will *prove* them correct. Again, it is up to the researcher to relate an internal thought process to people who were not part of it originally but are now trying to understand its developmental path. The reader must be able to see through the presentation of the material how the researcher connected one dot to the next and made sense of all the material presented. Why were these specific categories chosen over others? What led to interpreting participants answers in this way and not that? What other questions were asked and materials gathered to confirm or disprove the researcher's hunch about this idea? How exactly did the researcher get from the initial research questions to the conclusions presented at the end of the study? The more spelled out and clear this is the more the validity can be assigned by the reader (McCracken 1988:48–52).

Matching the questions to the purpose of the research begins long before any data are gathered. It happens in the earliest stages of the project design, when the researcher is asking larger questions of interest and conducting the literature review. Identifying the purpose of the study clearly outlines the parameters of the literature and defines the scope of the questions to be asked in the interview schedule or by the case study methodology. The purpose of the study then functions through the entire research process as a compass guiding the formation of data-gathering questions as well as categories for interpretation of transcribed data and theory formation. A continuous spiraling process is formed as the purpose informs the questions, data gathered raise new questions, and these questions go back to the purpose of the study to determine whether they are relevant or should be set aside for study in a different project. The depth to which this process can take a researcher is one of the strengths of qualitative research.

Qualitative research, particularly interview methods, uses the researcher as the actual data collection instrument. The researcher comes to this role with all the biases and assumptions every person carries. It is essential that the researcher do as much as possible to bring those assumptions about cultural categories, personal beliefs, research preferences, and preformed theories to conscious recognition and acknowledge them in the research process. Without this critical self-examination and internal critique, important aspects of the research are likely to be missed. "Individuals raised in other research traditions are encouraged to treat their own experiences as bias and to set them aside. In the qualitative case, however, this material is the very stuff of understanding and explication. It represents vitally important intellectual capital without which analysis is the poorer" (McCracken 1988:34). As McCracken points out, the researcher's intuition and self can be one of the greatest strengths of the research project, if consciously and openly used.

SUMMARY

Case studies, focus groups, and long interviews are promising avenues of research for studying multiracial religious organizations. Sufficiently focused research projects with well-crafted questions can provide deep and rich data for understanding how people are living in harmony without the deep racial divides commonly seen in our society.

A case study offers a unique real-life setting for exploration and understanding. Focus groups open a space for a collective story of this phenomenon to be brought to the surface, shaped, examined, and recorded by members of that community.

The process involved in focus groups can give members of the group confidence in speaking about difficult topics, like race, and jog memories of stories that involved more than one person in the group. It also allows multiple perspectives to be stated about what happened in particular circumstances.

Long interviews create a different type of space where the most personal and deep thoughts and stories may be told in confidence and the researcher can probe issues of interest that emerged during focus group conversations. The individual nature of the long interview allows for privacy that does not exist in focus groups. In situations where the presence of others may prevent a person from speaking their thoughts or experiences in the focus group, she or he may feel able to relate those things to the interviewer in confidence during a long interview.

RENEWING LIFE AND SOCIETY

The learning path about race in religious organizations eventually led me to look for a racially inclusive Protestant evangelical organization where I explored the lived experience of belonging to such a community using case study, focus group, and individual interviews.

The case study method helped me look at a racially inclusive organization because it allowed me to look at one unique organization and search for new understandings of this type of organization. I was also able to test whether the theories of racially inclusive organizations were consistent with other types of similar organizations. Multiple levels of organizational life and group process created much complexity that needed a way to surface. Case study allowed me to remain in context, which was important because the human system required a context for meaning to be made of relationships and interactions (Lincoln & Guba 2000; Yin 1994).

The case used for study was a unique example of a racially inclusive Protestant evangelical parachurch organization. Less than 10% of religious organizations are considered to be racially inclusive (DeYoung et al. 2003:3). In this case, though, over 30% of the organization was not part of the racial majority group. This membership was achieved through intentional change driven by a mission and vision aimed at racial inclusion rather than a population shift in neighborhoods surrounding the organization which is typically the case (Becker 1998).

The topic of race posed a significant challenge in protecting the anonymity and confidentiality of participants in this study. A pseudonym was chosen, which at the time of writing could not be matched to another organization through numerous searches on different Internet search engines. The names of all participants and people or places referred to by participants were changed to protect the confidentiality and anonymity of those interviewed. For the same reasons, some defining characteristics of the organizations—such as precise locations, exact document titles, defining details of participants' positions, and names of affiliated denominations and churches—were purposefully left vague. The details of stories, quotations, and statistics about the organization and individuals involved were checked by the participants both for accuracy and to ensure that the essence of their words, experiences, or the organization were not lost. When quotations were used, it was important to know more about the racial identity of the person, in which case a code was used rather than a name (POC = person of color; W = white; F = female; and M = male. For example, POC-F indicates a person of color who is also a woman). The term "person of color" was being used in this case, rather than specifically identified racial identities, because the number of people interviewed was small enough that knowing the racial identity of participants with the organizational position or conversational context would potentially reveal the identity of the speakers.

Talking about personal experiences of race and racism posed the risk of emotional, psychological, and spiritual discomfort for participants. Race is a difficult topic in normal conversation, but in the workplace difficulty increased because the possibility existed of losing resources gained from employment, particularly if one's views differed, or were perceived to differ, from the organizational expectations. For some participants, the risk of this was greater than that experienced in everyday circumstances; for others, it posed no risk at all. In either case, protecting the reputation and integrity of each participant was an ethical concern. The reliability of the research also rested largely on the assumption that the participants interviewed were honest in their responses. Fear of being identified in the final report was expressed by a number of participants. Ensuring anonymity where possible and confidentiality in all cases was a priority.

Individual interviews took place early in the process as a way to get to know key people in the organization and build trust. A nomination process was used to identify potential participants, therefore it was necessary to build trust with leaders in the organization so they felt confident in giving me access to other people in the system. Participants appreciated having the interview questions in advance to know what to expect and to mentally prepare to talk about race. Most interviews took place in a private room in the organization's facilities. Email communication of transcriptions and regarding data was sent to the email account given by each participant. All audio recordings and data files were stored in the researcher's possession in accordance with all Internal Review Board (IRB) requirements. Most participants wanted the specific IRB requirements because of their anxieties about discussing issues of race within the organization.

A focus group enabled me to have conversation with the participants as well as listen in on conversations by the participants with each other. This type of fluid conversation allowed a collective story to grow out of the group and provided a space for discussion about organizational culture and dynamics that had not occurred before that. The focus group was held toward the end of the research process for a couple of reasons. Coordinating the necessary schedules took longer than anticipated, and I felt that building rapport with participants through individual interviews and talking about the research project would build confidence and trust in me and the research process, making the space of the focus group safer for honest discussion. The focus group lasted three hours, which was enough time for the group to become comfortable, speak in depth on topics together, and come to appropriate closure. As themes emerged during the initial stages of data collection and analysis, further questions were formed, and the focus group became a forum to discuss them. The focus group was key to the research in allowing some important topics to surface that were explored in follow-up interviews and later became crucial pieces to a theoretical model explaining a hidden process of race in the organization.

Religious organizations are not immune to the power of racialization, and it has been argued that they contribute to that socialization process

(Emerson & Smith 2000; Heffner 2005). Despite this, the number of multiracial organizations in the United States is increasing (Christerson et al. 2005; DeYoung et al. 2003; Marti 2005; Yancey 2003), and such organizations are important sources of information about organizational change, social change, and racial interactions.

Research on multiethnic and multiracial religious organizations has used mixed methods of survey data supplemented by individual interviews, participant observation, and ethnography. Face-to-face interviews were used in the first national study on race and evangelicals (Emerson & Smith 2000) to better understand and clarify the initial survey research. Smaller studies of specific multiethnic religious organizations (Becker 1999; Christerson et al. 2005; Marti 2005; Yancey 2003) used individual interviews as well, sometimes blended with ethnography and participant observation, to gather data. It is difficult to tell from the methodological description if these studies used the long interview as described by McCracken (1988), or some variation leaning more toward an individual interview. Interviewing now tends to become a kind of hybrid between different methodologies, and the strength of the data is judged by the craftsmanship of the questions and how well the methods fit the research purposes and knowledge desired.

The multiracial status of religious organizations—the majority of those studied were congregations—depends on their location within urban areas, vision and leadership of pastors, number of minority group members already within the congregation, ability to incorporate diverse worship styles and music, ability of minority group members to find significant friendships within the congregation, and ability of members to find places of inclusion around common interests with other people (Christerson et al. 2005; DeYoung et al. 2003; Marti 2005). These are challenges to typical congregations whose membership is often formed around principles of homophily and rooted in long historical traditions that resist change. Religious organizations and congregations, in particular, tend to be culture keepers for groups that want to preserve traditions and cultural values of their heritage (Brotherton 2010; Christerson et al. 2005). Other types of religious organizations not defined as congregations have not been a focus of study in relation to race, with the exception of Christerson et al. (2005) and Brotherton (2010).

Such growth and change calls for more study to better understand how these changes are happening, the effects multiracial organizations have on the people in them, the benefits and struggles of creating and maintaining them, and the different organizational forms and management styles being created. For these to be accomplished, unique challenges presented by studying race must be met through the methodology used in the research process.

Focus groups offer potential for gaining insight into different ethnic, racial groups, and otherwise defined subgroups (i.e., leadership, middle management, pastoral staff, etc.) of multiracial organizations. Focus groups and long interviews give opportunities to investigate how individuals within a racially inclusive community have experienced racial healing, how the process began and continues, and what pieces of the process have worked for different group members in the organization. And case studies are needed to provide full-orbed pictures of the complexities of organizations and for comparison points between organizations that are able to create spaces where communities of people are able to live outside the dehumanizing processes of race, racialization, and racism.

REFERENCES

Barndt, J. (2007). *Understanding and dismantling racism: The twenty-first century challenge to white America.* Minneapolis: Fortress Press.

Becker, P. E. (1998). Making inclusive communities: Congregations and the "problem" of race. *Social Problems, 45,* 451–472.

Becker, P. E. (1999). *Congregations in conflict: Cultural models of local religious life.* Cambridge, MA: Cambridge University Press.

Bentz, V. M., & Shapiro, J. J. (1998). *Mindful inquiry in social research.* Thousand Oaks, CA: Sage.

Brotherton, D. B. (2010). Renewing life and society: The lived experience of racial inclusion in a Protestant evangelical parachurch organization. Ph.D. dissertation, Fielding Graduate University.

Chappell, D. L. (2004). *A stone of hope: Prophetic religion and the death of Jim Crow.* Chapel Hill: The University of North Carolina Press.

Christerson, B., Edwards, K. L., & Emerson, M. O. (2005). *Against all odds: The struggle for racial integration in religious organizations.* New York: New York Oxford University Press.

Christerson, B., & Emerson, M. (2003). The costs of diversity in religious organizations: An in-depth case study. *Sociology of Religion, 64,* 163–181.

Cornell, S. E., & Hartmann, D. (1998). *Ethnicities and race: Making identities in a changing world.* Thousand Oaks, CA: Pine Forge Press.

Denzin, N. K., & Lincoln, Y. S. (2000). *Handbook of qualitative research.* 2nd ed. Thousand Oaks, CA: Sage.

DeYoung, C. P., Emerson, M. O., Yancey, G., & Kim, K. C. (2003). *United by faith: The multiracial congregation as an answer to the problem of race.* New York: Oxford University Press.

Du Bois, W. E. B. (1903). *The souls of black folks: Essays and sketches.* Forgotten Books. http://forgottenbooks.org/info/9781606801611 (accessed November 2010).

Ellis, C. F., Jr. (1996). *Free at last? The gospel in the African-American experience.* Downers Grove, IL: InterVarsity Press.

Emerson, M. O., & Kim, K. C. (2003). Multiracial congregations: An analysis of their development and a typology. *Journal for the Scientific Study of Religion, 42,* 217–227.

Emerson, M. O., & Smith, C. (2000). *Divided by faith: Evangelical religion and the problem of race in America.* New York: Oxford University Press.

Feagin, J. R., Orum, A. M., & Sjoberg, G. (Eds.). (1991). *A case for the case study.* Chapel Hill: The University of North Carolina Press.

Hamel, J., Dufour, S., & Fortin, D. (1993). *Case study methods,* vol. 32. Thousand Oaks: Sage.

Heffner, G. G. (2005). Developing eyes to see: A study of multi-congregational anti-racism initiative. Ph.D. dissertation, Michigan State University.

Horton, J. O. (2003). *Interview with James O. Horton.* http://www.pbs.org/race/000_About/002_04-background-02-04.htm (accessed February 19, 2009).

Katz, J. (2003). *White awareness: Handbook for anti-racism training.* 2nd ed. Norman: University of Oklahoma Press.

Lincoln, Y. S., & Guba, E. G. (2000). *Naturalistic inquiry.* Newbury Park, CA: Sage.

Madriz, E. (2000). Focus groups in feminist research. In N. K. Denzin & Y. S. Lincoln (Eds.), *Handbook of qualitative research,* 2nd ed. (pp. 835–850). Thousand Oaks, CA: Sage.

Marti, G. (2005). *A mosaic of believers: Diversity and innovation in a multiethnic church.* Bloomington: Indiana University Press.

Maylam, P. (2005). Unravelling South Africa's racial order: The historiography of racism, segregation, and apartheid. In J. Lee & J. Lutz (Eds.), *Situating "race" and racisms in space, time, and theory: Critical essays for activists and scholars* (pp. 138–160). Montreal: McGill-Queen's University Press.

McCracken, G. (1988). *The long interview.* Thousand Oaks, CA: Sage.

Morgan, D. L. (1997). *Focus groups as qualitative research.* 2nd ed., vol. 16. Thousand Oaks, CA: Sage.

Myrdal, G. (1944). *An American dilemma: The Negro problem and modern democracy.* New York: Harper and Row.

Omi, M., & Winant, H. (1994). *Racial formation in the United States: From the 1960's to the 1990's.* 2nd ed. New York: Routledge.

Sanders, A. E., Jr. (2006). The spirit is willing but the flesh is weak: Understanding racial diversity on a Christian college campus. Ph.D. dissertation, Miami University, Oxford, Ohio.

Spickard, J. V. (2007). Micro/qualitative approaches to the sociology of religion: Phenomenologies, interviews, narratives, and ethnographies. In J. A. Beckford & N. J. Demerath (Eds.), *Handbook of the sociology of religion* (pp. 121–143). Thousand Oaks, CA: Sage.

Stake, R. E. (2000). Case studies. In N. K. Denzin & Y. S. Lincoln (Eds.), *Handbook of qualitative research,* 2nd ed. (pp. 435–454). Thousand Oaks, CA: Sage.

Stake, R. E. (2003). Case studies. In N. K. Denzin and Y. S. Lincoln (Eds.), *Strategies of qualitative inquiry* (pp. 134–164). Thousand Oaks, CA: Sage.

Stanfield, J. H., II. (1993). Epistemological considerations. In J. H. Stanfield, II & R. M. Dennis (Eds.), *Race and ethnicity in research methods,* vol. 157 (pp. 16–36). Newbury Park, CA: Sage.

Stanfield, J. H., II. (1995). The myth of race and the human sciences. *The Journal of Negro Education, 64*, 218.

Stanfield, J. H., II. (Under review). *Enduring hope of the faithful: Probing the theological sociology of racial justice.*

Staub, E., & Pearlman, L. A. (2001). Healing, reconciliation, and forgiving after genocide and other collective violence. In S. J. Raymond, G. Helmick & R. L. Petersen (Eds.), *Forgiveness and reconciliation: Religion, public policy, and conflict transformation* (pp. 205–227). West Conshohocken, PA: Templeton Foundation Press.

Volf, M. (1996). *Exclusion and embrace: A theological exploration of identity, otherness, and reconciliation.* Nashville: Abingdon Press.

Williams, C. L. (1991). Case studies and the sociology of gender. In J. R. Feagin, A. M. Orum & G. Sjoberg (Eds.), *A case for the case study* (pp. 224–243). Chapel Hill: University of North Carolina Press.

Yancey, G. (2003). *One body one spirit: Principles of successful multiracial churches.* Downers Grove, IL: InterVarsity Press.

Yin, R. K. (1994). *Case study research design and methods.* 2nd ed., vol. 5. Thousand Oaks, CA: Sage.

12 Psychohistory: The Triangulation of Autobiographical Textual Analysis, Archival and Secondary Historical Materials, and Interviews

John H. Stanfield, II

This exploration of the psycho historical analysis of the autobiographical text authored by Benjamin Elijah, *Born to Rebel,* stems from a mysterious Fed-Ex package that appeared in my office one day in 2000 when I was chair of the Department of Sociology and Avalon Professor at Morehouse College in Atlanta, Georgia. It was a contract application from the Martin Luther King, Jr. National Park Service for a consultant to assist the Park Service historian in updating park exhibits about Dr. King as a child and adolescent and when he returned to Atlanta in 1960. This updating would require interviewing persons who knew Dr. King during those periods of his life. I applied and was awarded the contract. This resulted in me finding and interviewing twenty-four persons. I also consulted archival and secondary sources and had the good fortune of seeking and receiving advice from old time Atlantans, especially those familiar with Morehouse and with the Auburn Avenue community where Dr. King grew up. The more I dug, the more I became intrigued by the value of psychohistory theory and methodology in writing a chapter such as this on Dr. King and those who influenced his development before he was twenty-five years old. This was especially interesting to me given my long time interest in developing and testing sociological theories of the community contextual development of intellectually gifted Blacks, especially black males.

LIFE HISTORICAL ANALYSIS

Life historical analysis, as a methodology in sociological research, places the case study of one or more lives in the shaping of formally or informally structured human experiences such as institutions, communities, systems, societies, movements, or stratified social orders in the center of inquiry (Stanfield 1987a, 1987b). Thus, it is not surprising that it was a common methodological tool developed and utilized in the emerging race and ethnicity field by W. E. B. Du Bois and William I. Thomas, early twentieth-century sociologists.

Even after Thomas's dismissal from the University of Chicago in 1918, his former colleagues Robert E. Park and Ernest Burgess continued to stress the value of the life history case study. Their African American students E. Franklin Frazier and Charles S. Johnson, the most prolific Chicago students trained in the 1920s, fine tuned and applied life historical analyses to urban and rural community settings to explore issues such as African American family dynamics, adolescent identity, and stratification.

Chicago School mentors and their students used life historical case materials without paying much attention to the external social, economic, political, and cultural environments, the standard criticism of biographical/life historical case study methodologies in sociological research (Stanfield 1985). Where is the context? How do contexts act as dynamic-changing externalities impacting life histories as unfolding phases of human development? These are critical questions to be asked and addressed by sociologically oriented scholars interested in using such case studies in their research designs.

An additional problem was that most Chicago sociologists—teachers and students—took a dim view of using psychoanalysis in life historical case studies. This was more than apparent in their criticisms of the psychoanalysis of southern racial caste, which began to be published in the 1930s and 1940s (with the significant exception of Fisk's Charles S. Johnson; see Johnson 1987). The general tendency in academic sociology was to reject psychoanalytical approaches. Perhaps this is because by the 1930s, emerging third-generation sociologists wanted to legitimate sociology as a positivistic science. A heavily nonempirically oriented field such as psychoanalysis was viewed as being unscientific and thus not worthy of being incorporated into the evolving science of sociology. In any case, the long-term consequence of this rejection is that, among other things, the deep unconscious and conscious emotionality of race as a dehumanizing experience has either been ignored or played down for years. Only recently has the sociology of emotions begun to develop a noticeable literature.

I have become increasingly concerned with how much sociological theories and methods of scholars interested in racial issues have failed to take into account the obvious roles of the unconscious and emotions in the creation, stabilization, and transformation of race-centered institutions, communities, systems, movements, societies, and human developmental phases (Stanfield 2006). My concern stems from my growing awareness that the mixed record of the outcomes of the Brown decision, affirmative action, and other post-1960s attempts to bring about racialized change and the personal attacks on President Barack Obama are indicative of the depth of multigenerational racialism and racism. They are forms of grotesque dehumanizing societal experiences in America that are deeply rooted in the collective and individual unconsciousness, semi-consciousness, and consciousness of most Americans (see Chapter 1 in this book for my definitions of race, racism, and racialism). My comparative research on anti-black racism in Brazil and South Africa and the widespread persistence of white anti-black racism in the United States and of how African Americans internalize their own racial oppression have further deepened my belief in the need for psychoanalytical approaches for understanding and eradicating the dehumanizing monster of race and its outcomes—racialism and racism.

These observations are offered as explanations for my interest in psychohistorical analysis, the focus of this chapter, and my growing interest in holistic restorative justice as a healing methodology. Psychohistory attempts to use historical events in the life of a person or a community or generation to make sense out of personal or collective decisions, priorities, values, leadership styles, and identity. It is a methodology first used by Erik Erikson (1994), who developed a six-stage theory of life historical development grounded for the most part in secondary historical sources. Other prominent psychohistorians who have written in the racial and ethnic studies field include child psychiatrist Robert Coles (1967), a close colleague of Erikson, and anthropologist Allison Davis (1983). James Fowler's (1981) Eriksonian stage theory of spirituality in human development is prominently applied in this chapter.

Erkisonian psychohistory has the methodological strength to encourage the exploration of unconscious and conscious emotional states in human development, but it also has two weaknesses. The first is the analytical framework itself, since there are attributes ascribed to any stage that can actually occur earlier or later in a person's life. The second criticism is the usual one that life historical case studies scholars ignore external environmental factors. In other words, there is a need for sociologically and culturally grounding life historical case studies for placement in broader societal contexts. I attempt to correct this weakness here and check, confirm, or question points made by an author in an autobiographical text through grounding my analysis in context-building archival and secondary historical sources and one-on-one interviews with people who knew the author and others related to him.

THE AUTOBIOGRAPHY BY BENJAMIN E. MAYS AND HIS LEGACY AS MENTOR TO MARTIN LUTHER KING, JR.

In life historical case studies, little stress is placed on the macro roles of social webs of relationships in and through which the individual grows cognitively, emotionally, socially, and spiritually. That is, as much as we cannot ignore the interior life concerns of Freud and Piaget, it is also important to bring into focus those researchers who explore how social contexts—primary and secondary institutions, communities, societies, and world-systems and most fundamentally, "chains of mentors"—all play crucial roles in the development of the self and its relationship to others.

Chains of mentors was one of the most vital social attributes of Martin Luther King, Jr.'s development in traditional and nontraditional learning and educational spaces from infancy through early manhood (age twenty-five) and beyond. Mentorship as a form of social capital as well as a type of social relationship is more than apparent in Dr. King's developmental phases, although little formal theoretical analysis has been applied to narratives about his chain of mentors. In fact, much of the impressionistic and scholarly historical literature on King and his mentors are wrapped in folk wisdom, myths, and in hearsay rather than first-hand evidence from those who knew him gathered through oral historical analysis and other forms of autobiographical accounting.

Through psychohistorical methodology, I will attempt to analyze Benjamin Elijah Mays's autobiography *Born to Rebel* (1971). I will contend that book was a double-edged production in myth and needs to be to unraveled to understand the real relationship between Mays and King and the psychohistorical generational context and consequences for Mays's development as a black who came of age in the ascent of Jim Crow America. I examined archival records and interviews with those who knew Dr. King during his childhood to age twenty-five as well as rare secondary sources (e.g., Carter 1998).

Why ML?

ML was Martin Luther King Jr.'s Auburn Avenue neighborhood nickname during his childhood and adolescence in Atlanta, Georgia. There are several reasons why studying young ML is important. First, King was an intellectually gifted black male. Sociologists and other social scientists interested in the contexts and external social conditions of human development rarely study the intellectually gifted and talented insofar as historically reconstructing their communities and networks (Bloom 1985).

Even social scientists rarely study intellectually gifted black people individually or contextually (but see Bond 1972; Stanfield 1999). The rarity of such studies has much to do with the norms and values that shape race research in the social sciences and in professional school education. These are embedded in caricatures of blacks as social problems and as intellectual inferiors. This is particularly the case in studies of black males. It is much easier to get a grant to study black male underachievement than to look at intellectually brilliant black males.

Those social scientists who have focused on black male giftedness have examined the sociology of sports or on bright black males who end up as criminals. There have also been historical and sociological studies of blacks in the musical arts such as jazz, blues, and rap. This interest in the development of intellectually gifted black males has, at best, been excellent ethnography but with little historical sociological reconstruction on the level that I suggest needs to be done.

The negative view of rural and urban black communities has been pervasive in sociological literature. It has made many scholars feel that there is nothing good in the "hood" or the rural countryside to support the positive development of residents there (Stanfield 1955/2008). This has promoted a magical perspective (i.e., a romanticized version that ignores structural and other empirical factors) on the mobility of talented blacks out of communities into circles of prominence in larger society. The contributions of powerful institutions such as elite white colleges and universities and philanthropic foundations are acknowledged as places where black youth from predominantly black communities are polished and anointed. However, little credit has been given to the networks and mentoring experiences that occur within the communities of origins of the high-achieving black person.

EXPRESSIVE AND INSTRUMENTAL MENTORS

This lack of credit was driven home to me almost twenty years ago when I did a study of the social origins of black medical doctors who were largely from poor rural and urban communities. I asked: Who discovered your talents as a child and adolescent and encouraged you to be all you could be (Stanfield 1999)? I discovered that each doctor in this sample of twenty-one had what I came to call through grounded theory data analysis "a chain of expressive and instrumental mentors"—no matter if they came from two- or one-parent households or from child-sharing communities in which parents regularly circulated their kids around the community for child care and development purposes.

The social capital of expressive mentors, such as a parent, grandparent, neighbor, barber, hairdresser, or play uncle or aunt, was the deep love and affection they had for their protégé. Expressive mentors were significant motivators who did not have contacts in the larger world; in some cases, they were not able to read or write. However, their deep love for the protégé provided the encouragement for him or he to achieve. An example of an expressive mentor would be a God-fearing, illiterate grandmother who is crazy about her baby. She may not know anything about any universities but she knows that her baby can do anything and encourages the grandchild to shoot for the stars beyond the immediate conditions of the community, however dismal they are.

Instrumental mentors are those who have social capital in terms of material resources, which literally opens up the community for the protégé and facilitates mobility opportunity—they have, in other words, contacts with the outside world, money to send the protégé to summer science camp, knowledge about college admission processes, ability to fill out the application for the protégé, etc.

No matter the location of the community, the structure of immediate and extended families, the socioeconomic characteristics of care-givers, and the gender, each doctor I interviewed in oral history format pointed to a string of instrumental and expressive mentors who discovered them, nurtured them, and became a vertical chain of sponsorship leading outside their community of origins.

But what is most amazing was my finding that mentoring is a symmetrical social relationship. Not only do mentors seek out protégés, but protégés seek out mentors and keep them in their lives as they continue to mature. Each doctor I interviewed was not only mentored but picked his or her mentors and kept them on as advisers.

ML and the Rebel

ML also had the emotional intelligence to select and sustain relationships with mentors such as his paternal grandmother, his mother, and members of his church such as his father's long-time church secretary. His surviving papers are replete with letters and other documents that illustrate the deep ties he developed and kept with instrumental mentors such as John Dobbs, J. Pius Barber, and Sam Williams.

As the common legend alleges, no one was as monumental as a mentor in King's life as Benjamin Elijah Mays (1894–1984), the president of Morehouse College between 1940 and 1967 (Stanfield 2003). Mays admitted that "It must be said in all candor that I feel that Martin Luther King, Jr. did as much for me, if not more, than I did for him" (Mays 1971:265). This was an important point, since if it were not for King, Morehouse would have probably remained an obscure black college; perhaps it would have closed during the initial phases of the desegregation of American higher education during the post-1970s. Mays, too, might have remained in obscurity.

Mays was already known in international church circles as a public sociologist of religion and of civil rights (Mays 1971) by the time Martin Luther King, Jr. arrived in 1944 as an early admission student to Morehouse. But Mays's career may not have continued to soar if Martin Luther King, Jr. had decided not to lead a bus boycott that caught national attention and quickly transformed ML into an international figure. That is why it is important to examine words and silences in *Born to Rebel*. The book clarifies how Mays's development impacted King so significantly. More importantly, it illuminates the developmental challenges and dilemmas of Benjamin Elijah Mays himself.

BORN TO REBEL

Born to Rebel is a classical autobiography in black male studies. The book is actually a personal commentary on race relations issues, with very little direct autobiographical information offered by Mays beyond his days as a Bates undergraduate. Other than making points about personal encounters with race and racism, Mays's self all but disappears.

Reading *Born to Rebel* even casually, it is easy to assume that all Mays cared about his entire life was race. He displays no emotion or insight about the death of his first wife, who he only mentions in passing a few times. His brothers and sisters and other relatives are not fully developed figures (except slightly in the first chapters about his childhood); they are just mentioned in passing to make general points. He does go into detail about the dire condition of Morehouse College when he became president in 1940 (Mays 1971:170–195), but is silent on the Morehouse years for the most part. He says nothing about his administrators, his faculty, and his students except again, in passing, to make a general point here or there.

What is of interest to me is that *Born to Rebel*, like Mays's rather stiff, defensive presentation of self, like so many autobiographies, is a shield meant to produce an image for historical immortality. It is a shield for a deeply injured man who, though extraordinarily successful, was still pained by the crucifixion of racial caste in childhood and adolescence at age seventy-seven when his autobiography was finally published. He remained crippled by an esteem problem; he never felt he was quite good enough, so he needed to dominate the limelight at the expense of others who were more talented than he was and accomplished much more.

Mays barely mentions the work of his predecessor President John Hope (Torrence 1948), who actually laid the foundations of the social justice orientation of the Morehouse institutional culture. He gives scant attention to Howard Thurman, the Morehouse Board first choice for president (Carter 1998). Thurman turned them down, making Mays a second or a third choice. Mays does not mention that Thurman, like himself, had contributed to the development of the Howard University School of Religion during the 1930s and had actually met Gandhi in India before he died. Since Mays was not a Morehouse man, he resented prominent Morehouse administrators and faculty (such as Brailsford R. Brazeal, the dean of men) during his presidency, with whom he had a love/hate relationship.

These observations were made to me by Dr. X. a distinguished Morehouse man at age ninety-five, was usually cordial about everyone whenever we spoke throughout the years. During this three-hour interview, the last one before his death soon after, his candid perspective on Mays as a "John Hope" student was quite surprising but illuminating since most commentaries about Mays have been made by "Bennie Boys"[1] of the 1950s rather than "Hope Boys" of an older generation.

These observations are not meant to be unduly negative about Mays. Instead, they are meant to pave the way to understand the social contexts of his long life, which took him from a childhood in dirt-poor rural South Carolina to being a world traveler who dined with heads of power states in his adult years during a very difficult time in U.S. race relations history. Mays's birth year, 1894, was in the midst of the ascent of Jim Crow after failed Reconstruction marked by *Plessey versus Ferguson* the following year, the lynchings of Blacks, and the crystallization of the separation of the races in thought, custom, policy, and public life.

Mays's mention of witnessing a lynching early in life that would shape his racial world view was a common comment in the autobiographies of Blacks of the time as were comments on witnessing or experiencing other grotesque examples of horrible acts of white violence against Blacks. Mays's preoccupation with recording how easy and routine it was for Blacks to be mistreated by white Americans at home and abroad was also a common theme in autobiographies of Blacks who were born in the decades immediately following Reconstruction (Mays 1971:1–49).

The ideology of biological inferiority and Social Darwinism that rationalized and routinized the transformation of a post-Civil War America from an agrarian slave-based society into a racial caste-ridden emerging urban industrial society influenced the unfolding of the twentieth century for elite and impoverished black people in similar and different ways. The similarity was that unless a black person had phenotypical features that could easily mistaken to as white, whatever the person's socioeconomic status, Blacks were subjected to overt acts of discrimination and to random acts of white violence at least up through the 1960s with public approval and little or no legal recourse for the victim or victim loved ones. In a region in which Blacks had no voting rights, were explicitly excluded from most white institutions of higher learning, were normally refused service in white-owned restaurants and hotels, and had to sit on the back of the bus and in the theatre balcony, the contemporaneous problem of being profiled driving while black took on the more basic problem of living while black, especially in the south. The emotional and mental tolls it took to be a black person were tremendous; among other things, Blacks had to develop coping mechanisms to avoid being insulted by Whites.

Mays paints a dismal picture of what it meant, on a daily level, to be a black person in Jim Crow America (also see Chafe et al. 2008). His portrait of the gendered normality of being a black woman who has to learn how to avoid being raped by white men and of being a black man who has to learn how to avoid being lynched by a white mob is a theme running through the book, from his earliest days in rural South Carolina through incidents with gas station attendants in the 1960s as president of Morehouse.

In the Jim Crow era, the captains of the industrial racial caste order created urban and rural labor markets that exploited unskilled black labor. When national political leaders expanded the financial security of workers during the New Deal, those low-service occupations dominated by Blacks were exempted to appease southern congressmen and state and local government leaders.

For the black elite, it was frustrating being one of the very rare few Black people who were well educated and still routinely treated as inferiors by their white peers and Whites of higher and of lower social standing. Being an adult man or women and being called a boy or a girl or having Whites avoid calling you by your first name or uncle or auntie rather than by your title of Mr., Mrs., or Dr. was particularly unsettling for the black upper crust.

The scars of this institutionalized degradation were more than apparent in Mays's preoccupation with this pattern of social disrespect. Although he attempted to come across as being a modest man, the book is sprinkled with instances of Mays patting himself on the back and in other ways reassuring himself that he was worthy of the respect so often denied him throughout his life.

For a seventy-seven-year-old distinguished man to still feel so inadequate that he writes a book to celebrate what has such a dismal theme strikes me as a semiconscious expression of Eriksonian despair. But it is understandable, given that what desegregation yielded in Mays's latest years was more cause for worry: Since the breakdown of Jim Crow, black community life and black identity itself have been dismantled. And on the other end, the Black Nationalist movement Mays so opposed disrupted the final years of his presidency at Morehouse, tarnishing his hope of ending his long tenure uneventfully.

Mays's autobiography reminds us that there are two dimensions of any institution or group. There is the actual physical location of the entity and its composition based on birth right or on achieved status after entry and there are members who symbolize the highest values of it—the symbolic entity.

There have always been two Morehouses. There is it physical location as an underresourced institution of higher learning for young black men. For decades, Morehouse has graduated thousands of black men who completed degree requirements. And there are the attendees and graduates who exemplify the highest values of Morehouse men: cosmopolites who rise above the parochial characteristics and the otherwise racially restrictive limitations of their era and live lives that are quite uncommon for black people. John Hope, Mordecai Johnson, Howard Thurman, Benjamin Mays, Martin Luther King, Jr., Mordecai Johnson, Hugh Gloster, T. M. Alexander, James Nabrit, and Samuel Nabrit are just a few Morehouse men who, though subjected to Jim Crow, came to live extraordinary lives.

Mays's most vivid stories in his autobiography are about his experiences while working as a summer Pullman porter as a college student at South Carolina State College for Negroes, when he transferred to Virginia Union, which had white faculty, and as an undergraduate student at Bates. It was quite a feat in the 1910s to transition from being a rural black adolescent to being a student at a historically black college (HBC) on two campuses to transferring to Bates College hundreds of miles away in a region with only a handful of Blacks.

With the support of his mother and despite the opposition of his father, Mays was determined to make the best out of being from a poor family. He enrolled in an HBC with even bigger dreams. What helped him construct such a vision for himself was working as a Pullman during summers while attending college high school in South Carolina and then college in Virginia. His observations and experiences of life outside the South made him yearn for integration and to leave home for New England to experience it (very much an Eriksonian desire for a break from home and realize an outward search for identity). The collaborative problem solving (see Van der Veer & Valsiner 1994) involved mentors at his colleges helping him find financial assistance to continue in school and map out his plans, allowing Mays to cleanly break away from a father who was not interested in his education and tried to block his efforts.

Bates became a successful social experiment for this provincial southern rural black male. He had a talent that made him popular on campus: his debating ability, a skill put to good use when Mays was debate coach for the undefeated Morehouse debating team in the 1920s when he was there for a few years. The good race relations experience of Bates inspired Mays to venture further into upper-middle-class white culture through the collaborative problem-solving assistance of Bates's professors in religion who sponsored Mays to the University of Chicago to pursue a doctoral degree in religion.

The University of Chicago idea came from one of his HBC professors who spent a summer at the University of Chicago and raved about it to the impressionable young Mays. His doctoral work would be an off-and-on again venture for years until he completed it in the mid-1930s. The interruptions were times in which Mays was involved in domestic and international church and YMCA work as well as social research activities.

These activities enabled him to polish his interpersonal and political savvy skills through observing the conduct of Whites who gave him access to national and international circles. His international YMCA work, which required him to go to India and to Europe, greatly influenced his views on integration during a time when everyday America was very much segregated in word and deed. Later, in the late 1930s through the 1950s, his World Council and Federal Council of Churches work would transform him into a leading world authority on anti–Jim Crow and anti-apartheid in integrated social spaces. One

member and friend in Mays's international network was Alan Paton, the renowned white South African human rights activist. Paton visited Mays at least
once in Atlanta during the 1950s (Paton 1980).

These experiences, plus Mays's increase exposure to affluent Whites after
becoming president of Morehouse created the duality in his life, which I call
the other symbolic Morehouse. Increasingly, while Mays continued to live the
life of a black man in a Jim Crow society, he was not totally of it and actually
lived at times outside it, mentally if not physically. This in-and-out of a societal body enabled Mays to be bold and socially prophetic in his ethical stands
that were so instrumental in the 1950s as there was a growing demand for
intellectuals to make ethical and moral sense out of the death of Jim Crow and
the painful birth of a new kind of society, an integrated/desegregating society
which progressive thinking people viewed as the realization of a distant dream
while conservatives viewed this transition as the spawning ground for much
spilt bloodshed between the races.

Mays's international lifestyle is why he encouraged his Morehouse men
to be global in their thinking, a most unusual thing for a black college president of his generation to do during an era in which it was daring to take the
risk of developing a liberal arts curriculum premised on the University of
Chicago model. His international lifestyle explains the study abroad program
in India that Morehouse did in collaboration with Spelman College in the
1950s and the international fellowships Morehouse students could compete
for in the 1950s and 1960s that would produce some of the first Morehouse
(and first black American) foreign service professionals. This also explains
why Martin Luther King, Jr. could expand his social justice concerns from
civil rights in the South to civil rights in the nation to the human rights dilemmas of the war in Viet Nam. He was a product of the global thinking of
Mays's Morehouse culture—even though he lacked mentorship from the man
himself, as we shall see.

It is important to sketch the social origins of Mays's racial integration life
since by precept it became a role-modeling attribute for Morehouse students
during his mandatory Tuesday chapel talks to the young men. Both in his autobiography and in interviews I have had with Morehouse men of the 1940s and
1950s, Mays's chapel talks railed against Jim Crow and insisted that students
not indulge in what he considered to be voluntary segregation such as sitting
in theater balconies. He also discussed his regional leadership role as an integration civil rights leader, which converged nicely with his reports of the pro-
racial integration stances he took in international conferences. Such chapel
talks could not help but give Morehouse students alternative visions of what
society could be other than a Jim Crow–infested America.

Mays's preoccupation with race left him distrusting Whites and not being
very respectful of a father he observed bowing and scraping before hostile
white men. Watching his father and other older black males being humiliated

and even killed made Mays feel a shame that he hid throughout his life, developing a "born to rebel" persona. As he became older, he confronted racism head on. However, if he was discriminated against, including being physically struck when outnumbered, he again expressed social impotency. This happened when he was struck by a white man as a teenager "just because," and dared not to strike back and when he backed down from eating in a white-only train dining car as president of Morehouse as he backed out with a gang of white men pressing him to leave.

As he went through Bates and then through his experiences with the YMCA as a student secretary in his twenties, he slowly began to develop into an integrationist as he began to realize that not all Whites were to be feared or were enemies. This "sorting out" of the structure of white racism from morally good white individuals, which deepened as Mays became involved in international church and YMCA conferences, had an interesting impact on Mays's Christian faith and on his black identity as a kind of faith.

Fowler's (1981) definition of faith is:

People's evolved and evolving ways of experiencing self, others, world (as they construct them) as related to and affected by the ultimate conditions of existence People's evolved and evolving ways of experiencing self, others, and world (as they construct them) and of shaping their lives' purposes and meanings, trusts and loyalties, in light of the character of being, value and power determining the ultimate conditions of existence (as grasped in their operative images-conscious, and unconscious-of them). (pp. 92–93)

Mays's Christian faith evolved from a simple rural black Baptist conception of a God limited by the racial caste line as represented by the black pastor of his childhood and adolescence. The pastor was a good moral leader within the social restrictions of caste, as were most southern black pastors who spoke against caste only at great risk of their lives and those of their congregations. At Bates, Mays became acquainted with social gospel-oriented religious leaders and writers who began to liberate him from his conventional rural Baptist beliefs in a God rendered impotent because of caste.

Mays's years at Chicago moved him even deeply into the social gospel camp. His YMCA work in the South and with the Commission on Interracial Cooperation during the 1920s and 1930s began to shape his moral and social justice orientation toward the moral contradictions of the white church preaching Christ and Christian love while upholding segregation. For decades, he used his brilliant oratory skills to pound away at such contradictions internationally as well as nationally as he confronted white South African church men who claimed to personally disagree with apartheid but argued that it was essential.

Mays's theology of racial justice and the church in his more mature years was light years from the timid rural Baptist faith he was socialized into as a child. His personal transformation was assisted by participating in and developing social circles of integration-oriented clergy and other civic leaders regionally, nationally, and internationally, and developing a persistent critique against leaders, black as well as white, who taught and preached separation. Mays's moral stand on the white church was not lost on Martin Luther King, Jr. His Birmingham Jail letter to white clergy has a Mays ring to it, even though Dr. King did not enjoy the mentoring attention of the Morehouse president.

Mays's transformation was accented with his unprecedented sociological survey of the black church in the 1930s (Mays 1988), which argued for the functional importance of the black church in creating a healthy sense of empowering black identity. This study refers more his firm identity as a black male adult who was becoming comfortable as an integrationist and as a black man who was very clear about who he was. In this sense, as Mays clearly explains in great detail in the last two chapters of his autobiography, he was a desegregationist and integrationist, not an assimilationist. Today, he would be considered a cultural pluralist—that is, a believer in an America in which it is possible to be culturally different as expressed by participation in culturally different communities and institutions while at the same time participating in larger society. This became even more clearly clarified when in his seventies he advocated for the survival of black colleges in the midst of desegregation of institutions of higher learning.

The issue of Mays's racial identity is important since it is another way to apply Fowler's definition of faith. Mays never lost a basic value system in regard to self and others when it came to being an ethnically black person. Although he evolved in other ways, becoming a more educated person, a well-traveled person, and a person who could mingle with kings and queens, he never lost his personal touch as a country preacher, as seen in his use of everyday language when he preached. He made it clear that he moved into an integrated neighborhood to get resources rather than from a desire to move away from black people. He was just as committed (i.e., faithful) to black people as he was to God.

Just why Mays had this steadfast racial identity has much to do with his experiences with white people early in his life. No matter how many honors he received and no matter how many white friends he accumulated, the emotional damage was done, never to be fully overcome. During his old age, rather than being at peace about the death of Jim Crow and the emerging desegregated society, he became quite worried as the gains by the Negro were offset by continued white resistance to change. After his autobiography was published, Mays was caught up in a controversy as Atlanta School Board chair in the early 1970s after he retired as Morehouse president. He struck a deal with the Atlanta NAACP to delay school desegregation, which he regarded as simply a way of patiently waiting for who he considered to be well-intending white leaders; the national media took the view that he sold out to segregationists.

But we must remember that Mays's golden years at Morehouse were actually right on developmental phase target, middle age, the generative years in the Eriksonian perspective. It is no wonder that 1940–1950 were actually the years in which Mays produced the greatest number of students who went out and changed the world, especially King's 1948 class and the 1949 class. Also, 1950–1964 became the time in which Mays became the active mentor and power broker for his former students. For example, he defended Martin Luther King, Jr., in 1955 when King's father tried to convince MLK, Jr. to return to Atlanta rather than go through with the Montgomery bus boycott. As president of Morehouse in the early 1960s, Mays was also an important behind-the-scenes supporter of student activists who wanted to demonstrate against segregated businesses in downtown Atlanta.

Still, Mays was a product of his age, well in keeping with the psychoanalytical analysis of racial caste in southern communities so aptly portrayed in John Dollard's (1937/2006) *Caste and Class in a Southern Town* and Allison Davis et al.'s (1941/2009) *Deep South* , both based on inter–world war research. Dollard and Davis et al. employ the theories and methods of psychoanalysis and anthropology to explore how racial caste causes a pathological form of repression that results in the exertion of white violence at privileged will. At the same time, black populations become psychologically and socially castrated lest they become targets of such frustration-aggression.

Mays's deep unconscious, semiconscious, and conscious fears as well as his insecurities led him to write a self-celebratory book. It had an interesting though lightly touched on sociological analysis of race rather than really being about himself and the full-bodied human networks of his development from childhood through late adulthood. Because of his hunger for the spotlight, he did not give credit where credit was due. So, he did not discuss in any great detail those who outshone him in significant ways such as Charles S. Johnson, Howard Thurman, and W. E. B. Du Bois. The case of Thurman, as earlier mentioned, is particularly telling since Mays was Thurman's Morehouse debate coach in the 1920s (Carter 1998). Thurman surpassed Mays in having met Gandhi first, went to Howard first, was the first choice to be president of Morehouse, and became the first black dean of a chapel of a white university— an honor never extended to Mays. Probably the greatest irony, though, is the guilt I am sure Mays felt when King became such an eminent national and international figure.

The editor of *The Papers of Martin Luther King, Jr.*, Volume I (Clayborne 1992) writes "Mays inspired a generation of Morehouse students who gathered for his Tuesday morning lectures in which he stressed intellectual excellence, religious piety, and commitment to racial advancement."

Mays later recalled King was an eager listener, often responding to his lectures by debating certain points. These contacts led to a "real friendship," which was strengthened by visits to his home and by fairly frequent chats—*Born to Rebel* (p. 265) was the reference used for this point rather than other persons who were at Morehouse or in other areas of King's life while King was a student there.

In *Stride Towards Freedom*, King's (1987) autoethnographic account of the Montgomery bus boycott, Clayborne (1992) also writes that "King later described Mays as 'one of the great influences in my life'" (King 1987:145). This may have been more King's gratitude for Mays supporting his decision to stay in Montgomery in the midst of the boycott more than an indication of Mays being a pre-Montgomery strong instrumental or expressive mentor. Clayborne's remarks include a mixture of historical accuracy regarding the Mays-King relationship in the Morehouse context and a failure to understand that King's sociability was an integral part of a deep intellect highly recognized by his peers, his family members, and neighborhood leaders, such as John Dobbs who only allowed one neighborhood boy, King, to visit one of his six daughters due to his impressive intellectual gifts. "King's enthusiasm for Mays's teachings developed only gradually. There is little evidence that King exhibited serious interest in his studies during most of his stay at Morehouse. Younger than most of the other 204 students in his class and uncertain about his career plans, King initially paid more attention to his social life than to his class work" (Clayborne 1992:38).

Although Mays claimed that King and he were friends at Morehouse, *The Papers of Martin Luther King, Jr.* (Clayborne 1992) reveals otherwise. It makes clear that Mays did not send King a strong letter of recommendation to Crozier Seminary in 1948 during King's senior year since King was not a sterling student or in any other way one of Mays's pet young men. Indeed, if we consider the close-knit cultural context of Morehouse during the King years there (Stanfield 2003), Mays's letter and that of Brazeal express subtle indifference regarding a student they presumed was marginal at best rather than confidence in a student they knew well personally:

Benjamin E. Mays to Charles Batten (Dean of Crozer Theological Seminary):

I want to endorse the applicants for both Martin Luther King, Jr. and (name deleted). I have no reservations in recommending these two men. Both of them should graduate from Morehouse College in June. They are men of good integrity; they adjust well, and I believe, that they would do a good job at Crozer. You will see from their records that they are not brilliant students, but both have good minds. I believe they have academic averages around B-, certainly between C and B. I am of the opinion that they both can do substantial B work and with good competition, they may do even better. I hope you will see your way clear to admit them. (Clayborne 1992:152–153)

Brailsford R. Brazeal to Charles Batten:

Your letter to President B. E. Mays about Mr. M. L. King and (name deleted) who are seniors at Morehouse College has been referred to my office for consideration because Dr. Mays is out of the office. I regret that I cannot at the moment let you know where Messrs. King and (name deleted) rank in relationship to the other members of the senior class because we are not able to compile a list until the end of the present semester. We have checked on the record of each one of the men involved. Mr. King has a quality point average of 2.48 which is virtually midway between a "C" and a "B" average. (sentence deleted) I might state that these two young men have developed considerably since beginning their studies at Morehouse College. They both had to work hard in order to overcome a comparatively weak high school background. I believe that Mr. King has succeeded in doing this to a slightly greater degree than has (name deleted). I believe that these young men will take care of themselves scholastically and otherwise if they are given the chance to study at Crozer, and I also believe that they will mix well interracially. (Clayborne 1992:56–57)

One would expect a letter from a college president, *especially a Morehouse president,* who knew a student and his family, to write a letter like the following that Martin Luther King, Sr., wrote about his son to Charles Batten, dean of Crozer, an impression of ML confirmed in interviews who knew him as a child and adolescent. Notice as well, King, Sr.'s mention of Mays being on his son's ministerial ordination committee, a point Mays himself does not even mention.

To Dean Batten:

In reply to your letter relative to Martin Luther King, Jr. He is completing his college work at Morehouse in June. He entered college at age 15, is a good student and very conscientious in his work. In my opinion he is above his age in thought. In fact he always was a very steady child, quite scholarly. From childhood he always wanted (to) possess scholarship.

He was licensed to preach June 1947, and was voted Associate Pastor in the Ebenezer Baptist Church. He was ordained February 25, 1948. Serving on the council were Dr. B.E. Mays, President Morehouse College, Reverends Samuel Williams, L.M. Tobin, Morehouse College and Dr. L.A. Pinkston, President State Baptist Convention and several of our local pastors. This is stated merely as a suggestive background of his Christian ministry. (Clayborne 1992:153)

Furthermore, one would think that as college president, if Mays was as close to King as he claimed much later, he would have written the following letter rather than George Kelsey, director of the Morehouse School of Religion:

The academic record of Martin Luther King, Jr. in Morehouse College is short of what may be called "good"; but I recommend that you give his application serious consideration. King is one of those boys who came to realize the value of scholarship late in his college career. His ability exceeds his record at Morehouse, and I believe his present attitude will lift his achievement to the level of his ability. He impresses me as being quite serious about ministry and having a call rather than a professional urge. His record as a citizen in Morehouse is good. He gets along well with people, is friendly and courteous. (Clayborne 1992:155)

Nor did Mays visit King while King was at Crozier or Boston University, attention he extended to his prize students. If they had a close professor-student relationship, it was not because Mays respected King's intellectual promise. If Mays had such high respect for King, he would have sent King off to Crozier with a sterling letter and certainly would written him a letter to Boston University to pursue doctoral studies after Crozier, which did not happen.

More than likely, Mays became an essential instrumental mentor of King after King became the leader of the Montgomery bus boycott, not before. It was in this sense that Mays greatly benefited from the rise of ML. Another reason why I submit that Mays did not embrace King until after his fame is because Mays was the math teacher at Morehouse for the class of 1931, which included T. M. Alexander, Martin Luther King, Sr., and Hugh Gloster (who Mays chose as his successor as Morehouse president).

In the interviews I conducted with those who knew ML as a child and adolescent in Atlanta, there is no evidence that Mays reached out to ML in any significant way as ML grew up, and he was not close to Martin Luther King, Sr. either. Nor is there any evidence that King was very close to Mays when he returned to Atlanta to live in the 1960s. Unlike in the cases of ML's parents, John Dobbs, T. M. Alexander, and William Borders, I have yet to find evidence of Mays in a collaborative problem network (i.e., a chain of mentors) prior to ML's admission into Morehouse. And I have yet to hear a member of ML's Morehouse brother circle mention an unusually close friendship between Mays and ML while ML was at the "House."[2] King did absorb the climate that Mays created at Morehouse but he did so on his own, without the caring interest of Mays as a instrumental or expressive mentor.

Did King become an instrumental mentor for Mays? As alluded to above, even after fame crossed ML's path in the 1960s, there is no evidence that the mentor-protégé relationship between Mays and ML was all that essential. It wasn't as important as the relationship ML had with Mr. Alexander, John Dobbs, Howard Thurman, Sam Williams, John Pius Barbour, and other expressive mentors from his neighborhood or from Morehouse, which in many ways was like the other Atlanta black colleges learning spaces that extended into the Auburn Avenue community. ML did more for Mays than vice versa, as Mays confessed without understanding too clearly what he was really saying. As a black man whose manhood like the manhood of most black men no matter his status or stature remained ever so fragile to the very end of what should have been a long life becoming increasingly enriching and grounded in a social identity graced in wisdom. But, for the articulated reasons, for Mays and for so many other black men of his generation and before and after him, such a lovely rather romanticized ascent into the pleasures of old age as the graceful wise one proves to be improbable due to the persistent psychological groundings which come with racial caste in its continued historically specific contexts from a black man's infancy through old age if he is so fortunate to live that long.

I conclude this psychohistorical analysis by saying that ML is a superb example of Fowler's stage six since he broke through the sociological sound barrier of race and fashioned a doctrine of all-inclusive love. However, the deeply festering scrapes and scratches of Benjamin Elijah Mays prevented him from breaking out of the prison of race that pinned him down and weighed him down in such great embitterment and despair until he died as a caste-ridden caged rebel still on the outside trying to break in. I would say Mays attained stage five at best.

Yet, perhaps the human development perspective of Bruno Bettelheim on what happens to those who grow up in war-torn traumatic environments is a more fitting way to interpret the developmental plight of even the most distinguished black men as they age than the much more overly optimistic perspective of Erik Erikson, James Fowler, and other Eurocentric life formation stage theorists. Benjamin Elijah Mays may be representative of how much black males in the United States for generations have lived in a world that is like a daily routinized highly traumatic war zone. Consistent positive development over a life span is indeed a rarity as is grasping and embracing an empowering sense of peace, accomplishment, and something worthwhile to pass down to one's children and children's children.

Conclusion: Prospects, Concerns, and Considerations

In race-centered societies, individual and collective unconsciousness, semi-consciousness, and consciousness ground the reproduction, stabilization, and transformation of multiracialization. Psychohistorical analysis of autobiographical texts of human beings who live in race-centered societies can provide great insight about how race is emotionally crippling and dehumanizing for all societal members. As this analysis of Benjamin E. Mays illustrates, and as documented elsewhere, racializaion is a devastating experience that impacts its victims well into old age in ways that have to be fully examined by sociologists, psychiatrists, and psychologists.

When we triangulate autobiography textual analysis with primary and secondary historical sources and with interviews, the researcher can construct the sociological and cultural external environmental context of the autobiography. Such triangulation also allows the researcher to confirm or question claims made by the author, an imperative given the tendency of these authors to over-embellish the positive and underrate or omit the negative.

When using primary and secondary sources and interviews to weave the social and cultural contexts of the autobiographical text, it is important to remember some rules of reliability and validity. For instance, for archival sources, as I have pointed out elsewhere (Stanfield 1987a), make sure that a contention in correspondence is based on more than one document. As an another example, face-to-face interviews reported here were done with older people. Most of them, now in their post-seventies and eighties, knew John Hope, Benjamin Mays, and Martin Luther King, Jr. personally. Forgetfulness and emphasizing issues not really important "back then" or downplaying issues that were quite important "back then" are major pitfalls in interviewing older persons. This is especially true when so much is at stake, such as the historical reputation of a famous person such as Hope, Mays, and King. But that is why it was important for me to confirm comments in interviews with other interviewees if at all possible as well as using primary and secondary sources. At the same time, old age often becomes a time of liberation in which interviewees assume they have nothing to lose by telling it the way it was.

It helped being a Morehouse faculty member while doing this research. That generated the ideas and data for this chapter since I could gain access to networks that allowed me to confirm and question information both in writing and in oral tradition just because I was blessed to become a trusted brother of the House. I will always be most appreciative of that brotherly embrace.

Notes

1. Bennie Boys refers to those men who attended Morehouse while Dr. Mays was president.

2. House is a nickname for Morehouse.

References

Bloom, B. S. (1985). *Developing talent in young people*. New York: Ballantine Books.

Bond, H. M. (1972). *Black American scholars: A study of their beginnings*. Detroit: Balamp Books.

Carter, L. E. (1998). *Walking integrity: Benjamin Elijah Mays, mentor to Martin Luther King Jr.* Mercer, GA: Mercer University Press.

Chafe, W., Gavins, R., & Korstad, R. (Eds.). (2008). *Remembering Jim Crow: African Americans tell about life in the segregated South* (with MP3 Audio CD). New York: New Press.

Clayborne, C. (1992). *The papers of Martin Luther King, Jr.* Vol.1. Berkeley: University of California Press.

Coles, R. (1967). *Children of crisis.* Vol. 1, *A study in courage and fear.* Boston: Atlantic-Little, Brown.

Davis, A. (1983). *Leadership, love, and aggression.* New York: Harcourt Press.

Davis, A., Gardner, B., Gardner, M., & Wallach, J. (1941/2009). *Deep South: A social anthropological study of caste and class.* Southern Classics Series. Columbia: University of South Carolina Press.

Dollard, J. (1937/2006). Caste and class in a southern town. ACLS History E-Book Project.

Erikson, E. (1994). *Identity and the life cycle.* New York: W. W. Norton & Company.

Fowler, J. W. (1981). *Stages of faith: The psychology of human development and the quest for meaning.* San Francisco: Harper.

Johnson, C. S. (1987). *Bitter Canaan.* Ed. and intro. essay by J. H. Stanfield, II. New Brunswick, NJ: Transaction Books.

King, M. L., Jr. (1987). *Stride towards freedom: The Montgomery story.* New York: Harper Collins Childrens Books.

Mays, B. E. (1971). *Born to rebel: An autobiography.* New York: Charles Scribner's Sons.

Mays, B. E. (1988). *The Negro's church.* Salem, NH: Ayer.

Paton, A. (1980). *Toward the mountain: An autobiography.* New York: Charles Scribner's Sons.

Stanfield, J. H., II. (1985). *Philanthropy and Jim Crow in American social science.* Westport, CT: Greenwood Press.

Stanfield, J. H., II. (1987a). Archival materials in race relations research. *American Behavioral Scientist, 30,* 366–379.

Stanfield, J. H., II. (1987b). Life history analysis and racial stratification. *American Behavioral Scientist, 30,* 430–440.

Stanfield, J. H., II. (1999). Before the rescue squad arrived: The indigenous origins of black physicians from poor communities. *Challenge: A Journal of Research on African American Men,10,* 61–77.

Stanfield, J. H., II. (2003). Editor, teaching sociology. Teaching sociology in historically black colleges and universities: A neglected chapter in the history of the scholarship of teaching sociology. *Teaching Sociology, 31,* 361–365.

Stanfield, J. H., II. (2006). Psychoanalytic ethnography and the transformation of racially wounded communities. *International Journal of Qualitative Studies in Education,19,* 387–399.

Stanfield, J. H., II. (1955/2008). *Introductory essay, Black ways of Kent by Hylan Lewis.* Columbia: University of South Carolina Press.

Torrence, R. (1948). *The story of John Hope.* New York: The MacMillian Company.

Van der Veer, R., & Valsiner, J. (Eds.) (1994). *The Vygotsky reader.* Oxford, UK: Blackwell.

Part III: Comparative and Cross-National Studies

13   Bush, Volvos, and 50 Cent: The Cross-National Triangulation Challenges of a "White" Swede and a "Black" American

L. Janelle Dance and Johannes Lunneblad

Introduction

Promising School Practices, Two Countries, and Two Ethnographers

Since the summer of 2006, we have been part of a six-nation research project titled "The Children of Immigrants in Schools" (CIS). With Richard Alba as the lead principal investigator (PI), the CIS project is driven by ten co-PIs and fifteen research fellows conducting binational comparative research on schooling and second-generation immigrants in the United States and Europe (U.S.-Great Britain, U.S.-France, U.S.-Spain, U.S.-Holland, U.S.-Sweden). As part of the five-member U.S.-Sweden team, we were two of the research fellows who collected data on "promising practices" in schools with high enrollments of immigrant students.

Instead of the usual focus on immigrant students and failure, we and the other members of the U.S.-Sweden team documented examples of successful school practices. Most of our ethnographic field research took place during the 2006/2007 academic year, with follow-up visits in 2008 and 2009. Thus far, our team has completed several preliminary reports, a final report, and manuscripts for journal publication. However, one story will not be elaborated on in any of these documents: the research design choices made to keep the cross-national research sites in sync and how racial/ethnic and national identities impacted this process. In this chapter, we tell that story. From among our many research experiences, we cull a saga about triangulation that is methodologically revealing, reflexive, and constructively critical. In the pages that follow, the pronoun "we" is a reference to the specific activities of L. Janelle

Dance and Johannes Lunneblad, not the broader activities of the U.S.-Sweden team.

The topics that comprise this triangulation saga range from things manageable to things unexpected. To capture both manageable and unexpected experiences, we will share etic and emic vantage points. We move among methodological perspectives that are "experience distant" from our research sites and those that are "experience near" (Beach 1997). Etic perspectives tend to focus on "categories meaningful to the [researchers and are] useful for initial data gathering as well as for cross-cultural comparisons"; emic perspectives focus on "the identification of categories which are meaningful to members of the [researched] community" (Keating 2001/2007:288).

As many methods texts attest, abstract-etic plans for ethnographic research are always subject to change based on the actual-emic chemistry of research sites (Atkinson et al. 2001/2007; Creswell 2007; Emerson 2001; Hammersley & Atkinson 2007; LeCompte & Schensul 1999). Although etic and emic conceptualizations typically refer to the analytic outcomes of data analyses, here we use them to frame reflections on our triangulation approaches. Our main objective is to examine the national and ethnic/racial identities of researchers that transcended triangulation. These identities emerged in the field and seemed to matter to the students, teachers, and other school staff.

With 20/20 hindsight, we add our voices to the growing chorus of scholarly critiques about researcher objectivity. We share the sentiments of John Stanfield and others who take as a given "that the autobiographies, cultures, and historical contexts of researchers matter; these determine what researchers see and do not see as well as their ability to analyze data and disseminate knowledge adequately" (Stanfield 1994). In short, we do not believe that researchers can ever be purely objective but we borrow a strategy similar to that used by economists: "Let's assume that all things/researchers are equal." In altering this strategy, instead of assuming all researchers are (or were) equal, the assumption is that we and the other members of the U.S.-Sweden team were good reflexive researchers who minimized the impact of our perspectives on the research process. Would that suffice as a good enough approximation of objectivity? The answer elaborated here is a resounding "No!" Please keep reading to find out why.

In the pages that follow, we tell our triangulation saga in a straightforward manner but admit that the process was more back and forth than documented. In the next section, we provide a brief literature review that defines our use of the concept "triangulation" and our view of the relationship between triangulation and researcher roles. At the end of this section, we provide background information about the broader project in which our two-school study is a part. In the third section, we revisit our research sites and methods by comparing our plans to the actual triangulation outcomes. Then we get to the heart of the chapter. We turn our focus away from the aspects of triangulation that we sought to influence to those aspects of ethnic/racial/national identities that influenced our researcher roles in the field. Therefore, the fourth section of this chapter provides our candid acknowledgment about the lack of triangulation in terms of emergent identities of race, ethnicity, and national origins.

We are critical education theorists who share many fundamental methodological, philosophical, and theoretical perspectives. In other words, we "look" a lot alike on the inside. BUT, as elaborated in the fourth section, we neither share racial/ethnic/national origins nor outward appearances. So, in the conclusion, we revisit what a "white" Swedish male and a "black" American female learned about triangulation, racial/ethnic/national identity, and respondents' influence on researcher roles.

First, here, in brief, is how we became interested in cross-national research.

Dance became interested in it back in the 1990s while working on her doctoral dissertation. During a two-week pleasure trip to visit a friend in Gothenburg, Sweden, Dance learned that Gothenburg and other large cities in Sweden had significant immigrant populations with persons whose continental origins included Latin America, Africa, Asia, and the Middle East. An interest in how the life-experiences of minority group members in Sweden compared to those of minorities in the United States inspired Dance to seek grant funding to return to Sweden and conduct qualitative research within minority communities. Since 2004, Dance has worked on and off as a visiting researcher and lecturer in Sweden.

Lunneblad, who grew up in a working-class fishing community in Sweden, is greatly interested in how differences of class, geographical origins, and ethnicity affect school success. More specifically, growing up outside the Swedish mainstream inspired Lunneblad's interests in dominant versus subordinate cultural codes. Dating back to his dissertation research, Lunneblad is interested in how teachers in Sweden navigate multicultural contexts. When the CIS project offered an opportunity to compare pedagogical practices in large city high schools in Sweden to those in New York City, Lunneblad expanded his research interests to the cross-national level.

In this chapter, we use cross-national comparisons to explore researcher identities at a more global level. Our focus is on the perspectives of the researched rather than on the perspectives of the researchers.

SCHOLARLY PERSPECTIVES AND RESEARCH SITES

Defining "Triangulation"

In navigation and surveying contexts, triangulation refers to using three fixed points or landmarks as more reliable indicators of a geographical position than a single point. In regard to qualitative methods, definitions of triangulation refer to the use of multiple aspects of the research process to cross-check research results instead of relying on one single aspect (Beach 1997; Bryman 2004; Denzin 1978; Hammersley & Atkinson 2007). A broad definition of triangulation lists the multiple aspects as multiple sources of data, multiple researchers, multiple theoretical perspectives, or multiple methodological approaches (Denzin 1978). A common usage of triangulation more narrowly refers to multiple methodological approaches. It is generally held that when multiple methodological approaches "involve different kinds of validity threat [these multiple approaches] provide a basis for checking interpretations" (Hammersley & Atkinson 2007:184). It is argued that in this way, the triangulation of methodological approaches improves positivistic measures of reliability and validity in the research design.

We use the broader definition of triangulation, which embraces multiple research sites, multiple methods and sources of data, multiple indicators of the phenomena under investigation (namely, promising practices), and multiple researchers (Beach 1997; Denzin 1978; Hammersley & Atkinson 2007). During the research process, we did not expect this broader approach to lead to more reliable and valid findings in a positivistic sense but to plausible findings and explanations of phenomena worthy of further analysis and substantiation. So, instead of using triangulation as a means to positivistic validity control, we used it as an engine that drove analyses. As argued by Dennis Beach,

> triangulation is best viewed and exploited ... as a means by which to both invent, refine, and test the stability of an explanation ... via the production and comparison of different images of understanding by utilising, following up and capitalising on both consistencies, inconsistencies and contradictions in and between data, data categories or emerging ideas. (1995, 1997:48–49)

We were particularly interested in the convergence of promising school practices that were consistent across the U.S.-Sweden team's four school sites. For consistencies found at the two schools that are central to the methodological reflections of this chapter, we tested the plausibility of the concept "performativity" (as defined by Stephen J. Ball). Due to the demands of performativity, teachers are forced to pay less attention to the actual academic and pedagogical needs of students and more attention to "impression management" (Ball 2006:12). Given the methodological focus of this chapter, we do not elaborate findings about promising practices or performativity; they are delineated elsewhere (Lunneblad et al. 2009; Suárez-Orozco et al. 2009). We mention them to provide an example of findings facilitated by our triangulation techniques.

Triangulation and Researcher Roles

As mentioned above, one approach to triangulation can be the use of multiple researchers. This may seem straightforward in theory, but it has many obstacles in practice. For example, different researchers may approach the same research topic from different roles and these differences may affect data outcomes. A classic typology, offered by Raymond L. Gold, holds that researcher roles range on a continuum, from being a complete participant to being a complete observer (Gold 1958; and see Hammersley & Atkinson 2007:82–86). Or researcher roles may differ by degrees of membership that range from peripheral membership to active or complete membership (Adler & Adler 1994:380). These conceptualizations of researcher roles, even at the complete membership end of the continuum, assume a somewhat neutral and unobtrusive observer. Adler and Adler affirm:

> Observers can thus take roles that range anywhere from the hidden or disguised voyeur, who watches from outside or with a passive (even electronic) presence, to the active participant, involved in the setting, who acts as a member and not as a researcher so as not to alter the flow of the interaction unnaturally. (Adler & Adler 1994:380)

There are numerous postmodern, poststructural, feminist, and critical theoretical critiques of researcher neutrality and objectivity (Caughey 2007; Collins 2000, 2003; Denzin & Lincoln 2005; Stanfield 1994; Twine & Warren 2000). Nonetheless, objectivity remains a tenacious aspiration "central to the self image of most practitioners of the social and behavioural sciences" (Angrosino 2005:730). As "good reflexive researchers," we have no grand delusions about objectivity, but we sought to manage certain aspects of our sites and methods to create consistency (or the illusion thereof). We did this even though we eschew notions of researcher roles and "ethnographic truth" and are more concerned with how "ethnographic observers ... enter into dialogic relations with members of the group being studied" instead of the traditional preoccupation with process and methods that ensure objectivity (Angrosino 2005:734).

A noticeable feature of this triangulation saga is that we do not share ethnic or national origins; that in and of itself is a threat to consistency. However, threats to objectivity and ethnographic truth as well as to consistency remain even if multiple researchers share national, ethnic, and gender backgrounds. As argued by Twine and Warren, although multiple researchers may share racial or ethnic backgrounds, "[race/ethnicity are] not the only relevant social signifier(s). ... [T]he meanings and impacts of racial difference [or similarity] are complicated by age, class, accent, education, national origins, region, as well as sexuality" (2000:9). Consequently, researcher roles and identities are situational (Angrosino 2005; Caughey 2007; Twine & Warren 2000). No matter how much a researcher attempts to objectively manage her or his role in the field, and no matter how similar two or more researchers are, this role is partially dependent on how respondents subjectively read, react, or interact with a researcher according to social signifiers of race/ethnicity, accent/dialect, personality, national origins, and so on. Therefore, if our "good reflexive researcher" strategy does not suffice, this insufficiency would remain whatever backgrounds or traits we share.

It is apparent that a black American woman and a white Swedish man could not have synchronized identities. In other words, we could not use our identities as fixed points because our identities vary with regard to gender, ethnicity, and nationality. However, our research design could have been more attentive to how our identities might be influenced by field dynamics beyond our control. Moreover, though some of our respondents seemed to assume the existence of essential "gender-ness" (i.e., essential aspects of "manliness" or "womanliness"), essential "black-American-ness," or essential "white-Swedish-ness," we eschew essentialist notions about race, ethnicity, gender, or nationality. Instead, we agree with scholarly claims that when ethnographers—even good reflexive researchers with clearly defined roles—enter the field they do *not* arrive in bodies that signify objectivity, translucence, or neutrality (Stanfield 1994; Troyna 1998; Twine & Warren 2000).

We are not suggesting that a research design should never attempt to synchronize researcher identities about gender, and/or ethnicity, and/or nationality, or other types of social background characteristics. Synchronized identities can be an important feature of a research design. We are arguing that researchers must always be mindful that field-based identities are situational, emergent, and interactive. To belabor this argument, imagine if instead of Dance and Lunneblad, two researchers who shared gender, ethnic, and national backgrounds had been the subject of this chapter. Imagine if Condeleezza Rice and Michelle Obama—(or Olof Palme and Fredrik Reinfeldt)—had been the good reflexive researchers studying promising school practices. (Of course, to better parallel Dance's and Lunneblad's social status, the research would have to have occurred before Rice and Obama became world famous or while Palme was still living and before he and Reinfeldt became prominent political leaders.) In any event, Rice's and Obama's shared outward identities would not guarantee more objective or consistent data collection outcomes because, as stated above, identities can be inconsistent markers of one's social location. Although Rice and Obama (or Palme and Reinfeldt) share racial/ethnic, gender, and national origins, inconsistent aspects of their identities—deriving from differences such as age, personality, and political perspectives—might emerge in the contexts of field dynamics.

Background on a Two-Nation Research Project

Four Research Sites at a Distance

The U.S.-Sweden Research Team of CIS included two research directors who were co-PIs and three research fellows who collected ethnographic data. The research directors of the team chose four research sites: two high schools from New York City and two high schools from large Swedish cities. All four schools had been recognized within their respective cities as innovative educational sites for students of immigrant origins. From an etic, "experience distant" perspective, the research team was interested in several aspects that indicated the schools could be useful sites for a cross-national, comparative study: (1) each of the four schools served immigrant origin youths; (2) each one was a non-exam, nonselective school that served many students from the local school community; (3) each school was known within the educational community for its innovative approaches; (4) in terms of criteria like low teacher-student ratios, high student stability rates, high graduation rates, and superb teacher qualifications, all four schools surpassed those that usually served immigrant youth (Suárez-Orozco et al. 2006, 2009). Aspects such as these allowed the U.S.-Sweden team an adequate degree of certainty that the team could collect data on promising practices that would be useful and comparable. In writing this chapter, we draw on the research activities that took place at two of the four research sites, specifically the two schools where we were the lead researchers.

TRIANGULATION PLANS AND TRIANGULATION OUTCOMES

Aspects of the Research Process Amenable to Triangulation

The directors of the U.S.-Sweden team were the first to draft the research design for the study of promising practices. However, before the data collection process began, the directors and researchers worked collaboratively on the final version of the research design. Though the directors had the greatest influence over the selection of the schools sites and the researchers who would collect data, the directors *and* researchers had a say in the research methods that were to be used and the additional site and methods triangulation that would take place in the field.

Etic-Plans for Site Triangulation

Site triangulation was an important aspect of our research design. To examine promising practices, the research directors chose multiple schools that had a lot in common in regard to educating immigrant origin students. Given that the research team only had about four months to conduct ethnographic research, the team deliberately planned to compare apples and apples instead of apples and oranges. In other words, our research sites did not include schools that lacked indicators of promising practices. The research directors of the team reasoned that the use of comparable schools sites might allow the team to uncover and learn more about commonalities instead of inconsistencies among schools with promising school practices. But as revealed by the following discussion of two of the four schools, no two apples are exactly alike. Therefore, site triangulation at a distance often required additional refinements when researchers began on-site research activities.

The Emic-Realities of Site Triangulation

World Citizens High School (WCHS), located in New York City, and Bergslunden Gymnasium (BG), located in a large Swedish city, are two upper-secondary schools with disproportionately high enrollments of immigrant students, nearly 100% and 70% respectively. At WCHS, all teachers worked with new arrival, immigrant students who were second language learners; in the United States, these students are called English Language Learners (ELL). At BG, teachers worked with four distinct groups of students: students who were mostly ethnic Swedes; students who were mostly second-generation immigrants; students with physical handicaps; and immigrant students who were both new arrivals and second language learners. At WCHS, most students traced their geographical origins to Asia, the Caribbean, and the Middle East; at BG, most students traced their origins to the Middle East, South America, Africa, and Asia.

Lunneblad was the lead researcher at WCHS; Dance was the lead researcher at BG. According to the initial research design, Lunneblad was to conduct research with the teachers of new-arrival immigrant students and the new-arrival students themselves, but the teachers would be his primary respondents. Dance was to conduct research with students who were second-generation immigrants and with teachers. Dance's primary respondent group, however, would be the students. These plans would change. To create more research consistency across these two school sites, Lunneblad (while conducting research in New York) and Dance (while conducting research in Sweden) used email and phone conversations to refine the initial research design so that components of Dance's research would more directly parallel components of Lunneblad's. As Lunneblad's focus was on teachers of ELL students, Dance revised her research focus to include teachers who worked with newly arrived immigrant students who were also second language learners, known in Sweden as "Swedish 2" (S2) students. Hence, our research site triangulation was fluid and adaptable, instead of rigid and uncompromising.

Etic-Plans for Methodological Triangulation
During the initial research design phase, the research team planned to use ethnographic fieldwork as the overarching strategy for collecting data across the four sites. Our (Dance and Lunneblad's) decision to focus data collection activities more exclusively on two schools occurred after the planning phase. According to the initial research design, the methods used at the four sites were to include interviews/focus groups with teachers, students, *and* parents as well as field observations in multiple contexts including classrooms, working groups, discussion groups, faculty meetings, school corridors, and school cafeterias. Last, the initial research design included plans to administer school-wide surveys "to assess dimensions of student relational, behavioral, and cognitive engagement" (Suárez-Orozco et al. 2006:3).

As often happens with ethnographic projects, we were not able to reach all of our methodological goals (Emerson 2001; Hammersley & Atkinson 2007). When the research was complete, we had conducted interviews and observations in three of the four schools. Forced by circumstances to deviate from the initial research design, Lunneblad conducted interviews and observations in one of the New York schools and one of the Swedish schools. Similar to the initial research design, Dance conducted interviews and observations in the two Swedish schools, but spent less time in the second Swedish school than initially planned.

Emic-Realities of Methodological Triangulation
Consistent with the initial research design, our primary methods of data collection included ethnographic interviews with teachers and students (both focus groups and one-on-one interviews) and ethnographic field observations in classrooms. We also conducted observations in school corridors and collected data on school programs and practices designed to support the school achievement of ethnic minority students as well as data on student achievement.

The duration of our on-site research activities, including follow-up visits, was roughly four to six months. Also, methodological triangulation strategies were sometimes refined during follow-up visits. Though short of a full-fledged ethnography, the four-to-six month duration of data collection did yield rich ethnographic snapshots of the activities, practices, daily experiences, and perspectives of typical school days at WCHS and BG.

Hindsight about Site and Methods Triangulation
As discussed thus far, the U.S.-Sweden team research design triangulated research sites and research methods. To reiterate, the team sought to understand promising practice through using multiple school sites and multiple methods of data collection; we will discuss the use of multiple researchers in the next section. Despite methodological textbook directives about the ad hoc nature of ethnographic research, our less than ad hoc research design proved to be

useful, flexible, and largely productive (Hammersley & Atkinson 2007:21). Even if the team had proposed a more ad hoc, untriangulated research design, the politics and requirements of funding would not have endorsed this open approach (Cheek 2005). And given the initials plans that multiple researchers working at multiple sites would only have three to four months to collect data on promising practices, an open approach may have done more to hinder the data collection process than to facilitate comparable findings.

Though not perfect, the utility of the team's research design was its flexibility; research plans made from a distant or etic perspective were amenable to alteration or emic refinements once we were in the field. As stated above, we still attempted to be good reflexive researchers, with the understanding this could not ensure objectivity.

If success is measured by completing the data collection process, analyzing data, writing final reports, and writing manuscripts for presentation/ publication in scholarly venues, then the U.S.-Sweden team research design delivered these successful outcomes. While we (Dance and Lunneblad) neither strove for nor achieved objectivity, we could argue that the team's research design allowed us to be impartial enough, given the cross-national and cross-cultural contexts of the research sites, to achieve most of the team's research goals. We could also argue that the team's design thoughtfully and successfully triangulated sites and methods in a way that facilitated research consistencies among sites.

In spite of this success, we have a major shortcoming to report. The research design failed to take into account that minimizing biases and facilitating consistencies are not determined by research designs or researchers alone; respondents also play a crucial role. Respondents could be partial and their interactions with researchers could be inconsistent. Respondents could be influenced by, concerned about, or interested in researcher identities. The U.S.-Sweden team failed to consider that researchers' appearances/identities would be coded and/or read by respondents in the field, thereby introducing elements of inconsistency across the research sites. In the end, the major shortcoming of the research design was that in the face of broad-based triangulation techniques that thoughtfully relied on multiple sites, multiple methods, *and* multiple researchers, the team failed to take into consideration respondents' notions about researcher identities.

Bush, Volvos, and 50 Cent

The Nuances of Identity and the Limits of Triangulation

Theoretical triangulation is an approach to data collection inducing or deducing multiple theories (Denzin 1989; Hammersley & Atkinson 2007:165). As is typical for studies that employ ethnographic methods, and in contrast to the predetermined sites and methods, the initial research design had no predetermined theoretical base. Instead of setting out to test particular theories, the U.S.-Sweden team's research design identified testable propositions or guiding questions that were rooted, to some extent, in both theoretical and empirical claims from previous research. For example, the research design listed several guiding questions about whether the schools had a positive school ethos (Lightfoot 1985) and whether researchers could discern a "grand narrative" expressed by school officials and students (Postman 1996; Suárez-Orozco et al. 2006).

We used these guiding questions as loose hypotheses instead of definitive claims for theoretical triangulation. Given the cross-national, multi-site nature of the project, we needed the flexibility to decode, recode, and/or retranslate the meanings of the guiding questions within the actual contexts of the research sites. In that way, we were open to navigating toward these questions or away from these questions or down different roads than those suggested by the guiding questions. Once on site, we began to explore the applicability notions like "performativity." And, as elaborated below, we believe that our approach to theories—which respected the emergent attributes of perspectives and notions induced or adduced in the field—could have been a model for our approach to respondents' notions about researchers' identities.

Up to this point, we have told a triangulation saga with mostly successful outcomes that occurred largely by design. But unlike our accomplishments with sites, methods, and guiding questions, successes related to researcher identities occurred more by default than design. This failure to consider how researcher identities might impact the data collection process could have had devastating consequences.

Pre-Research Jitters: The "Strange" Swede and the "Warmongering" American

Before Dance entered the research site and surrounding community of BG in a large Swedish city and before Lunneblad entered the research site and surrounding community of WCHS in New York City, each had private worries. Lunneblad was worried about not making connections because English was his second language (Swedish is his first language) and that he might be perceived as "strange" because of his European/Swedish accent and origins. He also had minor concerns about the rumors he had heard that Americans often confused Sweden with Switzerland and more substantial ones that Blacks and Hispanic Americans at his research site might have a general dislike of Whites. Like Lunneblad, Dance was also worried about the obstacles presented by Swedish not being her first language (English is her first). Additionally, in light of the war in Iraq and the general disapproval across Europe of the presidential administration of George W. Bush and the American "empire," Dance was worried about being perceived as a warmongering American researcher in a school where many of the students were from the Near East or Middle East. At the very least, these private concerns meant that neither of us would enter the field with naive visions of being translucent or neutral researchers. Though we only shared these concerns with one another, we were aware that we would enter the field in nationalized-bodies.

As good reflexive researchers, we did our best to not project our concerns and biases on the research site and findings, but we did not pretend that we were impartial, apolitical, carefree, unbiased beings (Peshkin 1991). We should have been equally mindful that our respondents would not be apolitical, carefree, unbiased beings.

Respondents' Perspectives and Researcher Identities
As critical educational theorists, we resemble one another. However, in appearance, we differ. From the perspective of a camera lens, Lunneblad appears to be thirty-something years old, 5 feet 7 inches in height, slim build, around 130 pounds in weight, with curly dark brown hair, blue-eyes, lightly shaven beard/moustache, and a light peach-pink complexion. While in the field, Lunneblad often dressed in jeans, a comfortable dress shirt, and brown Chelsea boots. Dance also appears to be thirty-something in age (though she is in her forties), 5 feet 9 inches in height, athletic build, around 158 pounds in weight, with dark brown Afro hair that is braided, dark brown eyes, and a mahogany-brown complexion. While in the field, Dance often dressed in sporty pants, long-sleeve sports shirts, and Timberland boots.

Lunneblad's concerns about being perceived as a strange Swede from Switzerland who spoke English with an accent as well as Dance's concerns about being perceived as a warmongering American from George W. Bush's empire who spoke Swedish with an accent eventually gave way to actual opinions and stereotypes held by respondents. These emerged during the research process, opinions, and stereotypes that derived from our national/ethnic/racial origins.

For example, Dance actually encountered opinions linked to George W. Bush, though she never initiated these conversations. Once students learned that Dance was an American, they frequently volunteered their negative opinions about the American invasion of Iraq (several of these students were Iraqi immigrants; even those who were not Iraqis offered protests). Some students, namely Kurdish immigrants, volunteered positive opinions about the American invasion of Iraq. Dance also frequently encountered positive stereotypes about black American comedians and hip hop artists, as students asked "Hey, Lory [Dance], have you ever met 50 Cent/Eddie Griffin/Snoop Dog/

Tupac Skakur?" Again, it was the students, not Dance, who initiated these conversations. So, in building rapport with students, many topics arose that had little to do with promising school practices but much to do about how students perceive the researcher(s).

While attending an English-language class with new arrival students at BG, for example, a Kurdish male student asked Dance about the rapper 50 Cent. He wanted to know what this rapper's name meant. Using the question as an opportunity to assist the student with English and to build rapport, Dance showed the student two U.S. quarters (coins) and explained, using Swedish and English, that 50 Cent was a reference to "change"; a reference that had a double meaning. Dance also explained that rapper 50 Cent had told two different stories about how he got that name. In classrooms, corridors, and other school-based meeting places, several other students frequently asked Dance about various black American rappers or about other topics that they thought a black American might be uniquely qualified to answer.

Instead of George W. Bush or rapper 50 Cent, Lunneblad frequently encountered the specter of Olof Palme,[1] as some teachers seemingly assumed that as a Swede, Lunneblad was automatically a leftist scholar in favor of socialism, welfare, progressive education, and social justice. No teacher confused Sweden with Switzerland. The identities that teachers projected on Lunneblad had more to do with his gender and national-ethnic origins as a Swede than with race as a white person. For example, during small talk with Lunneblad, male teachers would often comment about going home and relaxing with a six pack of beer or ask Lunneblad questions about Volvos. Teachers in general, at this progressive school, seemed to have a largely positive image of Sweden. For example, they asked Lunneblad a lot of questions about the Swedish school system and the social welfare system. None of the teachers had been to Sweden but they had notions that Sweden was a social democratic country; teachers took liberties with Lunneblad that reflected their notions about Sweden.

Thus, a teacher who was thinking about buying a car asked Lunneblad about different models of Volvos. On another occasion, this teacher used the Internet to show Lunneblad the Volvo models about which he wanted Johannes' feedback. During lunch, discussions came up about cars and automobile inspections. Teachers also assumed that Lunneblad had common cultural reference points in terms of cultural capital. For example, teachers would engage him in conversations about artistic books and novels and popular music (i.e., independent rock artists like the Cardigans or the Hives from Sweden). Johannes was pleased that no one asked him anything about the Swedish singing group ABBA (or the movie *Mama Mia*, which is based on ABBA's songs) but they did ask him other questions that they thought a Swede might be uniquely qualified to answer.

The fact that teachers' comments seemingly had little to do with Lunneblad's "racial" appearance does not mean that they did not notice it.

It may mean that they took for granted that a Swede would be white. We can only imagine that the small talk could have been different if Lunneblad had been a second-generation Iranian immigrant from Sweden. Lunneblad believes that he may have benefited from white/European privilege because he had the boyish look of a young lost white male: Black school guards allowed him to by-pass the metal detector and black-Caribbean cafeteria workers mothered him. And though students' comments suggested that they did notice Dance's racial/ethnic appearance, she believes that she may have benefited from being perceived as a non-Swede. Students quickly treated her as an insider, joking with her in the corridors and sharing stories about their families with her.

We both appeared inconspicuous in the communities of our research sites. Dance often blended into the broader community of immigrants where she conducted research because she resembled an immigrant or non-Swede; she felt at home as she walked around the neighborhood. Lunneblad blended into the white American "hipster" community where he conducted research because he appeared European; living in that community gave him a sense of belonging during his time in New York. Hence, as we conducted research on promising practices, we did so in the context of the respondents' political perspectives, stereotypes, and national/ethnic opinions that were cast on us. The "ghosts" of George W. Bush and Olof Palme as well as the stereotypes and notions about Swedes and black Americans could have become poltergeists that wreaked havoc with the research process but they did not.

Respondent Rapport by Default Instead of Design

By chance, not by research design, Dance was a hip hop aficionado, though she had not personally met any hip hop artists. So, in discussions with students about hip hop artists, Dance could be genuinely engaged. Likewise, Dance shared the students' political critiques about the abuses of the Bush Administration. And, having spent extended periods of time (over nine months, all together) in a Swedish community with several Kurdish families by whom Dance had been well received, she was sensitized to the pro-Bush views of many Kurds. Again, Dance's sensitivities allowed her to engage in genuine conversations with both Iraqi Arab and Iraqi Kurdish students, in particular, and with immigrant studies, in general. By chance, students' preoccupations with black American hip hop artists and the Bush administration's policies did not hinder the research process as students "read," "coded," or "decoded" Dance's identity. If Dance had not possessed an appreciation for hip hop or sensitivities about the differing perspectives Middle Eastern and other students had about the Bush administration, her interactions with students could have become awkward and stressed. Building rapport could have been hampered if Dance either dismissed or feigned or fumbled interest in topics and issues that students presented to her.

Similarly, more by default than design, Lunneblad was a progressive scholar who shared many of the educational visions of the teachers at WCHS. He shared their beliefs that new arrival immigrant students deserved the best education that the U.S. public school system could muster. He shared their belief in a democratic school system that was not guided by blind devotion to capitalistic markets. He shared their beliefs that the government should actively address and alleviate social inequalities of race, ethnicity, gender, class instead of waiting on the "hidden hand" of capitalism. By chance, teachers' assumptions about Sweden did not hinder the research process as they coded/decoded Lunneblad's identity. If Lunneblad had not been a progressive scholar—not all Swedes are progressive—and had he not shared the Swedish social democratic ideals that Olof Palme made famous, he or the teachers could have become ill at ease as Lunneblad conducted research with teachers, thereby limiting his ability to build rapport.

Though discussions about topics like Bush, Volvos, and 50 Cent had nothing to do with promising school practices, such discussions were important to building rapport with students and teachers. Our otherwise well-planned research design could have unraveled had respondents pulled researcher identity threads that undermined rapport. In fairness to the research directors for the U.S.-Sweden team, they chose Lunneblad and Dance based on assessments that we were competent researchers. So, by research design, two competent and qualified researchers were placed in the field (three, when you count our third colleague). But, collectively, the team devised no game plan for dealing with potential threats to the research process that could have been related to respondents' regard for researchers' identities.

CONCLUSIONS AND LESSONS LEARNED

A Social Scientific Appeal for Triangulation Serenity in Cross-National Research

"Valid, Reliable ... Objective Findings"

> [Traditional assumptions about observation-based research hold] that it is both possible and desirable to develop standardized procedures that can "maximize observational efficacy, minimize investigator bias, and allow for replication and/or verification to check out the degree to which these procedures have enabled the investigator to produce valid, reliable data that, when incorporated into his or her published report, will be regarded by peers as objective findings".

—Gold (1997:397, in Angrosino 2005)

"Research Design Is Crucial"

> [W]e must recognize that, even less than other forms of social research, the course of ethnographic work cannot be predetermined, all problems anticipated, and ready made strategies made available for dealing with them. However, this neither eliminates the need for pre-fieldwork preparation nor means that the researcher's behaviour in the field can be haphazard, merely adjusting to events by taking "the line of least resistance." Indeed, we shall argue that research design is crucial to ethnography, but that it is a reflexive process that operates throughout every stage of a project.
>
> —Hammersley & Atkinson (2007:20–21).

"Fixation on Objectivity [Is Optional]"

> If the battle cannot be said to have been definitely won, there is no longer any doubt that the traditional view—with its fixation on objectivity—is now simply one point on a continuum and not the unique voice of reputable social research.
>
> —Angrosino (2005:734).

We would have said far more about the "fixation on objectivity" if this triangulation saga were a philosophical treatise about ethnographic fieldwork. As stated in the introduction to this chapter, we are among the growing chorus of scholars who critique post-positivistic claims about researcher objectivity. If this were a philosophical reflection, we would have also emphasized that due to the ad hoc nature of ethnographic research, a triangulated research design could have been an imposition on an otherwise dynamic and emergent process of data collection. But this is an account of an actual research project. Even more, it is the true story of a federally funded cross-national project that used multiple sites, methods, and researchers. Though we do not agree with the first quote above, as a result of our traditional methodological training and the requirements of a funded research project, we are more like recovering "objectivity-holics" than researchers cured of our fixation. Despite our wish to transcend the fixation on objectivity, we admit that the U.S.-Sweden team's research design had some definite post-positivistic, "objectivity-holic" tendencies; dominant pressures imposed by peer-review and funding requirements enable these tendencies.

Our view regarding objectivity leads to Lesson Number One. That is, Hammersley and Atkinson's conclusion in the second quote above is correct: Though the course of ethnographic research cannot be rigidly planned and objectively predetermined, *research design is crucial to ethnography*. And this is especially the case when researchers are conducting federally funded qualitative research. Our more philosophical reflection would have transcended the traditional fixation on objectivity without need for a caveat about "good re-flexive researchers." However, this reflection may have lacked viable proce-dures for fine tuning the triangulation strategies of a cross-national, multi-site, multi-method, multi-researcher project in a timely, productive, and relatively consistent manner.

Lesson Number Two is that an ethnographic research design that includes one-on-one interviews or focus group interviews implies that a researcher will not passively observe but will actively interact with respondents. *Rapport is im-portant to the interview process.* Rapport depends, in part, on how respondents view, read, or code/decode the researcher, and a researcher's identity is central to this process. From the etic perspective of the research design, rapport may be easy to ignore or inadvertently omit. But from the emic perspective, rapport—or the lack thereof—may thwart or facilitate the data collection process.

Lesson Number Three is that whether two researchers like Lunneblad and Dance appear different in regard to gender, ethnicity, and nationality or appear similar like Condoleezza Rice and Michelle Obama (our hypothetical researchers), *researcher identity is not a fixed attribute.* When using multiple researchers as a triangulation strategy, we must keep in mind that researcher identity is situational and emerges in the context of field-based interactions between researchers and respondents. Therefore, there is no way to predict ahead of time the exact notions, stereotypes, or opinions that respondents may hold about a researcher's identity. But it is safe to predict that respondents will have notions and opinions about researchers. Therefore, whether a research design involves one researcher or multiple researchers, there should be some degree of consideration for the likelihood that respondents will code/decode or read the researcher.

This brings us to Lesson Number Four. We have learned that researchers should make room in the research design for the likelihood that *respondents will hold notions about a researcher's identity.* However, researchers should do so without succumbing to essentialist views about nationality, ethnicity/race, gender, or other similar identities.

In looking more closely at the approaches to triangulation revealed in this chapter, there was often a difference between the etic/experience distant plans of the research design and the emic/experience near research activities in the field. From the start, the U.S.-Sweden team knew that the research design needed both directives and flexibility. However, the most flexible and open-ended aspect of the research design was the approach to theoretical triangu-lation. The team did not favor any particular theoretical perspective(s) in the initial research design but left room for theories or other notions to emerge. Likewise, the team did not need to ascribe any particular belief system to respondents as to how they would code/decode researchers' identities. But the team could have had a plan about what, if anything, could be done if respond-ents' views about the researchers became obstacles to building rapport.

This leads us to Lesson Number Five. As stated in the Scholarly Perspectives section, we used triangulation as an engine that drove our analyses. We have learned that in regard to the use of multiple researchers, *respondent's views about researchers could fuel or stall that engine*.

In conclusion, and in addition to the above lessons, what did a black American female and a white Swedish male learn about triangulation, racial/ethnic/national identity, and respondents' influence on researcher roles? Instead of borrowing and altering a strategy similar to that of economists and thereby fashioning the good reflexive researcher, we borrow and alter a poem and create a moral to this triangulation saga. We invite individual ethnographers—especially those who work in projects with multiple researchers and/or in cross-national as well as cross-cultural contexts—to seriously consider our social scientific appeal to serenity derived from Reinhold Niebuhr's famous "Prayer of Serenity": Grant me the social scientific grace to accept with serenity the aspects of the research process that I cannot triangulate, the foresight to triangulate the aspects that should be triangulated and the wisdom to distinguish the one from the other.

A research design can use multiple researchers as a means to enhance findings, and those researchers may or may not be identical in ethnicity/race, nationality, gender, class, and so on. Researchers do *not* enter the field in bodies that signify objectivity, translucence, or neutrality (Stanfield 1994; Troyna 1998, Twine & Warren 2000), no matter how hard they try or how reflexive they are, because respondents also—and rightfully—have a say in the matter.

NOTE

1. Sven Olof Joachim Palme, like Raoul Wallenberg and Dag Hammarskjöld, was a Swede of international acclaim. From 1969 to 1986, he was the leader of the Swedish Social Democratic Party and served as prime minister for 125 months. Palme was renowned for his outspoken criticism against the U.S. war in Viet Nam as well as apartheid in South Africa. In Sweden, he was viewed as a revolutionary reformist in dealing with social inequalities. This engendered deep support from leftist Swedes and hostility from more conservative Swedes. Palme was assassinated in 1986. Similar to the assassination of U.S. president John F. Kennedy, there are ongoing debates about who assassinated Palme.

REFERENCES

Adler, P., & Adler, P. (1994). Observational techniques. In N. K. Denzin & Y. S. Lincoln (Eds.), *Handbook of qualitative research* (pp. 377–392). Thousand Oaks, CA: Sage.

Angrosino, M. V. (2005). Recontextualizing observation: Ethnography, pedagogy, and the prospects for a progressive political agenda. In N. K. Denzin & Y. S. Lincoln

(Eds.), *Handbook of qualitative research* (3rd ed., pp. 729–745). Thousand Oaks, CA: Sage.

Atkinson, P., Coffey, A., Delamont, S., Lofland, J., & Lofland, L. (2001/2007). *Handbook of ethnography*. London: Sage.

Ball, S. J. (2006). *Education policy and social class: The selected works of Stephen J. Ball*. New York: Routledge.

Beach, D. (1995). *Making sense of the problems of change: An ethnographic study of a teacher education reform*. Gotenborg, Sweden: Acta Universitatis Gothoburgensis.

Beach, D. (1997). *Symbolic control and power relay: Learning in higher professional education*. Gotenborg, Sweden: Acta Universitatis Gothoburgensis.

Bryman, A. (2004). *Social research methods*. 2nd ed. Oxford: Oxford University Press.

Caughey, J. L. (2007). *Negotiating cultures and identities: Life history issues, methods, and readings*. Lincoln: University of Nebraska Press.

Cheek, J. (2005). The practice and politics of funded qualitative research. In N. K. Denzin & Y. S. Lincoln (Eds.), *Handbook of qualitative research* (3rd ed., pp. 387–409). Thousand Oaks, CA: Sage.

Collins, P. H. (2000). *Black feminist thought: Knowledge, consciousness, and the politics of empowerment*. Rev. 10th anniversary, 2nd ed. New York: Routledge.

Collins, P. H. (2003). Toward an Afrocentric feminist epistemology. In Y. S. Lincoln & N. K. Denzin (Eds.), *Turning points in qualitative research: Tying knots in a handkerchief* (pp. 47–72). Walnut Creek, CA: AltaMira.

Creswell, J. W. (2007). *Qualitative inquiry and research design: Choosing among five approaches*. Thousand Oaks, CA: Sage.

Denzin, N. K. (1978). *The research act: A theoretical introduction to sociological methods*. New York: McGraw-Hill.

Denzin, N. K. (1989). *The research act: A theoretical introduction to sociological methods*. 3rd ed. New Jersey: Prentice Hall.

Denzin, N. K., & Lincoln, Y. S. (2005). *Handbook of qualitative research*. 3rd ed. Thousand Oaks, CA: Sage.

Emerson, R. M. (2001). *Contemporary field relations: Perspectives and formulations*. 2nd ed. Prospect Heights, IL: Waveland Press.

Gold, R. L. (1958). Roles in sociological field observations. *Social Forces, 36*, 217–223.

Gold, R. L. (1997). The ethnographic method in sociology. *Qualitative Inquiry, 3*, 388–402.

Hammersley, M., & Atkinson, P. (2007). *Ethnography: Principles in practice*. 3rd ed. London: Routledge.

Keating, E. (2001/2007). The ethnography of communication. In P. Atkinson, A. Coffey, S. Delamont, J. Lofland, & L. Lofland (Eds.), *Handbook of ethnography* (pp. 285–301). London: Sage.

LeCompte, M. D., & Schensul, J. J. (1999). *Designing and conducting ethnographic research*. Walnut Creek, CA: AltaMira.

Lightfoot, S. L. (1985). *The good high school: Portraits of character and culture*. New York: Basic Books.

Lunneblad, J., Dance, L. J., & Alexandersson, M. (2009). Trapped in the culture of performativity: Teaching English and Swedish language learners in ethnic minority high schools. Manuscript being revised.

Peshkin, A. (1991). *The color of strangers, the color of friends: The play of ethnicity in school and community.* Chicago: University of Chicago Press.

Postman, N. (1996). *The end of education: Redefining the value of school.* New York: Vintage Books.

Stanfield, J. H., II. (1994). Ethnic modeling in qualitative research. In N. K. Denzin & Y. S. Lincoln (Eds.), *Handbook of qualitative research* (pp. 175–188). Thousand Oaks, CA: Sage.

Suárez-Orozco, C., Alexandersson, M., Dance, L. J., Lunneblad, J., & Martin, M. (2006). Promising schooling practices for children of immigrants. Research plan from Mohonk meeting in June 2006 (National Science Foundation, Children of Immigrants in School, PIRE: No. 0529921).

Suárez-Orozco, C., Martin, M., Alexandersson, M., Dance, L. J., & Lunneblad, J. (2009). Promising practices: Preparing the children of immigrants in New York and Sweden. Draft of final report, completed June 15, 2009 (National Science Foundation, Children of Immigrants in School, PIRE: No. 0529921).

Troyna, B. (1998). "The whites of my eyes, nose, ears...": A reflexive account of "whiteness" in race-related research. In P. Connolly & B. Troyna (Eds.), *Researching racism in education: Politics, theory, and practice* (pp. 95–108). Bristol, PA: Open University Press.

Twine, F. W., & Warren, J. W. (2000). *Racing research, researching race: Methodological dilemmas in critical race studies.* New York: New York University Press.

14 Weberian Ideal-Type Methodology in Comparative Historical Sociological Research: Identifying and Understanding African Slavery Legacy Societies

John H. Stanfield, II

Personal Background Statement

My interest in comparative historical sociological studies of race and ethnicity as an area of research in sore need of theory driven methodological studies stems from numerous sources worthy of mention. First, I was quite fortunate to have two undergraduate teachers at California State University Fresno (CSUF) in the social sciences who exposed me to both comparative race relations and to the history of sociological thought. The first was anthropologist Bill Beatty. By the time I landed in his minority relations class in the early 1970s, Beatty was the school's most distinguished social scientist. He was also the most difficult academically; S. J. Dackawich, my primary mentor and departmental chair, considered Beatty's class to be an informal litmus test to determine if a sociology major had what it took to make it to graduate school.

Even today, Beatty's pedagogy would be considered rare since he was a comparative sociologist and anthropologist of racial studies rather than someone fixated on the United States. The reason why his class was so incredibly difficult to get through (he only gave a handful of As per year, some Bs, the rest Cs and Ds) was not only due to his essay in contrast to multiple choice exams and extensive required reading but probably more important, he was so fascinating to listen to. There he was, with his bald head glistening with sweat and those sparkling eyes, dramatically telling his world-travel stories to us working-class youth who had barely been across the hallway to grab a gulp of water. Who could take notes?

It was in Bill Beatty's class we were required to read the recently published *Race and Racism: A Comparative Perspective* by a young sociologist named Pierre van den Berghe (1967). From that book, I learned about a country called South Africa, became aware that Brazil was not just the name of a nut, and became fascinated with comparative studies of racialization. Unfortunately, Northwestern, where I went to pursue doctoral studies in sociology, did not have a comparative race and racism emphasis but I kept my eye on the literature. For years after graduate school, I continued to read comparative race and racism literature and taught racial studies classes with a comparative perspective. This deep theoretical and historical interest regarding racial issues in other countries served me well later in life when I began to travel, live, and observe everyday multiracialization in countries such as Brazil, Germany, Great Britain, Jamaica, Sierra Leone, South Africa, and Thailand as well as ethnoregional patterns in the United States.

My long-time interest in the narrative contents of comparative racial studies would have remained convergent with where American sociologists interested in this field of research tend to remain if not for Dugan Weber. Robert "Dugan" Weber was the second undergraduate teacher who shaped my nearly four-decade interest in historical comparative sociological analyses in racial studies. He was an ex-Jesuit priest married to an ex-nun who taught the required classical theory course for sociology majors.

Dugan was a stunningly brilliant Marxist-oriented sociologist who did his dissertation under the great Warner Stark. He lost his job at CSUF a year or so after I had him as a teacher when he was forbidden to defend his dissertation since he had left the priesthood. Dugan Weber, like Bill Beatty, did not suffer fools lightly. His course was conducted like a graduate seminar in academic expectations. He had us reading authors in the sociology of knowledge who would not begin to become even marginally known in the United States until the 1980s and 1990s. We were required to read the then new book by Lewis Coser, *Masters of Sociological Thought*, which is still the seminal text in the history of sociological thought. Dugan's pedagogy of teaching epistemology, theory, method, and practical relevance is a model I use now when I teach classical or contemporary theory or logic of inequality, methods, or any other sociology-of-knowledge-related course.

I took to the sociology of knowledge like a fish to water, doing a seventy-page voluntary senior thesis under Dugan's supervision. It was a Shutzian phenomenological analysis of conflict dynamics in culturally pluralistic societies, which became the first paper I read at a professional sociology meeting in a regular session in my senior year. My sociology-of-knowledge interest has led me to the history, politics, and sponsoring of ideas in racial studies epistemologies, theories, and methods in sociology and other social sciences. This began with my 1977 dissertation "Race Rationalization as a Cohort Experience, 1928–1948." This is now called a postmodern critique of the sponsorship and institutional origins of black and white social scientists who helped shift the idea of the race paradigm from biological to environmental factors in preparation for the emergence of the idea of the racially integrated society. This social scientist effort would become a knowledge base for racial justice social movements and public policy-making in the1950s and 1960s.

Along the way, from my doctoral dissertation research onward, I became and remain interested in the politics behind the absence of theory in race relations sociology; the white privileging of who could define data, data collection, and data interpretation and the racial segregation of subdisciplines in sociology in terms of contents and career configurations. Although I was interested in comparative historical issues, my initial graduate studies and early postgraduate studies was on sociology-of-knowledge issues regarding racial matters in American sociology. Still, without traveling or living abroad, I maintained an interest in comparative racial and ethnic studies and incorporated cross-national studies in my teaching and some of my pre-1990s publications. As with American sociological studies of racial and ethnic issues, I was disturbed by the paucity of quality literature about epistemological, theoretical, and methodological issues in comparative historical sociological studies of race and still am.

Since the international impositions of the Park race-cycle model in the 1930s–1950s, American sociologists and foreign sociologists influenced by American ontologies have utilized American ideas to interpret racialization matters in other countries—including their own for non-American sociologists. A brief high point of comparative race studies flowed out of the pens of sociologists Michael Banton, Harry Hoetink, Leo Despres, Stanley Greenberg, Leo Kuper, David Lowenthal, Philip Mason, Michael Smith, and Pierre van den Berghe in the 1970s and early 1980s, and has yet to be matched. These writings stimulated debate among functionalists, pluralists, and Marxists but did little to advance sophisticated theorizing or methodological applications. This is largely because until very recently, comparative studies of race and ethnicity has been virtually segregated from the dominant comparative historical sociological literature.

Other than Immanuel Wallerstein, who began his career as an Africanist, the big names in comparative historical sociologists for the past forty years or so have tended to focus on state and society studies, with little or no interest in race, even when examining multiracial colonies and nation-states. It has not been uncommon for comparative historical sociologists who have paid attention to race to reduce it down to class or/and political ideological issues. Except for W. E. B. Du Bois, Orlando Patterson, and Immanuel Wallerstein, comparative historical sociologists have allowed historians to dominate the discourse about the comparative historical sociological study of African slavery.

I think there would be less rehashing of the same old stuff in comparative sociological studies of race if authors spent more time traveling and living in the societies they write about rather than depending on second-hand information packaged as "the literature." This is why I decided to write this chapter about a comparative historical sociological analysis of what I call the "African slavery legacy societies" (ASLS).

For the past twenty years, I have been a traveler and a resident of different multiracialized societies, especially Brazil and South Africa during the past ten years; I am turning now to India and Southeast Asia. The more time I spend in Brazil and South Africa and the more I learn about India in preparation of my visits there, the more I realize the danger in armchair theorizing. Much of what I have to say here can be taken as pages from my writing as an autoethnographer in a constant mood of comparing and contrasting what I have read, and what I see, feel, hear, and sense as I walk the streets of Jo'Burg, Cape Town, Bangkok, Rio, São Paulo, Salvador, London, Amsterdam, Salzburg, and one day I hope, St. Petersburg, Beijing, New Delhi, and Sydney.

Theory-Driven Weberian Ideal Typing

Pierre van den Berghe's *Race and Racism* (1967) was the first book-length comparative historical sociological study of multiracialized societies with a sophisticated theoretically driven methodology—the Weberian ideal type—published in the United States. No scholar since then has developed and used a theory-driven Weberian ideal-type approach as thought-provoking as van den Berghe's cross-national comparisons of social and cultural pluralism and patterns of dominance in multiracialized societies.

Weber's theory-driven comparative historical sociological methodology was designed and implemented to understand the characteristics of three major forms of societal domination legitimation: charismatic, traditional, and legal-rational (Roth 1978). Through exhaustive searches of historical literature, Weber identified numerous patterns of characteristics that he framed as "idealized attributes" of each form of societal domination. Weberian ideal typing was not meant to empirically test or predict listed attributes. Idealized attributes in the Weberian sense were meant solely to explore and identify concepts to generate understanding of a phenomenon.

Van den Berghe's use of the Weberian ideal-type reminds me of the need to develop a comparative historical sociological theory that attempts to reconceptualize multiracial societies that have deep African slavery legacies derived from European imperialism and nation-building efforts. The focal point in such ideal typing, slavery and its consequential long arm in the evolution of such societies, is the dependent variable. The basic research question is: What are the identifiable attributes of such sustained slave-based societies and how are similarities and differences in attributes explained through recovering different societal, historical, ecological, cultural, and racialized human development and identity? Such societies are sustained slave-based collectivities since, from a restorative justice perspective, they are composed of elites and masses who are in denial or are ignorant of the history of African slavery in their countries. Therefore, they see little or no reason for perpetrator-victim memory disclosures beyond academic studies and museum construction, no justification for perpetrator confession or apology or victim admission regarding contributing to their own enslavement, no reason to engage in mutual understanding (forgiveness) or reconciliation involving restoration of material, symbolic, and emotional human dignity (reparations). The notion that people can live in a society purged of its slavery past infecting the present and future is a non-issue to them as they have no understanding of the profound continued reach of slavery.

Thus, although African slavery legally ended generations ago in ASLS, the unrepentant if not indifferent attitudes of the majority of residents in these societies about the 400 years old dehumanizing system has resulted in African slavery as a horribly dehumanizing institution continues to have to an impact today. For example, some psychiatrists in the United States have connected the growing rate of suicide among Blacks as a continued impact of slavery on their mental health (Poussaint 2001). There is a critical need for analyses to be demographically expanded to more comprehensively explore how the continued impact of the massive African slavery past of the country profoundly influences societal as well as population specific trends. For instance, the tendency for slavery to be premised on masters as hyper violent prone patriarchal men and slaves as their grossly dehumanized property has had much understudied bearing on how women in ASLS, who have been historically treated like chattel and as sex objects and have been controlled through mental and physical abuse. In such societies, there has been a historical tendency to mistreat other populations that are stigmatized such as the poor, the mentally ill, and the disabled. And we should not forget the claims by some that the massive incarceration of black and brown males are a new form of slavery, what I would call the continuation of an ASLS.

The continuation of the United States as a non-repentant ASLS has recently been symbolized in the blatantly racist treatment of President Barack Obama. The magic of President Obama's ascent as the first noticeable African-descendant American to the U.S. presidency vaporized within eight months of his first year. Even though he did not come from an African American slavery background, his complexion and the social meanings attached to it were enough for his opponents to publicly racially stereotype him to the point of even disrespecting the very office of the U.S. president.

The treatment of President Obama represents perhaps the most deeply rooted idealized attribute of ASLS, namely, anti-black skin prejudice, which conjures up negative stereotypical images of the person as being a child, passive, irresponsible, untrustworthy, a crook, and immoral. The darker the skin color, the more the discrimination. This holds true in the United States and in South Africa. It has been empirically shown in both societies that the darker the skin, the more you are scorned by "your own" as well as by others in society (the long-ignored classic on the significance of skin color in African-descendant communities in the United States, which still holds true, is William Lloyd Warner and colleagues *Color and Human Nature* [1941]). This also is the case with other non-whites who are known to scorn their darkest children and to urge their kids to marry lighter.

Brazil is the same, but the racial paradise and racial fluidity mythologies cloud the fact that black-skinned people tend to get the brunt of prejudice there (Amado 1971; Butler 1998; Hanchard 1994; Marx 1998; Telles 2006). You can walk down the commercial district streets of every major city in Brazil, especially in the southeast and south, and rarely find a dark-skinned Brazilian working in a bank, restaurant, office, or elsewhere in the public sphere other than perhaps pushing a broom or a wheel chair. The extent to which you see dark-skinned Brazilians marrying white or brown people for that matter it is when the dark-skinned or brown-skinned person is wealthy. Inter-skin color let alone racial marriage and more casual inter-skin color and racial relationships which are public occur most amongst the poor and lower middle class at best in Brazil as it does in the United States and in South Africa. Indeed in Brazil as in the South Africa and the United States, it is not unheard of to hear stories of white- and brown-skinned Brazilians disowning family members who marry someone dark skinned.

In these three societies and in others with ASLS, different groups feel superior or inferior depending on their location on the skin color continuum with whiteness and blackness being on both polar extreme ends symbolizing white purity and black impurity which in different national cultural histories. In Brazil, the Portuguese were dominant; in South Africa, the English and Afrikaners were dominant; and in the United States, English. In each national context, over decades and centuries, white immigrants from eastern, northern, and southern Europe, would come to join the dominant "White" population with privileged social and cultural if not economic amenities which come with whiteness. On the other hand, first dark-skinned enslaved Africans and over time other African-descendant populations signified inferiority, laziness, and lack of worth and thus being completely devalued in cultural, social, and economic capital terms.

Pure white–impure black polar extremes as reflections of the African-descendant slavery past in ASLS indicates the need to search for ideal-type societal cases that are not ordinarily thought of when such societies are discussed. The search for such societies is possible through critically examining conventional, rare, and usually ignored primary and secondary historical sources and calling to question disciplinary canons about typified concepts and events.

I wish to demonstrate this through building the historical sociological case for calling India an ASLS, with widely ignored diasporic linkages to the United States as well as to the African continent, which has been much more frequently explored and documented. I will then introduce as food for thought the place of India in ideal-type schemata of ASLS that include South Africa, United States, and Brazil (Hamilton et al. 2001). This will demonstrate how methodology can be driven by a theory-building process that leads to developing a bullet-pointed narrative such as an ideal-type to understand a phenomenon. When African slavery legacy is placed in an ideal-type schemata, it can be used to generate comparative and contrasting understanding about the historical, cultural, and societal contexts that explain how attributes of African slavery that look the same across different societies have both similar and different manifestations embedded in national historical contexts.

My attempt to reconceptualize India as an ASLS will be grounded in the recently emerging Dalits (Untouchables) human rights literature in the social sciences, humanities, and literary studies, consultation with conventional, revisionist, and marginalized (if not ignored) secondary historical records. It will also involve questioning conventional concepts in American and other Western social sciences such as the geographical location of the invention and utilization of race. That is, contrary to popular belief, race is not just an invention in the West but also has historical origins in the East, with different twists such as the historical origins and rationalizations of caste systems (Kapoor 2004; Moon & Omvedt 2001; Prasad 2004; Rai 2003; Rajshekar & Kly 2009; Rao 2009).

INDIA AS AN AFRICAN DIASPORA COUNTRY WITH A SLAVERY LEGACY: MAKING THE CASE

Both Karl Marx (Marx & Avineri 1968) and Max Weber (Roth 1978) nineteenth-century European sociological thinkers agreed, but for different theoretical reasons, on a critical point. While both were change oriented about formations and transformations of social ranking hierarchies, they viewed India through static lenses. They could not see or understand how India could produce what they considered to be the essential material conditions for industrial capitalism. In Marx's view, India lacked the vital bourgeoisie class because of a seemly perpetual caste system. In Weber's view, the Hindu-derived caste rules of purity and pollution made it possible for people to work together but without the mobility flexibility essential for modern industrial capitalism to emerge and flourish as in Western Europe and America.

From the standpoint of the historical sociology of knowledge, the static view of caste-based India in European and American sociological thought stems for the most part from the views of Marx and Weber. And it continued to prevail through the twentieth century and into the present one. This static view has both persisted and changed as Western social scientists have tried to apply the concept of caste outside of India or have attempted to offer further clarification of what caste is within the context of the Indian subcontinent.

Perhaps the most important illustration of the attempt to extend the concept of caste outside of India is the controversy involving inter–world war anthropologists Allison Davis and colleagues (1941/2009) and Lloyd Warner and social psychologist John Dollard (1937/2006). These scholars claimed the concept of caste could be applied in southern community race relations experiences to interpret the structured relations between European Americans and African Americans. Gunnar Myrdal, in his seminal *American Dilemma* (1944), like many other progressive critics of white-black relations, applied the term "caste," with little understanding of what Indian caste is, let alone ever visiting the subcontinent.

Their most vocal opponents were members of the Chicago School, such as E. Franklin Frazier, St. Clair Drake, and Horace Cayton (Chicago trained Charles S. Johnson on the other hand supported the caste school argument). These sociologists and anthropologists denied the relevance of caste in interpreting European American/African American relations. Among other things, they pointed out that although limited because of Jim Crow restrictions, African Americans were not totally confined to their low dehumanizing status groupings by birth. This could be observed in the parallel though rare integrated upward mobility of African Americans, some even moving into high-status positions. The most comprehensive critic of the American caste school was Oliver C. Cox. In his masterful *Caste, Class, and Race*, published in 1948, Cox claimed that the Indian caste system was a system of lower caste compliant inequality, whereas racial inequality in America was rooted in brutal exploitation, again, allowing for some degree of class mobility.

The social science study that has mostly influenced debates about the sociological and anthropological nature of Indian caste and caste in other societies for over four decades is French sociologist and anthropologist Louis Dumont's *Homo Hierarchicus: The Caste System and Its Implications* (1970). Like Cox, Dumont argued that caste was a hierarchy and thus structured inter-corporate group relationships, rather than a reified socially constructed category. The Indian caste system, with the priestly Brahmins on top was, in Dumont's perspective, a consistent value system rooted in ritualized notions of purity and pollution embedded in routine notions of physical contact, food, occupations, marriage traditions, and taboos. Indeed, Dumont's major criticism of the American caste school and of Cox and Myrdal, which is similar to C. Van Woodward's *The Strange Career of Jim Crow* (1966) and Arthur Raper's *Preface to Peasantry* (1936), is that European American racial prejudice against African Americans is not a consistent value system that occurs everywhere in America. There are, in Dumont's perspective, regional, and local leaks in the Jim Crow system: So, just because someone is socially defined as being white or black does not mean they are destined to experience the objectified expectations of Jim Crow roles, norms, and values.

To expand a bit on Robert K. Merton's 1948 seminal article, "Discrimination and the American Creed," in racially based societies like Brazil, Great Britain, South Africa, and the United States, there are times, places, and circumstances in which some members of dominant populations may discriminate very little or not at all because of intercultural experiences they are exposed to in their daily lives. Likewise, oppressed racialized people can be routinely empowered in their intercultural life experiences rather than living as victims of their dehumanization. In this rather Mertonian perspective, unlike the inequality structuring that occurs in Brazil, South Africa, and in the United States, the Indian caste system is a much more rigidly permanent way in which people behave toward each other in unequal birth placement ways though the culture of those involved may differ due to being Muslim rather than Hindu or being urban dwellers rather than village dwellers or living in one of the far less caste based southern regions or in one of the more caste based Northeast regions of the country.

As Ramachandra Guha describes in *India after Gandhi* (2007), most Americans know little about India beyond the overly simplistic stereotypes of curry, incense, and mystical Eastern philosophies. The correct metaphors we should use to describe India is that of Africa or Europe, continents housing a complex mosaic of countries rather than a singular country as stereotypically imagined in many Western minds. Indeed, when the British granted India its independence in 1947, along with giving the Muslims what they wanted through the partitioning that created Pakistan, some 500 independent fiefdoms needed to be negotiated with by the new Indian national government to join the nation-state. These fiefdoms, vast and small, have contributed to the establishment of India into a highly pluralistic nation-state, the world's most populous democracy with strong socialist leanings, making India the most powerful nonaligned nation in the world.

The Indian caste system, which is stereotypically based on the four-tier Varna caste system, is actually much more complicated than that, with hundreds of local, regional, and provincial variations within and across castes. This includes even the Untouchables, now called the Dalit in political human rights terminology, who are dehumanized in hundreds of the lowest castes. As they have for centuries, Dalits are still experiencing dehumanizing conditions and are victims of upper-caste random and massive violence described in the 1990s by a human rights activist (Rashidi 1998):

The existence of Untouchability has been justified within the context of Hindu religious thought as the ultimate and logical extensions of Karma and rebirth. Hindus believe that persons are born Untouchables because of the accumulation of sins in previous lives. Hindu texts describe these people as foul and loathsome, and any physical contact with them was regarded as polluting.

Untouchables were usually forced to live in pitiful little settlements on the outskirts of Hindu communities. During certain periods in Indian history Untouchables were only allowed to enter the adjoining Hindu communities at night. Indeed, the Untouchables' very shadows were considered polluting, and they were required to beat drums and make loud noises to announce their approach. Untouchables had to attach brooms to their backs to erase any evidence of their presence. Cups were tied around their necks to capture any spittle that might escape their lips and contaminate roads and streets. Their meals were taken from broken dishes. Their clothing was taken from corpses. They were forbidden to learn, to read and write, and were prohibited from listening to any of the traditional Hindu texts. Untouchables were denied access to public wells. They could not use ornaments and were not allowed to enter Hindu temples. The primary work of Untouchables included scavenging and street sweeping, emptying toilets, the public execution of criminals, the disposal of dead animals and human corpses, and the clean-up of cremation grounds. The daily life of the Untouchable was filled with degradation, deprivation and humiliation.

The basis status of India's Untouchables has changed little since ancient times, and it has recently been observed that "Caste Hindus do not allow Untouchables to wear shoes, ride bicycles, use umbrellas or hold their heads up while walking in the street." Untouchables in urban India are crowded together in squalid slums, while in rural India, where the vast majority of Untouchables live, they are exploited as landless agricultural laborers and ruled by terror and intimidation. As evidence of this, several cases from 1991 can be cited: On June 23, 1991 fourteen Untouchables were slaughtered in the eastern state of Bihar. On August 10, 1991 six Untouchables were shot to death in the northern state of Uttar Pradesh. On August 16, 1991, an Untouchable woman was stripped in public and savagely beaten in the southern state of Andhra Pradesh. On September 6, 1991, in the western state of Maharashtra, an Untouchable policeman was killed for entering a Hindu temple. Official Indian figures on violent crimes by caste Hindus against Untouchables have averaged more than 10,000 cases per year, with the figures continuing to rise. The Indian government listed 14,269 cases of atrocities by caste Hindus against Untouchables in 1989 alone. However, Indian human rights workers report that a large number of atrocities against Untouchables, including beatings, gang-rapes, arson and murders, are never recorded. Even when charges are formally filed, justice for Untouchables is rarely dispensed. (Rashidi 1998:n.p.)

Such is the persistent, centuries-old tragic daily life of millions of Dalits each day, even though the Indian Constitution is one of the most sophisticated in the world regarding human rights guarantees and protections for all citizens. Dalits, their name meaning "downtrodden or broken down," but used with pride as a self-chosen name that reflects no idea of pollution and can include all who identify themselves as oppressed by the caste system (Moon & Omvedt 2001:xi), were called before the emergence of their political awareness in the 1970s, Untouchables, the depressed classes, and the scheduled classes. In previous centuries, there were efforts in some fiefdoms to do away with or at least reform Untouchable castes.

In the twentieth century, these Dalit human rights efforts picked up significant speed with the emergence of Dr. Bhimrao Ramji Ambedkar (1891–1956). Ambedkar was an extraordinary man of Untouchable caste background with degrees from distinguished American and British universities, who became from the 1920s to the 1950s, the foremost champion of Untouchable human rights and a chief rival of Gandhi. Some have claimed that Dr. Ambedkar's political awakening as a Dalit came when he spent from 1913 to 1916 at Columbia University, when the Harlem Renaissance and other black pride movements began to stir in New York City. That may have been true or he might have become aware in other ways of the grotesque Jim Crow dehumanization African Americans were experiencing (e.g., blatant discrimination, segregation by law, and lynching), since, while making his case for Untouchable rights while in the United States and after he returned to India in the early 1920s after spending time attending the London School of Economics, he at times equated the unjust treatment of Untouchables to African Americans during the Jim Crow era. S. D. Kapoor (2004:15–16) observes in his book, *Dalits and African Americans: A Study in Comparison*: "He made a comparison between the attitude of the Brahmins towards the (Dalits) Pariah and the attitude of the Klansmen toward the Negroes and found the latter more unjustifiable and crueler." Ambedkar wrote: "What are the caste cruelties of India put by the side of what the white man has done to non-white people." On this Ambedkar comments that the atrocities practiced by the Hindu on the Untouchables were no less than those practiced by the Americans on the Negroes. "If those atrocities are not as well known to the world as are those practiced upon the Negro, it is not because they do not exist. They are not known because there is no Hindu who will not do his best to conceal truth in order to hide his shame" (Kapoor 2004:15–16).

Ambedkar, who in the 1920s established an organization advocating for the human rights of Dalits similar to the NAACP in the United States and who established a pro-Dalits publication similar to the NAACP's *Crisis* is not as culturally palatable in the United States as Gandhi, so we do not read about him in American schoolbooks as much as we do about Gandhi. Ambedkar did not have the same inspirational ties to the civil rights movement in this country as Gandhi had with Howard Thurman and his Morehouse younger brother Martin Luther King, Jr. Gandhi was very much of a conformist reformer because, although he was against Untouchables being mistreated within the caste system, he was not an anti-caste system advocate. For those knowledgeable about southern civil rights movement history: Gandhi was very much a Will Alexander–type conformist reformer. Alexander, a Vanderbilt-educated minister and public sociologist, helped organize and lead the Atlanta-based Commission on Interracial Cooperation from 1919 to 1944 to fight for better accommodations for Blacks but was not an anti-segregation advocate from the separate but equal legal standpoint of his Jim Crow time. Ambedkar was an advocate for abolishing the caste system and for untouchable political and legal justice, even to the point of urging legislation for Untouchables to hold their own elections under British rule to make sure they received representation from within their own communities, which is very much of a political view falling outside the American paradigm of racialized politics then and now except perhaps in the most radical and therefore ignored wings of African American political activists and civil rights movement leaders.

With the clamor for Indian independence growing louder after World War II, Ambedkar had become so effective as a human rights activist for Untouchables that he was invited to become the first minister of law in the Nehru cabinet, with the primary responsibility to write the Indian Constitution. It was in that role, as architect of the constitutional framework of the new nation of India, that he wrote a national constitution that guaranteed legal rights for Untouchables as well as for all Indian citizens. Ambedkar's inspirational leadership as an Untouchable who ascended to the highest heights of his newly founded nation and assisted in shaping its modern state had a profound trickle-down impact, as seen in the emergence of the Dalit human rights movement in the 1970.

The political and legal branches of the post-1960s Dalit human rights movement are led by those who keep pressure on the national government to enact and reinforce Dalit human rights in all key sectors of the country such as affirmative action in education, the first such efforts in the world. The education and cultural branches are very much involved in developing higher education programs and projects such as advocating for the Ambedkar Distinguished Chair in social justice programs in Indian universities, which highlight Dalit histories, cultures, and justice movements. Gail Omveldt, an Indian American who emigrated to India after finishing her doctorate at UC-Berkeley in the late 1970s, has become one of the most foremost, and still rare, sociologists on Dalit concerns and translator of Dalit autobiographies. Recently, she was appointed to the Ambedkar Chair for Social Justice at Indiri Gandhi University in New Delhi.

During the past few years, there has been some debate about the pluses and minuses of developing Dalit Studies programs in universities, similar to the early black Studies debates in American universities and colleges in the 1960s and 1970s. In the 1980s, a Dalit theology movement emerged, greatly influenced by the African American liberation theology movement. This movement has been buttressed by the fact that 70% of Christians in India are Dalits, as some branches of Christianity, such as the Lutheran Church, allowed Dalits to escape from the caste system by converting to Christianity.

As has been the case for oppressed people around the world, especially those with some degree of African background, African Americans in the Dalit cultural movement are viewed as role models. In 1997, the Indian Institute for Advanced Study sponsored the first-ever comparative literature conference. It showcased the efforts of Dalit and Dalit-interested Indian scholars to compare and contrast Dalit novel, short stories, and poem themes with those of African American writers, themes such as Du Boisian notions of the veil and double consciousness and concepts about freedom, bondage, and identity drawn from the novels of James Baldwin, Ralph Ellison, and Toni Morrison.

On the social science end, there have yet to be many comparisons drawn between Dalit communities, such as urban slum or middle-class life. There is rich territory here to explore, as seen in the comparative content of the few urban-dwelling Dalit autobiographies translated into English such as Vasant Moon's (2001) *Growing up Untouchable* with African American or Afro-Brazilian or black or colored South African writers describing what it was like growing up in their poor urban neighborhoods, exemplified in historical comparative novel literature such as Peter Abrams's (1989) *Mine Boy* in South Africa, Jorge Amado (1971), *Tent of Miracles* in Brazil, and Richard Wright's (1944) *Black Boy* in the United States. Sociological observations made by Ambedkar in his collected writings and other Dalit activists about what happens when Dalits become well-assimilated middle-class people could be compared to observations of African-descendant middle-class critics such as W. E. B. Du Bois, Franz Fanon, E. Franklin Frazier (1957), and Carter G. Woodson about upwardly mobile African American and African diasporic people who forsake or evade their racialized group identity by ignoring or avoiding all things stereotypical black or by passing into another ethnic group.

What remains an interesting question in the emerging Dalit human rights movements is the degree to which India is a deeply African diasporic nation and what this means in historical, sociological, and anthropological terms. In what ways have the African presence in India become part and parcel to the building and sustaining of castes? Some of the more radical branches of the Dalit human rights movement such as V. T. Rajshekar, publisher of the American Afro-centric-influenced *Dalit Voice* newspaper, and authors such as Runoko Rashidi, author of "The African Presence in India: A Photo Essay" (1998) claim that the majority of the Dalit people are of African descent. They illustrate this claim with evidence of ancient African settlements in India as well as such black race consciousness movements such as the development of the Dalit Panthers in Mumbai (Bombay) modeled after the Black Panthers in the United States. But, to date, the mainstream Dalit movement has rejected this argument, preferring to view African Americans as role models rather than as being connected through ancestry.

Nevertheless, mostly outside the Dalit movement, more in the global Afro-centric community, a small number of scholars have begun to reconstruct the European- and African-derived slave trade eastward from the east coast of Africa to various points in Asia, including India, as well as to documents ancient African settlements. This focus in the global history of African slavery in India and other areas of Asia is symbolized in a map in the Afro-Brazilian Museum in Salvador, Brazil. The map, which geographically lays out the pre-twentieth-century global African slave trade with the expected arrow lines exiting the west coast of Africa and landing in the southern states, the Caribbean, and northeastern Brazil geographical regions, has a peculiar arrow leaving somewhere on the east coast of Africa and stopping in the middle of the Indian Ocean.

Though there is a growing number of narrative descriptions of such African-derived experiences in Indian Ocean islands and on the subcontinent, we do not have the sophisticated historical sociological reconstruction scholarship documenting the social and cultural consequences of, for example, the structuring of the blending of Africans into Indian indigenous populations. We have narrative-based suggestions, but no data about the centuries-old caste-making processes of invading Aryans from the north who imposed their prejudicial coding with regional correlations and caste correlations according to skin color.

As a side bar, the long neglect of Africans in Asia, especially in India up until fairly recently in global historical and social scientific accounts, including in African and African Diaspora Studies, becomes quite intriguing when we consider the views of Paul Robeson written in the 1930s. Robeson, an astute anthropologist as well as athlete, actor, and political activist, contended that rather than looking to the West for inspiration, African-descendant people may have much more in common culturally with Asia, so perhaps they should look eastward. Du Bois certainly thought so. In an article on the radicialization of Du Bois (Stanfield 2010), I discuss how much Du Bois, like other pre-World War II African and African American public intellectuals—enamored with Japan, the most powerful non-white country prior to World War II, and with Indian activists such as Gandhi—were more profoundly influenced by Asian leaders and their movements than what has been written about them thus far.

There is also little research about what I call the looping back of enslaved mixed Africans/Indians, Indians, or other Asians who were sent on slave ships going east to west and landed in slave-holding cities such as Cape Town and then continued on ships up the African West coast and then across the Atlantic—let alone free Indians and African Indian people who did the same. If we look hard enough, we just might find in the surviving records of slave traders who used both South African and West African slave shipping connections that there were such African Asian and Asian slaves in the mix of those who were sold in bondage in various points of the Western hemisphere.

This idea occurred to me when a friend of mine in Cape Town took me on a tour of a museum he is designing to remind Cape Townians of their slave history past that has been so deeply buried and thus forgotten about. On a map visualizing the eastward slave trading of Europeans, he pointed to arrows that began on the eastern and southern coasts of Africa, heading to India and then back again. I began to wonder if the ships with their dehumanized human cargo just continued on around the southern bend of the continent up the west coast, and he agreed. Then he pointed out the importance of South Africa to the Confederacy during the American Civil War, which had actually sent a war ship to Cape Town. A piece of comparative sociological history could look at the relationship between slave traders and owners in the United States with those in the Western Cape region where Cape Town lies. This suggested historical reconstruction work is very much of an extension of the long-forgotten circuit Gerald Horne has reconstructed between Brazilian and American slave traders and plantation slave owners.

Another form of this looping back is the needed study of emigration records of Indians to the United States in the eighteenth and nineteenth centuries and in the earliest twentieth century decades who went on to contribute to African American and other ethnic communities. After all, about two years ago, the African Methodist Episcopal Church, one of the most distinguished African American denominations, fondly called the AMEs, sent a delegation to India to fulfill the vision of a church connection with India set forth by

> William Paul Quinn (1788–1873) who was the fourth bishop of the African Methodist Episcopal Church. Quinn was born in Calcutta, India. He was at the organization of the AME Church in 1816, ordained a deacon in 1818, and an elder in 1838. The General Conference of the church elected him a bishop on May 19, 1844. He became the Senior Bishop of the church in May 1849 and served until his death in Richmond, Indiana, United States. (Quinn [n.d.])

IDEAL TYPING INDIA WITH BRAZIL, SOUTH AFRICA, AND UNITED STATES AS AFRICAN SLAVERY LEGACY SOCIETIES

Let's get back to Dalit issues in relation to India as an African Diaspora society with an African slavery legacy.

First, it is usually controversial to claim that other parts of the world besides the United States and other Western societies and regions have forms of race, racialism, and racism (racialization). We are comfortable as historians and as sociologists of knowledge involved in the history of race studies restricting racialization as a form of dehumanization to the West rather than looking eastward and to other non-Western global places. Prominent Duke University sociologist Edgar Thompson embraced a more universal understanding of the race-making processes of Japanese plantation owners in Taiwan many years ago. His view was that dehumanization based on race occurred in many places in the world, long before major Western intrusions, but in different ways that may dramatically vary from what goes on in the West. We have yet to come to terms with that as we venture outside the gates of the West.

Second, although there is disagreement with evidence that Dalit status in India has nothing to do with being of at least partial African ancestry somewhere in their family and community historiesy, there is still acknowledgment that untouchable status, no matter what the Indian Constitution says and the piles of laws passed, is an intensely dehumanizing experience for millions of Indian citizens so marked through horribly dehumanizing hereditary traditions. The gap between the constitution and actual practices is largely ignored in Indian universities. Most of the Dalit Studies knowledge is produced by Indians and non-Indians outside India or if inside the country, outside the academy through NGOs and independent efforts. This is similar to the marginalized if not ignored scholarship of W. E. B. Du Bois and Carter G. Woodson and others during the Jim Crow era unable to gain appointments in prominent white universities and who were confined to becoming marginally and temporally employed in historically black universities and colleges and established their own knowledge-producing associations hidden from the mainstream of historically white universities. It is also similar to studies about South Africa during apartheid and before: The vast majority of the critical historical and social science studies of the country was produced by South African and non-South African scholars and commentators outside South Africa.

Third, and most important for this chapter, there is the issue of the impact of the demographic history of Africanization of subcontinent local areas and regions, when we consider as Ambedkar did, the Dalit caste as a form of slavery enforced with the brutal force of violence, which he equated with the Ku Klux Klan. In this regard, if we consider India as a deeply African slave-based society rooted in the Untouchables, how does it compare and contrast with other nation-state-building efforts centered on significantly large African-descendant populations with a significant slavery past that has endured until today, such as Brazil, South Africa, and the United States?

Using a Weberian ideal schemata, is it feasible to contend for the sake of further empirical research that all four nations are largely what can be called, in restorative justice terms, unrepentant slave societies with profound societal and population specific implications along a continuum of transformation or lack thereof—with India at one end and South Africa on the other and the United States much closer to the South African end and Brazil much closer to the India end? When we go through the historical records of each country—biographies, demographic and geographical data, secondary histories, fictional accounts, and social science studies, it is more than apparent that each country has the following attributes that enable them to be typed as ASLS, with the described differences along an ideal-type continuum:

1. engagement in African slave trading between 1600s and 1900s, creating and transforming slave-exploiting institutions and communities;

2. white purity–black impurity polarities, with vast intricate and paradoxical complexion;

3. incorporation of anti-black racialization into religious belief systems and into routinized public and private cultures and in multigenerational everyday life experiences and decision-making about mate selection, faith community participation, employment and promotion, educational access, and political authority; the ritualization of segregation and dominance and subordination in daily life, customs, values, and traditions;

4. organized white violence movements and institutions and individualized white violence, with no legal repercussions, to keep racialized people under control and for economic and political exploitation (in Brazil, military and civilian police, rural organized crime and vigilante groups, and white individuals with no legal repercussions; Brahmin individuals and organized groups and law enforcement agencies in India, apartheid government and Afrikaner brotherhood societies and white individuals with no legal repercussions in South Africa and Ku Klux Klan and other white supremacy groups and individuals with no legal repercussions; historical local, state, and federal law enforcement agencies in the United States);

5. hyper-patriarchy derived from autocratic slave owner resulting in overflows to other forms of paternalistic and violent forms of control such as sexism and cultural normalization of male violence against female such as rape and domestic violence and other treatments of women as noncitizens and as commodities and objects—as slaves;

6. African-descendant liberation struggles and national state actions to extend democracy to African-descendant people and to Untouchables; abolition movements (abolishment of slavery in Brazil, South Africa, and United States; abolishment of Untouchable caste in India); revolts (African slave revolts in Brazil, South Africa, and United States); riots (slave and Untouchable); civil rights movements, black power movements (in Brazil, India, and South Africa modeled after American civil rights and black power movements); voting suffrage movements (ex-slaves and Untouchables); state sanctioned actions—rewriting constitutions, constitutional amendments, affirmative action; and

7. during times of formalized anti-black prejudice and segregation, critical scholarship on ASLS tends to be produced by scholars and commentaries within such societies in marginal and in excluded roles and institutions or by scholars and commentaries in other countries who may be in highly visible academic and nonacademic organizations.

This contention is in keeping with the post-1990s comparative sociological historical literature on Brazil, South Africa, and United States (see, e.g., Butler 1998; Hamilton et al. 2001; Hanchard 1994; Marx 1998; Telles 2006), with the addition of India. Other sources, including fiction, that offer national focus on issues of racialization in ASLS can be utilized to construct cross-national comparisons.

The problem, of course, is locating reliable and valid historical sources for constructing ideal-type schemata. In a controversial area such as the study of ASLS and the more general study of racialization, researchers must use historical documents extraordinarily carefully while at the same time being flexible about the kinds of sources they choose to use since standard sources may not exist may be steeped in cultural biases. Further, information may be found in sources that are not considered appropriate by mainstream perspectives but actually are quite adequate knowledge acquisition sources. For instance, fictional accounts and the arts such as novels, plays, poems, songs, oral tradition stories, paintings, and sculpture may be just as valuable as reliable and adequate data for a sociologist as a primary or secondary historical document such as a letter or a statistically or ethnographically grounded study.

There is also the need to learn how to distinguish between a document that is poorly written and documented from one that may be negatively criticized because it calls into question canonical perspectives crafted and institutionalized by representatives of dominant groups, including those who come from oppressed backgrounds but who identify with the status quo. This is especially a problem when those on top of a society feel threatened by the attempts of the oppressed to find their voices and do all they can to pick apart their attempts to challenge standing paradigms.

Ideal-type schemata are meant to promote cross-comparative understanding rather than be empirical tests. This makes ideal-type methodology a powerful way to map out the contours and bullet-pointed contents for deeper attempts to understand a phenomenon across societies or to compare and contrast different kinds of societies within a particular kind of society such as ASLS or to present a strategy for future empirical study. In either respect, this means that when used properly, theory-driven ideal types grounded in idealized attributes drawn from extensive literature reviews can be creative ways to understand very complex societal issues in very coherent ways.

REFERENCES

Abrams, P. (1989). *Mine boy.* Portsmouth, NH: Heinemann.

Amado, J. (1971). *Tent of miracles.* New York: Knopf.

Butler, K. (1998). *Freedoms given, freedoms won.* Piscataway, NJ: Rutgers University Press.

Cox, O. C. (1948). *Caste, class, and race:* A *study in social dynamics.* New York: Monthly Review Press.

Davis, A., Gardner, B., Gardner, M., & Wallach, J. (1941/2009). *Deep South: A social anthropological study of caste and class.* Southern Classics Series. Columbia: University of South Carolina Press.

Dollard, J. (1937/2006). Caste and class in a southern town. ACLS History E-Book Project.

Dumont, L. (1970). *Homo Hierarchicus the caste system and its implications, including caste, racism and "stratification": Reflections of a social anthropologist.* Chicago: University of Chicago Press.

Frazier, E. F. (1957). *Black bourgeoisie* (translation of *Bourgeoisie noire*). Glencoe, IL: The Free Press.

Guha, R. (2007). *India after Gandhi.* New York: Ecco.

Hamilton, C. V., Huntley, L., Alexander, N., & Guimaraes, A. S. A. (Eds.). (2001). *Beyond racism: Race and inequality in Brazil, South Africa, and the United States.* Boulder, CO: Lynne Rienner.

Hanchard, M. (1994). *Orpheus and power: Afro-Brazilian social movements in Rio de Janeiro and Sao Paulo, 1945–1988.* Princteon, NJ: Princeton University Press.

Kapoor, S. D. (2004). *Dalits and African Americans.* Satyawati Nagar, Delhi: Kalpaz.

Marx, A. (1998). *Making race and nation.* Cambridge, MA: Cambridge University Press.

Marx, K., & Avineri, S. M. (1968). *Karl Marx on colonialism and modernization.* New York: Doubleday.

Merton, R. (1948). Discrimination and the American creed. In R. M. MacIver (Ed.), *Discrimination and national welfare* (pp. 99–126). New York: Harper & Brothers.

Moon and Omvedt (2001). *Growing up Untouchable in India.* G. Omvedt, Trans. New Delhi: Vistaar Publications.

Myrdal, G. (1944). *An American dilemma: The Negro problem and modern democracy.* New York: Harper Brothers.

Poussaint, A. F. (2001). *Lay my burden down: Suicide and the mental health crisis among African-Americans.* Boston: Beacon Press.

Prasad, C. B. (2004). *Dalit diary, 1999–2003: Reflections on apartheid in India.* Chennai, India: Navayana.

Quinn, W. P. (n.d.). Wikipedia. http://en.wikipedia.org/wiki/William_Paul_Quinn (accessed March 24, 2011).

Rai, L. L. (2003). *Unhappy India.* New Delhi: Low Price Publications.

Rajshekar, V. T., & Kly, Y. N. (2009). *Dalit: The black Untouchables of India.* Atlanta: Clarity Press, Inc.

Rao, A. (2009). *The caste question: Dalits and the politics of modern India*. Berkeley: University of California Press.

Raper, A. (1936). *Preface to peasantry*. Chapel Hill: University of North Carolina Press.

Rashidi, R. (1998). The African presence in India: A photo essay. The Global African Community Lecture Notes. http://www.cwo.com/~lucumi/india.html (accessed March 24, 2011).

Roth, G. (1978). *Economy and society*. Berkeley: University of California Press.

Stanfield, J. H., II. (2010). W. E. B. Du Bois on citizenship. *Journal of Classical Sociology, 10*, 171–188.

Telles, E. (2006). *Race in another America: The significance of skin color in Brazil*. Piscataway, NJ: Princeton University Press.

van den Berghe, P. (1967). *Race and racism: A comparative perspective*. New York: John Wiley & Sons.

Warner, W. L., Junker, B. H., & Adams, W. A. (1941). *Color and human nature*. Westport, CT: Greenwood Publishing Group.

Woodward, C. V. (1966). *The strange career of Jim Crow*. New York: Oxford University Press.

Wright, R. (1944). *Black boy*. New York: Perennial Classics.

ABOUT THE AUTHORS

Eduardo Bonilla-Silva is professor of sociology at Duke University. He has published numerous articles and five books, including *White Supremacy and Racism in the Post-Civil Rights Era* (co-winner of the 2002 Oliver Cox Award by the American Sociological Association), *Racism Without Racists: Color-Blind Racism and the Persistence of Racial Inequality in the United States, White Out: The Continuing Significance of Racism* (with Ashley Doane), *White Logic, White Methods: Racism and Social Science* (co-winner of the 2009 Oliver Cox Award), and *State of White Supremacy: Racism, Governance, and the United States* (with MoonKie Jung and Joao H. Costa Vargas).

Dawn B. Brotherton is a training specialist, leadership coach, and mentor. She teaches in the School of Business and Leadership for Nyack College's Washington, DC. campus. Her doctoral dissertation on race in an evangelical parachurch organization was completed at the Fielding Graduate University School of Human and Organizational Development (Santa Barbara, California) in 2010.

L. Janelle Dance is an associate professor of sociology and ethnic studies at the University of Nebraska, Lincoln. **Johannes Lunneblad** is a lecturer and researcher in the Department of Education, Communication, and Learning at the University of Gothenburg in Sweden. As fellows and co-researchers on the U.S.-Swedish Team of the Children of Immigrants in Schools six nations' study (NSF, PIRE, No. 0529921), Lunneblad and Dance have coauthored several scholarly works. Among other interests, they both study how social differences (e.g., class, nationality, ethnicity) affect school success and how researcher-respondent interactions impact the data collection process.

Mary Jo Deegan is professor of sociology, University of Nebraska, Lincoln. A specialist in feminism, race, social theory, disability, and the history of sociology, she has authored or edited twenty books and numerous articles on these topics. She was accorded the Distinguished Scholarly Career Award by the History of Sociology section of the American Sociological Association, among her other honors.

Elizabeth Hordge-Freeman is a doctoral candidate in the Department of Sociology at Duke University. Her dissertation, "Battling the Enemy Within: Racial Socialization in Brazilian Families," explores the practices and ideologies associated with racial socialization. She is also a coauthor on a recent article in the *Journal of Marriage and Family* that addresses colorism in U.S. families.

Sarah Mayorga is a doctoral candidate in the Sociology Department at Duke University. Her dissertation research focuses on multi-group segregation in Durham, North Carolina. She is specifically interested in the effects of Latina/ Latino migration on neighborhoods in this historically black and white city.

Eileen O'Brien is an associate professor of sociology at Saint Leo University, Virginia campus. She is the author of *Whites Confront Racism: Antiracists and Their Paths to Action* and, with Joe Feagin, *White Men on Race*. She is the coeditor, with Joseph Healey, of *Race, Ethnicity, and Gender: Selected Readings*.

Abigail A. Sewell graduated summa cum laude from the University of Florida, Gainesville, and is a doctoral candidate in the Department of Sociology at Indiana University. Her areas of interest include medical sociology, social psychology, race/ethnicity, and quantitative research methods. Her primary research question concerns the ways in which race and ethnicity function as structural sources of cultural attitudes, social change, and health disparities. She is a Ford Foundation Predoctoral Fellow, a National Science Foundation Graduate Research Fellow, and a Ronald E. McNair Graduate Fellow.

Stephen Small, associate professor of African American Studies, University of California, Berkeley. His research concentrates on analyzing links between historical structures and contemporary manifestations of racial formations and racialized relations.

John H. Stanfield, II is professor of African American and African Diaspora Studies, Philanthropic Studies, Sociology, and director of The Research Program on Transcultural and Intercultural Philanthropic Studies, Indiana University, Bloomington; a member of the Consulting Faculty on Advanced Studies, Fielding Graduate University School of Human and Organization Development; and 2007–08 Distinguished Fulbright Chair, Catholic University– Rio de Janeiro. He has taught at Yale University, the College of William and Mary, the University of California, Davis, and Morehouse College, among others. Recent publications include: *Historical Foundations of Reflective Black Sociology* and *Reflective Black Sociology:Epistemology, Theory and Method*, both published in 2011 by Left Coast Press, Inc.

Quincy Thomas Stewart is an associate professor of sociology and a Faculty Fellow in the Institute for Policy Research at Northwestern University. Professor Stewart completed his undergraduate training (B.S.) in Interdisciplinary Studies at Norfolk State University (1996). He completed his Ph.D. in Demography and Sociology from the University of Pennsylvania (2001). Professor Stewart was a 2006 recipient of the Robert Wood Johnson Scholar in Health Policy Research fellowship at the University of Michigan. His research interests pertain to demography, social inequality, and methodology. Specifically, he is interested in the dynamic social processes that create inequalities in socioeconomic status, health, and mortality.

Teun A. van Dijk is Professor Emeritus of Discourse Studies at the University of Amsterdam and currently a visiting professor at Pompeu Fabra University, Barcelona. After earlier work on literary theory, text grammar, and the psychology of discourse processing, since the 1980s he has explored several topics of Critical Discourse Studies, such as discourse and racism, ideology, context, and knowledge. He founded and edited the international journals *Poetics, Text* (now *Text & Talk*), *Discourse & Society, Discourse Studies, Discourse & Communication*, and *Discurso & Sociedad* (www.dissoc.org), of which he still edits the latter four. For a list of his publications, see his website www.discourses.org.

Henry A. Walker is Professor Emeritus of Sociology at the University of Arizona. Previously, he taught sociology at Stanford, Cornell, Arizona, and several other academic institutions. His published research on legitimacy processes, power, inequality, and theoretical methods appears in leading journals and research annuals. Professor Walker has designed and run experiments that test ideas drawn from legitimacy theory, network exchange theory, status characteristics theory, and theories of collective action. The Chinese edition of *Building Experiments* (with David Willer) was published in May 2010.

Yvonne Walker is a doctoral candidate at the Fielding Graduate University School of Human and Organization Development.